Michael Grant

CLEOPATRA

Simon and Schuster
New York

First U.S. printing
SBN 671-21521-3
Library of Congress Catalog Card Number: 72-12428
Manufactured in the United States of America

Passages from *Cleopatra* by J. Lindsay are
quoted by permission of Constable and Company;
passages from *Josephus*, Vol. VIII (translated
by R. Marcus) by permission of The Loeb
Classical Library; passages from The Aeneid
(translated by Patric Dickinson), by permission
of The New American Library; and passages
from *Plutarch: Makers of Rome* (translated by
Ian Scott-Kilvert) by permission of Penguin
Books Limited.

Contents

Acknowledgments   xi
Foreword   xiii

PART ONE: CLEOPATRA'S FIRST TWENTY-ONE YEARS
1 Cleopatra's Father   3
2 Cleopatra Gains and Loses the Throne   30

PART TWO: CLEOPATRA AND CAESAR
3 Cleopatra and Caesar in Egypt   61
4 Cleopatra and Caesar in Rome   83
5 Cleopatra after Caesar's Death   95

PART THREE: CLEOPATRA AND ANTONY
6 Cleopatra Summoned by Antony   109
7 Cleopatra Abandoned by Antony   125
8 Cleopatra Revives her Ancestral Kingdom   135
9 Cleopatra Receives Antony Back from the Wars   145
10 Cleopatra Queen of Kings   161

PART FOUR: CLEOPATRA AGAINST ROME
11 Cleopatra Declared Rome's Enemy   185
12 Cleopatra's Escape from Actium   203
13 Cleopatra's Death   216
14 Cleopatra's Conqueror in Egypt   229
15 Cleopatra's Position in History   233

BIBLIOGRAPHY
A Ancient Sources   239
B Modern Sources (Books)   246
List of Abbreviations Used in Notes   249
Notes   251

CONTENTS

Note on Money 281
Table of Dates 283
Genealogical Tables 287
Index 291

Illustrations

Between pages 144–145

1 Ptolemy I Soter, who seized Egypt after the death of Alexander the Great. (*From a sale catalogue*).

2 Gold coin showing the great figures of the Ptolemaic cult, on which Cleopatra's regime was based: Ptolemy I Soter with his wife Berenice I, and Ptolemy II with his sister-wife Arsinoe II. (*From a sale catalogue*).

3 Cleopatra's great grandfather Ptolemy VIII Euergetes on a temple at Ombos (Kom-Ombo). (*Popperfoto*).

4 and 5 Statuette of Ptolemy XII, Cleopatra's father. (*Collection of Professor Henri Seyrig, Neuchâtel*).

6 Funeral relief of Egyptian dance. (*Museo Nazionale Delle Terme, Rome*).

7 The temple of Horus at Apollinopolis Magna (Edfu) in Upper Egypt, completed by Cleopatra's father. (*Popperfoto*).

8 Roman lamp showing the harbour of Alexandria, first century AD. (*Hermitage Museum, Leningrad*).

9 Silver plate from Boscoreale, near Pompeii. (*Louvre, Paris*).

10 Head of an African; a popular subject for Alexandrian art. (*British Museum, London*).

11 Personification of the Nile, from a temple of Isis in Rome. First century AD. (*Vatican Museum*).

12 The bull god Buchis of Hermonthis (Armant), near Thebes. (*Alinari, Florence*).

13 Sarapis, the god who was invented or adapted by the Ptolemies to bridge the gap between the Egyptian and Greek religions. (*Guildhall Museum, London*).

14 One of the Ptolemaic queens whom Cleopatra was brought up to emulate: perhaps Berenice II (d. 221 BC), wife of Ptolemy III Euergetes. (*Antiquarium Communale, Rome*).

15 Arsinoe II Philadelphus, one of Cleopatra's greatest predecessors. (*From a sale catalogue*).

16 Chalcedony intaglio of Julius Caesar. (*Collection of Professor Henri Seyrig, Neuchâtel*).

17 Portrait bust of Julius Caesar. (*Castello di Aglie, Italy*).

18 Silver coin (38–37 BC) of the harbour city of Ascalon, showing Cleopatra at the age of thirty-two. (*From Ars Classica sale catalogue, Geneva 1933*).

vii

19   Bronze coin of Cleopatra issued at Alexandria. (*British Museum, London*).
20   Silver coin of Alexandria showing Cleopatra when she was twenty-four. (*British Museum, London*).
21   Marble head found at Caesarea (now Cherchel). (*Cherchel Museum, Algeria; photo by Roger Wood*).
22   A young woman with the hair style of some of Cleopatra's coins. (*Vatican Museum; photo by Scala*).
23   The orator Cicero. (*Capitoline Museum, Rome; photo by Alinari*).
24   Aerial view of modern Alexandria. (*Radio Times Hulton Picture Library*).
25   Isis and the Baby Horus. (*Metropolitan Museum of Art, New York*).
26   Ptolemaic priest from Hermonthis. (*Louvre, Paris*).
27   The temple of Isis on the island of Philae. (*Photo from the Donald McLeish Collection*).
28   The temple of the Egyptian goddess Hathor at Tintyra (now Dendera). (*Photo from the Donald McLeish Collection*).
29   Coin issued in Cyprus showing Cleopatra with an infant at her breast. (*British Museum, London*).
30   Carnelian of Sextus Pompeius. (*Staatliche Museen, Berlin*).
31   Mosaic from Antioch in Syria, showing Dionysus (Bacchus). (*Metropolitan Museum of Art, New York*).
32   Coin issued in Eumenia, showing a portrait of Antony's wife, Fulvia. (*British Museum, London*).
33   Painting from Herculaneum showing a priest of Isis performing the afternoon service. (*National Archaeological Museum, Naples*).
34   The meeting of Antony and Cleopatra, by Giovanni Battista Tiepolo. (*National Gallery, Edinburgh*).
35   King Orodes II of Parthia. (*British Museum, London*).
36   Polychrome statue of Isis. (*Cyrene Museum, Libya; photo by Alinari*).
37   Bronze coin of Antony with his wife Octavia. (*British Museum, London*).
38   Sard ringstone probably representing Octavia. (*Metropolitan Museum of Art, New York*).
39   Silver coin of Asia Minor showing Antony with his wife Octavia. (*British Museum, London*).
40   The triumph of Dionysus, from the Tomb of the Egyptians, St Peter's, Rome. (*Photo from the collection of Professor J. M. C. Toynbee*).
41   Alexander the Great. Roman copy of a bust of the late fourth century BC by Lysippus. (*Louvre, Paris*).
42   The jackal-headed god Anubis. (*Egyptian Museum, Cairo*).
43   Mosaic of the first century BC from Pompeii. (*National Archaeological Museum, Naples*).
44   Silver coin of Antony and Cleopatra issued in Syria in *c.* 34 BC. (*British Museum, London*).
45   Cleopatra 'Thea'. (*British Museum, London*).
46   Silver *denarius* of Antony (*c.* 34 BC). (*British Museum, London*).
47   Gold coin showing Antony and his son Antyllus. (*British Museum, London*).
48   Ptolemaic jewellery. (*Metropolitan Museum of Art, New York*).

ILLUSTRATIONS

49 Pendant worn by Ptolemaic lady. (*British Museum, London*).

50 Terracotta drinking cups from Arretium (Arezzo). (*From casts in the Museum of Fine Arts, Boston*).

51 Coin issued by Antony just before Actium to honour his legions. (*British Museum, London*).

52 Marcus Vipsanius Agrippa. (*Uffizi Gallery, Florence*).

53 Onyx cameo celebrating the victory of Octavian at Actium. (*Kunsthistorisches Museum, Vienna*).

54 Relief from Praeneste (Palestrina) showing a Roman warship. (*Vatican Museum; photo by Alinari*).

55 Statue of Octavian (Augustus) from Arsinoe (Fayum). (*Ny Carlsberg Glyptothek, Copenhagen*).

56 Gold coin of Octavian (Augustus) in one of the eastern provinces, celebrating his annexation of Cleopatra's Egypt. (*British Museum, London*).

57 Procession of Isis; second century AD. (*Vatican Museum; photo by Alinari*).

58 *Cleopatra*, by Michelangelo. (*Casa Buonarroti, Florence; photo from Mansell Collection*).

59 *The Death of Cleopatra*, by Guido Cagnacci. (*Kunsthistorisches Museum, Vienna*).

60 Portrait-bust of Cleopatra's grandson, Ptolemy of Mauretania. (*Louvre, Paris*).

Maps

Plan of Alexandria   32
Egypt   39
Egypt and the Roman Provinces at the Accession of Cleopatra   50
  (51 BC)
Italy   56
Greece   104
Asia Minor, Syria, Judaea and the East   136–7
The Donations of Alexandria (34 BC)   167
Actium   210

Acknowledgments

I owe a profound debt of gratitude to Mr Tony Godwin of Messrs Weidenfeld and Nicolson for many careful and penetrating suggestions, without which the book would have been a great deal worse than it is. I also want to thank Miss Gila Curtis of the same firm for the invaluable assistance she has given as editor, Mrs Marigold Johnson for all her helpful criticisms, Mrs Jane Dorner for collecting the pictures and Mr Claus Henning for drawing the maps. I have also to express my warm appreciation to the following for their contributions: Dr T. J. Cadoux, Mrs Bezi Hammelmann, Mr G. K. Jenkins, Mr Jules Leroux, Mr K. Nikolaou, Mr S. E. Rigold, Professor H. Seyrig, Dr C. H. V. Sutherland and Mr A. Tillotson. And without my wife's help, of very many kinds, this book would never have been written, or revised, or completed.

Foreword

The story of Cleopatra is the story of a woman who became utterly involved, in her public and private life alike, with two men, one after the other, Julius Caesar and Mark Antony. But it is also one of the most moving and astonishing stories in all history, because both she and they were persons of entirely exceptional qualities, who held the fate of the Greco-Roman world in their hands.

It was a world controlled by the Romans, but the inhabitants of its eastern and richer half were mainly Greeks, or people who belonged to some more easterly race but spoke Greek as their first language. Cleopatra, too, was a Greek much more than anything else. Though queen of Egypt, she possessed not a drop of Egyptian blood in her veins. The last ruler of the dynasty of the Ptolemies, she was of wholly Greek upbringing, and to a very considerable extent of Greek race.

She was consumed with perpetual ambition to revive the former glories of her Greek kingdom and house. But these great glories, which had extended the Ptolemaic empire far beyond the Egyptian borders, could only be revived by co-operation with the Romans. It is true that Egypt was, officially, an independent kingdom, but it survived on Roman sufferance. Cleopatra, therefore, was well aware that her kingdom could only be restored to its earlier grandeur by co-operation with Rome. She inherited this view from her father, Auletes, a complex individual whose influence upon her development is often underestimated. He had passed on to her a policy of collaboration with the Romans, and this she maintained. It was a policy which horrified a large part of the ruling class of her own country. Yet in face of the overwhelming predominance of Roman power, anything else would have been suicidal.

To ask what Cleopatra thought of the Romans is a question without a simple answer. She devoted a great part of her life to striving for the cause of her fellow-Greeks; and they had absolutely no cause to love Romans. Obviously, she must have agreed with most other Greeks in believing certain of Rome's imperialistic attitudes to be wholly deplorable and all too likely to lead her own country into the subjection into which others had already been plunged. Nevertheless, she took individual Romans as she found them, liking some and disliking others. And the only two men, other than her father, who played a really important part in her life were both Roman.

When she was still a girl, Rome fell under the absolute domination of the most powerful and intelligent leader it had ever produced, Julius Caesar. In the course of a Roman civil war, he happened to arrive at the Egyptian capital, Alexandria, and he and Cleopatra became lovers. Then she followed him back to Rome. But while she was still there, some of his fellow-Romans, who longed to restore the Republic he had destroyed, plotted and carried out his assassination.

The extent to which she had guided Caesar's opinions and judgements is difficult to assess; but she probably influenced him more than is often nowadays believed. Although thoroughly Roman, he was at the same time by no means averse to Greek ways of living and thinking. And this was an even more conspicuous characteristic of Mark Antony who, after a period of civil war, took over the eastern part of the empire, and, in the process, took over Caesar's role as Cleopatra's lover. In Antony, once again, she found a man who was singularly lacking in current Roman prejudices against the Greeks.

Indeed, there seems to have emerged from their association a genuine and viable concept of a new sort of Greco-Roman world. Cleopatra had aims which rose beyond the purely dynastic ambitions of her own country, for they took account also of the Roman empire, and envisaged that this whole vast territory, together with the external regions dependent upon it, should no longer be under the sole, exclusive domination of Italians, as it had been hitherto. Instead it should be a partnership, in which the Greek and Hellenized orientals who inhabited the regions east of the Adriatic were to be associates of the Romans rather than merely their subjects, enjoying a status almost equal to theirs. This was an aim for which her whole upbringing and natural inclination prepared and encouraged her.

It was also, however, an aim which presents us today, if we are trying to study her career, with a very serious problem. For the Romans appreciated, not altogether clearly perhaps but quite clearly enough, what she was about; and it terrified them. Against her, consequently, as one of her best twentieth-century historians, W. W. Tarn, has observed, 'was launched one of the most terrible outbursts of hatred in history; no accusation was too vile to be hurled at her, and the charges which were made have echoed through the world ever since, and have sometimes been taken for facts'.[1] Our problem, then, consists of the fog of fiction

and vituperation which has surrounded her personality from her own
lifetime onwards.

The first effect of this propaganda, from its very beginnings, was to
create the impression that the predominant element in her character
was sexuality, directed towards the ensnaring of noble Romans. This
has meant that a miasma of romance, glamour, sentiment and prurience
descended upon her amorous relations with Julius Caesar and Antony,
and prevented other aspects of her character from being seen. The ancient writers embarked immediately and wholeheartedly on this sort
of presentation, and they have been followed by a whole host of historians, dramatists and poets of later Europe, including William
Shakespeare in his *Antony and Cleopatra* and Bernard Shaw in *Caesar and
Cleopatra*. As Shakespeare declared, embroidering imaginatively upon
Plutarch,

> Age cannot wither her, nor custom stale
> Her infinite variety: other women cloy
> The appetites they feed, but she makes hungry
> Where most she satisfies: for vilest things
> become themselves in her.[2]

And innumerable biographers of later times, joined by innumerable
painters, have dwelt feverishly upon the same theme. Not that they are
altogether wrong to do so. Although many of her own Greco-Egyptian
upper class viewed Cleopatra with hatred, Caesar and Antony both
found her an altogether exceptional mistress, as well as an exceptional
companion and friend, and this is a matter of real historical importance.
Nevertheless, over-emphasis on such a personal factor makes it easy to
lose sight of a second, equally real, even more important, Cleopatra: the
Cleopatra who had ideas.

The ideas failed to take practical effect because, in a series of naval
manœuvres off the west coast of Greece, Antony and Cleopatra were defeated by their enemy and rival, Octavian, the future Augustus, who
had come after them from Italy. After their defeat, Antony and Cleopatra fell back together upon Egypt. And there, a year later, when
Octavian reached Alexandria, they died.

So profoundly relieved were the Romans that they magnified the final
engagement at Actium, off Greece, into one of the greatest battles of all
time. And in loading a somewhat unimpressive clash with this vast symbolic significance they were not completely mistaken. For they interpreted the whole struggle between the two sides as an integral part of the
millennial, perpetual strife between east and west. And that, if by 'east'
one understands the Greek world, is what it was. The Greeks lost. But
the proof that Cleopatra's aim was not, after all, so impracticable is

provided by the Greco-Roman world of several centuries later, in which it was the Greeks, not the Romans, who supplied the dawning Byzantine empire with its dominant language and culture.

If the campaign had ended in victory, Cleopatra, as long as she lived, would have had a major part to play in the imperial régime of the future. Her Roman enemies knew that this would be so, and when they dwelt fearfully upon the prospect it was not just unfounded war-hysteria. But the thought, implying the modification of their own supremacy, was so distasteful that there rapidly grew up a legend that the defeat of Antony and herself had been entirely inevitable, a working out of manifest Destiny. This legend was all the easier to create because of the ready conviction of the Italians that westerners, represented by themselves, were superior to easterners, represented by Cleopatra – who was depicted, for the purpose, as exotically oriental rather than Greek.

Modern historians, too, are inclined to concur much too rapidly with this retrospective, official Roman judgement of the inevitability of the outcome. For nothing succeeds like success, and we too are westerners. To myself, partly perhaps because I have lived for nine years in the near east, the picture looks somewhat different. There seems to me nothing in the policies of Antony and Cleopatra which made their defeat in-evitable. True, there were embarrassing factors, such as the position of Cleopatra herself. But Octavian also had his embarrassments to con-tend with, notably a grave shortage of money. In my view he won the battle of Actium for quite another reason: because, during the im-mediately preceding months, his admiral, Agrippa, had proved himself a far better commander than anyone on the other side. If that had not been so, if that is to say Actium, or more precisely its decisive prelimin-aries, had gone the other way, we should all be saying today that the victory won by Antony and Cleopatra had been inevitable owing to the flaws inherent in Octavian's policies!

The ancient sources upon which every such inquiry has to be based are tantalizingly fragmentary, intractable and enigmatic. Yet although I realize all too well how inadequate any new survey is bound to be, I believe that the evidence is at least sufficiently extensive and varied to justify this further attempt to describe the sort of woman that Cleopatra was.

Gattaiola 1972   MICHAEL GRANT

Part One

Cleopatra's First Twenty-One Years

1

Cleopatra's Father

When Cleopatra was born at the end of 70 or the beginning of 69 BC, Egypt had already been a united nation, under its Pharaohs, for over three thousand years, and the Macedonian, Greek-speaking dynasty of the Ptolemies to which she herself belonged had been ruling the country since the death of Alexander the Great in 323. As for Rome, its huge Mediterranean empire was reeling into the last turbulent phase of the Republic. The orator Cicero, who came to dislike Cleopatra very much, was thirty-seven; Caesar, who did not share his view, was thirty; Antony was about thirteen.

Cleopatra's father, a strange and complex man, was Ptolemy XII. Fortunately for us, each of the Ptolemies was known by additional titles. Ptolemy XII was Theos Philopator Philadelphus Neos Dionysos – the God, Lover of his Father, Lover of his Sister (or Brother), the New Dionysus. The people of his capital, Alexandria, however, who liked to call their monarchs by undignified nicknames, named him Nothos the Bastard, and Auletes the Piper or Oboe-Player. Such designations pleased the Alexandrians' taste for the grotesque, shown also in their caricatured terracotta statuettes.

Auletes appears to have had six children. The eldest was another, different Cleopatra, Cleopatra Tryphaena; for a short time in 58–57 BC, she became Queen Cleopatra VI Tryphaena. Next there was a second girl, Berenice IV. Then came the Cleopatra with whom this book is concerned, the future Cleopatra VII, who was queen from 51 to 30 BC. After her followed a fourth daughter, Arsinoe IV, born some time between 68 and 65. And finally there were two boys, born in 61 and 59. Later they became fellow-monarchs of Cleopatra, Ptolemy XIII and XIV, but neither survived adolescence.

We do not know who Cleopatra VII's mother was. In view of her daughter's subsequent fame this is rather strange. The mother of

Cleopatra VI and Berenice IV was a certain Cleopatra V Tryphaena, who was both sister and wife of King Auletes – more will be said of these brother–sister marriages later. The mother of the two boys, Ptolemy XIII and XIV, was a second wife of Auletes, whose name is unknown. Auletes' first wife Cleopatra V died, or at least vanished from the scene, some time before 25 February 68 BC. Her name appears at the head of papyri as late as 7 August 69,[1] but such headings sometimes display brief time-lags, so this does not rule out her disappearance at a slightly earlier date. However, since Cleopatra VII was conceived not later than the spring of 70 BC, it is on the whole simplest to assume that Cleopatra V Tryphaena was still alive and in the palace at that time – and was her mother.

The supposition that Auletes may have had two wives at the same time can be rejected since the Ptolemies were normally monogamous, and if Auletes had provided an exception to the rule, information to this effect would probably have survived. When, therefore, an Egyptian temple inscription records that he visited the ancient Egyptian capital of Memphis 'with his wives',[2] this is either an archaic mechanical survival of the phraseology of the ancient Pharaohs or another way of saying 'the Queen and the ladies of her court'. A further complication might seem to be raised by Strabo, a Greek writer and geographer of Asia Minor who was some six years younger than Cleopatra VII. 'Auletes' only legitimate daughter', he remarks, 'was his eldest one.'[3] But this suggestion that all his other daughters were illegitimate, including the Cleopatra with whom we are concerned, is an unlikely one. No one in all history has had more hostile propaganda directed against her than Cleopatra VII, and if there had been the slightest suspicion that she was illegitimate, her numerous Roman enemies would have told this to the world in no uncertain fashion. As it is, their attacks on her, many of which have survived, do not include this particular charge at all, which we only hear of from this one casual statement by Strabo. For the same reason we should probably rule out the hypothesis that Cleopatra VII was conceived by the second wife-to-be (name unknown) while the first wife Cleopatra V Tryphaena was still upon the scene, and subsequently and retrospectively, after her mother had become queen, legitimized. For then she would still have been born a bastard, and her Roman foes would not have missed the point. On the whole, then, it seems most likely that Auletes' first wife and sister, Cleopatra V Tryphaena, was the mother of our Cleopatra.

*

Racial investigation of eminent personages does not generally serve much purpose. But in the case of Cleopatra VII it does at least suggest that she had a fairly dark complexion – or at least not blonde hair, such as was ascribed to her in one Stratford production of Shakespeare's *Antony and Cleopatra*. Her remote Macedonian forebears must have been of various complexions, since the Macedonians were of very mixed blood.[4] Not all of them, clearly, were fair-haired – though apparently her ancestor Ptolemy II Philadelphus (282–246 BC) was a blonde.[5] But her great-great-grandfather Ptolemy V Epiphanes (205–180 BC) married into the house of the Seleucids – the other great successor-state of Alexander, reigning over Syria and other parts of the near east – and this Seleucid wife of his, Cleopatra I, was partly of Persian and other Iranian blood.[6] And Cleopatra VII's grandmother, too, the mother of the illegitimate Auletes, is quite likely to have been a Syrian – though it is possible that she was also partly Greek. Certainly she was not an Egyptian, because although Egyptian women had for centuries been renowned for their skill at making love, we only know of one Egyptian mistress of a Ptolemy, and she was an exceptional figure who had lived a great many years earlier[7] (no Ptolemy, as far as we know, had an Egyptian wife). So when Robert Greene in 1589 wrote of Cleopatra VII as 'black Egyptian',[8] the second of these terms was wrong, for she probably did not possess one single drop of Egyptian blood; and the first was exaggerated, like the blackness sometimes attributed to her in modern African school-books. Dark, however, she probably was, as Shakespeare appreciated: for this is what he means when one of his characters calls her 'a gipsy'.[9]

Cleopatra VII would have described herself as a Greek. Whatever the racial ingredients of her Macedonian ancestors, her language, like theirs (though they had spoken a dialect), was Greek, and so was her whole education and culture. Educated Greeks or Hellenized easterners of her time were staunch admirers of classical Hellas, which may be regarded as having come to an end at the time of Alexander the Great (336–323 BC) when it was replaced by what we know as the Hellenistic age. But the attitudes of Cleopatra's contemporaries were also conditioned by the startling career of Alexander himself who, more than two hundred years before their time, had brought about that vast change in the Greek civilization which we describe as the transition from classical to Hellenistic Greece.

One of the principal features of this new era was an immense geographical explosion, so that Hellenism, which had formerly been restricted to the shores of the Mediterranean and Black Seas, now extended as far afield as Afghanistan and India. This expanded Greek civilization was remarkably uniform: the spread of ideas was not hampered by the frontiers that hamper it today, so the Greek way of life had extraordinary success in reaching untutored barbarians; and it also seeped rapidly into the older cultures of the east – taking much from them in a reciprocal process, for never before had Hellenism been so tolerant and receptive. There was a great mingling with Syrian and Hebrew traditions, and with the traditions of the Iranian and Egyptian worlds as well. And yet, paradoxically, the Greeks all the time remained very conscious of their Hellenism, and very proud when they repelled its enemies, such as the relatively primitive Gauls (Galatians) who had flooded into Asia Minor in the third century BC.

The Galatians were defeated in great battles. Yet one of the major gains of Hellenistic times was a diminution in the total number of wars. In classical Greece every tiny region had been more or less constantly at war with its neighbours. In the vast expanses of the Hellenistic world, during the third and second centuries BC, there were, it is true, always people fighting somewhere, as there are today, but there was peace over enormous areas, and the improvement over the previous anarchy was great. There were also still scientists, writers and artists of the utmost distinction. The classical Greek world of the immediate past had become a bankrupt concern, ruined by perpetual strife between the city-states: but the Hellenistic Greeks who took it over managed to restore it to a new kind of cultural as well as political solvency. It is only in quite recent years that we have begun to understand the manifold glories of this later Greek world – and indeed, even now, history books often come to an abrupt stop just at its starting-point.

For this, the Romans are largely to blame. They admired ancient Greek culture, but did not much care for the Greeks of their own day whom they saw around them; with the result that they saw ancient, classical Greece as good, whereas Hellenistic Greece appeared to be an inferior article. Moreover, many Greeks all over the Roman empire accepted precisely the same view, so that the greatness of their Hellenistic compatriots, who had come between the classical Greeks and themselves, was allowed to fall into oblivion. A woman like Cleopatra VII, looking back upon all that her ancestors had done during that time, was not likely to make the same mistake. But she and her contemporaries of the first century BC had another, peculiar, problem of their own. Could the 'Hellenistic Age' (which we ourselves often regard as coming to an end in about her time) still be said to exist at all, could *any* Greek Age, now that the Romans were the dominant power? This was a question never far from Cleopatra's mind. But it is quite certain that she considered the Greek epoch to be by no means finished, and intended to do everything in her power to ensure its perpetuation.

The reason why the Hellenistic world had succeeded, except in its most bellicose moments, in restricting the number and the impact of wars was because it had replaced a multitude of city-states by a few states of very large size. Or rather, the old city-states still existed, but their capacity for strife was much diminished, because they were hence-forward under the shadow and domination of the great new Hellenistic powers. These were the 'successor states' that had divided up the herit-age of Alexander the Great after his death. Each of these, perpetually, made wide and mutually incompatible territorial claims. But, although their frontiers fluctuated, the core of the Antigonid realm remained Alexander's Macedonia, the Seleucid kingdom extended through much of western Asia, and the Ptolemies were based on Egypt.

We know these empires by the names of their dynasties, for monarchy was their form of government. The various forms of oligarchy, or demo-cracy, which had characterized the old city-state system were left in the powerless hands of the city-states that had invented them. But these old types of government were not imitated by the great new Hellenistic realms. In taking over the legacy of Alexander, they took over his monarchic form of government as well. And from that time onwards, it became the normal form of political life, and remained the normal form for over two thousand years – until our own century.

*

Cleopatra VII was a part of this tradition. Among her proud Hellenistic inheritances was a monarchy which went straight back to Alexander. She was the sole source of law within her dominions, for Hellenistic sovereignty was a highly personal affair, the private property of the sovereign.[10] She was The Queen – not even queen 'of' any place, even of Egypt, contrary to what Shakespeare and many others lead us to suppose.

Nor, indeed, would she ever have agreed that Ptolemaic rule ought to be restricted to Egypt. In this respect she modelled her views on those of the original Ptolemy I, Alexander's staff-officer, general and historian. It is true that Egypt had been his headquarters. For after his master's death, he had established his rule in that country, which Alexander had conquered from the Persians nine years earlier. Once in Egypt, Ptolemy I proceeded to establish as his capital the greatest of the cities Alexander had founded, Alexandria, declaring himself king there in 304 BC. Later known as Soter (the Saviour), Ptolemy I was the son of a not particu-larly distinguished personage named Lagos, after whom, subsequently, the dynasty was sometimes known as the Lagids. Alone of Alexander the Great's successors, however, Ptolemy possessed the advantage of some degree of kinship with the family of Alexander himself: his mother Arsinoe was the second cousin (or mistress) of Alexander's father, Philip II. His personal badge was an eagle, as befitted this eagle-nosed man, and the eagle remained for ever afterwards the emblem of the Ptolemaic house which he had founded.

But Ptolemy I Soter had no intention of limiting himself to Egypt. It was an antique tradition of the Egyptian Pharaohs to seek to conquer considerable tracts of territory far away to the west and north-east of Egypt's own borders. Aggressive monarchs, such as Thothmes III and Rameses II in the sixteenth and thirteenth centuries BC respectively, had habitually allowed themselves to be depicted crushing hordes of Asians and other foreigners, and seizing them by their collective hair. Indeed, in even earlier days, Sesostris III had recorded the view that 'he who goes no further than his own frontier is a real —', the missing word being an obscenity which Egyptologists have modestly preferred to conceal from the uninitiated.[11] Ptolemy I felt just the same, if indeed he recognized the existence of any frontiers or territorial limitations at all. He conquered Cyrenaica, the eastern half of the modern Libya. He occupied southern Syria. Indeed, he repeated this latter operation on no less than four occasions – and the country remained a permanent bone of contention with the adjoining Seleucid empire. Ptolemy I Soter also seized Cyprus (owned by the Pharaoh Aahmes [Amasis] in the sixth century BC), and it was to stay, for the most part, under Ptolemaic rule for nearly two and a half centuries to come. Then he moved forward to the islands of the Aegean, and put garrisons on the Greek mainland. His influence extended right up to the kingdom of the Cimmerian (Crimean) Bosphorus on the northern shores of the Black Sea.

Such were the exploits which Cleopatra VII was taught about in the days of her youth. Ptolemy Soter had far exceeded any Pharaoh in his exploitation of Egypt's Mediterranean frontage. And the glamorous *roi soleil* who followed Soter, his son Ptolemy II (282–246 BC) who was known after his death as Philadelphus (Lover of his Sister), from time to time deserted the peaceful pursuits his more delicate constitution preferred – study and womanizing – in order to continue the work of expansion. Later generations, and Cleopatra herself, felt that his name was the symbol of the Ptolemaic empire at its zenith. Well might his court poet Callimachus voice Egypt's imperious claims to world rule,[12] while artists exalted the sea-power of the Ptolemies, which guaranteed their people's wealth, abundance and merriment. For now came the climax of the resplendent Ptolemaic luxury, which although somewhat diminished still seemed extremely impressive to Romans in Cleopatra's time. The unique Pharos lighthouse outside Alexandria harbour towered into the sky, and directed the shipping that brought prosperity. The Museum and adjacent Library, with their fine gardens, fountains, colonnades and restaurants, became the research centres of the Mediterranean world, where scholars lived tax-free and at the state's expense, as befitted the subjects of a monarch who himself was learned in geography and zoology. 'Victory odes, Funeral dirges, Marriage-hymns, genealogical trees, medical prescriptions, mechanical toys, maps, engines of war: whatever the palace required it had only to inform the Museum, and the subsidized staff set to work.'[13] Thus E.M. Forster, but he is not quite fair: the Museum and Library played an enormous part in the conservation and evolution of Greek culture, and in its transmission to the modern world.

The dominions of Ptolemy II Philadelphus were expanded to even greater dimensions by his son Ptolemy III Euergetes (The Benefactor) (246–221). He temporarily occupied the whole of Syria – the nucleus of the rival Seleucid kingdom – right up to the Euphrates; it was a part of a vast expedition which almost reached the borders of India and was regarded as the greatest of all Ptolemaic military triumphs, earning him the title Conqueror of the World. His son Ptolemy IV Philopator (Lover of his Father) (221–205) has been represented as a contemptible victim of drink and sex, but he was more than that. For example, he fought off the inevitable Seleucid counter-attack – though the strain meant that Upper Egypt (the Thebaid), southernmost of the country's three governor-generalships, became gravely disaffected. And then his child Ptolemy V Epiphanes (God Manifest) (205–180) before he even came of age lost most of his dynasty's possessions outside the Egyptian borders. The tide had begun to turn.

Most serious of all, Rome had come on to the scene, having defeated Carthage in two wars and asserted its claim to be the principal Mediterranean power. Earlier, Ptolemy II had made a treaty with Rome, and now, in 200 BC (so the Romans liked to believe),[14] they sent a nobleman to Egypt as guardian for the young Ptolemy V, in the name of the Roman Senate. The belief was mythical. But soon afterwards Egypt had become little better than one of Rome's numerous puppet states. Probably it was not a full 'client', which was the technical term used for thoroughly dependent kingdoms,[15] but all the same, in 168 BC, the Romans directly intervened to 'save' Ptolemy VI Philometor (Lover of his Mother) from invasion by the Seleucid Antiochus IV Epiphanes when Gaius Popilius Laenas turned Antiochus IV back only four miles from Alexandria.

Ptolemy VI's reign witnessed a complicated coming and going of simultaneous, rival Ptolemaic rulers, who represented the most perfidious and murderous side of Hellenistic rule. They culminated in the appallingly savage figure of Cleopatra VII's great-grandfather, Ptolemy VIII Euergetes (146–116), whose monstrous bulk, clothed in transparent gauze, earned him the nickname of Physcon (Fatty). Nevertheless, he finally enforced internal peace – and was the last monarch who managed to do so until Cleopatra. Yet he had felt compelled to appeal to the Romans against his own rebellious relatives in 162 BC, and again in 145.[16] When the glorious Scipio Africanus the younger (Aemilianus) paid him a visit in 140 or 139, Scipio observed under his breath to a companion, as the king waddled along beside them, 'we have given the Alexandrians a new experience – the sight of their king taking a walk.'[17] For the greatest of living Romans to snigger at the ruling Ptolemy was a foretaste of many future humiliations by Scipio's anti-Egyptian compatriots. Egypt was still officially a sovereign state, but only in the sense that many such states today have the same title, though they are in fact dependent, in their external policy, upon one of the great powers.[18] We can well imagine the visit a Roman senator, Lucius Memmius, paid to Egypt in 112 BC: a papyrus has survived in which the Egyptian prime minister (*dioecetes*) instructs a provincial official to receive him deferentially, and to give him a view of the sacred crocodiles at their feeding time.[19]

But the habit of appealing to Rome was perilous. Early in the first century BC, monarchs of semi-dependent nations all along the imperial frontiers were finding that if the Romans helped an 'ally', they expected to be rewarded. And this was the fate that now befell the Egyptians, whose weakness had by this time made them intensely vulnerable to predatory Romans. Competing against Cleopatra's grandfather Ptolemy IX Soter – nicknamed Lathyrus (Chick-Pea) – her great-uncle Ptolemy X Alexander I found it necessary to borrow a large sum from Roman financiers in order to raise a fleet and regain the throne (88 BC). Then, immediately afterwards, in order to appease his creditors, he made a will, or was said to have made a will (we shall never know the truth), bequeathing the entire country to the Roman people.[20]

If so, this was not the first time that eastern monarchs dependent upon Rome had left such directions, which sometimes seemed to them the only way to protect their supporters after they themselves were dead. But Egypt was far the richest legacy of the kind that had ever looked like coming the way of the Romans, even exceeding the kingdom of Pergamum in western Asia Minor, which had been bequeathed to them by its last king in 133 BC, becoming the Roman province of Asia. Ptolemies, too, had indulged in this type of gesture – for example Physcon, when he made the Romans heirs to Cyrenaica (to which he had been temporarily relegated) in the event of his death without issue (154). Nothing came of this bequest, but his bastard son, Ptolemy Apion, repeated it in 96. The Romans, however, although they duly claimed Apion's own royal lands in Cyrenaica, again did not accept the country as a whole. And now once more, in 88, the Senate still did not attempt to annex Egypt either, although it had been left, or allegedly left, to them by Ptolemy X Alexander I. They had their reasons for caution. For one thing, annexation would give whatever Roman was given the task of enforcing it the chance to acquire too much power and money for himself – and Rome's provincial governors of the period were frequently dishonest. Secondly, Ptolemy x Alexander i had scarcely been entitled to make the bequest at all, since his brother Ptolemy ix Soter (Lathyrus), who was still alive, had successfully prevented him from coming back to Egypt. So the Romans let Lathyrus stay there and reign, and contented themselves with collecting the debts they claimed he owed them.

But when Lathyrus died in 81, Lucius Cornelius Sulla, who had now become dictator in Rome, interfered sharply in Egyptian affairs. He still did not go so far as to annex the country. But he placed a new Ptolemaic king on its throne (80 BC). This new king was the late ruler's nephew Ptolemy xi Alexander ii (son of Ptolemy x Alexander i). Sulla compelled Ptolemy xi to marry his own elderly stepmother and cousin, who had been in charge meanwhile. Nineteen days later, however, the new monarch put her to death, and then the people of Alexandria, exercising their ancient Macedonian right to participate in the selection of kings, struck him down, murdering him in his turn.

It was now that Cleopatra's father, Ptolemy xii Auletes, the Piper, gained the throne. His other nickname, Nothos (Bastard), was accurate, since he was the illegitimate son of King Lathyrus by a concubine. When Ptolemy xi was assassinated it was feared in Alexandria that Sulla, who seemed to regard Egypt as a sort of personal dependency, would be angry about this violent suppression of his nominee, in which case it appeared all too likely that he would decide to annex the country after all, on the pretext that it no longer possessed a rightful king of its own. In order, therefore, to forestall any such intervention, Auletes, who was perhaps in his early twenties or younger, found himself hastily summoned from Syria and made king of Egypt. It was possible to cite the precedent of the Pharaohs for the elevation of a concubine's son to the throne in the absence of any legitimate heir. And to shore up his doubly dubious position – dubious on grounds of illegitimacy and dubious because of Sulla's foreseeably hostile reaction – Auletes incorporated among his official names the designation Philopator, Lover of his Father.

In fact, Sulla abdicated from his dictatorship and died, and Rome's restored republican government decided to let the Egyptian situation be. But in 75 BC two princes in exile from the neighbouring Seleucid state, sons of an aunt of Auletes called Cleopatra Selene, visited Rome to press their own claims to the Ptolemaic throne. However, although they presented a splendid candelabrum to Capitoline Jupiter, the Roman Senate did nothing to help the princes against Auletes. Moreover, during their return journey to Syria, they were robbed of their possessions by the Roman governor of Sicily.

*

Six years later, Cleopatra was born. While she was still a young child, Egypt came to the forefront of Roman politics: for to power-seeking Romans the temptation to annex the country had now become almost irresistible. Not only was it very wealthy, but it had actually been bequeathed to Rome (or so it was said) by one of its own monarchs – and then its leaders had actually dared to flout Rome's will! The Roman Senate, on the whole, reinforced by the orator Cicero,[21] was still against annexation. But the *populares* – those senators and others who were happy to obstruct the Senate, calling on the Assembly of the People when necessary – welcomed the idea, and the influential leaders of their group, Crassus and Pompey, were particularly eager to carry out the job themselves, since they saw it would bring them extensive profit and patronage. Rumour also extended similar ambitions to a rising younger politician, Julius Caesar.

Pompey's possible claim to undertake the task in person looked much stronger when, after defeating an inveterate enemy of the Romans in Asia Minor (Mithridates VI of Pontus), he descended on the Levant to suppress the decaying Seleucid kingdom, annexing it under the name of the province of Syria (63 BC). The way in which he got rid of this historic part of the heritage of Alexander the Great, after Rome had sat back and watched its prolonged enfeeblement by internal struggles, was an evil omen and warning for Auletes, king of the only surviving major realm of Alexander's former empire; he may even have regretted, rather late in the day, that the Ptolemies had so often been glad to foment civil strife among their Seleucid neighbours.

Pompey next turned his attention to the Jewish kingdom of Judaea. Until 200 BC, this had formed part of the Ptolemaic kingdom. Then it had fallen to the Seleucids, but during the second century the Jews (under the native Hasmonaean or Maccabee dynasty) had thrown off their control. Now, however, Pompey reduced Judaea to a virtual dependency of Rome: so that the Roman empire henceforward bordered upon Egypt. Auletes had thought it advisable to safeguard himself during the campaign by giving a lavish dinner in Pompey's honour, at which each of the thousand guests had his gold cup changed at every course. Furthermore, he had contributed to the maintenance of eight thousand cavalry in Pompey's service upon the borders of Judaea.[22] These gestures helped to save his own throne from Roman annexation. But they did not endear him to his own subjects, who remembered that Judaea had once belonged to the Ptolemies. Feeling in Egypt, in these years, was running strongly against the Romans. At Alexandria, in 60 BC, a visitor from Rome who had killed a cat – an animal which, like many others, was considered sacred in Egypt – narrowly escaped a lynching at the hands of the city crowd.[23]

It was the sort of incident likely to impress a child of nine, Cleopatra's age at the time. But in any case she must have become aware, as time went on, of the strength of anti-Roman feeling. And she gradually learnt of the unprecedented brutality, faithlessness, incompetence and corruption that Roman policy was displaying during these last years of the Republic – if 'policy' is any longer the right word at a time when ruthlessly acquisitive personal interests very largely prevailed, however much they might masquerade under sanctimonious slogans.

*

As Cleopatra became old enough to understand international affairs, relations between Rome and Egypt were entering a rougher phase which imposed new humiliations upon the Egyptians. In 60 BC Pompey, Caesar and Crassus joined forces in the 'First Triumvirate' which from now on unofficially ruled the Roman world, making nonsense of Republican institutions. In the next year Pompey and Caesar agreed to back Auletes' tenure of the Egyptian throne against the increasingly formidable rebellious elements in his own country. However, the Roman leaders also demanded a price. It was a very high price indeed, for the unprecedented influx of wealth into Rome after Pompey's eastern campaigns had enlarged the financial ideas of leading Romans, causing the prices for such services to rise considerably. And so Caesar, who was consul at the time, consented to pass a law confirming the kingship of Auletes as 'friend and ally of the Roman people' if the latter was prepared to hand over to Caesar and Pompey the sum of six thousand talents, a figure which, although such equivalents are inexact, can perhaps be thought of in terms of approximately seven million pounds or seventeen million dollars. This has been roughly estimated as the equivalent of the entire revenue of Egypt for six months, or perhaps even for a whole year.

Caesar and Pompey required the money immediately. So Auletes needed to find it immediately. On the other hand, he was anxious that the embarrassing task of raising it from his subjects should be postponed. So instead he borrowed the whole sum, turning to a Roman speculator and financier who specialized in such deals, an eminent banker's son named Gaius Rabirius Postumus.[24] Having laid hands on the money in this way, Auletes wondered how to prepare the Egyptians for the shocking news that it would be up to them to contribute its equivalent (plus interest) in order to repay Rabirius. As a first step he declared a general amnesty, cancelling all impending prosecutions; and then he waited for this declaration to have a favourable effect on Egyptian public opinion.

Meanwhile, however, further trouble was brewing for the Ptolemies, this time in Cyprus. This island was Ptolemaic property, but it was not ruled by Auletes; its ruler was his brother, who was likewise called Ptolemy. In 58 BC, the year after Auletes' deal with Rome, Cyprus attracted unwelcome attention in Rome. A young Roman politician named Publius Clodius Pulcher, ambitious and radical, was one of the occupants of the tribunate, an annual elective office which offered opportunities for influencing the city populace. He had sought to win their favour by pushing through an unprecedented measure with authorized free distributions of grain. However, this placed a hopeless strain on the Roman treasury, and if the measure was ever to be implemented it was imperative to raise funds elsewhere. So Clodius hit on the idea of annexing Cyprus: its monarch, unlike his brother, Auletes, had never purchased recognition by Rome, so there was a good cause for evicting him. So Ptolemy of Cyprus found himself accused, rightly or wrongly, of collusion with the pirates who had in recent years been Rome's enemies in the eastern Mediterranean; and it was announced that his kingdom was going to be taken over by the Romans. This, it was pointed out, had already been the intention of his uncle Ptolemy X Alexander I, whose doubtful bequest of the Egyptian dominions to Rome in 88 BC was alleged to have included Cyprus.

To undertake the annexation of the island, Clodius decided to appoint his political arch-enemy, the austere though hard-drinking conservative Cato, in order to get him out of the way. The possibilities of Cypriot plunder, joked Clodius, were so tempting that no one except the most honest man in Rome was fit to organize the take-over; and the joke had a sting in it because four years earlier Cato, abandoning his high principles, had himself tried to conciliate the people of Rome, in anticipation of Clodius, by increasing the doles of cheap corn. Cato duly started for Cyprus, where its king Ptolemy, accused of a host of vices, rejected the offer of the high-priesthood of Aphrodite at Paphos and chose to commit suicide instead.

So Cleopatra, at the age of eleven – and it is justifiable to suppose she was a very precocious eleven – heard how Roman imperialism of an exceptionally cynical kind had brought about her uncle's humiliation and death. And she also became aware of the further degradation of her father. For, in the summer of the same year, Auletes found he was unable to hold on to his throne after all. The Alexandrians would not put up with him. For one thing, the repayments of his debt to Caesar and Pompey had inevitably necessitated the infliction of new taxes, to which his subjects greatly objected. Secondly, they resented his failure to take any action whatever to save Ptolemaic Cyprus from its aggressor. What was the use of being called 'Lover of his Brother' if their king could not, in fact, take the smallest step to rescue his brother from such abominable treatment? The people of Alexandria had not yet accepted the idea that Egypt was entirely subject to the power of Rome.

Auletes, however, was fully aware of this hard fact, and so when his subjects now began to revolt against him it was to Rome that he fled for help. When he got as far as Rhodes, he found Cato there, on his way to Cyprus. Displaying little respect for the king's dignity, the Roman refused to call on him, indicating that since he was taking a course of laxatives, Auletes must come to him instead. When he arrived at Cato's residence, his host did not rise from his seat (perhaps his lavatory seat) to greet him. Moreover, all he felt inclined to say was that Auletes had better cancel his proposed journey to Italy, and instead go back to Egypt and concentrate on conciliating his own people, since if he really intended to ingratiate himself with the principal Romans he would need all the Egyptian wealth he could get. This was, in theory, not such bad advice, though Cato's manner of giving it was offensive. But Auletes did not at all like the idea of returning to Egypt, and instead went on his way to Rome. The treasure of his late brother, seven thousand talents of cash and bullion, in addition to lavish supplies of plate, furniture, jewellery and fabrics, was shortly afterwards dispatched by Cato from Cyprus in the same direction.[25]

Meanwhile the Egyptians, having got rid of Auletes for the time being, had given the throne to his eldest daughter and Cleopatra's sister, Cleopatra VI Tryphaena. It would appear, however, that allegiances within the country were confused and divided. Inscriptions from Apollinopolis Magna (Edfu), dated 5 December 57 BC, show the local priest describing Cleopatra VI Tryphaena and her father as joint monarchs.[26] These priests of Upper Egypt, which had received great benefactions from Auletes, evidently did not like to think of him as deposed, even though he had, in fact, been chased out. But Cleopatra VI Tryphaena was not the only one of his daughters who remained in Egypt, for her sister Berenice IV stayed too; and in certain circles or regions it was she, rather than Tryphaena, who was regarded as queen. A letter of 23 October 57 BC, to Theadelphia beside Lake Moeris (Fayum) in Middle Egypt, is in Berenice's name alone, without any reference either to Cleopatra VI or to Auletes.

But Auletes' third daughter, Cleopatra VII, with whom this book is concerned, may well have left the country with her father. That could be the explanation of an epitaph set up at Athens by a 'Libyan princess' in honour of one of her ladies-in-waiting who had died there.[27] Greeks used the term 'Libyan' loosely for their compatriots and others from any part of north Africa – and it is very likely that Auletes did not think it advisable to leave *all* his three daughters behind among his political foes in Alexandria. If this interpretation is correct, the inscription dates from a brief stay in Athens by Auletes and Cleopatra on their way from Rhodes to Rome.

If she was with him – or indeed even if she was not – the experiences of these years were giving her an exceptionally sharp and grim political education. She must have been very different from the ignorant, kittenish adolescent of Bernard Shaw's *Caesar and Cleopatra*.

*

Auletes' visit to Italy started well, with Pompey hospitably accommodating him and his retinue at his mansion in the Alban hills. But the king's pressing problem was how to return to Egypt. Pompey and Caesar (who was now away fighting in Gaul) had received their money, in exchange for Rome's recognition of his royal claims. But Rabirius Postumus, who had lent him the vast sum he needed to pay the Roman leaders, was surely now reminding them in no uncertain terms that he would not be repaid until the monarch was restored to his kingdom. Meanwhile Auletes' enemies at Alexandria had sent a deputation of a hundred men to Rome in order to present the case against him. However, Auletes had a number of the envoys assassinated as they landed at Puteoli (Pozzuoli), and then he arranged that their leader, a philosopher named Dio, should likewise be murdered in Rome. Various Romans, including Pompey, were said to be involved in the crime, though it was clear enough that Auletes was chiefly responsible.[28] No doubt he was satisfied with the result, since those of the hostile envoys who had survived now felt a marked disinclination to speak against him. Consequently, at the end of 57 – after distributing large bribes at Rome, and leaving an agent, Hammonius, behind in the city to see that the money did not go astray – he retired to the sacred precinct of Artemis, at Ephesus in Asia Minor, to wait until the Romans had decided who would restore him to the throne.

After prolonged intrigues and quarrels a henchman of Pompey named Aulus Gabinius, governor of the recently established province of Syria, took on the role. For this service, however, Auletes was to give him and others (with Pompey and Caesar again taking their cut) the fantastic sum of ten thousand talents, nearly twice the total already borrowed from Rabirius and paid to Caesar and Pompey three years earlier. It was an appalling burden for Egypt, and we do not know how Auletes proposed to raise the sum; perhaps he expected Gabinius, when he arrived, would raise it himself by looting. But in any case Auletes was not altogether sorry to have incurred such an enormous debt, because it meant that leading Roman businessmen had an interest in putting him back on the throne and keeping him there. Indeed, Rabirius was even now demonstrating how accurate this supposition was, for he insisted on accompanying Gabinius to Egypt, in order to make sure of the money Auletes still owed from the earlier loan.

The Roman Senate had been very reluctant all along to sanction a military invasion of Egypt by Gabinius or anyone else. But Gabinius, though himself nervous of the project for military reasons, wanted the money, and argued that invasion was a necessity on the rather dubious grounds that current Egyptian leadership posed a naval threat to the eastern Roman provinces.[29] In fact, the internal situation in Auletes' absence had been so chaotic that Egypt can hardly have been regarded as menacing anyone. Disturbances are recorded in 58 BC from the region of Heracleopolis Magna (near Beni Suef) in Middle Egypt – hardly surprising in view of the differences between Auletes and his two eldest daughters Cleopatra VI Tryphaena and Berenice IV. Before long, Cleopatra VI was dead or in retirement, and Berenice had emerged as the temporary victor. Since, however, Ptolemaic queens could not reign alone, strenuous efforts were made to find her a husband. Plans to secure two successive Seleucid princes failed, because one died and the other was vetoed by Gabinius, who had presumably not announced his intention of dismissing Berenice in favour of Auletes at this stage. A third candidate named Seleucus, who was possibly a royal Seleucid bastard, proved such a coarse creature that the Alexandrians called him Salt-fishmonger (Cybiosactes), and Berenice's impatience with him was such that she had him strangled after only three days. Then, in the second year of her reign (56–55),[30] without consulting Gabinius, she chose and married a certain Archelaus from Pontus in northern Asia Minor, who may have been the illegitimate son of its former king, Mithridates VI. Archelaus had been well thought of by Pompey, but now that he was King of Egypt without Roman permission Pompey's henchman Gabinius became his enemy, and marched against him from Judaea. Gabinius' chief cavalry officer, Mark Antony, now twenty-five or twenty-six years old, gallantly led the way, capturing the frontier-post of Pelusium. Then Gabinius himself moved into Egypt and with the aid of a contingent of Egyptian loyalists reinstated Auletes upon his throne.

Archelaus had fallen in battle, and against Auletes' wishes Antony gave him an honourable burial, since he had enjoyed the dead man's hospitality in Syria. This made Antony popular in Alexandria, and so did his protection of Egyptian prisoners from Auletes' vengeance. But the restored king's daughter, Berenice IV, was executed by her father's order. What his next daughter, the fourteen-year-old Cleopatra VII, thought about this slaughter of her sister we do not know, though she was later to imply a criticism of Berenice's unfilial usurpation. In any case the death of Berenice left Cleopatra as heir-apparent to her father's throne. This must also have been the occasion when she first met Antony, fresh from his brave exploits during the campaign.

Gabinius and Rabirius now extracted from Egypt all the money they could. Although the country was nominally independent, Rabirius managed to acquire for himself a dominant official post in its government, either the prime ministership itself or, more probably, a special job of economic overlord (April 55–end of 54).[31] He requisitioned supplies of every kind, and dispatched a merchant fleet home to Puteoli with saleable cargoes of cheap cloth, linen and glass.[32] Finally his depredations caused such discontent that he was obliged to leave Alexandria in a hurry. When he and Gabinius reached Rome, each of them had to face prosecution for financial misbehaviour. Cicero, although he had earlier described Gabinius as a treacherous, thieving, effeminate ballet-boy in curlers, now agreed to defend them both in court. Gabinius, in spite of feverish distributions of bribes, was condemned (at the second attempt) on at least one of the charges brought against him, and had to go into exile. But Rabirius seems to have got off. He claimed, no doubt falsely, that he was now a poor man: he said he had failed to collect the repayment of his debt from Auletes. And apparently Caesar, turning his attention from his Gallic War, agreed to take on the obligation of eventually collecting Rabirius' 'unsatisfied' claim. His acceptance of this responsibility could be made to look fair and chivalrous enough, since it was only because Caesar had taken so much of Auletes' money in 59 that Rabirius was pleading this predicament now. But it may be suspected that Rabirius paid Caesar heavily for assuming the task on his behalf. The fact that Caesar agreed to do so was destined to play an important part in Cleopatra's life and reign.

And so, as recent research has increasingly shown, did another heritage of this murky period: for Gabinius left behind him in Egypt a substantial army, consisting of Gaulish and German troops, supplemented, now and later, by various other elements. These 'Gabinians' stayed on, not as a Roman army of occupation, since the country was still formally independent, but as mercenaries in the employment of the Egyptian crown. Ever since the third century BC, the Ptolemies had relied greatly on foreign mercenaries – indeed for nearly a thousand years past the native Egyptians had hardly ever proved good enough soldiers for their monarchs to depend upon. But the mercenaries had proved hard to control, as a dangerous revolt in 274 BC showed; and in the next century, under Physcon, these foreign soldiers had got out of hand again. They were frequently at odds with the other royal units, and particularly with the Macedonian Household Troops who were supposed to guard the persons of the Ptolemaic sovereigns. Now, however, the Gabinians provided yet another, new, mercenary force. They must have been quite formidable. Caesar, when he later became their enemy, considered them worth an extended mention in his *Civil War*. The Egyptian army, he said, was 'by no means contemptible', and its nucleus consisted of the Gabinians. 'Gabinius' men,' Caesar continued,

had grown accustomed to the lax way of life at Alexandria. They had ceased to think of themselves as Roman, forgotten the standards of discipline of the Roman people, and had married and mostly had children by their marriages. Added to these were men collected among the brigands and pirates of Syria and the province of Cilicia (south-eastern Asia Minor) and the neighbouring areas; and many condemned criminals and exiles had joined them. All our runaway slaves had found a safe refuge and an assured livelihood, if they enrolled as soldiers. If any of them was arrested by his master, his comrades would unite to rescue him, resisting violence to any of their number inasmuch as it was a threat to themselves, since they were all in a similar situation. These men had been accustomed to demand the execution of royal favourites, to plunder the property of the wealthy, to besiege the palace for a rise in pay, to drive some from the throne and summon others to fill it, according to some ancient tradition of the Alexandrian army.[33]

Caesar might also have mentioned that these Gabinians were an indispensable, though often uncomfortable, prop for the restored Auletes régime. Indeed, it was a considerable achievement on Auletes' part to have converted them, by a mixture of discipline and concessions, into a force which both before and after his death continued to fulfil a significant role.[34] Caesar does go on to say, however, that at some point this royal army based on the Gabinians had occasion to 'make war upon the Egyptians'. He may be alluding to strife which was to arise after Auletes' death. But he could also be referring to severe internal troubles which characterized the period of Auletes' restoration to the throne. For not only were there disorders at Alexandria – the cause of Rabirius' hasty departure – but, before that, disturbances had been once again recorded from Heracleopolis, and from the adjoining regions of the Fayum and Oxyrhynchus (Behnesa) as well. The farmers were demanding protection from Rabirius and threatening, unless they received it, to neglect the maintenance of the canals, dams and dykes, while Rabirius and the government insisted that the provincial officials were not acting with sufficient vigour against the agitators.

*

And yet, after extraordinary convulsions, Cleopatra's father Auletes had to some extent become master of his own house once again. This much maligned man did not seem to everyone, and probably not to his third daughter Cleopatra VII either, just a mere stooge who had been

19

humiliated by the Romans. His own ferocious treatment of his opponents, and his development of the Gabinians into a fighting force, suggest that he was more positive than that. He had an impressive record as a builder and restorer of temples. His external policy, too, may have been characterized by ambitious action beyond his southern borders – as befitted the man who arranged for his daughter Cleopatra to learn more than one African tongue, in addition to the language of the Egyptians themselves (for Cleopatra's languages, see p. 256 n. 42).

Auletes' portraits on his coins, notably those issued in 53 BC, show that it was from her father that Cleopatra derived her hooked nose.[35] These coins also make it possible to recognize him in the bony profile, petulant mouth and weary, disillusioned expression of a bronze statuette recently identified at Alexandria.[36] Murderous when he needed to be – though not as consistently murderous as some of his ancestors – he was crafty and calculating in his determination to retain the Ptolemaic heritage: a determination which remained resolute in spite of all his weaknesses.

One of these weaknesses, although he achieved the paternity of Cleopatra and other offspring, was perhaps homosexual vice. This is suggested by inscriptions from the Nile island of Philae engraved by at least two and probably three men who claim to have been the king's passive sexual partners.[37] The names given by two of these individuals seem to be pseudonyms deliberately suggestive of lechery. But it is also fair to point out that the term by which they describe themselves, *kinaidos*, is sometimes used to mean, not only a passive homosexual, but also some sort of dramatic or musical performer – probably a dancer of obscene dances. There was a tradition of this kind of dance in the Ptolemaic house, since Cleopatra's great-uncle Ptolemy x Alexander I, though extremely stout, had himself been an agile practitioner of the art.[38] A Platonic philosopher Demetrius was said to have danced at Auletes' court, after first refusing to put on the appropriate feminine costume; subsequently he was forced to comply, and danced wearing a fashionable dress from Tarentum (Taranto).

This evidence concerning Auletes' taste for dancing fits in well enough with another of his principal interests, which was music. The reason why his subjects called him the Piper (Auletes) was because he loved accompanying choruses on the *aulos* or pipes, an instrument related to the clarinet or oboe.[39] Voltaire applauded Frederick the Great's skill on the pipes by declaring that even Auletes would not have dared play his *aulos* after hearing the Prussian king's performance. In ancient times this sort of activity incurred a good deal of disapproval, especially if carried to excess by monarchs who ought to have other matters to think about. The Romans, in particular, considered that vocal and instrumental music led to immorality,[40] a conclusion which received some support from the tastes of Auletes. However, he must have gained quite a reputation, for he was described as being 'not man but *auletes* and magician (*magos*)'.[41] An element of fashionable mysticism entered into the pipe competitions he organized, and we can see something of this spirit from a statuette of an enraptured, strangely costumed Alexandrian piper of the time.[42]

*

The Romans, however, believed that no one dances unless he is drunk. The Greek philosopher Demetrius, too, who objected to taking the floor at Auletes' court, classified drinking with dancing as one of the undesirable features of the palace. The bracketing of these activities was appropriate enough, and for a significant reason: dancing and drinking alike formed part not only of the amusements of the Ptolemies but also of their religious background, and even (conveniently enough) of an official religious policy that consecrated the rulers as gods. This was a doctrine that fulfilled a vital role in the policies of Auletes, and subsequently in those of his daughter Cleopatra.

During the centuries that spanned the beginnings of Christianity, paganism was still very much alive. This Greco-Roman period was the epoch of passionate belief in the Mystery religions, stressing initiation, purification, mystic communion, redemption in this world, and salvation in the next. But it was also a great age of ruler-worship. For many centuries past the Greeks had been prepared to envisage superior personal gifts as something supernatural, so that they regarded certain individuals as more than human, as geniuses deserving to be set apart.[43] Thus the poet Sophocles, for example, after his death, was allotted a shrine. But after the classical Greek city-states had been eclipsed by the Hellenistic kingdoms, this idea was even more readily applicable to the new national rulers, since 'god is the helping of man by man', as a philosopher observed,[44] and these were men who possessed enormous power to save or destroy. In consequence, they were hailed as 'Epiphanes', God made Manifest in living kings,[45] or 'Neos Theos', the New God, a young and approachable incarnation of the Olympians, his 'newness' incorporating divine magic power.[46] And the new manifest God was also 'Soter', the Saviour, or 'Euergetes', the Benefactor, terms which acknowledge past protection and benefit, and express the hope that these will continue in the future.

All these titles were incorporated in the titles of the Ptolemaic monarchs of Egypt, who from the very beginning had led and guided the rest of the Greek world in the various manifestations of ruler-worship. The idea, in Egypt, was a very ancient one, since the Pharaohs had been god-kings for many centuries.[47] So significant was the national kingship for the people of Egypt that deification was inevitable. But it was in Ptolemaic times that the institution assumed the new forms which spread far and wide into other Hellenistic territories. The first step had been taken shortly after the death of Alexander the Great (323 BC), when Ptolemy I diverted his corpse to Egypt. It lay at the ancient capital, Memphis in Middle Egypt, the site of Alexander's formal recognition as Egypt's king, until it could be installed in a magnificent new tomb at the new capital he himself had founded, Alexandria. There and elsewhere in the country he was venerated as a god in a variety of different ways.[48] The next stage was the worship of Ptolemy I and his step-sister and wife Berenice I as Theoi Soteres (Saviour Gods). Ptolemy I was first called 'Soter' in his lifetime as a voluntary act of homage by the people of Rhodes, because of services rendered to their community. Others followed their example, and finally he and his wife, after their deaths, were made the objects of a major state-cult by his son and heir Ptolemy II Philadelphus. Right down to the reigns of Auletes and Cleopatra, the head of Ptolemy I, with its pronounced features and deep-set eyes, continued to appear on Ptolemaic coins.[49] But meanwhile Ptolemy II and his sister-wife Arsinoe II Philadelphus had taken the final step of allowing themselves, while they were still alive, to be officially honoured as gods. They were known as the Theoi Adelphoi, Brother and Sister Gods.[50] From then onwards, at least four sorts of cult were devoted to all living Ptolemies during their lifetimes.[51]

Ptolemy III (246–221 BC) was specifically known as Euergetes. Ptolemy V (205–180 BC) described himself as Epiphanes. Ptolemy VI (180–145) places the plain designation Theos (God) on his coins, and Ptolemy VII (145–4) bore the title of Neos. Then Cleopatra's father Auletes adopted a whole row of such designations. Moreover, whereas his predecessors had been hailed as 'Our Lord the King', records and petitions to Auletes describe him as 'Our God and Lord the King'. Even his daughters and sons were called goddesses and gods while he himself still lived;[52] and the Alexandrians dedicated a precinct to Auletes and his children as 'Our Lords and Greatest Gods' (52 BC). So Cleopatra was a goddess before she even ascended the throne. To those brought up with transcendent ideas of godhead, all this procedure seems empty flattery. But it was a deliberate policy designed to canalize loyal and patriotic emotions.

*

The best clue to Auletes' policy towards ruler-worship is provided by his most characteristic title Neos Dionysus (the New Dionysus),[53] a designation which he adopted from at least 64–63 BC onwards. He claimed to be the incarnation of this god, the Roman Bacchus or Liber, a claim reflected in the Dionysiac wreath of ivy which adorns his portrait statue, and in the Dionysiac wand or *thyrsus*, an ivy-wreathed fennel stalk with a pine-cone on its tip, which accompanies the ivy-wreathed head on certain of his coins. Such ideas and associations were far from new. But they acquired fresh significance under Auletes, and again under Cleopatra, whose policies, like those of her father, they help to elucidate.

It is a popular misconception of European literature to regard the ancient Dionysus–Bacchus as little more than the god of wine and revelry – though this is hardly a mistake that will be made by any reader of Euripides' *Bacchae*, which reveals the universal, irresistible force of the god. Dionysus was not just the patron of wine, but the god of the great waves of religious emotion which were never far below the surface in ancient Greece,[54] and from time to time rose formidably into view. The ritual included an impressive series of ceremonial initiations into increasingly intimate circles of the god's devotees, culminating in final mystic union. This cult was at its height in the Hellenistic age, when frenzied anxiety to ascend beyond the human body led millions of people into a devoted and ecstatic acceptance of the Dionysiac escape from worldly bonds. And, most of all, the men and women of Hellenistic times clung to Dionysus' promise that his worshippers would be rewarded, not in this life, or not only in this life, but after death, when salvation for the whole of eternity would be theirs.

Such promises, it is true, were the essence of all the Hellenistic Mystery religions. But they figured most dramatically of all in the worship of Dionysus, which at this time almost eclipsed the old Olympian cults as the religion of the Mediterranean world. Any tendency to underestimate its magical force is dispelled by the Dionysiac wall-paintings of the first century BC still to be seen in the Villa of the Mysteries outside Pompeii, with their strangely moving parade of the rituals, terrors and mystical glories of Initiation.[55] The central figure in these paintings, reclining with Dionysus, is usually believed to represent Ariadne, representative of the female sex which played so prominent a part in this emotional religion. Abandoned by Theseus on the island of Naxos, Ariadne has awakened to wed Dionysus, just as the soul of the initiate, too, will be roused from the slumber of death to union with the god, and to eternal triumph, and to the Symposium of the Blessed. Or perhaps the woman at the god's side may be his mother Semele, whom he descended to the Underworld to seek.[56]

Dionysus was victorious even over death, and that is why he can ensure the same victory to his devotees. But in this world, too, he was thought of as the mightiest of conquerors – a fitting tribute to the god whose worship, at this time, seemed the only religion capable of vanquishing the whole world.[57] Already in Euripides' *Bacchae*, Dionysus, by magical rather than warlike arts, was held to have assumed the lordship over vast territories of Asia, and this image was intensified after the conquests of Alexander the Great, whose identification with the god led to the creation of many new sagas of triumphal Dionysiac progress throughout the east.[58] Assimilated among a host of local deities, Dionysus seemed to the successors of Alexander to provide a ready-made means of communication between their Greek and native subjects. Many, therefore, were the Hellenistic rulers who chose to link their names with his.[59] They liked to be thought of as Dionysus, not only because it was convenient to harness these potentially destructive psychological forces to their own purpose, but because such an assimilation indicated that they themselves and their kingships were endowed with the typical Dionysiac virtues. These included benevolence and generosity on an imperial scale, and the equally grandiose encouragement of the dramatic and musical arts.

Seleucid monarchs were among the Dionysiac devotees, and so was Rome's enemy Mithridates VI of Pontus. But once again it was the Ptolemies who led the way, and it was in Alexandria that large parts of the myth took shape, embroidering lavishly upon the eastern conquests of the god. Ptolemy I Soter actually claimed descent, on his mother's side, from Dionysus himself.[60] The great four-yearly festival of the Ptolemaia, introduced by Ptolemy II Philadelphus and celebrated not only in Egypt but in many other parts of the Greek world, included the most resplendent of all processions, led by a poet as Dionysus' priest.[61] The procession culminated in an enormous effigy of the god wearing his sacred ivy-wreath and carrying his wand. Borne along in a carriage shouldered by eighty men, the effigy was accompanied by huge tableaux of world conquest depicting him as lord and master of mankind and of the whole animal world; and exotic animals were carried along in his procession. The people of Alexandria, remarked a later observer, Dio Chrysostom, were as completely carried away, while watching a show of this kind, as if they were intoxicated by drink.[62]

The Dionysiac character of these displays reflected an element which dominated the royal Ptolemaic religion throughout the whole history of the dynasty. Ptolemy II Philadelphus, in addition to the special religious features with which he endowed the Ptolemaia, prepared for the winter festival of Dionysus by erecting a banqueting pavilion of unsurpassed magnificence, supported on inner columns resembling the god's sacred wand.[63] His wife Arsinoe II, too, was a devotee of the same cult. Ptolemy IV Philopator (221–205 BC) sought to prevent undesirable, possibly seditious, deviations among his people by instituting a careful registration of the Dionysiac votaries.[64] But he also identified himself so closely with his divine ancestor that he celebrated the god's Mysteries in his palace, and had the god's ivy-leaf tattooed on his own body. Indeed, he evidently dreamt of making Dionysus the unifying force of his whole empire, the heavenly representative and guarantor of the Ptolemaic house.

When, therefore, the Platonic philosopher Demetrius refused to drink and masquerade at Auletes' court, he was doing more than expressing a puritanical distaste for the royal amusements. The activities he was objecting to were religious, dynastic manifestations, and his refusal was political opposition to the royal godhead. Ranged on the other side, loyally supporting the Ptolemaic régime in many centres, were officially-sponsored Dionysus clubs, each with its own sacred writings and ritual books – and Dionysiac guilds of actors and musicians.[65]

*

This was an age when people increasingly felt that there was perhaps one god instead of many, or at least that the different Olympian deities were not as distinct from one another as had hitherto been generally believed. It became easy, therefore, to merge one deity with another, and this was often done. Dionysus proved the easiest of all to assimilate with his fellow-deities, becoming identified, for example, with Pan as the best dancer, and even with the supreme Zeus himself as arbiter of war and peace.[66] Moreover, such assimilations not only took place within the Greek cults, but provided bridges with the foreign faiths which proliferated among the native, non-Greek populations of the great Hellenistic states. It was agreed that the most ancient and venerable of these was the religion of the old Pharaonic Egypt. There was therefore a widespread process of equation between Egyptian and Greek deities. In the fifth century BC the historian Herodotus had consistently tried to identify each Egyptian god with a Greek one, and in the Hellenistic epoch the process continued. At Sais (Sa-el-Hagar) in the north-western part of the Nile delta, a festival calendar of about 300 BC shows that the native Egyptian priests fully recognized such absorptions, for they listed the names of the Egyptian and Greek gods side by side.[67]

Dionysus, accordingly, was assimilated with the great Egyptian god Osiris. The identification appears in Greek literature from at least the time of Herodotus, and was worked out in detail by the historian Diodorus Siculus who lived in the times of Auletes and Cleopatra, and devoted the first book of his *World History* to Egypt.[68] The same point is made by the wall-paintings of a recently discovered house in Pompeii, where a room is devoted to the depiction of Dionysus–Osiris in both his Greek and his Egyptian forms.[69] And this process was also applied to ruler-worship, so that Auletes, the New Dionysus, is represented in Egyptian texts as the New Osiris.

Osiris, Us-yri (throne, eye), means the Occupier of the Monarchy, the Pharaoh. For very many centuries all classes of the Egyptian population had believed that the king was the god Osiris upon earth. It was thought that Osiris himself had once been a worldly king, a hero who conquered and cultivated the land, and introduced the blessings of civilization. He had then been granted immortality, and so became the god of life's everlasting renewal. His death was bewailed afresh every year, and at a series of imposing annual festivals his rebirth and resurrection – mirrored alike in the Nile and its flood, and in the seed corn, and in the life of man himself – were celebrated with thanksgiving in a series of liturgical dramas, attended by huge throngs of participants and spectators, displaying intense, exuberant emotion. Moreover, although the cult of Osiris extended back to remote antiquity, its importance had increased greatly during the centuries preceding the Christian era. Out of all the multitudinous male deities of Egypt noted by Herodotus, Osiris, he found, was the only one whom men and women worshipped throughout the length and breadth of the land. And later, too, the Ptolemies lavished devout attention upon his worship. They had good reason to do so, since they themselves, in the eyes of their people, were Osiris upon earth.

*

If the king was the god Osiris, the queen was the god's partner Isis, with whom Cleopatra came to identify herself passionately. Moreover, this pair of heavenly prototypes provided the theological justification for what seems to us one of the strangest of Ptolemaic institutions, the marriages of the kings with their sisters. For Osiris and Isis were not only husband and wife but brother and sister, firstborn children of the god of the earth and goddess of the sky.[70] This view of the two deities as brother-husbands and sister-wives goes back to the earliest Pharaonic times, and helped to induce many Pharaohs, who were so closely identified with Osiris, to marry their own sisters or half-sisters. Such marriages preserved the divine royal blood from contamination – and served a practical purpose by cutting down the number of potential pretenders. The Egyptian monarchs were very content to 'keep the business in the family by keeping the family in the business'.[71]

Marriages between full brother and sister, though not unknown in other cultures, were alien to Greek ideas.[72] Yet in this respect the Ptolemies chose to follow the Egyptian rather than the Greek tradition – and for the same political reasons. Thus in about 276 BC Ptolemy II Philadelphus (Sister-Loving) married his masterful sister Arsinoe II

Philadelphus (Brother-Loving),[73] and this was why, in due course, they became the Theoi Adelphoi, Brother-and-Sister Gods. But when this marriage took place, the Greek aversion to such practices found strong expression from the poet Sotades of Maronea, whose observations on the subject were so coarse that he was punished, and perhaps executed.[74] But court poets rallied round the monarchs, explaining that the theology of Greece, as of Egypt, offered highly suitable models, the most notable of all being the marriage of Zeus himself to his sister Hera.[75] Since the time of Ptolemy II there had been many more brother–sister marriages in the same royal house, and, in spite of obscurities regarding her pedigree, there is no doubt that Cleopatra VII, for all her outstanding intellectual and physical endowments, was the product of generations of incest. As those who breed cattle are well aware, the marriage of near relations, although it gives a double chance for blemishes to appear, also makes the recurrence of initial excellences more probable, without necessarily impairing fertility.[76]

It is doubtful, however, if the Ptolemies escaped genetic trouble altogether, for a number of them were abnormally fat. This characteristic had been present in the family since its first emergence upon the historical scene, and then Ptolemy VI Philometor, and Cleopatra's great-grandfather Ptolemy VIII Euergetes (Physcon), and her great-uncle Ptolemy X Alexander I, were all monstrously overweight. It is not clear if this disability also appeared on the female side of the family; at any rate there is no record of Cleopatra, who only lived to the age of thirty-nine, becoming gross. Nevertheless, it is a possibility that certain elements in her character may have been due to this persistent in-breeding – notably her total absence of moral sense, and a tendency to murder her brothers and sisters which may have been partly an inherited family habit.

Cleopatra later followed precedent by contracting two successive marriages with half-brothers, in name at least; they were Osiris to her Isis. But meanwhile, in the years before she became queen, it was her father Auletes who was king and therefore Osiris. This, it is true, like his identification with Osiris' Greek counterpart Dionysus, had not always helped him in his vicissitudes upon earth. Yet such assimilations exercised a more potent influence upon the populations of Egypt and other eastern countries than we can readily imagine. Indeed, it may well have been largely due to such beliefs, quite as much as to Roman arms and money, that Auletes ended up once again on his antique but precarious throne, and stayed there until he died.

*

In the late fifties BC Auletes was only a little over fifty years of age or, younger. Yet after such an eventful and maybe dissipated life, it was hardly surprising if he was beginning to feel the strain. At all events, he began to think of the fate of his children after his death. This, surely, is the reason why the inscription of 52 BC which calls his children Gods also hails them, hopefully, as Lovers of their Brothers (or Sisters) (Philadelphoi). 'Philadelphus' was a noble title in Ptolemaic history, owing to its association with one of the régime's principal heroes, Ptolemy II. Auletes himself had taken on the same designation. And he attributes it to his daughters and sons in the hope of conferring upon them a glorious future.

These children were now four in number, two daughters, Cleopatra VII and her half-sister Arsinoe IV; and Arsinoe's brothers, the future Ptolemies XIII and XIV. Unfortunately the title of Philadelphoi, by which these children were now hailed, was belied by their subsequent careers; and no doubt Auletes was already aware that this mutual love – with special reference to his daughters, because of the boys' extreme youth – was singularly lacking. If so, his revival of the historic title Philadelphus for their benefit was an appeal for family solidarity, and a gesture to try to persuade the people that all was well within the royal house. The wording of the dedication speaks of his surviving off-spring in general terms; so it was presumably intended to refer to all four of them.

At about the same time, however, Auletes gave written expression to the wish that the successors to his throne were to be the elder of his two surviving daughters, Cleopatra VII, who was aged eighteen, and the elder of his two surviving sons, the later Ptolemy XIII, aged about ten. Arsinoe IV, although older than Ptolemy XIII, was omitted, but this need not be seen as a foretaste of her future bad relations with Cleopatra, since two women should not, indeed could not, reign together. A Ptolemaic queen must not reign without a male colleague, and temporary *de facto* exceptions had only been provided, in very occasional emergencies, by powerful, mature queens. There was no possibility of Cleopatra, still in her teens, being pronounced as the sole heir. So the older of her two half-brothers was declared to be her future colleague, and it was no doubt planned that in due course he should become her husband as well.

Auletes incorporated these intentions in a will which he then, according to a precedent that had become established in recent decades, dispatched for safe-keeping to Rome. But Rome, in the late fifties BC, was deep in crisis. As Caesar ended the Gallic Wars, it was clear that he was very soon going to clash violently with the other surviving triumvir, Pompey, who dominated the capital. 'One copy of Auletes' will', records Caesar, 'had been taken to Rome by his emissaries to be placed in the Treasury, but since, owing to the political troubles, this had proved impossible, the will had been deposited instead with Pompey. A duplicate copy was kept under seal at Alexandria.'[77] In this document, Caesar added, Auletes had appealed to the Roman people, by all the gods and by the treaties he had made at Rome, to ensure that the instructions it contained were carried out.

Although the Egyptological evidence is complex and dubious, consisting of problematical headings and datings of texts, certain papyri of 51 BC which refer to 'the thirtieth year of Auletes which is the first year of Cleopatra' suggest that early in that year she, as the older of the two designated heirs, found herself elevated to the rank of co-ruler with her father, so that they began to reign jointly.[78] Such a practice was by no means unknown in Egyptian history. If it was resorted to now, we may conjecture that Auletes may have been unwell – and perhaps that the onset of this illness was what had prompted him to draw up his will. But in any case the reign of Auletes was now drawing rapidly to an end.

2

Cleopatra Gains and Loses the Throne

If, as seems probable, the year 51 BC witnessed a joint reign of Auletes and his daughter, it did not last more than a few weeks, or at most a few months, because by May or even possibly before the end of March he was already dead.[1] However, papyri referring to the thirtieth year of Auletes which is the first year of Cleopatra continue as late as 15 July: which has suggested the possibility that, following earlier Ptolemaic precedents, she hushed up her father's death for a time in order to seize sole control.[2] At all events, the official reign of Cleopatra and her ten-year-old brother Ptolemy XIII began shortly afterwards, since Auletes' death was known to Roman politicians by 1 August.[3]

Ptolemaic dating systems, inconveniently for modern historians, started afresh at the begining of each new reign. According to ancient Egyptian tradition a new reign meant a new beginning, accompanied by gestures of goodwill and generosity – a rebirth of the kingdom necessitating a new era.[4] This renewal was given its specific character by the titles and new ruler selected. The monarchs who came to the throne in 51 BC, Cleopatra VII and Ptolemy XIII, not only retained the titles Brother- and Sister-Loving which they had already been optimistically given by their father,[5] but each took the additional title Philopator (Father-Loving) as well.[6] Philopator had been the title of the fourth and seventh Ptolemies, and Auletes too, had adopted it, since he was a bastard, to stress his royal paternity.

Cleopatra's revival of the same title was a deliberate expression of respect for her father's memory. She had lived through his bad times beside him, and may even have accompanied him in his exile. And he, for his part, had confirmed her position as his heir, and his senior heir at that, since the formal disadvantage of her female sex was outweighed by her colleague's extreme youth. Her older sisters had betrayed their father by accepting the throne when he was driven away, and her title Philopator was intended to show that she took her late father's side – appropriately enough, since her very name meant 'glory to her father'.[7] At a later date in her reign, the Phoenician city of Berytus (Beirut) inscribed one of its coins not only with the era of her accession, which was normal practice, but with that of Auletes, also, which was exceptional since he had been dead for so long.[8] This, too, surely, was a sign that Cleopatra proclaimed and felt a special attachment to the memory of her father. She was likely to be sympathetic to his ideas; and his harsh experiences, at the hands of his own people and of the Romans, were never likely to be far from her mind.

*

The dominant element in Egypt, the element which Cleopatra would find it most necessary to conciliate, consisted of the Greeks. In the wake of the Greek-speaking, Greek-educated Ptolemaic dynasty, many thousands of Greeks had flocked into Egypt during the previous centuries. They did not, for the most part, live in the self-governing city-states characteristic of their mother-country, but settled, under privileged conditions, among the natives. Four cities in Egypt, however, provided exceptions to this rule – cities which were inhabited by Greeks and approximated to the Greek model.[9] The oldest of them was Naucratis (Nabira) beside the westernmost (Canopic) branch of the delta, a settlement which went back to a Greek merchant colony of the seventh century BC. The newest of the four communities was Ptolemais (Psoi, Tolmeta) in Upper Egypt, established by Ptolemy I Soter. Two foundations dated from Alexander the Great: Paraetonium (Sollum) on the western border – the starting point for the desert journey to the oasis of Jupiter Ammon (Siwa) – and the infinitely more important city of Alexandria (332 BC).

Inheriting the trade of Phoenician Tyre which Alexander had destroyed, the Alexandrians eclipsed Carthage after its defeat by the Romans in the first two Punic Wars (264–241, 218–201 BC). From then onwards, until overtaken by Rome itself, Alexandria was the greatest city in the Mediterranean world. Constructed upon the site of an Egyptian village, Rhacotis, near the border of the western desert just beyond the Nile delta, it stood upon a narrow limestone strip between the sea and a coastal lagoon, Lake Mareotis. Alexandria's climate was attractive, supplies of fresh water were abundant, and a vast city rapidly became the centre of culture and fashion for the whole Greco-Roman world. Poets were very ready to sing its praises, and a papyrus declares that 'Alexandria is the whole earth'.[10]

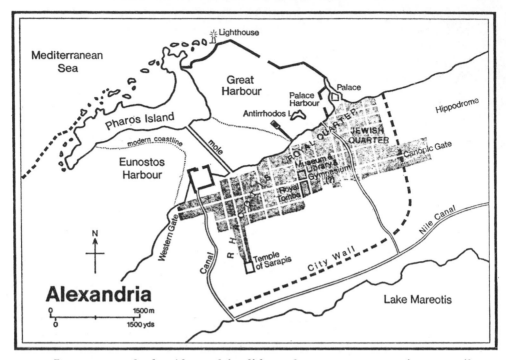

Immense, polyglot Alexandria did not have a representative council like other Greek cities, or at least if there ever was one it had vanished by Cleopatra's time. But the city gave the Ptolemaic kingdom a real capital, which none of the other major Hellenistic monarchies possessed. Yet it was a capital stuck loosely on to an undeveloped body. Like the other Greek towns and settlements in the country, it was an extension of Greece rather than part of Egypt, which really began only at Sais, several miles to the east. In the papyri, people speak of making the journey to Egypt from Alexandria; and the Roman régime which succeeded Cleopatra called its governor the 'prefect of Alexandria and Egypt'.

Because the eastern current carried the Nile silt away from the foreshore, Alexandria was built at the only place on Egypt's Mediterranean coast where a harbour town was a practical possibility. It became the most famous port of the entire ancient world, cut off and protected from the open sea and the north wind by a parallel ridge of reefs, and nearer the coast, three-quarters of a mile offshore, by the three-mile-long Pharos island. By an ingenious feat of planning, this island was joined to the mainland by the construction of a mole (the Heptastadion), which thus provided two superb harbours, one on either side. The eastern, or Great, harbour, was a creation of nature, but was defended by huge man-made

32

breakwaters. The western harbour (Eunostos), on the other side of the mole, was entirely artificial. The two harbours, each leading to a smaller interior basin, could hold as many as 1,200 ships at a single time. The incoming and outgoing of these vessels was controlled by that Wonder of the World the Pharos lighthouse, situated just beyond the eastern extremity of the island from which the lighthouse took its name. To the south, on the city's landward side, Lake Mareotis gave access to the Nile through a canal. And the traffic moving through the lake to and from the river was even more extensive than the shipping that came into the maritime harbours.

Dinocrates, the designer of Alexandria, followed the fifth-century tradition of Hippodamus which favoured a clear-cut grid plan. In contrast to the crooked alleys of Rome, there were straight, right-angled thoroughfares, based on the long latitudinal Street of Canopus running from west to east for a distance of more than three miles from gate to gate. Some way to the north of this street, reached through the Jewish quarter, lay the large, self-contained palace area, looking out upon the promontory which bounded the eastern harbour.

*

Though turbulent, the Alexandrians were industrious. They raised production and exchange to a volume and intensity quite unknown in the Mediterranean area ever before. Papyrus, a plant used for making paper and for a host of other purposes, was one of their principal exports, and virtually an Egyptian monopoly. Other exports included linen, scent, ivory, architectural and sculptural stones of many kinds, emeralds and a variety of less precious gems, and a famous range of metal utensils – particularly in silver, which was brought into the country in large quantities in order to be made into these graceful shapes. The Alexandrians also produced glass vases with paintings in gold or water-colours, perhaps, like glass-blowing, an invention of Cleopatra's time.[11] There was also a substantial export trade in woollen goods, including those manufactured at the queen's own wool-mill, run by slave-girls under the direction of a Roman senator, Quintus Ovinius.[12] At some time during the immediately preceding centuries Egypt had invented an improved vertical loom, and perhaps a horizontal loom as well: both types made their way to Greece and Italy, where there was a great vogue for elegant Egyptian rugs. The Ptolemaic authorities, with the help of a canal from the Nile to the Red Sea, were also very active in sending mass consignments of cheap clothing, glass and other inexpensive goods south to their African neighbours – the peoples of Ethiopia (North Sudan) and the Somali coast, the 'Cinnamon Country' which representatives of Ptolemy II and III had explored in order to fix stations for elephant hunts. Cleopatra herself learnt to speak the languages of the Ethiopians and of the Trogodytes who inhabited the torrid African coast from Upper Egypt down to the farther end of the Red Sea.

Evidently her father had foreseen, or hoped for, important developments in this area, and perhaps far beyond, since he had entrusted Callimachus, his governor-general of the Thebaid or Upper Egypt, with a commission described as the 'Command of the Red Sea and the Indian Sea'.[13] The post was designed to keep an eye on the rising south Arabian Himyarite state, which was eager to keep the Somali cinnamon trade in its own hands, out of the way of Ptolemaic encroachments. Furthermore, this governor-general of Upper Egypt was concerned with commerce as far away as India, and his instructions authorized him to employ naval patrols for the protection of Egyptian traders.

Ptolemy III Euergetes may have penetrated as far as the Hindu Kush. But it was not until the late second century BC that the Red and Indian Seas began to play an important part in Egyptian policy. For it was then that Cleopatra's great-grandfather, Ptolemy VIII (Euergetes Physcon), engaged a Greek explorer, Eudoxus of Cyzicus, to explore the open-sea route from Aden to India, under the guidance of an Indian stowaway who had offered to reveal the workings of the monsoons. This secret, as it happened, was not finally mastered until shortly after the end of the Ptolemaic era. Yet already under the Ptolemies there was a good deal of coasting along the southern Arabian shore outside the Red Sea. Moreover, the strait leading out of that sea into the Indian ocean was guarded by a party of Egyptian Greeks who, following an earlier exploration, colonized the island of Dioscuridou Nesos (Socotra),[14] probably in the time of Cleopatra's father Auletes and under his sponsorship.

They did not keep the island, which fell under the control of Arabian sheikhs, and the trading route was not fully exploited by the Ptolemies. Cleopatra's younger contemporary Strabo remarks that 'formerly not twenty ships ventured outside the Red Sea'.[15] Presumably he means twenty ships a year, though it is not quite clear what period he, or his source, is speaking about. But a good deal still had to be done before all the natural and man-made impediments to southern trade could be eliminated. Cleopatra did not, as far as we know, pursue her father's initiative. Until her very last desperate days, her eyes were turned instead towards the Roman north and west.

*

Cleopatra presided over one of the most rigidly centralized bureaucratic governments that the world has ever seen. It was largely the creation of Ptolemy I and Ptolemy II. Successive monarchs, through their ministers and agents, controlled virtually the whole of the country's revenue on either a monopoly or a percentage basis. Their economic aim was to accumulate the maximum of wealth with the minimum of expenditure, change and risk. The kings regarded Egypt primarily as a source of income, and the whole administration was directed to this end. 'No one', stated a Ptolemaic decree, 'has the right to do what he wishes, but everything is organized for the best.'[16] And it was organized under an array of provincial governors, grouped (at least from 178–7 BC) under three governor-generalships: Lower Egypt (Delta), Middle Egypt (including Memphis and Lake Moeris or Fayum) and Upper Egypt (Thebaid).

There had been bureaucracies in the ancient east before. But this was a far more sophisticated, logical and coherent system than any of its predecessors. And how fortunate for the bureaucrats (and ourselves) that Egypt, through its papyrus crop, produced a world monopoly of the papyrus on which they could write their minutes and memoranda and letters! In some ways, there was virtually a modern civil service. Its members (unlike officials of the Roman Republic) drew salaries, except for some of the most important of the functionaries, who enjoyed such large opportunities for gain that they were obliged instead to pay the king for their posts. Many of the papyri relating to the work of these civil servants deal with taxes, which were more highly developed in Egypt than anywhere else, with the help of an elaborate and ubiquitous police force. Taxation in kind was gathered by state officials, while monetary taxes, according to a widespread ancient practice, were often collected by private individuals who bought the rights from the state at annual auctions.

In the first days of the Ptolemaic régime, this Greco-Egyptian civil service was not very complicated, and more like a private business than a national organization, since its members were thought of as personal agents of the king and members of his own household.[17] But by the middle of the second century BC the bureaucracy had proliferated alarmingly. For example, a papyrus indicating the numerous formalities required to secure a state appointment[18] gives an impression 'of the stupendous amount of writing, of the circulation of papers, of the running of petitioners to and fro, which was always going on in Ptolemaic Egypt'.[19] Officialdom, combined with severity, became almost intolerable, and an edict of 118 BC gave a grim list of the depredations and injustices which had to be fought against.[20] Public and private papyri alike show that even the central government agreed with its subjects that far too many of the innumerable state functionaries were insubordinate, dishonest, arbitrary and violent.[21]

*

There were two main sources of the income of the Ptolemies. They were in control of the agriculture of the Nile valley. And they kept their hands on all the more important branches of trade.

Egyptian agriculture possessed unique advantages, because the Nile overflowed its banks every summer and receded every autumn, leaving behind it great masses of extraordinarily fertile mud. Consequently Egypt was renowned for the superb abundance of its grain.[22] The Ptolemies much improved its quality by acclimatizing Syrian and various kinds of Greek wheat, and they introduced numerous specialized improvements in techniques, methods of irrigation and types of equipment. Already at the start of the third century BC, in spite of all the expenses of transportation, it actually cost a Greek living in Greece one-fifth less to buy Egyptian wheat than to purchase the grain grown in his own country. Egypt became, in due course, the largest grain producer in the whole Mediterranean area, exceeding Sicily and Tunisia, and even the Black Sea kingdom of the Cimmerian (Crimean) Bosphorus, which drew upon the vast resources of south Russia. After the Romans took over Cleopatra's kingdom, the amount of grain regularly dispatched to Rome was enough to supply the needs of the whole city for four months of every year.[23]

In theory, the Ptolemies owned the entire soil as their own personal property. And in practice, too, they administered very large tracts, leasing out small lots to crown peasants who were not allowed to leave the land until after the harvesting was done. The monarchs were therefore landowners and agriculturalists on an unprecedented scale. The royal granaries lent seed to individual farmers, who paid one-quarter of the proceeds in tax, and also acted as banks for private grain repositories. The circumstances in which crops had to be bought, stocked and sold were laid down by precise rules.

The Ptolemaic régime's trading monopolies, too, were so comprehensive that almost every article in daily use was manufactured either in royal factories or under royal licences which laid down compulsory sale-prices. These monopolies included papyrus, wool, salt, cloth, scent and oil. Our surviving evidence (written on papyri) happens to tell us most about the oil, which was indispensable for food, body-care and lighting. Egypt was not, like other leading Mediterranean countries, dependent on olive oil, which could only be imported on payment of a 50 per cent duty, compared with $33\frac{1}{3}$ per cent on wine and figs. Vegetable oils, which played a much larger part, were extracted at state-controlled mills, and the workers, like the crown peasants, were never allowed to move elsewhere before the production season had finished. The right to sell oil was hired out to wholesalers and retailers, who were obliged, like other traders, to sell at fixed prices. The royal profit ranged from 70 per cent on sesame oil to 300 per cent or more on oil of colo-cynth (bitter apple); other vegetable oils in Egypt were croton, linseed and safflower. Only temples were allowed to possess their own private oil factory and they could use it for only two months in each year: for the rest of the time it had to be kept closed. Temples were also allowed to make linen robes for their own priests – on condition that they supplied the king with a further fixed amount of linen for purposes of export.

Banking was another state monopoly, and its efficient centralization in the hands of the government, which operated through a network of branch banks, was a novelty in the Mediterranean world. There were private banks also, but these were secondary and besides they, too, operated under governmental leases and regulations. As everywhere in the ancient world, interest rates were high – officially 24 per cent per annum – which kept labour cheap and money dear. In keeping with general Greek practice, the first Ptolemies issued a national silver coin-age, but later on it became more and more sporadic and debased and was largely superseded by a humbler coinage of bronze. This circulated only inside Egypt, and not very extensively even there, since the avail-able opportunities for using money were small, but at least it was un-challenged by foreign issues, since these were not admitted. The influx of capital was controlled by tolls, and foreign coins were restruck with Ptolemaic dies. Thus the national economy was deliberately isolated from the rest of the Hellenistic world, so that nothing should interfere with the completeness of royal control.

Ptolemy vi Philometor (180–145 BC) and his successors drastically lowered the already irregular weights of the bronze coins, which meant that the royal government declared a sort of state bankruptcy, hoping to make a heavy profit by the high purchasing value it attached to its light-weight token currency. But instead the expected gains were swamped in a general process of inflation which swept over the Mediter-ranean area, causing especially catastrophic hardship and unrest in Egypt. Before long, desperate and destitute individuals and groups were rioting and going 'underground' into the marshes of the Nile. And the oppressiveness and dishonesty of the Ptolemaic officials, operating with-in a vicious circle of ever-increasing taxation, did nothing to bring them back.

*

The principal result of these developments was that the poor became poorer, while the rich still continued to prosper: for the exports which gave them their wealth did not suffer as much as might have been ex-pected. It is true that Egypt's gradual loss of its external possessions cut off certain trading facilities in the Aegean, which passed successively to two rising commercial rivals, the island-cities of Rhodes and Delos. But the collapse of Rhodes at Roman hands (167 BC), followed by the destruction of Delos by Mithridates VI of Pontus and then again by pirates (88 and 69 BC), was helpful to Egypt. The Ptolemies still continued to export grain, papyrus, linen and glass to Greek lands – and compensated for any setbacks by new connections with those regions beyond their southern and eastern borders, in which Auletes took such a special interest. Moreover, Italian merchants became fascinated with the possibilities of purchasing Egyptian goods for Rome and other cities of Italy. The Ptolemies had maintained Italian links from an early stage of their régime,[24] and when Scipio Aemilianus visited Cleopatra's great-grandfather Physcon in 140 or 139 BC he returned to Rome with a vivid impression of Egyptian resources. From then onwards, as the excavations of Pompeii have confirmed, the Italian connection became more and more extensive, and inscriptions testify to the existence of a flourishing Italian business community at Alexandria.

In spite of the economic troubles of the two preceding centuries, Egypt's annual financial surplus was still large during the first century BC.[25] The financial difficulties of Auletes were particularly grave, but the king who staggered everyone with the lavishness of the dinner he gave to Pompey in 63 BC was not easy to reduce to penury, however hard Roman financiers might try. Ancient writers disagree whether Auletes' revenue was 6,000 or 12,500 talents (see Note on p. 281). These figures are almost valueless since we do not know what they comprised or how how they were reached,[26] but it remains clear that the wealth which Cleopatra inherited from him far exceeded that of any country that the Romans had hitherto contrived to annex.

She herself was said to be passionately eager to make profits.[27] One way in which she achieved this was by debasing her occasional silver coinages still further. In theory, these coins were supposed to be of good silver, intrinsically equal in value to the objects they purchased. But by Auletes' time the proportion of silver had sunk to 33 per cent, and Cleopatra lowered it still further to about 25 per cent. She also cut the weights of her father's already light-weight bronze coinage by three-quarters.[28] In the past, when the weights of coins were irregular, merchants had often preferred to assess their value by weighing them in bulk,[29] but Cleopatra safeguarded her profits by taking the step, unprecedented for the Ptolemies, of marking the denominations (80 and 40 drachmas) upon her bronze pieces, which no doubt had to be accepted at the official valuation, with extensive gains to herself.

But this was only a comparatively minor manifestation of her general financial acumen, which no doubt, in true Ptolemaic fashion, extended

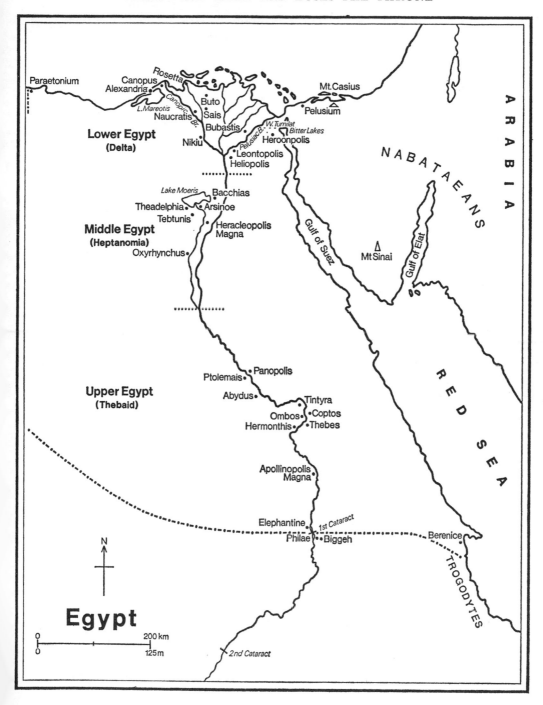

Paraetonium

Canopus
Alexandria
Rosetta
L.Mareotis
Canopic Br.
Naucratis

Buto
Sais
Bubastis

**Lower Egypt
(Delta)**

Nikiu

Mt.Casius
Pelusium

W. Tumilat
Bitter Lakes
Pelusiac Br.
Heroonpolis

Leontopolis
Heliopolis

N A B A T A E A N S

A R A B I A

Lake Moeris
Bacchias
Theadelphia
Arsinoe
Tebtunis

**Middle Egypt
(Heptanomia)**

Heracleopolis
Magna

Oxyrhynchus

Gulf of Suez

Mt Sinai

Gulf of Elat

Panopolis
Ptolemais

**Upper Egypt
(Thebaid)**

Abydus

Tintyra
Ombos
Hermonthis
Coptos
Thebes

R E D   S E A

Apollinopolis
Magna

Elephantine
Philae
Biggeh
1st Cataract
Berenice

TROGODYTES

N

Egypt

0   200 km
0   125m

2nd Cataract

through every part of her administration. A Greco-Egyptian author, apparently of Cleopatra's time, wrote a treatise on weights and measures, but thought it proper and plausible, and good for sales, to pretend that his essay was the work of the queen herself.[30] Moreover, the reference in one of the surviving extracts from this monograph, to a *Georgica*, seems to suggest that she was also credited with a treatise on farming. But much more indicative of her renown as a sharp financial operator is a further study, likewise bearing her pseudonym, which proclaims her skill in alchemy, and concludes with a boast that she could even manufacture gold.[31]

*

Cleopatra was a Greek queen, and her ruling class, who were allowed to share some of the monarch's riches, were men of Greek culture, descended from Greek and Macedonian settlers.[32] They enjoyed a superior status and special privileges, including law-courts of their own and exemption from the more degrading forms of corporal punishment;[33] and, unlike, for example, the Anglo-Saxons after their conquest of Britain, they never worked the land. There were also, of course, many other non-Egyptians in the country besides Greeks. In particular, the Jews were very numerous. And there were many foreign slaves, for although the domestic slaves of Alexandria were mostly Egyptians, those of the countryside came from Asia Minor and Syria and the African hinterland.

But the principal population of the country consisted of Egyptian peasants. In Cleopatra's time, these *fellahin* probably numbered between seven and nine million. Although they fared no worse and perhaps a little better than in Pharaonic times, and some of the Ptolemies showed a genuine interest in doing something to protect their interests, a very large proportion of this native population lived barely above subsistence level. Except for a relatively few collaborating priests, they were wholly excluded from power, and could only note, across a wide gulf, the many privileges which the other communities possessed and they themselves lacked. The behaviour of the foreign upper class, it may be assumed, added fuel to the flames. As a Macedonian once remarked, 'against men of other race, against barbarians, all Greeks wage eternal warfare'.[34]

Perhaps as early as the third century BC Egyptian dissatisfaction began to show itself. Underground nationalist pamphlets, one of which is known as the Potter's Prophecy,[35] assail the Greeks, and declare that Greek Alexandria, attacked by a native monarch from the south, is destined to yield its pre-eminence once again to ancient Memphis in Middle Egypt, south of where Cairo stands today: and in those eagerly awaited days the City beside the Sea 'shall become a place where the fishermen dry their nets'. In Egyptian religious liturgies, too, this xenophobic spirit was on the increase.[36]

During the crises of the middle Ptolemaic epoch, however, the monarchs began to reflect that the Hellenistic states destined to last longest were probably those which managed to effect some compromise with the native cultures. Even if the memory of common hostility to the temporary Persian occupation of Egypt before Alexander had worn somewhat threadbare as a bond between Greeks and Egyptians, it was only by the pooling of Greek skill with Egyptian experience that the great wealth of the country could be fully exploited. Nevertheless, it needed an external menace to introduce an effective measure of liberalism into the government's policy: in order to beat back the Seleucids at Raphia (Rafah) in 217 BC, Ptolemy IV Philopator was compelled to admit native Egyptian troops to military service, a privilege (for so it was regarded) which had previously been reserved for settlers. The result, however, was that the Egyptians wanted other privileges as well, and started a wave of rebellions which made Upper Egypt virtually independent for two decades or more.

In the middle of this period (196 BC) Ptolemy V Epiphanes made a gesture to the natives by staging his coronation at the old capital Memphis – where his father Philopator may perhaps have been crowned too – and celebrating the appropriate Pharaonic rituals which went back three millennia. The Rosetta Stone (from Rashid on the Mediterranean), now in the British Museum, significantly celebrates the event not only in Greek but in the official (hieroglyphic) and popular (demotic) Egyptian scripts. Things were changing. The Egyptians were accustomed to complain of discrimination against themselves because they were not Greek. But by the mid-second century BC the Greeks, too, were beginning to protest about discrimination. For example, a Greek woman tells how her son learnt Egyptian in order to better himself in the world.[37] Rival claimants to the throne needed the help of the Egyptians, and in 130 BC an Egyptian, Paos, became governor-general of Upper Egypt. Cleopatra's great-grandfather Physcon, although himself the product of a learned Greek education, favoured the Egyptians so much that the Alexandrian Greeks turned against him; whereupon he expelled the Greek intelligentsia from the city; and Athens, in disapproval, omitted to celebrate the festival of his royal house, the Ptolemaia.

The separateness of the Greek and Egyptian communities must not, however, be regarded as absolute. In spite of everything, there is evidence of friendly relations between members of the two communities. And the art and architecture of the country, especially in the days of

Cleopatra and her immediate forebears, displays some curious and significant blends of Greek and Egyptian traditions.[38] There had also been a great increase in intermarriage and racial fusion. In the second century BC the historian Polybius found that even at Alexandria where, as in the other Greek cities of Egypt, mixed marriages remained illegal, none of the Greeks were any longer ethnically pure. Except in the royal house itself, where no Egyptian blood can be traced, they are better described as Greco-Egyptians than as Greeks. The papyri record families in which one brother has a Greek and the other an Egyptian name. Indeed, sometimes a Greek and Egyptian nomenclature are combined in a single person.

Nevertheless, community interchanges and bilingualism remain the exception rather than the rule;[39] it is clear enough that these blurrings of distinction did not suffice to bring the two communities very much closer together. For one thing, the more the local Greeks became Egyptianized, the more firmly, indeed stridently, they clung to Greek institutions and culture. And as for the Egyptians, in the time of Herodotus they had looked on the Greeks as unclean foreigners, and so they did still. On the temple at Tintyra (Dendera) in Upper Egypt an inscription forbade all entry not only to Asians and Syrians and Arabians, but also to Greeks. The inscription dates from shortly after Cleopatra's death, but no doubt similar vetoes had existed in her time, and probably much earlier as well.

For the Egyptians were singularly tenacious. Hellenistic culture overlaid but never eradicated the stubborn Egyptian traditionalism, which 'ran so deep and nurtured a plant so oddly resistant to many of the blandishments of classical civilization'.[40] Indeed, their sardonic gusto, as well as their racial type, still survives intact today.[41]

*

This, then, was the strange national structure which Cleopatra inherited She herself, during her reign of twenty-one years, was too heavily preoccupied with her relations with Rome, political and personal, to be able to devote a great deal of time to internal affairs. But from such slight evidence as has survived, her relations with the native Egyptians seem to have been good. When she got into trouble with the Alexandrians shortly after her succession, it was in Upper Egypt that she found refuge and support; and in her final defeat the Egyptians, or some of them, are said to have offered to rise in her favour. We cannot, perhaps, deduce any special goodwill towards the Egyptians from her instruction that a decree should be published in their tongue as well as in Greek, for this was in her own interests, and had been done before. But Plutarch preserves a significant tradition that, in addition to all her other African and Asian languages, she spoke the Egyptian tongue – which not a single one of her Ptolemaic predecessors had managed to learn.[42]

But it was chiefly in the religious field that those Ptolemies who were most interested in Egyptian support had tried hardest to make contact, and this, probably, was the policy of Cleopatra too. The founder of her line, Ptolemy I Soter, had sought to forge a theological link between the two communities by more or less inventing a god who could become a leading divinity of both the Greek and the Egyptian religion at one and the same time. This was Sarapis (Serapis), who was deliberately evolved from the native cult of Osor-Hapi (Apis), a bull associated with Osiris.[43] Partially Hellenized for the purpose, and established in a huge temple four miles from Memphis, Sarapis became an oracular god of healing, a wonder-worker superior to fate, whose great statue, with its golden head and jewelled eyes, gazed out of a darkened shrine equipped with all the sensational miraculous effects which were a speciality of the age – conjuring tricks, scientific devices and every sort of visual illusion. At Alexandria, too, the shrine of Sarapis, situated upon a rocky hill overlooking the city and Lake Mareotis, was believed to be the grandest building in the world after the Temple of Capitoline Jupiter at Rome. Sarapis belonged to a Trinity with the goddess Isis and the god Anubis, a jackal-headed deity who conducted the souls of the dead to immortal life.

Sarapis combined the mystery and glamour of ancient Egyptian religion with an iconography recalling the chief god of Greece, Zeus, with whom he was often regarded as identical. The cult of Sarapis continued actively throughout both Ptolemaic and Roman times. But as a link between the Hellenic and Egyptian pantheons, the innovation hardly proved a success, for he did not exercise much appeal outside Memphis and Alexandria, and the Egyptians paid him little attention. Although sometimes proclaimed the universal ruler, he was never invoked apart from Isis, and indeed she tended to eclipse him, because of the greater emotional satisfactions she could offer – satisfactions of which Cleopatra was very well aware. What the worship of Sarapis did achieve, however – and this, too, had clearly played an important part in the original conception – was to provide a cult suitable for exportation to the Greek or Hellenized subjects and friends of the Ptolemies outside Egypt. To them the new god seemed an admirable representative of the twin traditions over which the Ptolemies presided, the traditions of Greece and of Egypt.

*

Yet the two national strands, on the whole, remained obstinately apart, and the Ptolemies were obliged to recognize the fact. For example, they were crowned as Egyptian Pharaohs quite separately and distinctly from whatever inaugural ceremonies they celebrated as Greek monarchs. At their Egyptian coronations, the priests invested them with the royal crook, sceptre and whip, and crowned them with the double Pharaonic crown: the red cobra crown of Lower Egypt which was the Lady of Spells, and the white, conical, bulbous-tipped vulture crown of Upper Egypt, the Lady of Dread. Ptolemy II Philadelphus already bore a Pharaonic royal name, and no doubt Ptolemy I Soter had possessed one before him. The Egyptians still saw their rulers, foreign though they were, as a continuation of the Pharaohs who had been their indispensable links with the gods.

The most distinctive, urgent and pertinacious feature of the Egyptians was their religion. Being uniquely attached to the past, they had long been intensely proud of their traditional rites, and of the venerable, multifarious, bewildering antiquity of the whole business. This religion survived Cleopatra's time for half a millennium or longer still, until unremitting Christian pressure finally brought it more or less to an end. The Persians, during their brief occupation of Egypt sharply terminated by Alexander, had been remiss about the honours they paid to the Egyptian gods. Alexander did not make the same mistake. He had been saluted as king at ancient Memphis, and Ptolemy I, before moving to Alexandria, settled for a time at the same place, adorning it with Sarapis' shrine. Later Ptolemies, too, resided for short periods in Memphis. This was to show how much they revered the religious traditions of their Egyptian subjects – however badly these fared on the material plane.

The leaders of the Egyptians were their priests, identifiable by shaven heads and white linen robes, very different from the woollen clothing of the Greeks. There were also important native officers of the army, but they were very few; and if there was still a lay Egyptian aristocracy, it no longer had a representative role. As for the priests, the Ptolemies favoured them on condition that they contributed to the régime, by paying their taxes on temple manufactures. These contributions being assured, the monarchs welcomed a few of the leading priests at court, and conferred lavish and much publicized benefactions upon the temples. It had always been regarded as the essential duty of the Pharaohs to build temples and see to their upkeep; and still the temples remained the chief centres of the national civilization, repositories of its writing and art. The Egyptian priests lost no opportunity of reminding the Ptolemies about the gifts allegedly showered on their shrines by the monarchs of old: a papyrus of about the time of Cleopatra stresses that prosperity is only possible if many offerings are made to altars and festivals.[44] In response to these suggestions, the Ptolemies did much to restore the temples to their former glories, and allowed them the right of asylum, to protect the people against bureaucratic oppression. Ptolemy I Soter had already maintained close relations with the native priesthood, and on the Rosetta Stone the priests of Memphis, showing a new degree of self-assertion, congratulate Ptolemy v Epiphanes on the honour he has paid to the Egyptian divinities.

By the time of Cleopatra the hereditary high priests of Memphis, tracing their descent back to earliest Ptolemaic times, had become extremely grand personages, almost as grand as they had been under the Pharaohs; and they worked very smoothly with the régime. For the first ten years of Cleopatra's reign this high priest was a man named Pshereniptah.[45] Records relating to his revenues suggest that at this time, as perhaps earlier, Memphis exercised primacy over the whole Egyptian priesthood. However, since the Egyptian priests were supposed to be strictly monogamous, Pshereniptah seems to go a little too far when he boasts of his 'excellent harem'. He was only forty-nine or fifty when he died, having held the high-priesthood ever since his boyhood. The reign of Auletes, in which he first took up office, must have been a good time for such men, for Auletes, in spite of all his extensive disbursements to the Romans, was a large-scale builder and restorer of temples. Even if most of his restorations were surface work, they were extremely widespread. They can still be recognized at a considerable number of Upper Egyptian sites,[46] and he was probably just as active in Lower and Middle Egypt, where all the ancient buildings have now been washed away by the Nile. On the temple walls Auletes is shown as Pharaoh smiting his enemies to the ground, like a Rameses or Thothmes. Although these reliefs present a romantically inaccurate picture of his sometimes undignified reign, they are also reminders of the glories of millennial Egypt which Cleopatra was brought up to revere, and which she felt proud to inherit from her father.

One of the places enriched by Auletes' building activities was Karnak, the north-eastern part of the ancient city of Thebes on the east bank of the Nile. Thebes had been the capital of Egypt in 1600–1200 BC, a royal capital such as the world had never seen before and would never see again. Homer called it the city of a hundred gates. The local god Amon, after whom the place took the name of No-Amon, had absorbed the northern sun-god Ra, transforming himself in the process into a great imperial deity, the King of the Gods: the wealthiest religious force in the world. In those days it had been the chief priest of Amon-Ra at Thebes, not the high priest of Memphis, who was the primate of all Egypt, and at certain times, for example in the early eleventh century BC, he was even more powerful than his royal master. The temple of his god Amon-Ra at Karnak was the largest place of worship the world has ever seen;

and its restoration by Auletes no doubt brought great credit to himself and his family.

The Pharaohs were widely believed to be the offspring of Amon-Ra, and the Ptolemies took over this claim; at Thebes Ptolemy I Soter was worshipped in conjunction with the god. Yet under his successors the Thebaid, or Upper Egypt, was often insubordinate and seditious. The top crust of Hellenism was thinner there than anywhere else in the country, for the Thebaid contained few Greek settlers, and many Egyptian priests. Its people felt a great distaste for Alexandria, as they still do today, and took advantage of the frequent strife within the Ptolemaic house. The native disturbances that broke out soon assumed the scale of patriotic rebellions. Under Ptolemy IV and V, when the territory suffered from prolonged revolts, it actually asserted its independence under a native dynasty. In the time of Cleopatra's grandfather Lathyrus a further obstinate rising in the same area ended, after three years, with the partial destruction of the legendary city of Thebes itself. Henceforward it was only an insignificant town – except for the four great temples, and the City of the Dead. All these monuments still remained, not only as tourist centres, but as continuing embodiments of the obstinate tradition.

*

At the very outset of her reign Cleopatra decided to associate herself with this native sentiment in a striking gesture. The occasion was provided by a fortunate chance. One of the holy places adjacent to Thebes was Hermonthis (now Armant), fourteen miles to the south of the city on the west bank of the Nile.[47] Its most famous divinity, at this time, was a bull named Buchis or Bakis or Pakis. And at precisely this time the reigning bull very conveniently died.

The large number of different animals worshipped by the Egyptians was one of the many aspects of their religion that the Greeks and Romans found baffling and shocking.[48] To the Egyptians, on the other hand, this practice seemed entirely natural and inevitable. From the earliest times, for example, they had worshipped bulls. This was a fertility cult, and in some cases its performance included erotic practices. At least four provinces of the country chose the bull as their emblem, and at least four regions worshipped different bulls of their own. The most famous was Apis of Memphis, a black bull with white spots whose name and cult had contributed to the creation of the god Sarapis. But there was also the more warlike holy bull Buchis of Hermonthis, honoured as the living soul of Amon-Ra.

In view of the recent death of the last Buchis, a new animal had to be installed. The installation ceremonies duly took place on 22 March,

51 BC,[49] and there is a good reason to believe that Cleopatra attended the rites in person: an inscription on the shrine of Buchis, the Bucheum of Hermonthis, declares that 'the Queen, the Lady of the Two Lands, the goddess who loves her father, rowed the Bull in the barge of Amon to Hermonthis'. The conventions of Egyptian terminology are hard to understand and sometimes surprising; for example she is also described as 'king'. Nevertheless, in spite of arguments to the contrary, it does seem probable that the reference is not just a figurative statement, and that she herself led the river procession upon the sacred vessel, and conducted the new Bull to its sacred home amid a vast concourse of priests and state officials.[50] It may well be that she was the first Ptolemaic monarch ever to take part in this ceremony, and that her ancestors had hitherto been content to dispatch royal functionaries as their deputies.

There is no mention of Auletes in the inscription, and it is possible that he was already dead; though if Cleopatra was pretending, at this time, that he was still alive, she presumably explained that illness kept him away, and that she, the elder of his heirs and perhaps his co-monarch, was representing him. The inscription does not refer to her half-brother Ptolemy XIII either, but if his father's death had not been announced he was not yet co-monarch, and would not necessarily have been expected to attend, especially in view of his youth.[51]

However, that was only in March, and a much more significant indication of the boy's position is provided by a contract document dated 28 August of the same year. For this, too, is headed by the name of Cleopatra, and makes no mention of her half-brother at all.[52] A reference by Marcus Caelius Rufus, in one of his letters to Cicero, makes it certain that Auletes' death had been publicly announced at this time. Auletes had declared Cleopatra and Ptolemy XIII to be his joint heirs; but people were afraid that Cleopatra intended to supplant her young half-brother, and the papyrus of 28 August suggests that they may have been right. Such an attitude was against the wishes of her beloved father. But he was dead, and she could always argue that in the new political circumstances it had become impracticable to retain a minor on the throne: a minor had to have a Regency Council, and he would be at the mercy of unscrupulous councillors. It was all the more impracticable because she was female and he was male, and Ptolemaic custom insisted that queens, even when they were co-monarchs, took second place, in point of law, to the kings who were their colleagues.[53] This would have meant that her brother's Regency Council took priority over herself, a position which – as later events were to demonstrate – would make her position impossible. For she left it in no doubt, at all stages of her reign, that even if convention required her to have a younger male co-monarch, she was never disposed to allow him superiority or even equality. Unlike previous Ptolemaic queens, whose portraits had never normally appeared alone on Egyptian coins,[54] she habitually coined with her own head and name, omitting any mention of her juvenile male colleagues.

And yet those earlier queens had not been demure violets. Indeed, some of them can more accurately be described as murderous tigresses.[55] At any rate they were often exceedingly powerful characters. The royal women of the successor states of Alexander in general, and of the Ptolemaic house in particular, had frequently shown energy, foresight, daring and courage to a degree 'greater than the measure of women'.[56]

For example, Arsinoe II, the sister–wife of Ptolemy II Philadelphus, though she had never become joint ruler in the same sense as some later queens, would have been difficult to surpass either in power or strength of personality or renown. As the 'Lady of Abundance', she had placed double cornucopiae on her coinage,[57] and Cleopatra VII, to show her consciousness of this heritage, deliberately repeated her design. Berenice II (c. 273–221 BC), wife of Ptolemy III Euergetes, had likewise been justly praised by the court poet Callimachus as an exceedingly masterful woman.[58] Cleopatra I, of Seleucid birth, survived her husband Ptolemy V Epiphanes and controlled the affairs of the Ptolemaic kingdom for four years as Regent for her infant son. And he, Ptolemy VI Philometor, later became the first to associate his queen-consort in the dating formula with himself, a custom which henceforth prevailed; his sister–wife Cleopatra II (Thea Philometor Soteira) gained the position of full co-monarch (132–1 BC). Such were the formidable women whom Cleopatra VII had been brought up to regard as her models. But now already she was going farther than any of them in her determination to establish sole, unhampered control.

*

At the very outset of this attempt, Cleopatra encountered a perilous and unforeseeable difficulty owing to external circumstances. A short time previously, the Romans had suffered a catastrophic defeat at the hands of their only formidable neighbour, the Parthian empire which bordered upon the recently established Roman province of Syria. In 53 BC Crassus, colleague of Pompey and Caesar in the Triumvirate, had been overwhelmed by the Parthians at Carrhae (Haran) in northern Mesopotamia. He perished, and Rome was terrified that the Parthians would sweep straight on into Syria. Fortunately their invasion, when it finally took place in 51 BC, was only a small affair. Nevertheless, when a new Roman governor of Syria, the honest, stubborn and ill-tempered Marcus Calpurnius Bibulus, reached his province later in the same year, he still found part of the Parthian army entrenched within its borders. Desperately short of troops, he pitted his hopes upon the legionary force which

Gabinius had left in Egypt as mercenaries in the service of Auletes: a force which Cleopatra had now inherited. Bibulus dispatched his two sons to arrange with Cleopatra that these Gabinians should be ordered to join him and help defend Syria against the Parthian menace. But the Gabinians felt so reluctant to leave Egypt for active service under an austere Roman commander that they refused to obey Bibulus' sons, and murdered them instead.

Cleopatra arrested the men responsible for the murders, and sent them in chains to Bibulus. This must have been a very difficult operation. Not only was there a grave risk of the whole Gabinian army rising in revolt, but such a rising could easily have been joined by all the numerous and powerful Alexandrians who had violently objected to the pro-Roman policies of the queen's father Auletes. Bibulus, as it turned out, refused to punish the killers of his sons, indicating that the Roman Senate would have to deal with the matter.[59] But that did not make their surrender by Cleopatra any less perilous for herself.

She was barely nineteen, and although at this age she did not require the guidance of a Regency Council, she was presumably backed and advised by her prime minister of the time, whose name was Protarchus.[60] However, he also had other troubles on his hands, for the papyri of this period display signs of considerable tension in the country, aggravated, it would appear, by a bad harvest. The priests of an island temple (Hiera Nesos) in Middle Egypt, in a document dated 51–50 BC, complain that for some reason all the inhabitants of the village have moved off, leaving the priests quite alone, and they express anxiety about the temple treasures.[61] Then in 50–49 we learn that a drought has caused all strangers temporarily resident at another place in the area, Tinteris, to abandon their village.[62]

But crop failures were not by any means the only trouble. A further papyrus, dated 27 October 50 BC, hints at wider and more alarming implications in the political field.[63] This is a royal decree (*prostagma*) which forbids the transportation of grain from Middle Egypt to Lower and Upper Egypt, and orders that all grain should be dispatched to Alexandria instead. The terms of the decree are sharp and oppressive, threatening transgressors with confiscation and even death, and offering encouragement to spies and informers.

Clearly, harvests had been unsatisfactory, and there was a danger of famine in Alexandria. But something else was happening as well, because the decree is issued not in Cleopatra's name alone, as had been customary since her accession, but in the name of ' the King and Queen': her half-brother Ptolemy XIII, pushed completely into the background since their accession (or rather hers), has emerged on to the surface of the political scene as Cleopatra's colleague.[64]

The correctness of this interpretation is confirmed by a further set of papyri dating from this same third year of her reign (which ran, according to the Egyptian method of calculation, from September 50 BC until September 49 BC).[65] Hitherto, since the announcement of her father

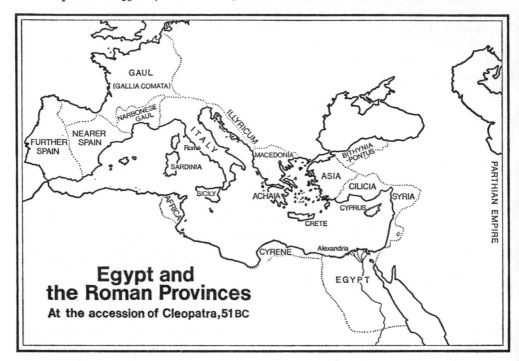

Egypt and the Roman Provinces
At the accession of Cleopatra, 51 BC

Auletes' death, these documents had been dated from Cleopatra's accession in 51. Now, instead, we find some dated 'in the first, which is also called the third year'.[66] The 'third' year is still Cleopatra's, but the 'first' refers, once again, to the young Ptolemy XIII. What apparently happened is that Cleopatra, shaken by the national crisis caused by her handing over of the *assassins* of Bibulus' sons, was compelled to accept the boy as her fellow-monarch, in accordance with Auletes' will. The admission that this was only Ptolemy's first year, not his third, is merely a recognition that it had not hitherto been possible (ostensibly, no doubt, owing to his youth) for this portion of the will to be carried out immediately. But the change seems to represent a serious weakening of Cleopatra's position. The Regency Council who represented her thirteen-year-old brother had taken effective charge.

In the light of this conclusion let us take one more look at the decree of 27 October 50 BC. In view of the current developments regarding the throne, the reason for the veto on moving grain from Middle Egypt to

Lower or Upper Egypt could have been something more than economic. It is a tempting hypothesis that Cleopatra and Ptolemy XIII, though officially exercising joint rule in accordance with their father's will, had in fact split up, that the queen had been compelled to leave Alexandria (as she certainly was before long, for Caesar tells us so),[67] and that the royal decree was not merely designed to avert famine but was also intended to secure the city against siege from Cleopatra by denying her supplies – the areas to which shipments were prohibited, the Delta and the Thebaid, being those controlled or threatened with occupation by her supporters.[68]

*

Yet such local happenings shortly afterwards waned to insignificance beside the shattering events that were taking place within the borders of the Roman empire. Throughout the later fifties BC, the world of Rome had been rent by rivalry between the two surviving Triumvirs – Pompey who enjoyed a great position in the city and elsewhere, and Caesar who had strengthened and enriched himself by the conquest of Gaul. In 49, this rivalry at last broke out into civil war. The other leaders of the government were mostly on Pompey's side. Nevertheless, within the first months of the year he and his followers had been ejected from Italy by Caesar; and they left for the Balkans to continue the struggle from there.

Pompey was obliged to make every possible effort to whip up military, naval and financial support from the countries of the east. Among them was Egypt, a state friendly and allied to the Roman commonwealth – of which, with some measure of justification, he claimed to be the true representative. Pompey left Italy on 17 March. Thirteen days earlier his son, called Cnaeus Pompeius like himself, had also sailed from Italy, with instructions to proceed to Egypt and seek reinforcements.

This Cnaeus Pompeius the younger found Ptolemy XIII and Cleopatra officially in occupation of the throne as joint monarchs – though, if the present interpretation is correct, Ptolemy's Regency Council was at this stage virtually in charge. The Roman visitor was given a good reception,[69] because the royal government remained grateful to his father Pompey for the part he had played (however profitably to himself) in opposing the annexation of the country and guaranteeing Auletes' will. So the Egyptian authorities – presumably Ptolemy's Council – provided Cnaeus Pompeius with sixty ships and five hundred Gabinian soldiers, who, this time, were at last persuaded to move out of Egypt. Furthermore, supplies of grain were sent to the Pompeian base at Dyrrhachium (now Durrës or Durazzo in Albania).

In autumn or winter of the same year the Roman Senate, or the large proportion of its members who had left Italy at about the same time as Pompey, met at Thessalonica (Salonica) and passed a complimentary resolution thanking Egypt for its response to Pompey's appeal. In appreciation of what Ptolemy XIII's government had done, they decreed that Pompey should be appointed guardian of the young king.[70] There was a dubious precedent, nearly a century and a half old, for such Roman guardianships of youthful Egyptian monarchs, and it had been recalled within living memory. Auletes' will may already have enjoined Pompey to assume such a responsibility, though this cannot be confirmed.[71] At all events he assumed it now.

The apparent absence of any reference to Cleopatra in the Senate's resolution does not necessarily mean that she was no longer officially joint monarch, since at the age of nineteen she did not require a guardian as her brother did.[72] However, it remains possible that another reason why the Senate did not bother about her was because she had not only fled from Alexandria but had also subsequently been deposed. This new situation is mirrored in the headings of papyri, which now abandon the double dating of joint monarchs, and no longer refer to Cleopatra at all, instead displaying the name of Ptolemy XIII without an associate. The old double dating was still to be seen in June 49 BC, but then the sole name of Ptolemy begins to appear before the end of the Egyptian year (September).[73] Cleopatra, that is to say, was deprived of the throne at some time between June and September of this year; and incidentally, the latter papyrus now attributes 'year 3' (not, as hitherto, 'year 1') to Ptolemy, so that his supporters were now, it seems, taking the retrospective view, justifiable on legal though not on factual grounds, that he had been king ever since the death of Auletes.

A Byzantine writer, Malalas, declares that Cleopatra took refuge in Upper Egypt.[74] Late though this evidence is, it may come from a good source, and it seems acceptable. Upper Egypt was one of the regions to which the royal decree of 27 October 50 BC, perhaps directed against her, had forbidden the dispatch of grain; and it was a part of the country with which she had personal links. In the previous year, she had apparently taken part in the ceremonies at Hermonthis, and her father had been a great benefactor of the temples of Upper Egypt; it is a reasonable deduction that Cleopatra, too, possessed powerful supporters in the region. Perhaps she fled to them as early as 50, and then, after her official deposition in 49, she may have relied on them to put her back on the throne.

At first sight it might seem that an argument against the deposition of Cleopatra as early as June–September 49 BC is provided by the terms in which Caesar alludes to her departure. In referring to events at the end of September 48, he states that Ptolemy XIII had 'expelled her from the kingdom a few months beforehand'. Now June–September of 49 BC, it is true, cannot be regarded as 'a few months before' September 48. But Caesar himself provides a likely solution by his very next words, from which we learn that, in October 48, Cleopatra was no longer in Upper Egypt but away on the far side of the eastern borders of the country.[75] If this reconstruction of events is correct, she had fled to Upper Egypt in 50 BC; in 49 she had been deposed; and in 48, finding it impossible to maintain herself any longer on Egyptian soil, she had withdrawn to a point outside Egypt altogether.

This was by no means the first time that one of Egypt's Ptolemaic queens had been in such a situation. The formidable Cleopatra IV, whom Cleopatra VII's grandfather Ptolemy IX Soter (Lathyrus) expelled, had found herself in very much the same position in 113 BC. Cleopatra also owed to her grandfather something else, of more practical use than a historical precedent: namely, the support of a powerful and ancient city-state just beyond the Egyptian frontier, between Egypt and Palestine. This was Ascalon (Ashkelon), a Philistine foundation which Lathyrus had rescued from the clutches of the Judaean kings (103 BC). In consequence, though the city remained free, it placed his head on its silver coins (together with the Ptolemaic emblem of an eagle on a thunderbolt), and then honoured Auletes in the same way. Now, in 49/8 and probably in 48/7 as well, Ascalon displayed the head of Cleopatra.[76] Its government was evidently on her side against her half-brother Ptolemy XIII, and this must have provided her with the base she needed to get herself restored to the throne, with the help, presumably, of Arabs from the neighbouring Nabataean Arab kingdom, of which Petra (now in Jordan) was the capital.[77] The army of Ptolemy XIII was ranged against her on the Egyptian border, some thirty miles beyond the frontier post of Pelusium upon the lower slopes of Mount Casius (Ras Baron). The core was provided by the Gabinians, other than those who had left to join the Pompeian cause. Caesar's remark, speaking of a period a few months later, that the Gabinians had already seen 'wars against the Egyptians', may perhaps have been a reference to skirmishes against Cleopatra's supporters at this time.

Seeing that she had handed over to the Romans the two murderers of the sons of Bibulus, the Gabinians had good reason to dislike her. But they were not powerful enough to account, by themselves, for the wave of hatred that drove her off the throne and out of the country. She was also very much disliked in leading Greco-Egyptian political circles at Alexandria. Every identifiable politician and government official was against her. There were two reasons for this. First of all, they must have disliked her surrender of the two murderers quite as much as the Gabinians did, since the surrender was a pro-Roman act.

They had hated and driven out her father Auletes for his pro-Roman behaviour. Cleopatra, deliberately, behaved as her father's daughter, in this as in other respects, and so they were only too happy to expel her as well. But there was also a second reason for their animosity. At the time of her accession her half-brother Ptolemy XIII was only ten, but she had already turned eighteen. A boy of ten could obviously not prevent the leading Alexandrians, serving on his Regency Council, from doing whatever they pleased. A girl old enough to rule without a Regency Council to guide her might well be a different matter – and, since she was Cleopatra, we can confidently suppose that even at that comparatively early age she did not suffer from any lack of determination. And so the courtiers and politicians rallied round the boy against his half-sister, and she was turned out, as Caesar puts it, by her brother 'acting through his relatives and friends'.[78]

*

The Ptolemaic court was an elaborate and colourful affair, full of dignitaries sporting robes of different colours according to their gradations of rank. Ptolemy II Philadelphus had already employed a Chief Huntsman, Chief Seneschal, Chief Physician and Chief Cupbearers. Subsequently, in keeping with the general rule that diminished power means an increase in pomp and display, Ptolemy V Epiphanes (205–280) introduced further complications into the court hierarchy. At its summit were the Kinsmen (*syngeneis*) including honorary kinsmen – addressed by the monarchs as 'brother' or 'father'.[79] Next came First Friends, and then Friends. (These are the categories of 'relatives and friends' to whom Caesar was referring.)

The Kinsmen were entitled to adorn themselves with 'the Splendour of the Head-Band, sacred appanage of the Glory belonging to the Monarch's Relatives', and with a gold brooch that he himself bestowed upon them. The First Friends dressed in purple robes. Nearly all the Kinsmen, First Friends and Friends claimed Greek or Macedonian origin, and most of the highest functionaries wore the wide-brimmed felt hats, small oblong mantles and high laced boots of a Macedonian country gentleman. A certain number of Egyptian faces (besides those of priests) were nowadays to be seen at court, since it had become advisable to bestow the title of Kinsman upon a sprinkling of native senior officers. But they, too, probably dressed in the Greek style.

The most important of the Kinsmen were those who served as ministers of the crown. The principal state official, the prime minister, was known as the *dioecetes* or 'manager', a title deriving from the theory that the whole of Egypt was one huge royal estate. It was the prime minister's job to administer and exploit this estate, through his representatives,

54

who were known as *oeconomi*; but we must suppose that the prime minister himself was almost continually in attendance upon the monarch.

During the second century BC the custom arose of appointing eunuchs to ministerial offices, and particularly to the post of prime minister. From remote antiquity in eastern kingdoms, and subsequently in Greek lands as well, eunuchs had been employed to take charge of the women in the palaces; and they had also graduated to more general duties as court chamberlains. Their confidential position often enabled them to gain great power, and Herodotus, noting the situation in Persia, observed that they tended to be conspicuously loyal. That was one of the reasons why the Ptolemies, too, came to depend so very largely upon eunuchs. They could be relied upon not to render the royal princesses pregnant; and popular prejudice against their physical condition – illustrated by the sneering remarks of Horace[80] and many others about Egyptian officials of this category – made it impossible for them to seize power for themselves. For such reasons the Ptolemies, like other Hellenistic monarchs, often appointed them not only as generals – the first great Ptolemaic eunuch Aristonicus (*c.* 186 BC) was an excellent commander – but actually as prime ministers of the whole country. Usually these premiers were Alexandrian Greeks or Greco-Egyptians. But sometimes Hellenized Asians of various origins were found in this key post.

Normally, unless the prime minister was some exceptionally powerful figure, he held office for a single year like the Roman consuls, although, like them again, he might well be reappointed at a later date. Our ignorance of the personalities of Cleopatra's successive prime ministers is one of our most serious historical losses. In the year September 52–September 51 BC, when she ascended the throne, the holder of the post may have been a certain Hephaestion, who had also perhaps performed the same functions in 54 at the time when Egypt was compelled to appoint the Roman financier Rabirius Postumus as its economic overlord. If these datings are correct, Hephaestion served as chief adviser to successive rulers in two years of grave emergency. Protarchus was the head of Cleopatra's government during the crisis caused by the murder of Bibulus' sons (51–50). In 49–48, when she was deposed, a man named Ptolemaeus, but probably not a member of the royal family, seems to have been prime minister; and we must conjecture that he took the side of her temporarily successful half-brother and his regents.

But easily the most important politician of the period was a certain Pothinus. He was also the person who disliked Cleopatra most. His opposition to her rule and her person was the decisive political theme of the years 51–48. Not only did he become prime minister in 48, in succession

Italy

to Ptolemaeus, but until then he had been chairman of Ptolemy XIII's Regency Council, a position which out-ranked the prime ministers of that time. The chairman, as well as certain further members of the Council, and perhaps a number of others entrusted with the care and education of the young king, traditionally bore the especially privileged title of 'Foster-Father' (*tropheus, tithenos*), a poetical term linked with the cult of Dionysus which played so large a part in the religion and ruler-worship of the court.

*

Meanwhile, in the Roman civil war, there had been a rapid and apocalyptic movement of events. After Caesar's occupation of Italy, he had successfully invaded Spain. Then he pursued Pompey to the Balkans, where on 9 August 48 BC (7 June according to the seasons, with which the calendar had got out of joint) the decisive battle was fought at Pharsalus in Thessaly. Pompey was overwhelmingly defeated, and fled from the country. Compelled to find a new base from which new armies could be raised, he came to the conclusion that the best country for this purpose was Egypt, officially independent though it was. Its monarch, Ptolemy XIII, who was at this time sole ruler of the country, had been placed under Pompey's guardianship by the Roman Senate when it met at Thessalonica in the previous year. And now the time had come for him to claim Ptolemy's assistance, in repayment of the hospitality and friendship Ptolemy's father Auletes had received from him in Italy (58 BC). Pompey believed that the Gabinians, whose creator Aulus Gabinius had been his follower, could form the nucleus of his new army to carry on the fight against Caesar. He was also, of course, attracted by the great wealth of the country – a first instalment of which he had diverted into his own hands when he agreed to the recognition of Auletes eleven years previously.

So Pompey sent an envoy ahead of him to approach the advisers of King Ptolemy, who were with their monarch and his army at Mount Casius,[81] facing Cleopatra and whatever force she had collected. On 28 September 48 BC, Pompey's small flotilla approached the shore where the king's army had its camp, and a boat was rowed out from the harbour to meet him. It contained three passengers. One was Achillas, a Greco-Egyptian senior officer in Ptolemy's army, perhaps with special over-all responsibility for the Gabinians.[82] His two companions were Roman officers. One was a certain Lucius Septimius, who had once served under Pompey and was now apparently in command of the Gabinian contingent on Mount Casius. The other was a centurion named Salvius. Leaving his wife on board his flagship, Pompey stepped into the boat, accompanied by four attendants. As they reached the shore, Septimius stabbed him, and he fell dead. Egyptian battleships, which were cruising not far off, destroyed a number of his ships and killed one of his relatives, and another leading supporter who landed the next day encountered the same fate. The rest of the Pompeian vessels got away as rapidly as they could.

The murder of Pompey earned the fifteen-year-old Ptolemy XIII a place in Dante's Inferno, in company with Judas and Cain. Cicero, on the other hand, although he had been one of Pompey's supporters, remarked that after the defeat at Pharsalus such a conclusion, at some time or other, was inevitable.[83]

The government of Ptolemy XIII, led by Pothinus, had not felt sufficiently impressed by the bonds of Pompey's friendship and hospitality to accept the idea of Egypt as the headquarters of major international operations – on behalf of a cause which they rightly judged to be doomed. Internally, too, they were at this moment in a weak position. Not only was there the threat from Cleopatra, but this year 48 BC had proved catastrophic for Egyptian agriculture. When the Nile began to rise two months previously, its rise was the smallest on record.[84] Faced with such an unprecedented disaster, likely to bring starvation to millions, the government needed all its energies to cope with the home front. In these circumstances, the prospect of becoming Pompey's headquarters was particularly appalling. And the well-founded idea that Caesar would rapidly come to Egypt in pursuit of his defeated enemy was equally abhorrent. That is why the decision to murder Pompey was reached. According to the poet Lucan (who may or may not be inventing the story), the high priest of Memphis, Acoreus or Anchoreus, advised that Pompey should be given a friendly reception.[85] But the opposite counsel prevailed, so that when Caesar should arrive, and find his enemy dead, he would no longer have any excuse to prolong his stay in Egypt.

Part Two

Cleopatra and Caesar

3

Cleopatra and Caesar
in Egypt

Only four days after the murder of Pompey on Egypt's eastern border, Caesar arrived in Alexandria harbour, with ten warships from the maritime city-state of Rhodes, and a force of 3,200 infantry and 800 cavalry. A boat came out to meet him, bringing a leading member of Ptolemy XIII's court. He was Theodotus, a professor of rhetoric from Samos or Chios, who was one of those in possession of the elevated title of royal Foster-Father; he probably held the post of the king's tutor, and was one of the leading court-chamberlains. Theodotus had favoured the decision to murder Pompey, and now he offered Caesar not only the dead man's signet-ring, but also his severed head, which had been embalmed, he explained, on his royal master's instructions.[1]

However, the hope that Caesar would now move elsewhere proved mistaken. He had no intention of doing anything of the kind, since Egypt was the richest country in the world and he needed money. Furthermore, he maintained that the Egyptian government owed him a very large sum. Five or six years earlier, when the financier Rabirius Postumus had claimed that Auletes had failed to pay what he owed him, Caesar had graciously but greedily taken over the responsibility of extracting the alleged debt. On the death of Auletes, however, he had been good enough to reduce the obligation of the new monarchs to only a little more than half what was supposedly owed. This sum, he now said, he had come to collect, since he needed it to pursue the fight against Pompey's sons and supporters, if need should arise. In the words of the poet Lucan,

> He saw the Egyptian wealth with greedy eyes
> And wished some fair pretence to seize the prize.[2]

One very fair pretence, indeed quite a plausible pretext, was the behaviour of the Egyptian government in the previous year. For they had given men, ships and money to Pompey's elder son Cnaeus Pompeius. Caesar was also proposing to remind Pothinus and his colleagues that the late king, Auletes, had specifically and solemnly called upon the Roman people, 'by all the gods and by the treaties he had made at Rome', to see that his will was carried out. The will had enjoined that Ptolemy XIII and Cleopatra should succeed as joint monarchs. That was not, at present, the situation. Caesar, during his first consulship in 59 BC, had played a leading part in the restoration of Auletes, and now, being consul once again, he felt able to claim it was his bounden duty to ensure that the will was duly honoured. He was a friend of both sides, he wrote afterwards, and in consequence felt particularly anxious to arbitrate in the dispute between Ptolemy and Cleopatra.

With this intention in mind – though he had not, of course, been able to explain it to the Alexandrians yet, except perhaps by an advance letter to the Regency Council – Caesar decided it was appropriate to land in the insignia of a Roman consul, escorted by the statutory twelve official attendants carrying the *fasces*. However, this caused the people of Alexandria to demonstrate violently against him. His conduct seemed to them a gross infringement of Egyptian independence, and released all the anti-Roman sentiment which was strong not only in the Regency Council but among the entire population of the city, including the royal troops.[3] As he landed, angry Egyptian soldiers and agitators surged towards him. Soon afterwards the civilian population started to riot and went on rioting for several days, killing a number of Caesar's soldiers in various parts of Alexandria.

This was a dangerous situation in such a large and excitable place. The Alexandrians, at this time, numbered something between half a million and a million.[4] Ancient observers unanimously agreed that this polyglot population was fanatical and treacherous, and abnormally disposed to commit violent atrocities when its passions were aroused – as happened all too readily, and was happening now.[5] Caesar's force, on the other hand, was a small one, and even if this hostile reception disposed him to favour withdrawal after all – which is unlikely, in view of his pertinacity – he could not in any case get away, since north winds were to be expected off this coast for the next couple of months.

So Caesar stayed, moving straight into political and diplomatic action. First he summoned Ptolemy XIII from his royal army on the eastern frontier. About a fortnight after Caesar's landing the boy-king duly arrived in Alexandria. Pothinus, who accompanied him, at once raised every possible objection to Caesar's fund-raising aims, suggesting that urgent business surely needed his attention elsewhere. He also arranged that inferior grain should be served to the Roman troops for their food, since they were not entitled to Egyptian supplies and should therefore consider themselves lucky to have anything at all. Common, broken crockery was placed on Ptolemy's table, so as to insinuate that Caesar had laid hands on all the precious plate. Perhaps he had.

Soon, Cleopatra also arrived from her headquarters beyond the Palestinian frontier. Whether she came on her own initiative or at Caesar's bidding remains uncertain. Certainly, it was in her interests to come, because she wanted him to hear her case. She had already presented it to him by letter, but, as the historian Dio Cassius observed, she believed that her arguments were more likely to prevail if she could obtain the opportunity to exercise her personal charm.[6] On the other hand, it is by no means unlikely that Caesar summoned her. His arbitration could hardly be made to look at all plausible unless he interviewed both the parties concerned.

At all events her journey to Alexandria was not at all an easy one. Her half-brother's army on Mount Casius barricaded her access by land, and his fleet blocked her approach by sea. Nevertheless, she took a ship, transferred herself into a small boat off Alexandria, and somehow managed to make her way inside the harbour. The poet Lucan later asserted that she had bribed some of her brother's troops to unchain the boom across the harbour.[7] Her landing is immortalized by the story, which may well be true, that a Sicilian merchant Apollodorus smuggled her past the coastguards in a carpet or a roll of bedding.[8]

However this may be, she arrived at the palace, and appeared in Caesar's presence. And although, according to Lucan's feverish imagination, she pretended to tear her hair in grief at her predicament, it was not sufficiently disarranged by this action, or by the uncomfortable journey, to have lost its attractiveness. As the world knows, this twenty-one-year-old girl rapidly captivated the experienced womanizer of fifty-two, and they embarked on a love-affair in the palace. No doubt he conducted the love-making in his excellent Greek, since Latin is not mentioned among Cleopatra's numerous languages.[9] Caesar appreciated her looks and intelligence, but no Greek or Roman, with their uncomplicated respect for splendid lineage, could forget that she belonged to the most royal of the world's royal houses. Napoleon was pleased enough to secure an Austrian imperial princess for himself, and although Caesar was no upstart he was exceedingly insistent upon the value of glorious ancestry, and must have liked the idea of associating with a woman descended from Ptolemy I and related to Alexander the Great. Moreover, as queen of Egypt, she was the descendant of the Pharaohs whose three-thousand-year history cannot have failed to seem glamorous to any Roman with Caesar's strong historical sense.[10] Indeed the entire life of ancient Egypt, including its art, exercised a potent influence on Roman minds of this epoch,[11] and when, from time to time, the authorities of Rome displayed a xenophobic desire to eliminate Egyptian shrines in Italy, they encountered a sharp and superstitious resistance. Caesar, too, was to show later that he felt no reluctance to learn from all that Egypt had to offer.

However, it was primarily the fascination of the young queen herself which caused him, at this juncture, to take her political side against Ptolemy XIII. It would have saved Caesar a good deal of trouble to have sided with Ptolemy instead, for the king was supported both by the Alexandrian political leadership and the Egyptian army, whereas Cleopatra enjoyed no such backing. As an ally, therefore, she was a considerable liability to Caesar. However, quite apart from sexual or emotional considerations, the hostile attitude of Pothinus left him no alternative. Pothinus was a genuine nationalist, anxious to keep the Romans out, and convinced that he himself, as Ptolemy's representative and an experienced politician, was better equipped to achieve this than Cleopatra. But he was wrong to suppose that Caesar could be fobbed off so easily.

Pothinus' judgement was probably impaired by intense dislike of the Romans. Such an attitude was characteristic of educated Greeks or Hellenized foreigners of the time.[12] It was prompted partly by the cultural deficiencies of the all-too-powerful conquerors, but mainly by their aggressiveness and arrogance – and above all by the malice that the Romans so often showed towards the Greeks. Already in about 200 BC the Latin comic dramatist Plautus was attacking a multitude of their supposed national deficiencies, and, later on, Cicero, in spite of his deep admiration of classical Hellenic culture, had a great many unpleasant things to say about contemporary Greeks – unless they were servile household dependents, and even then they were often described as 'ungrateful'. It was usual for Romans to describe Greeks as men of words and not deeds, untrustworthy, cunning, unscrupulous, frivolous, boastful, inefficient, lecherous, quarrelsome and bloodthirsty. All these generalizations can readily be documented in Latin literature, and Cicero gave currency to the term 'Graeculus', dirty little Greek. Moreover, especially derogatory terms were reserved for those Greeks or Greek-educated people who came from lands east of Greece itself, such as Pothinus and his fellow Greco-Egyptians.

Not very surprisingly, therefore, the Greeks hated the Romans just as much as the Romans hated the Greeks. Their monarchs frequently described Romans as barbarians, and any Hellenistic king who fought against them, such as the Seleucid Antiochus III who tried to bar their way during the second century BC, or Mithridates VI of Pontus who massacred Italian businessmen in Asia Minor (88 BC), could be sure of enthusiastic support from very many Greeks. As Cicero was well aware, they produced malignantly anti-Roman writings:[13] which the Romans did their best to suppress. Such was the tradition working on Pothinus. It only served to sharpen his indignation over Caesar's financial claims, his fear of further claims ahead, and his detestation of the man who had chosen to become the lover of Cleopatra – especially as he himself, being a eunuch, found it easier to resist her charms. The reports that Pothinus intended to murder Caesar are very probable. Why he did not do so we cannot tell, but no doubt Caesar took measures to protect himself; and anyone who murdered him, or attempted to, would scarcely have been able to escape without retribution.

Cleopatra, on the contrary, had various reasons for wanting an accommodation with Caesar. For one thing, she must have responded to the extraordinary quality of his personality – even though he was so much older than herself. But an association with such a man also corresponded with the policy she had inherited from her father. The other great Hellenistic dynasties, the Antigonids in Macedonia and the Seleucids in Asia, had both tried to fight Rome, and in due course both had succumbed to its power. The Ptolemaic state alone had hitherto survived as a country independent enough to govern itself without Roman officials or tax-collectors, under its own historic monarchy. It had survived because the Ptolemies had never taken up arms against Rome. If they had done so, it would have meant a rapid end to their kingdom. They owed their unique survival to outward passivity and collaboration; and Cleopatra intended to follow the same policy.

But she also proposed to give it a new purpose, which only she, with her personal allure, was in a position to contribute. For she intended not only to collaborate with the greatest Roman of the day, like her ancestors, but, by becoming his mistress, to ensure the restoration of the Ptolemaic kingdom to its former splendours. If Rome's treatment of her country and family had partially broken the spirit of her ancestors and her father, she would show the world it had not broken hers; and by her devotion she would perform her duty to their memory. This was a new and more formidable version of the appeals for help which so many of her predecessors had directed towards eminent Romans.

The famous personal qualities which she exploited to achieve these ends were analysed subsequently by Plutarch. 'Her own beauty, so we are told, was not of that incomparable kind which instantly captivates the beholder. But the charm of her presence was irresistible, and there was an attractiveness in her person and talk, together with a peculiar force of character which pervaded her every word and action, and laid all who associated with her under its spell. It was a delight merely to hear the sound of her voice....'[14]

Shakespeare, who had read this account in Sir Thomas North's translation, interpreted it as meaning that her supreme gift was vitality – in the form which the dramatist most admired, 'the nobleness of life'.[15] As for her looks, although these, Plutarch suggests, were not her principal charm, it is disappointing that there is not one single surviving portrait-bust that can be confidently believed to represent her.[16] There are, however, several portraits upon her coins. Some of these representations seem so unworthy of the famous temptress that an over-ingenious theory once proclaimed them to be enemy propaganda. But an optimistic appraisal can find something quite attractive about certain of the portraits – for example the head on an Alexandrian coin of 47–6 BC, when she was twenty-two.[17]

In general, however, we get little more than an impression of a *belle laide* with a rather large mouth, and, on some specimens, a long hooked nose which she had inherited from her father – this feature becomes even more pronounced on coins issued later in her life. When Pascal once remarked 'If Cleopatra's nose had been shorter, the whole face of the earth would have been changed', he might not have commented in quite the same way if he had studied some of these coins and seen just how pronounced her nose really was.

At Alexandria, the portraits are in the Greek style. They show her wearing a metal head-band, elaborately tied by a ribbon at the back. The form of this head-band is not very clear from the coins, which are usually, nowadays, in poor condition, but it was probably reminiscent of the circlets worn by earlier Ptolemaic queens and kings. Those, in their turn, went back to the diadem of Alexander the Great, which was thought to be derived from a diadem associated with Dionysus.[18]

Cleopatra's hair-style at this time shows three of the large artificial waves which had become a feature of Hellenistic fashion, terminating in a rather substantial chignon low down behind her head, with a few curls allowed to escape in front of her ears, and behind them. Smart Greek women in Alexandria, who led the fashions of the Mediterranean world, did their hair in styles as varied as those of modern Europe and America,[19] and no doubt the queen, too, who gave them their lead, did not limit herself to a single, invariable style. Like her diadem, the coiffure she favours on these early coins deliberately recalls Ptolemaic queens of the past, such as Arsinoe III, wife of Ptolemy IV Philopator. Or was the whole thing, or part of it, a wig? The possibility cannot be excluded, for wigs had long been known, and a later pamphlet by Maecenas, praising the beautiful Octavia who became Cleopatra's

66

hated rival in the following decade, took care to point out how *natural* Octavia's hair was.[20]

Cleopatra's make-up was probably elaborate. Complicated cosmetics were an ancient Egyptian custom, as the discovery of many ebony, alabaster and glass boxes, bottles and paint-pots clearly indicates; and Cleopatra, though no Egyptian, is unlikely to have been uninformed about this national tradition. Antimony (replacing malachite) and lamp-black were applied to the eyebrows and eyelids with round-ended rods, ochre was applied to the lips with a brush, and the nails, soles of the feet, and palms of the hands were dyed orange red with henna. But it was not only in Egypt that women took care over their make-up; this was also the practice throughout the Hellenistic world. Paint and powder had been employed both by prostitutes and married women as early as the fourth century BC. White lead, too, was rubbed into the skin to make it seem fairer; plants, seaweeds and mulberry juice were all called upon to produce different shades of rouge.

The general likelihood that Cleopatra knew all about such methods is perhaps corroborated by the ascription of an ancient work on cosmetics to her authorship. There is no reason to suppose that the attribution is correct, but it was made because she seemed the right person to have written such a work. A somewhat cryptic excerpt from the treatise has survived:

For bald patches, powder red sulphuret or arsenic and take it up with oak gum, as much as it will bear. Put on a rag and apply, having soaped the place well first. I have mixed the above with foam of nitre and it worked well....

The following is the best of all, acting for fallen hairs, when applied with oil or pomatum; acts also for falling-off eyelashes or for people going bald all over. It is wonderful. Of domestic mice burnt, 1 part; of vine-rag burnt, 1 part; of horse's teeth burnt, 1 part; of bear's grease, 1; of deer's marrow, 1; of reedbark, 1. To be pounded when dry, and mixed with lots of honey till it gets the consistency of honey; then the bear's-grease and marrow to be mixed (when melted), the medicine to be put in a brass flask, and the bald part rubbed till it sprouts.[21]

Even if Cleopatra did not need the recipe about falling hair, her lover Caesar certainly did; it was his custom to adjust his laurel-wreath to cover his bald head.

*

Inside the royal palace of Alexandria, with Caesar and Cleopatra, was the thirteen-year-old king Ptolemy XIII. It must have come as a terrible surprise to discover that his hostile half-sister had arrived, and a worse shock to learn that she and Caesar had become lovers. When he was invited to attend Caesar the morning after her arrival, and found them together on plainly intimate terms, he rushed straight from the room, shouting to his friends and supporters who were waiting outside that he had been betrayed and his cause was lost. Hastening out into the streets, he tore the royal diadem from his head and dashed it to the ground in a spectacular rage, appealing for popular support against the couple. The past history of Ptolemaic precocity suggests that he may well have been capable of taking such action on his own account. Nevertheless, his gesture, like most of the agitation against Caesar, was probably prompted by Pothinus, who was busy telling the Alexandrians that Caesar intended to make Cleopatra the sole ruler.[22] Ptolemy's dramatic appearance in the city immediately aroused a public uproar, and an angry crowd, including soldiers of the royal army, began to surge towards the palace. Caesar's legionaries, however, succeeded in dragging the boy back inside the gates, and Caesar himself hurried out and soothingly addressed the demonstrators, promising to make some settlement that would be to their satisfaction.

Until this violent outbreak, he had thought it best to adopt a nonchalant attitude, making a number of sightseeing trips in the city, and attending university lectures. But now he redoubled his attempts to explain and pursue his mission as arbitrator. Finally, an ostensible reconciliation was enforced on the royal brother and sister, and celebrated, according to Lucan, by a memorable banquet.[23] Caesar made the arrangement palatable by declaring that Cyprus, annexed by the Romans ten years previously, was to be returned to Ptolemaic rule. But it would be a separate Ptolemaic kingdom, as it had been before, for instead of handing over the island to Cleopatra and Ptolemy XIII, Caesar bestowed it jointly upon two of Auletes' other children, Arsinoe IV who was aged between seventeen and twenty, and Ptolemy XIV, who was eleven. This, Caesar hoped, would win favour among the Alexandrians, especially as Roman oppression in Cyprus, including depredations by financiers, had been singularly deplorable.[24] Only Cleopatra's feelings must have been mixed, since although the restoration of Cyprus to the Ptolemies was in accordance with her policy, she got on extremely badly with her half-sister Arsinoe IV who was now proclaimed its joint ruler. Presumably Caesar pointed out to her that it would be best to have Arsinoe out of the way. However, until the current Egyptian crisis was over, it seemed best that she and Ptolemy XIV should remain inside the palace at Alexandria under the eye of Caesar himself.

Nevertheless, Caesar had made a striking gesture. The alienation of a territory from Roman rule, even if so far an unrealized project, was certain to incur severe Roman criticism. His announcement was a sign that even so imperturbable a man as Caesar felt that his present situation, and the hostility of Pothinus, gave reason for some anxiety.

*

The position inside the Royal Quarter of the city, the Brucheion, must have been tense. Situated on the eastern, or Great, harbour, the Quarter extended a mile or more along the shore, occupying between one-third and one-quarter of the total area of the city (see Plan, p. 32). It was a place of many temples and porticoes, full of spacious gardens studded with statues. Among the trees and flowers stood the Museum and Library, the quarters of the royal guard, and the tombs of Alexander and the Ptolemies. Presiding over the whole imposing scene, out on Cape Lochias (Silsileh) at the entrance to the harbour, stood the Palace itself, probably the most luxurious and elegant building in the world. 'No Latin ruler', remarked Ernle Bradford, 'gasping for air in the hot Roman summer, had nearly as attractive a situation as these Greek rulers of the Egyptian people.'[25] The plan of this noble residence has so far evaded reconstruction,[26] but we can perhaps get some idea of its spacious entrances, impressive halls and internal colonnades from another palace of Hellenistic times which has recently been excavated near Palatitza in Macedonia.[27] That, however, seems to have been a single royal residence, whereas the palace of Alexandria, like ancient palaces of the east, the Imperial City at Peking, and the Ottoman Scraglio at Istanbul, probably comprised a number of mansions and pavilions distributed about an extensive park.

During the events of 48 BC it is to be supposed that Caesar and Cleopatra, although they spent such a large part of their time together, occupied, for official purposes, separate wings or even separate buildings, while Ptolemy XIII occupied yet another. Each of the three potentates, living in such close proximity to one another, was surrounded by a separate entourage, including, no doubt, numerous security guards because many rumours of assassination were in the air. Caesar's court consisted largely of his own officers, and Ptolemy's comprised the ruling class of Alexandria under the direction of Pothinus. Cleopatra's retinue must have been a good deal more modest, because the Alexandrian leaders did not care for her – unless a few were sufficiently impressed by her prospects as Caesar's protégée to go over to her cause. Besides, she had left behind most of her own advisers, such as they were, on the other side of the eastern frontier, and it must have taken them some time to filter back to Alexandria.

After the ostensible reconciliation between Cleopatra and Ptolemy XIII, there followed a short lull, during which the two of them may have gone through the traditional ceremony of brother-and-sister marriage – unless this had already been celebrated at an earlier stage of their troubled joint reign. But by the end of October it was already clear that the peace was hollow. For Caesar discovered that Pothinus, with the probable cognizance of the boy-king, had secretly ordered the army to come back from the eastern frontier to Alexandria. Pothinus had also entrusted the supreme command to Achillas, who after superintending Pompey's murder had resumed his duties with the army.

In about mid-November, it was reported to Caesar, whose intelligence service had apparently been at fault before, that Achillas was approaching the city with twenty thousand men. It was a very mixed force, including Gabinians, refugees, guerrillas, outlaws, retired pirates and runaway slaves. The infantry column was accompanied by two thousand cavalry. Caesar, outnumbered five to one, dispatched appeals to his representatives in Asia Minor and Syria for reinforcements. At the same time, he sent envoys to Achillas. He selected two eminent doctors, Dioscurides and Serapion, both of whom had performed important missions for Auletes.[28] Achillas, however, arranged for them to be attacked. One was killed – we do not know which – while the other was severely wounded and left for dead, though his friends carried him away and he survived.

Achillas and his army marched onwards into Alexandria. Caesar, whose own *Civil War*, together with the much later history of Dio Cassius, is our authority for these events, does not tell us whether his own legionaries put up any resistance at this stage. But he does make it clear that he himself, with Cleopatra and Ptolemy XIII, was penned into the palace compound and subjected to a siege.

This sharp transformation of their situation must have caused Cleopatra, and perhaps Caesar as well, considerable dismay, especially as Achillas' appeal for help against Roman oppression was warmly received by the Alexandrians. In order to deprive them of a possible figurehead Caesar decided to place Ptolemy XIII under house arrest. He indicated that the defective education of the youth needed remedying. But he also recorded that, by taking this step, he hoped to blame the warlike actions of his enemies upon the private enterprise of a few ruffians rather than upon the initiative of the king, whose name carried great weight among his people.

Almost at once Achillas launched a full-scale attack on the palace quarter;[29] and now began one of the most remarkable periods of Cleopatra's life. At night she was with Caesar, while by day he went out among his troops and sailors, and the battle raged by land and sea. Within Alexandria itself, Achillas failed to force his way into the palace because Caesar had posted soldiers who, amid savage street-fighting, held off the attack. But very soon it became clear that the warfare at sea was going to be more serious. As Cleopatra looked out from her palace, she could see in the Great Harbour seventy-two royal Egyptian ships – more than twice the number of Caesar's own. And Achillas was now making the most determined attempts to seize them. If he managed to do so, it would mean that Caesar would be hopelessly out-numbered at sea, and his communications with the outside world cut off.

But Achillas' plans were thwarted, for Caesar moved to the attack, and succeeded in capturing the entire Egyptian fleet. There are times such as this when one regrets the laconic brevity of his *Civil War*, and would have preferred to hear the full story that he was able to tell Cleopatra that evening. Whether he himself took part in the operation we do not know; at all events, his ships must have rowed out from the private palace harbour behind the island of Antirrhodos,[30] and deliberately grappled with the much larger Egyptian fleet, successfully overcoming its resistance; although the Egyptians were excellent sailors they were not so good at fighting hand to hand. Cleopatra no doubt watched this, and what she saw next must have shocked her. Since Caesar, at this stage, could not be sure of holding the Great Harbour indefinitely, his men were ordered to set fire to all the ships they captured, and every one of them went up in flames. The flames extended to the quays and dock buildings of the Great Harbour, and in the course of the conflagration a large number of books were destroyed – not the great Alexandrian Library itself as has often been believed, but probably a consignment awaiting either transportation to the Library or export overseas.[31]

Caesar's sudden seizure of the Egyptian ships enabled him, on the very same day, to bring off another spectacular success, and this too was clearly visible to Cleopatra. Where the Great Harbour narrowed to its entrance, and the palace rose up on its eastern side, the western end of the entrance was formed by the greatest lighthouse in the world, the Pharos; and this too now became the target of an adventurous operation. 'Because of the narrowness of the strait,' observed Caesar, 'there can be no access by ship to the harbour without the consent of those who hold the Pharos.' In view of this, Caesar took the precaution of landing his troops while the enemy was preoccupied with fighting, seized the Pharos, and posted a garrison there. The result was that safe access was secured for his grain supplies and reinforcements.[32]

Meanwhile fighting also continued by land, but without any decisive result since the streets provided little space for manœuvre. At this stage, however, Caesar took the opportunity to build regular defences round a portion of the palace area, including the Theatre of Dionysus – where he established his command post – and a fort which had access to the harbour and the docks.

But within the palace, all was not well. Cleopatra was not the only Ptolemaic woman confined there. Her young half-sister Arsinoe IV, who hated her and her pro-Roman attitude, felt frustrated because she had not been allowed to go and occupy the throne of Cyprus, and was by no means satisfied with her subordinate role. So she secretly escaped from the palace, and fled to Achillas. Thereupon the army of Achillas and the people of Alexandria, delighted with this defiance of the Romans and Cleopatra, declared her queen of Egypt. This was a serious blow for Caesar, since it meant that the war could no longer be regarded as a purely private revolt against royal authority.

Cleopatra must have been enraged. But she could take comfort from what happened next. Arsinoe IV had an adviser and Foster-Father, the eunuch Ganymedes, whom at this stage she presumably promoted to be her prime minister. But friction rapidly arose between Ganymedes and Achillas, and the two rival groups competed with each other in bestowing gifts upon the troops. Pothinus, and his protégé Ptolemy XIII whom Caesar still retained under house arrest, were watching these developments closely from the palace. Whether they knew in advance about Arsinoe's escape or not – and it is supposed that they did – they had no reason to be anxious so long as she co-operated with their nominee Achillas. Indeed, Arsinoe, who being a woman was obliged to accept a male colleague on the throne, at first probably declared herself joint monarch with her brother Ptolemy XIII.

When Pothinus learnt that Ganymedes and Achillas had quarrelled, he secretly sent messengers to Achillas pledging him his continued support. He is also likely to have assured Achillas of his own intention to escape from the palace with the young Ptolemy as soon as possible, in order to join the army before Arsinoe and Ganymedes could take control. However, as a result of information received from his barber, the messengers were betrayed to Caesar, and he seized the opportunity to have Pothinus arrested and executed. In view of the victim's official position as principal royal functionary, Caesar no doubt announced that the execution was on the orders of Cleopatra, or even perhaps, fictitiously, on the joint order of Cleopatra and Ptolemy XIII. Caesar also declared that if he had not killed Pothinus, then Pothinus would have killed him. Whether Pothinus had, at this stage, really embarked on a plot to murder Caesar we cannot tell; but he had to die, because his attempts to keep Egypt out of Roman hands had been defeated.

A second important casualty was Achillas. He had failed to assert effective control over the undisciplined Alexandrians, and soon, after the death of his political chief Pothinus, he succumbed in the power struggle with Ganymedes, and was murdered. Ganymedes, now in complete charge of the anti-Roman forces, continued to fight aggressively against Caesar, bringing a new fleet into action, surrounding the palace quarter with military posts and road-blocks, and pumping sea-water into the Roman wells. But the legionaries dug all night to sink new wells, and two days later a flotilla carrying a very welcome Roman legion from Asia Minor appeared off the coast near Alexandria.[33]

It may have been at about this time, December 48 BC, that Cleopatra, shut up within the palace, discovered that she was pregnant. Meanwhile, however, the fighting went on, and it continued to prove singularly intractable. It was comforting for Caesar that in early February of the following year[34] his Rhodian admiral, Euphranor, at last succeeded in extending his control from the Pharos lighthouse to the adjoining island of the same name, where the houses of wealthy Alexandrians were ransacked and destroyed.

Since they were mostly her political enemies, this cannot have unduly troubled the watching Cleopatra. But what followed on the next day must have caused her acute anxiety, because it very nearly cost Caesar his life. The crisis occurred during an attempt to follow up the occupation of the Pharos island by the capture of the Heptastadion mole which linked it to the Alexandrian foreshore. As Caesar's troops, under his own personal command, proceeded along the mole to the point where it joined the mainland, and started to seal it off by erecting a barricade, Egyptian soldiers landed on the mole behind him. His warships, which had been accompanying the operation, prudently started to move away. This caused great alarm among Caesar's men, who believed they were being cut off. They hastily abandoned their unfinished fortification and boarded any available boats, or dived off the mole into the sea, in a mad rush to get to their ships.

What happened to Caesar himself is recounted by the unknown officer (possibly Aulus Hirtius) who took up the story where his commander's *Civil War* came to an end, and wrote the *Alexandrian War*. 'Caesar, so long as he was able by exhortation to keep his men by the mole and the fortification, was exposed to the same danger, and when he saw that they were all giving ground, he withdrew to his own vessel. He was followed by a crowd of men who began forcing their way on board and made it impossible to steer the ship or push it off from land; whereupon Caesar, who had guessed that this would happen, jumped overboard and swam out to the ships farther off. From there, he sent small boats back to pick up his men in difficulties and saved a considerable number. As for his own ship, it sank under the pressure of numbers and was lost, with all the men on board.'[35] A man of fifty-two wearing armour, Caesar was obliged to swim two hundred yards. 'This was the time', reported Plutarch, 'when, according to the story, he was holding a number of papers in his hand and would not let them go, though he was being shot at from all sides and was often under water. Holding the papers above the surface with one hand, he swam with the other.'[36] It was also said, though the writer of the *Alexandrian*

73

War was too loyal to mention it, that he fled in such a hurry that he left his purple cloak behind as a trophy for the enemy.[37]

Caesar now turned his attention once again to the domestic problems of the palace. One source of irritation for Cleopatra was gone, since Arsinoe had deserted to the enemy. But her young fellow-monarch and half-brother Ptolemy XIII was still under guard there, and his bad relations with Cleopatra, when they were living in such close proximity, must have been a constant source of intrigue and dissension. Following upon the disaster at the mole, Caesar decided to exploit this situation with the idea of weakening the enemy. He took the remarkable step of freeing Ptolemy from house arrest and sending him into the city 'to take command of the royal army', this is to say the army commanded by Ganymedes. Caesar indicated that since the war could no longer be regarded as a private rebellion Ptolemy's male authority, young though he was, should help to bring the people to their senses and secure the restoration of order. However, he cannot seriously have believed that this would be the result of the boy's release, and the *Alexandrian War* suggests various other possible motives for his gesture.[38] But its real intention, surely, was to provoke dissension between the advisers of Ptolemy XIII and Arsinoe IV, since this was Caesar's best hope of counteracting his own numerical inferiority. It must also have occurred to him and Cleopatra what an excellent thing it would be to give Ptolemy the chance to put himself in the wrong. Once that had happened, it would be easier, at a later date, to eliminate him and make her the sole ruler.[39]

The attempt to cause dissension, however, does not seem to have had any useful military effects since the Egyptians continued the war with unabated ferocity. And although, according to Caesar, Ptolemy wept when they parted, he was obviously eager enough to prevent Arsinoe from obtaining a free hand. When the king arrived at Ganymedes' headquarters, he immediately assumed supreme command of the royal army, though not as a friend of Caesar: on the contrary, he became Caesar's open enemy. Perhaps it was at this point that Cleopatra divorced her brother; under Egyptian law husband or wife could divorce the other. As for Ganymedes, he does not figure as commander in our sources any more, and his protégée Arsinoe, whether under protest or not we cannot say, presumably took second place to Ptolemy.

*

Early in March 47, Caesar's relieving army began to arrive on Egypt's eastern frontier. Since it was undesirable, in face of the continuing Parthian menace, to withdraw Roman legionaries from Syria, the force consisted of Asian, Syrian and Arabian troops, under a Greco–Iranian commander, Mithridates of Pergamum. At Ascalon, we learn from

Hebrew sources that it was joined by a contingent of Jewish troops from Judaea.[40]

The Jews could be expected to come to the help of the Roman who was the conqueror of Pompey, since when Pompey suppressed the remnants of the Seleucid state (63 BC), he had not only profaned the Jerusalem temple by setting foot in the Holy of Holies, but had reduced Judaea to the status of a 'client' dependency of Rome. He debarred its Hasmonaean priest-king Hyrcanus II from the use of his kingly title, which he was obliged to exchange for the inferior designation of 'prince' (ethnarch); and even this he lost eight years later, retaining only his high-priestly office. Moreover, Pompey deprived Judaea of a great deal of territory, including the entire coastal region and much else. Indeed, the principality was actually divided into two separate parts. It only held together at all because Hyrcanus, a very weak man who owed everything to his glorious Hasmonaean descent, possessed an astute minister and adviser. This was Antipater, who came from Idumaea in southern Judaea, a borderland which had only been converted to Judaism in the late second century BC. A great landowner in that region, with family connections in the free city-state of Ascalon, Antipater had made himself the dominant figure at the court of Jerusalem, and it was due to him alone that the diminished Jewish state survived the difficult years since Pompey's harsh settlement. Nor had its chances of survival been assisted when Antipater, like Egypt, made the mistake of taking Pompey's side at the beginning of the Roman Civil War in 49 BC. Probably he had no alternative, but his decision cannot have endeared the Judaeans to Caesar. Now, however, they had been given a chance to put themselves in the right again. For when, besieged in Alexandria, he appealed for help throughout the Levant, he appealed to Judaea as well, and Antipater responded. As soon as the relief column reached Ascalon, and found that its forward path was blocked by Ptolemy XIII's troops, Antipater, accompanied by Hyrcanus himself, arrived in time to clear the way ahead. And during the five to eight days' desert journey into Egypt, it was he, once again, who kept the army supplied with food and drink.

The presence of this Jewish force, escorting the high priest in person, did a great deal to win over the very large body of Egyptian Jews to the cause of Caesar and Cleopatra. There had been Jews in Egypt as early as the second millennium BC, as the Old Testament records; and in the sixth century, Jewish mercenaries and their descendants had lived in a settlement on Elephantine island (Abu, opposite Aswan). Ptolemy I Soter had brought other Jews to Alexandria, regarding them as useful army material, and there they became the largest Jewish community in any city in the world. They occupied a large area behind the royal

75

palace, possessed their own communal organization, and comprised as much as two-fifths of the total Alexandrian population.

Throughout the third century BC Jews continued to flock into Egypt, and in *c*. 160 Ptolemy VI Philometor, to show his sympathy with the Hasmonaean rebellion against the hated Seleucid empire on his frontiers – the empire which forty years earlier had seized Judaea from the Ptolemies – allowed the refugee high priest to convert a ruined shrine at Leontopolis (Tell-el-Yahudiyeh, north-east of Memphis) into a partial replica of the Jerusalem temple.[41] Ptolemy VI and his daughter Cleopatra III also employed Jewish generals to conduct battles against their own relations, and it was during one of these crises that the friction between Egyptian Jews and Greeks, which was to remain a dominant factor in the country's history for centuries, really became violent.[42] The Jews, in addition to their hatred of native Egyptian cults, had displayed open distaste for the Ptolemaic brand of paganism and ruler-worship, and were also increasingly conscious of their exclusion from many of the privileges of the Greek settlers in Egypt.

Cleopatra's relations with the Jewish state of Judaea were to be complex and unsatisfactory for the greater part of her reign. She could never forget that it had once been Ptolemaic property. Moreover, she was able to cause trouble through her powerful friends in the Hasmonaean family itself, and at the free city of Ascalon as well. The Jews in Alexandria were reported to have taken a dislike to her during one of the famines of the reign, because she excluded them from grain distributions, presumably on the correct but unendearing pretext that they did not belong to the Alexandrian citizen body, which was restricted to Greeks or those who were accepted as Greeks. For this and other reasons her relations with the Egyptian Jews were often strained, though the Greco–Egyptian writer Apion, in the first century AD, was prepared to say that the friction was their fault and not hers.[43] However, the ill-will of the Jews towards her must not be exaggerated, because she is also recorded by an inscription as sponsoring the construction of a synagogue.[44] Plutarch states that the numerous languages learnt by Cleopatra included Hebrew;[45] if this was so, then the queen, or her father who arranged her education, must have envisaged a serious effort to conciliate this large section of opinion in the country.

*

As the relief force approached Egypt, it found Ptolemy XIII's frontier outpost, Pelusium, in its path. The fortress was protected by marshes and a desert belt, and could, perhaps, have been defended. But it had often fallen to invaders before, and now it succumbed to Mithridates' attack. His Jewish contingent was well to the fore (though the Roman sources say nothing about its contribution), and here and in other parts of Egypt, notably at their own temple city of Leontopolis, the large local population of Jews gave Hyrcanus and Antipater an enthusiastic welcome.

Skirting the Nile mouths, Mithridates marched round the apex of the delta and turned northwestwards in the direction of Alexandria. At a point not far from Lake Mareotis he found that the generals of Ptolemy XIII, accompanied by the king in person, had brought their Nile fleet out of the city through the waterways, and were confronting him with a greatly superior force. However, Caesar, leaving a tiny garrison behind in Alexandria to guard Cleopatra, now proceeded rapidly on his way to meet Mithridates. The enemy had seen his flotilla leaving Alexandria, and since it turned east out of the harbour they deduced that Caesar proposed, after landing, to march southwards along the east bank of Lake Mareotis. Instead, however, silently and secretly, the ships turned back after dark with their lights out, and disembarked Caesar to the west of the city and the lake. From there he hastened inland, eluding the royal forces, and joined up with Mithridates. On 27 March 47 BC the decisive battle took place. A Roman pincer movement proved too much for the Ptolemaic army, which fled headlong to its camp. Caesar took it by storm, and on the very same evening he triumphantly re-entered Alexandria. It was the first time the city had ever fallen to a foreign foe, and a suppliant population brought out the statues of their gods to meet him. Then he passed through the former enemy barricade to greet Cleopatra and the handful of troops he had left in the palace to protect her.

During and after the engagement, there had been a massacre of Ptolemy's soldiers, including the Gabinians. When the slaughter was over, the young king was nowhere to be found. According to information brought to Caesar, however, he had escaped as far as the Nile but the boat he had climbed into got overloaded with fugitives and sank, and the king was drowned. This was an appropriate enough fate for an Egyptian monarch, since there had been a belief for at least four centuries past, and probably much longer still, that to drown in the Nile conferred on the victim the Blessing of Osiris and the status of a god; indeed the belief, though no longer, presumably, connected with Osiris, still exists.[46] It is true that no Egyptian monarch, whether Pharaoh or Ptolemy, had lacked divinity even while he was still alive; nevertheless such a death added an aura of sacred mystery. In particular, it was likely to lead to rumours that the dead man had risen again and reappeared upon earth. Caesar, well aware that this sort of legend was likely to spread, felt it desirable to prove that Ptolemy was indubitably dead, and had experienced no bodily resurrection. He therefore gave orders that the Nile should be dredged. The king's body was duly found, and his golden armour was placed on show for all the Alexandrians to see.

Ptolemy had been the half-brother, husband, fellow-monarch and fellow-deity of Cleopatra. Yet his short life, one may guess, did not seem to her in any way sacrosanct. She had very unpleasant memories of him as a colleague, and he was much better dead.

*

It must have looked to some Romans that the time had come to annex Egypt at long last. In spite of frequent temptations to take this step, the Romans had always concluded, in the time of Auletes, that an easier way to obtain some of the country's immense wealth was to accept the king's money and keep him on the throne. And now Caesar made a similar decision in favour of Cleopatra. No doubt he collected from her government the large sum of money he had initially come to collect. But he rejected annexation.

This was partly because of their close personal relationship. According to the official version, she 'had remained loyal and had stayed with his forces',[47] while he for his part had continued, throughout the Egyptian war, to keep her under his protection, and did not intend to jettison her now. But there was also another reason why he rejected annexation, and it is recorded by his biographer Suetonius. He was afraid that, if he made Egypt into a Roman province, a headstrong governor might one day use such a wealthy, centralized country as an effective centre of rebellion.[48] This was an argument which had weighed with the Senate in previous decades, and it remained cogent now. Rome's continued fear of such a development was clearly shown after it did finally annex Egypt seventeen years later, for the very first governor of the new province was accused of over-reaching himself. And that was at a time when the empire had, at last, become durably united under one man. In 47 BC, on the other hand, there was civil war of the most perilous kind, for although Pompey was dead his sons were planning to continue the fight in Africa and then Spain. In these circumstances there was no Roman in the world whom Caesar felt he could trust as governor of Egypt.

So Cleopatra was retained as queen. Since, however, according to Ptolemaic practice, a male co-monarch was needed, Caesar arranged that her surviving half-brother, aged about twelve, should be elevated to this position; and he ascended the throne as Ptolemy XIV. The *Alexandrian War* indicates that this arrangement was in accordance with Auletes' will. If that is correct, Auletes must have given instructions that if his older son were to die, this younger boy should take his place.

Cleopatra and Ptolemy XIII, when they ascended the throne jointly in 51, had described themselves as Lovers of their Father Auletes, and now her second partner Ptolemy XIV assumed the same designation. The new joint reign was also apparently signalized by their adoption of a further title, Philadelphus, Brother- and Sister-Loving.[49] This was an appellation which their father Auletes had borne, echoing the great imperial ruler Ptolemy II Philadelphus, and it had unofficially been awarded to all his children before his death. Cleopatra and Ptolemy XIII had continued to call themselves Philadelphi after they ascended the throne. In the context of 47 BC the title implied a criticism of the conduct of the late Ptolemy XIII, to whom the term Sister-Loving hardly applied.

Like the older boy, Ptolemy XIV presumably married his half-sister. The presence of her twelve-year-old husband and colleague, however, does not seem to have weighed very heavily with the queen. She never placed his head on the coinage, but continued to portray her own head alone; and inscriptions of the new joint reign present her regnal dates without making any mention of his. If he possessed a Regency Council, it was clearly under her thumb. Since the time when Caesar had nominally presented Cyprus to Ptolemy XIV and Arsinoe IV, circumstances had changed because Arsinoe had become a traitor. But Ptolemy XIV was still available, and Caesar now bestowed the island upon him and Cleopatra in their capacity as monarchs of Egypt. Arsinoe, who had failed to evade capture, found herself placed under arrest, and soon afterwards she was transported to Rome.

The decision about Cyprus must have added greatly to Caesar's prestige in Egypt. This was useful, since he also had less welcome steps to take. For one thing, he was obliged to reward the Jews who had so greatly assisted him in his Egyptian campaign. At Rome, he arranged for the Senate to exempt their synagogues from a general ban on associations. He also took decisive steps to rescue the little state of Judaea from the insignificance to which it had been reduced by Pompey and his successors. It recovered the port of Joppa and other sections of its lost territory, and Hyrcanus was given back the title of prince (ethnarch); while the powers of his chief minister Antipater, who had led the successful Jewish contingent in Egypt, were increased.[50] This deliberate bolstering up of the state of Judaea, which had once been Ptolemaic territory, cannot have been palatable to Cleopatra and her government. Nor can they have been too pleased by further benefits conferred by Cleopatra at Caesar's request upon the Jewish community in Alexandria, who, like other Jews in the country, had no doubt rallied to Caesar's cause.

But we do not know the precise details of these privileges.[51] Their foreseeable unpopularity, among Greeks and Egyptians, no doubt contributed to Caesar's decision to leave Roman troops in the country, in place of the Gabinians who had ceased to exist. When his departure from Egypt became imminent, he decided he would take only one legion with him, leaving three others behind as a force of occupation. It is true that Egypt was officially independent, but one could cite numerous precedents for the posting of foreign garrisons in independent states, and Rome had a special interest in Egypt and its régime. As the *Alexandrian War* explains, this army of occupation was intended 'to give support to the power of the monarchs who could neither have the affection of their own people, because they had remained loyal supporters of Caesar, nor the authority of long usage, since they had been made rulers only a few days before'.[52] Cleopatra, who had never been popular in Alexandria, must have agreed that the Roman occupying force was desirable, and indeed could not be avoided.

But Caesar also had it in mind, the same writer adds, that 'if the rulers of Egypt remained loyal, they should have the protection of our forces, while if they proved ungrateful, these same forces could constrain them'. For Caesar's personal association with Cleopatra during the previous months would not necessarily ensure her obedience to Rome for all time. Moreover, he could not necessarily trust her ministers – not to speak of her possible successors. The army left in Egypt was not to be another mercenary force like the Gabinians, controlled by the Egyptian government; it was to be under a Roman commander responsible to Rome. However, this raised a problem. For if annexation was impracticable because no potential Roman governor of Egypt could be trusted, there was equally little reason to feel confidence in any important Roman officer who was left there in charge of a substantial force. According to precedent, he would have to be a senator, since the commanders of legions and groups of legions were always members of the Senate. But senatorial generals, with predictable ambitions, had to be avoided. That was why, when Egypt finally suffered annexation seventeen years later, it was arranged, quite unexceptionally, that the combined governorship and military command should never be allocated to a senator. In 47 BC Caesar set a precedent for this cautious attitude; however ungracious it might seem to the Roman Senate, he left his three legions, not under a recognized officer of senatorial status, but under a certain Rufio who had once been a slave – a member of the non-political class of freedmen which had hitherto never been entrusted with Roman armies.

*

Early in the year 47 BC, Caesar went with Cleopatra and a considerable

number of ships and troops on a cruise up the Nile.[53] Our information
on the subject is extremely scanty. This is largely because at a later date
Octavian (subsequently the emperor Augustus) was anxious to play
down his adoptive father Caesar's association with the queen, which he
regarded as calamitous. To fill the gap, however, biographers and
painters of more recent times have dwelt most imaginatively on this
trip.

In reaction against such an approach, some modern scholars have
made little of the event, minimizing both its length and its importance.
But the scope and political significance of the journey were considerable.[54] Such a parade played an essential part in the pacification of
Egypt, and provided a necessary means of strengthening Cleopatra's
pro-Roman régime. It is true that urgent crises awaited Caesar's
attention in other parts of the world; and while spending so long in
Egypt (a delay Napoleon found amazing) he had been cut off from
Italy ever since December. All the same, it would still be as well for
him to settle Egyptian affairs before leaving; and he hoped his journey
with Cleopatra would do this. Caesar knew very well that Alexandria
was not Egypt. There were also the Egyptians of the countryside in their
millions, including the people of Upper Egypt with whom Cleopatra
possessed special ties. After a famine in the previous year, it was advisable for her to renew those ties by a personal visit, and highly
appropriate that she should travel in the company of the great Roman
who guaranteed her régime.

Our few pieces of information about the Nile cruise now begin to
make sense. Appian, in the second century AD, tells us in his *Roman
History* (*Civil Wars*) that four hundred ships were involved: Caesar's
biographer Suetonius declares that they carried 'an army'.[55] It is
likely enough that the expedition was a large one, and since Caesar and
Cleopatra had so many enemies, it must have included a large force of
troops. Nor is Appian just retailing a casual rumour, for he adds that
he has given a detailed account of the whole enterprise in the Egyptian
books of his *Roman History*, which are now lost. Suetonius indicates, in an
imprecise phrase, that the journey extended, or was meant to extend,
to the southern extremity of Egypt, which is perfectly probable. He
also reports that the tour was curtailed by serious unrest among the
legionaries accompanying the expedition. This may be a fictional echo
of the discontent among Alexander's soldiers in India; but it could also
well be true. It would not have been the only occasion when Caesar
had to face this kind of trouble, and after so long away from home the
Roman soldiery may have appreciated a cruise up the Nile less than
their master. To him, the journey was politically useful. But it was also a
celebration: an Egyptian intaglio of this time shows him wearing not

only his laurel-wreath but a garland of flowers, in Ptolemaic fashion.[56] Whether Cleopatra's pregnant condition, which had already lasted several months, affected her health adversely on the trip we are not told.

Cleopatra's state barge, on which she travelled with Caesar, was probably almost as luxurious as the most romantic imaginations have pictured. Magnificent Nile pleasure boats were a Ptolemaic speciality, and a description of Ptolemy IV Philopator's great floating palace gives us some idea of what Cleopatra's ship must have been like.[57] Constructed of cedar and cypress, Ptolemy IV's 300-foot-long barge had Greek furnishings, except for one dining-room in the Egyptian style. The vessel contained shrines of Aphrodite and Dionysus, the deities who were most closely associated with ruler-worship. There was also a grotto or winter-garden, and the decks were designed as arcaded courts.

*

Soon after they returned to Alexandria, Caesar finally departed from Egypt and from Cleopatra. Appian's statement about the duration of the Egyptian war records that 'he consumed nine months in this strife'.[58] On the assumption that Appian is referring not merely to the actual fighting but to Caesar's entire stay in Egypt, this would fix his departure at the beginning of July 47 BC. In fact, however, his subsequent movements suggest that he must have reached Syria towards the end of June.[59]

He left two monuments behind; one that was certainly his own, though unfinished, and another which was nearly ready, but of uncertain attribution. The first was the Caesareum, a splendid building on the seafront which Cleopatra began to erect in his honour; a large colonnaded precinct of Pharaonic layout and Greek architectural forms,[60] it rose high above the harbour, a wonder to behold, and, as a Byzantine rhetorician added, 'the hope and comfort of seafaring men, either coming in or going out'.[61] The second memento of Caesar's stay was a son born to Cleopatra not long after his departure. Or was the boy not Caesar's at all? That is the matter which will now have to be discussed.

4

Cleopatra and Caesar in Rome

When Cleopatra's son was born, the people of Alexandria facetiously called him Caesarion, little Caesar or Caesar's offspring. Cleopatra pointedly named him Ptolemy Caesar, likewise indicating that Caesar was his father.

Before other aspects of this vexed question of his paternity are considered, something must be said about the date of his birth. Certain of the ancient sources suggest that the infant was born in Caesar's lifetime. But an alternative version (Plutarch contradicts himself by giving both) indicates that he was not born until shortly after Caesar's death.[1] Most of the arguments on either side prove nothing. But Antony later informed the Roman Senate, citing witnesses, that Caesar had acknowledged the boy his son.[2] Whether Antony, when he said this, was telling the truth or not, or whether, if so, Caesar's claim to be the father was accurate or inaccurate, Antony surely could not have made such an assertion unless it was generally known that the child had been born in Caesar's lifetime. And since the ancient writers who accept this view maintain that he was born in 47 BC, this is the year which should probably be accepted.

An inscription from Memphis, now in the Louvre, indicates 23 June as the 'birthday of King Ptolemy Caesar'.[3] Now, it is conceivable that this refers to some later personage; for example a Roman emperor might have been described by such a title.[4] However, it seems probable, on balance, that the birthday in question is that of Caesarion. But it does not necessarily follow that the Memphis inscription was engraved in the year of his birth. Indeed, it probably was not, since it calls him 'king' (basileus) which he did not become until 44; though the title *basilissa* was sometimes given to princesses, the *basileus* is normally the reigning king. On the supposition, then, that the inscription belongs to a year subsequent to 47, its date, 23 June, probably refers to the *new* Roman calendar, adjusted to the seasons, which Caesar only began to introduce in 46 BC. If, therefore, *according to that subsequent calendar*, the date of Caesarion's birth was 23 June, his birthday, according to the reckoning still in force in 47 BC, fell during the first week of September;[5] and that is when we may suppose that he was born.

If so, he had been conceived at a time when Caesar and Cleopatra were together in the palace at Alexandria. But the sources are as much in disagreement about Caesarion's paternity as they are about the date of his birth. Even if Antony was right in saying that Caesar acknowledged the child as his, that would not, it might be repeated, prove that Caesar had been telling the truth.[6] After his death, this became a burning political issue, upon which the whole question of his heirship revolved. While Cleopatra was determined to assert that the boy was Caesar's child, many supporters of Octavian (Augustus), who claimed the inheritance because Caesar adopted him as his son in his will, issued equally vigorous denials. Indeed, one of Caesar's former friends, Gaius Oppius, seems to have held both views in turn, first expressing the conviction that Caesar was the father, and then, in Octavian's interests, writing a pamphlet to deny that this was so.[7]

Two further considerations may be added, one against Caesar's paternity and one in its favour. His only unchallenged offspring, in all his life, was his daughter Julia, born no less than thirty-six years previously.[8] Considering the large number of women who were reputedly his mistresses, and the inadequacy or non-employment of contraceptives at the time, this is an unimpressive result, and has led to suggestions that he was sterile. If Cleopatra, in the last weeks of 48 BC, had come to a similar conclusion, her desire, for political reasons, to have a son who could be regarded as Caesar's heir might possibly have induced her to seek a substitute lover as an emergency measure.

On the other hand, the princesses of the house of the Ptolemies had always apparently been very much averse to taking casual lovers, especially from outside the royal house. They were not, like later Roman imperial ladies, both murderous and adulterous. They were murderous and chaste. The same extreme pride in their families which caused these royal Ptolemaic women to enter into brother-and-sister marriages deterred them from promiscuous associations. Cleopatra's relationship with Caesar was adulterous in a purely technical sense, since she had gone through marriage ceremonies with her juvenile half-brothers. But her extra-marital associations seem to have been very far from casual, since, as far as we know, there were only two men in her life, Caesar and Antony. Such arguments, however, are not conclusive, and we still have no idea whether or not Caesar was the father of her son Caesarion.[9]

Cleopatra seems to have celebrated his birth by a coinage in Cyprus, over which her rule, in association with her surviving half-brother Ptolemy XIV, had recently been extended. The coinage is inscribed with her name alone, as usual. But for once her portrait is not quite alone, for she is suckling an infant, who must be Caesarion, shown very shortly after his birth.[10] She is Isis, and Isis, too, often appeared suckling the baby god Horus, a theme to which Cleopatra would later revert when her plans for the boy began to mature. In Greek terms, the mother and son were Aphrodite and Eros.

*

After bidding farewell to Cleopatra, Caesar had marched out of Egypt with his small force. His destination was Asia Minor, and his purpose the suppression of King Pharnaces II of Pontus, who showed defiance of the Romans in the spirit of his father, Rome's old enemy Mithridates VI. Caesar defeated Pharnaces at Zela (Zile) on 1 August 47 with a rapidity which inspired the conqueror to borrow the Greek epigram 'I came, I saw, I conquered.'[11] Then, returning at long last to Italy, he landed at Tarentum (Taranto) on 24 September. But he soon hastened back again to north Africa, where the sons and friends of the late Pompey, encouraged by Caesar's prolonged delay in Egypt, had raised a large army in the Roman province of Africa, which corresponds to the modern Tunisia. Caesar crushed the Pompeians on 6 April 46 BC at Thapsus (Ras Dimas), and was back in the capital by 25 July.

Between 20 September and 1 October 46 he celebrated four Triumphs in honour of his various victories, accompanied by an orgy of extravagant festivities and ceremonials. The obscene songs which the soldiers habitually sang on such occasions included spicy verses about his relations with Cleopatra and other women.[12] A mock sea-fight between the fleets of Egypt and Tyre, manned by numerous soldiers, was staged on an artificial lake, and the second of the four Triumphs was specifically devoted to the commemoration of Caesar's Alexandrian war. A model of the Pharos lighthouse, with imitation flames issuing from the top, was carried in the procession. A statue of the Nile-God was also to be seen, and huge framed pictures displayed the deaths of the treacherous, or patriotic, Pothinus and Achillas. These paintings were very well received by the Roman crowds. But the climax of the procession was the appearance of the captive Arsinoe IV. At the head of a group of Egyptian prisoners, including perhaps, her own former chief minister Ganymedes,[13] she walked, loaded with chains, in the triumphal parade.

It was not the first time that foreign princesses had figured in Roman

Triumphs, for Zosime, the widow of Mithridates, and his two daughters had experienced the same ordeal in Pompey's procession of 61 BC. But the sight of the princess Arsinoe, a girl of energy and courage, touched a chord of compassion in the hearts of the Roman populace, which showed itself displeased by her humiliation. However, Caesar imitated Pompey and spared Arsinoe the execution which so often befell Rome's captives immediately after their appearance in a Triumph. Whether Cleopatra favoured this act of mercy to her half-sister may be doubted. But Caesar probably felt it would not be in her interests if he inflicted such a penalty upon a member of her family, since he had decided to keep that family upon the Egyptian throne. So Arsinoe was allowed to leave for Asia Minor, where she found lodging and asylum (like her father before her) in the precinct of Artemis at Ephesus, the Diana of the Ephesians whose followers later resisted St Paul. What happened to Ganymedes is unknown.

*

And now Cleopatra came to Rome herself, accompanied by the thirteen-year-old Ptolemy XIV and an imposing entourage. With her also, no doubt, was her infant son Caesarion, so that she could emphasize her claim that his father was Caesar.

It is unlikely that the party arrived in time for the Triumphs; if it had, this would have been recorded. Her child was not much more than two weeks old when the festivities started. Besides, it would scarcely have been decorous for Cleopatra to join in the celebration of victory over her own country, a victory, moreover, which had caused such disasters to members of her own house.

One purpose of their visit – or rather of hers, since her half-brother was still so young – was to induce the Roman government to reaffirm the treaty of alliance and friendship which her father had arranged with Caesar during his first consulship, thirteen years earlier. A new treaty, which would safeguard Cleopatra in case of attempts to annex Egypt, was safely concluded.[14] At this time, the state was completely dominated by Caesar as dictator, and the new treaty was rapidly and successfully arranged. This was a relief to the queen, since there was always a section of influential Roman opinion which favoured the annexation of her country.

*

The main purpose of her visit, however, was to continue her close personal relations with Caesar, since it was on him, treaty or no treaty, that her whole position depended. This was a matter about which she had reason to feel anxious, because Caesar had other mistresses besides

Cleopatra. One of them, people said, was a queen of Mauretania, King Bogud's wife Eunoe, to whom Caesar was reported to have shown exceptional generosity. Indeed, he may well have been conducting this affair during his recent north African campaign.

Caesar hospitably lodged Cleopatra and the royal boys and their retinues upon his own estate across the Tiber, near the south-eastern corner of the Janiculum hill. The two monarchs, Cleopatra and Ptolemy XIV, occupied a special position as Caesar's protégés, and the welcome he gave them was a correctly courteous return of hospitality for all the months he had spent in the royal palace of Alexandria.

Installed in Caesar's mansion, Cleopatra must have maintained a spectacular and cultured court. We hear, for example, of a famous though temperamental singer and musician, Marcus Tigellius Hermogenes, whom she favoured with her patronage.[15] But her borrowed palace must also have been full of Roman statesmen anxious to ingratiate themselves with a woman who so obviously enjoyed Caesar's favour: though it is impossible to discover who they were, since later on, after Cleopatra had become Rome's enemy, no one was eager to advertise this former association. Antony she already knew, but whether she saw much of him in Rome we cannot tell; after serving in 48/7 as Caesar's deputy (Master of the Horse), he was temporarily out of favour until 44. The orator Cicero, however, was not one of her admirers. He cast a jaundiced eye on all this un-Roman pomp, referring unpleasantly to Cleopatra's arrogance (*superbia*).

It is ironical, however, that we have quite detailed information about the Alexandrian street-fighting of the previous years, but none at all about the queen's stay at Rome, though it must have been one of the most significant periods of her career; the last scene of Shaw's *Caesar and Cleopatra*, implying that the two did not meet again after Alexandria, is misleading. Caesar at once paid Cleopatra a very high compliment. As a sequel to his Triumphal celebrations, he staged the official opening ceremony of the Forum Julium, his grandiose annexe to the venerable but overcrowded Forum Romanum. The central feature of the splendid new precinct was a Temple of Venus the Mother (Genetrix), the goddess from whom, through Aeneas, the Julian family claimed descent. There was a superb image of Venus in this new temple: and beside it Caesar placed a gilt-bronze statue of Cleopatra herself.

This noteworthy gesture, it is true, possessed no constitutional significance. Still less did it imply any suggestion that Caesar was going to marry Cleopatra. He had a wife already, Calpurnia (whose opinion of Cleopatra is unrecorded), and bigamy was forbidden by Roman law. Nor, in any case, did the legal system recognize the marriage of a Roman with a foreigner. Nevertheless, that the queen should have her statue erected in a great Roman temple, a temple, moreover, which was the focus of an imperial cult already forming round the Julian house, was an unprecedented honour. In Ptolemaic Egypt it had long been customary to place the statues of kings and queens in shrines, so that they became Divine Temple Companions (*theoi synnaoi*) of the gods, who were, after all, only regarded as their senior colleagues.[16] Now, however, Caesar had extended the custom to Rome. He later allowed the practice to be repeated in his own favour, when his statue was erected in the Temple of Quirinus, who was Rome's deified founder Romulus. But the first person to receive the compliment was Cleopatra.

The statue, purely honorific though it was, provided a pointed and elegant allusion to her divine status as the reincarnation of Isis, who was identified with Aphrodite (Venus). It was also a mark of favour which raised her considerably above all the other monarchs who were dependent on Rome. But did Caesar also, at this stage, admit that he was the father of her son Caesarion? We do not know; and we are equally unaware whether the frenzied statements for and against the dictator's paternity had yet begun. It is quite probable that he already accepted, more or less openly, that he was the father. But, if so, this had no bearing on the Roman constitutional scene.

*

We should also like to know just how much Cleopatra influenced Caesar's official and imperial policies during her stay in Rome – or for that matter during their previous association in Alexandria.

The theory of the 1930s that Caesar remained uncompromisingly Roman at all times[17] was a reaction against the exaggerated view that he became thoroughly oriental. Nevertheless, it needs a certain amount of modification. The conflict in his heart between Roman traditional instincts and eastern autocratic ideas remained strong. A certain sympathy with the east helped to make him increasingly impatient and contemptuous of the conservative Roman nobility and its opinions. This impatience may have been fomented by Cleopatra, and perhaps this was one of the reasons why her visit, we are told, caused a good deal of offence.[18] It is by no means improbable that Caesar's introduction of certain rites of Dionysus[19] into Rome took place under her influence,[20] and the relationship of the Dionysiac religion to ruler-worship was close. As Cleopatra's later behaviour showed, she felt little sympathy for the brand of liberty that these Roman nobles professed – which meant free speech for themselves and their own class. In dealing with her own Alexandrian aristocracy, she had found that the only way to suppress its uncompromising hostility was by force. And she seems likely to have felt that its Roman counterparts could best be dealt with in the same way. As Octavian (Augustus) later showed, she may not have been far wrong. But, when his turn came, he concealed the iron hand decorously in a velvet glove – having learnt his lesson from Caesar, whose failure to do the same proved so disastrous. If Cleopatra encouraged Caesar to this intransigent attitude, which culminated in his appointment as Perpetual Dictator in February 44, she helped, unwittingly, to bring about his death.[21]

We can at least identify certain practical ways in which Caesar was indebted to Cleopatra's Alexandria, and therefore, directly or indirectly, to herself. The first was his reform of the calendar.[22] The reason why the Roman months and days, at this period, were a good deal ahead of the seasonal, solar year was because the calendar or lunar year consisted of only 355 days instead of 365 – augmented by an additional month in each alternate year, to make up the difference. But these additions, owing to political difficulties, had not been regularly made, so that the calendar year had drifted more than two months ahead of the seasons. Caesar therefore introduced a solar year of 365 days, made up to $365\frac{1}{4}$ by the introduction of an extra day every fourth year (Leap Year). In order to simplify the new arrangement, the year 46 BC was extended to 445 days.

This reform was carried out under the guidance of the Alexandrian astronomer Sosigenes. It is reasonable to suppose that Caesar had made contact with him in Egypt in 48–47 BC, and that Sosigenes then came to Rome with Cleopatra. His adoption of the solar year was owed to an astronomer of the fourth century BC, Callippus of Cnidus.[23] A great deal of research had also been done at the Ptolemaic Museum in Alexandria. Various forms of regular calendars, based on twelve months, had been tried since at least the third millennium BC, and a 365-day calendar may date to 3000 BC. Alexander the Great's Macedonian calendar had been a retrogressive step, since it involved synchronization of sun and moon which was not regularly effected in subsequent times. Ptolemy III Euergetes sought to introduce a solar year (239 BC),[24] but his reform did not achieve complete success in Egypt, though the idea of a solar calendar gained increasing currency in various Hellenistic lands. It remained for Cleopatra's astronomer Sosigenes, under the auspices of Caesar, to arrange for its effective introduction into the Roman empire, and so to the modern world.

A second project in which Caesar evidently owed much to Egypt was the building of canals. He proposed to dig a canal from the River Tiber near Rome to Terracina in order to drain the Pontine Marshes and form a new waterway. In Greece, too, he intended to construct a canal through the Corinthian Isthmus. The great mercantile centre of Corinth had been destroyed by the Romans when they annexed Greece and made it into the province of Achaia in 146 BC. Now Caesar planned to revive the city by peopling it with colonists, mainly ex-slaves from the surplus population of Rome. And in order to make the new settlement prosperous, he announced his intention of piercing the adjacent isthmus, in order to link the Ionian and Adriatic Seas with the Aegean through the Corinthian Gulf.

Again the ancient Egyptians had been the pioneers. As early as 2000 BC an artificial channel had been constructed to join the Red Sea to the Mediterranean. This waterway did not link the two seas directly, like the Suez Canal, but extended from the Red Sea to the eastern (Pelusian) branch of the Nile, by way of the Wadi Tumilat and the Bitter Lakes. The Persian monarch Darius I (522–486 BC) and Ptolemy II Philadelphus had undertaken restorations, and the latter built a lock system at the southern end. The canal may later have fallen into disuse, but it surely provided the model for Caesar's enterprise. Like the experts on the calendar, the advisers who guided him had been brought to his notice in Alexandria; and they too may have come to Rome with Cleopatra. She arrived in the city in 46 BC – a probable year for the launching of the Corinth settlement, because it was the centenary of the new provincial era introduced in Greece (Achaia) by the Romans. It was characteristic of Rome to seek a solemn anniversary of this kind for the new foundation, in order to contrast its own beneficence with the failures of previous régimes; Caesar's new colony on the site of Carthage was also to commemorate the centenary of the city's destruction.[25]

A third example of practical Alexandrian influence upon Caesar was his plan to create great public libraries in Rome. Presiding over this project, which envisaged the collection of the whole of Greek and Roman literature, was the polymath scholar Marcus Terentius Varro, who had fought against Caesar but subsequently gained his pardon. Varro was appointed in 47, and it is surely no coincidence that this is the very year in which Caesar returned from Alexandria. For there, beside the Museum, was the largest and most famous Library in the world, founded by Ptolemy I Soter and greatly extended by Ptolemy II Philadelphus. It was undoubtedly the exemplar for his Roman public libraries.

When Caesar owed practical measures of this kind to Cleopatra's Alexandria, one wonders whether he did not also owe her many of his more far-reaching and effervescent ideas, relating to the whole nature of government by one person.

*

While Cleopatra was staying in Rome, however, it is doubtful whether he was able to spend much time in her company, for he had an immense amount of business to transact. Moreover, in the recent African campaign his health had been giving him trouble. He appears to have become liable to attacks of epilepsy, and he suffered from headaches and fainting fits.

Besides, the Civil War was not over. Defeated in north Africa, the sons of Pompey had built up a menacing new army in Spain, and Caesar had to hasten abroad on yet another campaign in order to deal with them. He left the city late in 46, only four months after his Triumphs and perhaps only about ten weeks after the arrival of Cleopatra in Italy. Although he was old and worn for a man of fifty-four, he reached southern Spain in twenty-seven days, averaging fifty or sixty miles a day in a springless carriage. On 17 March 45 BC, after running great risks, he crushed his enemies at Munda, east of Seville. Before the end of the summer he was back in the neighbourhood of Rome.

Cleopatra was no doubt still surrounded by eminent Romans. Nevertheless, she was serving little useful purpose in Caesar's absence, and it is not certain that she remained in Rome all the time he was away. Cicero, writing in 44, seems to imply that her residence in Caesar's mansion across the Tiber had come to an end at some earlier date.[26] Suetonius, too, is under the impression that at some time or other, while Caesar was still alive, she departed from Rome, generously loaded with gifts.[27] It seems possible, therefore, that while he was in Spain she seized the opportunity to pay a short visit to Egypt, which surely needed her attention after she and so many of her principal advisers had been away for so long: it is true that Caesar's Roman legions were keeping order in the country, but no doubt some of her political enemies were still at large.

If she did go away from Rome, however, it is quite clear from Cicero's letters that she returned there before Caesar's death. She wanted to be close to the ruler of the western world, and this determination must have been strengthened by the news that the Mauretanian Bogud was playing an important part as Caesar's ally in the Spanish campaign. For if Bogud was by his side, then Bogud's wife, queen Eunoe, said to be Caesar's mistress, was likely to be by his side as well. Cleopatra would not have wanted to let her own influence go by default.

Caesar's return may have been disconcerting, for he did not enter the capital immediately. While he was at Corduba (Cordova), his health had failed him again. And now he withdrew to his estate at Lavicum (Monte Campatri), south-east of Rome, with the intention of making his will. This document was deposited in the official residence of the Vestal Virgins, as the custom was, on 13 September 45 BC. It was only concerned with his personal affairs and not with his official position, since dictatorships and consulships were not heritable. Nevertheless, although almost nobody knew the contents as yet, they were highly significant. For the will directed that his promising nineteen-year-old grand-nephew Gaius Octavius (later known as Octavian and then Augustus) should become his adopted son after his death, and inherit three-quarters of his huge estate. Of Cleopatra's son Caesarion no mention was made. This was inevitable, since even if the infant was Caesar's son, he was not legitimate, and Roman law made it impossible for a Roman to declare a foreigner his heir. Nor, for the same reason, could the will take any cognizance of the foreigner Cleopatra.

Nevertheless, when Caesar returned to Rome at the beginning of October 45 in order to celebrate a fresh Triumph, the queen's presence in the city stimulated various rumours. For example it was asserted that the dictator actually intended to move his capital from Rome to Alexandria – though other versions of the report preferred Troy, of whose mythical royal house he claimed to be a descendant. Such gossip was pure fantasy, the sort that came easily to the Roman populace. It was also said that he proposed to make Cleopatra his wife.[28] A more peculiar and circumstantial tale was associated with the name of a certain Helvius Cinna, a north Italian poet who held one of the tribuneships in 44 BC. This man, according to Suetonius, 'admitted to several persons that he had a bill drawn up in due form, which Caesar had ordered him to propose to the people in his own absence, making it lawful for Caesar to marry what wives he wished, and as many as he wished, for the purpose of begetting children'[29] – that is to say, legitimate children, for this is what the legal formula means.

Probably Suetonius' information is fictitious, associated with Helvius Cinna's name because Cinna was one of Caesar's most enthusiastic supporters.[30] Nevertheless, the story could only have been invented if it possessed some plausibility, and this gives some idea of the influence Cleopatra was exercising in Rome – and the likelihood that it might become inordinate.

Caesar himself was about to leave again for the east. Indeed, riled by a number of criticisms from the Republican opposition at Rome, he proposed to leave Italy almost immediately: the date was fixed for 17 March 44 BC. Regardless of his poor health, he planned to undertake an immense oriental military operation, an enterprise which would even dwarf all his others, so that he would become the equal of Alexander the Great. In revenge for Parthia's victory over Crassus nine years before, he envisaged nothing less than the conquest of the entire Parthian empire. An extremely powerful Roman army had been gathered together, and it was intended that this should avoid Crassus' disastrous Mesopotamian incursion by attacking the Parthians from the north instead, by way of Armenia. Operations of such vast scope would require supplies of men, ships and money from every one of the numerous dependent states along the empire's eastern borders, and most of all from the richest and most populous of these countries, Cleopatra's Egypt. The five months that had elapsed since Caesar's return to Rome had largely been devoted to planning this unprecedented expedition, and Cleopatra was no doubt brought actively into the consultations.

Once Caesar had left Italy there was no knowing when he would be back: and it is certain that Cleopatra, too, intended to leave at about the same time. She would then be in a position to play her part as Rome's ally in the impending campaigns. She would also be able to spend some time with Caesar, maintaining or even increasing her personal authority and ensuring that Egypt would be suitably rewarded for its role in his expected victories.

However, she had miscalculated. Alexandrian dissidents might be forcibly suppressed, but Caesar's methods could not cow men like Brutus and Cassius. They found the dictatorship bad enough, but felt that the dictator's prolonged absence in the east would be even worse; for, while he was away, he was going to leave Rome in charge of obedient lackeys (his secretaries Balbus and Oppius, under the titular direction of Lepidus who had succeeded Antony in 46 as Master of the Horse). And so, only two days before he was due to depart from the city, a group of Republicans decided to act. Caesar's aristocratic pride and nonchalance could not let him worry about such dangers, and he was careless about his own safety. No doubt he appreciated the possibility that he would be murdered, and regarded it with a mixture of fatalism and contempt: at a dinner-party on the evening before he died, he is said to have expressed preference for a death that would be sudden. It is possible that Cleopatra, who was accustomed to an atmosphere of lethal suspicion in Alexandria, was one of those who warned him that this careless attitude was rash.

There were sixty conspirators, so it was not surprising that word of the plot leaked out. A meeting of the Senate was called for 15 March. As Caesar approached the meeting-place, in the hall adjoining Pompey's theatre, a Greek who had once been Brutus' tutor tried to speak to him, and handed him a warning note. But it remained unread in his hand. The plotters had arranged that a group of gladiators, who were due to fight in a show that day, should be nearby in case of need. It was also planned that Antony, who had now been restored to Caesar's favour and was a man of great physical strength, should be detained in conversation at the door by Gaius Trebonius, who was in the plot.

Approaching the dictator, one of his enemies, Tillius Cimber, knelt before him as though to present a petition. Caesar motioned him aside, but Tillius caught hold of his toga and pulled at it. Then a friend of Cassius named Casca drew his dagger and wounded him just below the throat. The blow slipped, and Caesar, turning, pierced Casca's arm with his iron pen. But now his assassins came upon him from every side, and as Caesar, screaming, lunged first one way and then another, Cassius stabbed his face and Brutus struck him in the groin. Torn by twenty-three wounds, he covered his face with his robe and fell to the ground, against the pedestal of Pompey's statue.

The most redoubtable leader Rome had ever known was dead. And Cleopatra had lost her lover, patron and friend, on whom the fulfilment of all her ambitions had depended.

5

Cleopatra after Caesar's Death

Two days after the murder of Caesar, his will was read out, and soon it was generally known that Cleopatra and Caesarion were not mentioned. To Cleopatra, this was presumably no surprise; as her Roman legal advisers could have reminded her, their inclusion was impossible. But to the general public, less familiar with Roman law, her omission was a sign that she had not yet achieved the major ambitions which rumour attributed to her. Her only solid gain, ever since she had come to Rome one and a half years earlier, was the renewed treaty of friendship and alliance between Egypt and the Roman people.

For what happened next we are wholly dependent upon a few fragmentary and cryptic references in Cicero's letters to his closest friend, Atticus. First, Cicero reports that Cleopatra has departed from Rome and Italy, and being one of those Republican Romans who greatly disliked both Caesar and herself, he is glad. 'I see nothing to object to', he writes on 15 April 'in the flight of the queen.'[1] She had intended to leave Italy at about the same time as Caesar, and his death was no reason to change her decision. Indeed, the assassination made her presence in Rome an embarrassment, while the disturbances likely to ensue throughout the Greco-Roman world made her return to Egypt highly desirable.

Then, on 11 May, Cicero has something more to say about her. 'I am hoping it is true', he writes to Atticus, 'about the queen and about that Caesar.'[2] 'That Caesar' might seem to refer to her son Caesarion. Yet a better solution may be provided by the two immediately preceding sentences, which refer, with regret, to a miscarriage suffered by 'Tertulla', an affectionate diminutive name for Tertia, wife of Cassius and half-sister of Brutus. Although the style of Cicero's letters is often

95

telegraphically abrupt, this juxtaposition might be interpreted to suggest a rumour that Cleopatra had miscarried during her journey back to Egypt. If so, then 'that Caesar' may refer not to Caesarion after all, but to an unborn infant, a second child she had allegedly conceived by the dictator;[3] the poet Lucan, though admittedly writing more than a century later, refers to Caesar's extra-conjugal begettings in the plural.[4] At first sight, this theory of a miscarriage by Cleopatra appears weakened by Cicero's next observation on 17 May, when he writes that 'the rumour about the queen is dying down'.[5] Yet a week later some report about Cleopatra is still going the rounds after all, since on 24 May Cicero writes: 'I wish it had been true about Menedemus. I am hoping it is true about the queen.'[6] Menedemus was a Thessalian supporter of Caesar; Cicero wanted him out of the way, and had apparently heard some report that his hopes were fulfilled.

On 13 June, however, Cicero treated Atticus to his most lengthy observations about Cleopatra; and they are more revealing.

I hate the queen! And the man who vouches for her promises, Ammonius, knows I have good reason to do so; although the gifts she promised me were of a literary nature and not beneath my dignity – the sort I should not have minded proclaiming in public. Her man Sara too, beside being a rogue, I have found impertinent towards myself. Once, and once only, have I seen him in my house; and then, when I asked him politely what he wanted, he said he was looking for Atticus. And the Queen's insolence, when she was living in Caesar's house in the gardens beyond the Tiber, I cannot recall without indignation. So no dealings with that lot. They seem to think I have not only no spirit, but no feelings at all.[7]

Cicero detested most living Greeks, and especially those who came from farther afield than the Greek mainland. There were also abundant political reasons why he should detest any mistress of Caesar. But his letter makes it clear that he had additional, personal pretexts for disliking Cleopatra.

Her 'insolence', and the pomp and grandeur of her court at Rome, must have seemed to him utterly scandalous – especially as she was a woman. In spite of a literary friendship with one blue-stocking Roman lady, Cicero was never very good with women. His two failed marriages (one in the quite recent past) had indicated his inadequacies in this field, and perhaps they also made him particularly unwilling to see the attractions of a woman as glamorous as Cleopatra. For he is on record as displaying a particular animosity towards women with pasts, and indeed towards sex in general.[8] So the foreign queen, who had been the hated dictator's concubine, was unlikely to appeal to him in any way. As far as we know, Cicero did not venture to write anything against her in

Caesar's lifetime. But now, when the dictator was safely dead, his indignation broke out.

His impassioned reference to humiliations she and her ministers had inflicted on him rather suggests that he had tried to take a high line, and that this reigning monarch and goddess had snubbed him. The story about Ammonius, whoever he was, suggests that Cleopatra had promised Cicero certain presents, which Ammonius had failed to deliver.[9] The rest of the letter is a list of lamentations about financial problems which have nothing to do with Cleopatra. But the reference to the queen fits in well with this series of complaints, if the negligence of Ammonius or his queen had caused the orator to suffer serious loss because he had not received her gifts. There is also, perhaps, a suggestion that other Romans had sponged on the queen more effectively and disgracefully than Cicero. That seems to be the implication of his sour assertion that *he* would not have minded admitting to her presents in public. No doubt Cleopatra, during her stay in Rome, acted as her father had acted before her, and arranged the judicious distribution of presents and bribes to important Romans, whose assistance might be politically useful in the future.

*

Now that Caesar was dead, the temporary supremacy of the consul Mark Antony did not worry her, for presumably she knew him quite well and already liked him. Graver news was that the young Octavian, confounding forecasts and refusing advice, was determined to try to claim his heritage as the dictator's son. He had solemnly assumed the name of Gaius Julius Caesar, and counted on attracting to his cause the loyalty of many of the dead man's soldiers, who were appalled by the dictator's murder and could be expected to rally to his heir. Octavian had been completing his academic and military studies at the Adriatic town of Apollonia, now in Albania. But now he hastened home, sailing to Italy in late March or early April. His arrival posed an immediate threat to Cleopatra – and more especially to her son Caesarion. According to her, this boy who had been given the name of Caesar before Octavian was the only surviving child of Caesar's blood. But this might well seem intolerable to Octavian. His emergence and arrival made her departure from Italy imperative.

So Cleopatra now made her way back to Egypt, in the company of her fifteen-year-old half-brother and fellow-monarch Ptolemy XIV. Since a papyrus is still headed by his name (in addition to Cleopatra's) on 26 July of the year 44,[10] it is to be supposed that the boy survived the journey back to Egypt. But he must have perished very soon thereafter, for we are told that he was dead before September.[11]

Both the Jewish historian Josephus and the pagan writer Porphyry, who lived in the first and third centuries AD respectively, declare that Cleopatra murdered him. They refer to treacherous action on her part, and in another passage Josephus indicates that she employed poison.[12] There is no reason to believe that the accusation was untrue. If Cleopatra could demand the death of her half-sister (as she did three years later), she was also capable of murdering her half-brother. And his death was too opportune to be accidental, for during the crisis after Caesar's death her greatest remaining political asset, to which all else must be sacrificed, was the boy she declared to be his son, Ptolemy Caesar or Caesarion. It was consequently essential that Caesarion should be elevated to the throne of Egypt as her fellow monarch. But it was impossible for her to have two co-rulers, so the existing incumbent Ptolemy XIV, though he was her own half-brother and husband, had to be removed.

The age that produced Cleopatra was one in which self-preservation often meant the destruction of one's own kinsmen. For example, a man who was to ascend the throne of Parthia during the following decade only established himself by arranging the murder of no less than thirty of his brothers. It has been questioned whether the murder of a few dozen members of one's family, if they represented a genuine threat to one's position and one's life, was really much more deplorable than the slaughter of millions of foreigners in modern wars.[13]

It is true that Cleopatra was in no obvious danger, as far as we know, from this fifteen-year-old boy. Yet she herself might have been able to tell us otherwise. Only a very few years previously his brother, at the age of twelve, had become the focus and figurehead of a group of politicians violently unfriendly towards her. Now that Caesar had been murdered, there was every reason to expect a vigorous revival of the same sort of hostile element. Cleopatra may well have felt that her life was again being threatened by a half-brother. If so, his removal and replacement by her own three-year-old son Caesarion, the bearer of Caesar's charismatic name, may well have seemed an urgent political necessity.

At all events, shortly after her return, the death of Ptolemy XIV enabled her to place Caesarion on the throne as her associate and fellow-monarch, Ptolemy XV Caesar.[14] For the new reign, she not unnaturally dropped the title Philadelphus (Brother-Loving) but retained the designations Thea Philopator (Goddess who Loves her Father) while Ptolemy XV Caesar was called Theos Philopator Philometor (God who Loves his Father and Mother).[15] This reference to his mother was added because he was an infant, so that Cleopatra was obviously, in effect, sole ruler. Even in the days of her departed brother-husbands, she had not bothered to associate their heads with her own on the Egyptian coinage, and she does not depict her new 'colleague' either. It was with some reason that later chronologists, while speaking of her 'joint' reigns hitherto, indicate that at this point she now entered upon a period of sole rule.[16]

But the other title of Ptolemy xv, Lover of his Father, refers to Cleopatra's affirmation that he was the son of Julius Caesar. It implied that he was Caesar's only true heir, and that the counter-assertions of Octavian, who was only Caesar's great-nephew and adopted son, had far less justification.

*

For the benefit of the Egyptians, Cleopatra translated the same message into their native visual idiom, and engraved it upon the walls of their temples. At Tintyra (Dendera) in Upper Egypt she and Caesarion were represented together as Pharaohs in the traditional style. This relief appears on the wall of the shrine of Hathor, the female power of nature, who was assimilated to Isis or regarded as the wet-nurse of Horus, the divine child of Isis and Osiris.[17] The same message was conveyed even more clearly at the sacred place of Hermonthis, where 'Cleopatra had the birth of Caesarion unmistakably celebrated both in the pictures and in the text. His birth is realistically depicted alongside that of the God Horus.... Cleopatra is shown kneeling attended by goddesses, and above her is her new name "Mother of Ra (the Sun-god)" in hieroglyphs. Over the new-born child stands symbolically, the device of the scarab (sacred beetle), marking out the young Ptolemy Caesar as God of the Rising Sun. On a couch apart sit two cow-headed goddesses suckling two infants, clearly the young god Horus and the young Caesarion. In addition, not only the god Amon and the goddess Mut but also Cleopatra herself are shown appearing on the scene in response to the joyful event. An important official character was thus bestowed on the birth of Caesarion.'[18]

This shrine at Hermonthis was a 'birth-temple'. The Pharaohs and their wives had carried out elaborate rituals in connection with the births of their offspring, and the Ptolemies built special birth-shrines for these rites as annexes to the ancient temples, adorning them in the native artistic tradition. The essential theme of the reliefs engraved upon their walls was the birth of the god Horus, 'the young one with his finger in his mouth'.[19] Representations of Isis nursing him as an infant had long been a prominent feature of Egyptian art, and already Cleopatra had shown herself with Caesarion at her breast on a Cyprus coin. Throughout Ptolemaic and Roman times the baby Horus became continually more and more popular, and indeed Osiris, Isis and Horus became a Trinity which finally dominated the religion of the country.[20]

The king of Egypt was Osiris, the queen was Isis, and infant princes and kings were Horus, destined to grow up as The Powerful One, who would take his father's place.[21]

The birth-temples show the heavenly pattern re-enacted upon earth, but the scenes and texts displayed usually keep the imagery firmly upon a symbolic level, avoiding any direct reference to the birth of the earthly prince. The Hermonthis temple marks a novel and deliberate breach of this convention, because it displays not only the birth of Horus but the birth of Caesarion as well. This unprecedented directness may have a topical explanation. For one of the principal duties of Horus was to avenge the violent death that his father Osiris had suffered. There were many Egyptian stories of the obstacles Horus had to overcome in pursuing this task of vengeance; and in Ptolemaic times the child was still described as the 'Avenger of his Father'.[22] When Caesar was murdered, those who had honoured his memory dedicated themselves to a similar vengeance against his assassins. And since, according to Cleopatra, Caesarion was his only son, the Hermonthis sculptures, so emphatically identifying the boy with Horus, are deliberately asserting his claim to be his father's avenger. Like Caesarion's title 'Father-Loving', this was an implied slight upon Octavian, who had declared that vengeance for the death of his adoptive father was his own special task. It seems very probable therefore that the Hermonthis relief does not date from the time of Caesarion's birth in 47 BC, but from his elevation to the throne three years later, shortly after the murder of Caesar.

In siting one of these birth-temples at Hermonthis, which she had visited immediately after her accession to the throne, Cleopatra was continuing to show her special interest in Upper Egypt, where native Egyptian opinion remained so influential.[23] An inscription from Thebes, now at Turin, vividly displays the pretensions of the area under her rule. The relief was set up, perhaps in 43–42 BC, by the priests of Amon-Ra in honour of the local governor, Callimachus (perhaps the son of Auletes' governor-general of the same name), who had helped to restore the city after its destruction in a rebellion of the eighties BC, and had once again come to its assistance during a recent famine.[24] The inscription concentrates on the merits of Callimachus, but, except in the heading, refrains from making any mention of the queen and king. This unusual omission suggests that Cleopatra was allowing Upper Egypt, where she enjoyed political support, considerable autonomy.

*

In the violent crises that convulsed the Roman empire after Caesar's death, Cleopatra needed all the support from inside Egypt that she could possibly get.

The young Octavian, back in Rome to claim his heritage, began to pay off Caesar's legacies from his own resources, while Antony – deeply disappointed because the dictator had merely named him one of his secondary heirs – took steps to strengthen his own position. Meanwhile, in the summer of 44 BC, Caesar's assassins, Brutus and Cassius, left for the eastern provinces, and started to raise troops for the inevitable clash with Antony or Octavian, or both. But by the spring of the following year, grave additional complications had arisen. In the west, Antony found himself opposed by a coalition of Republicans and moderate Caesarians, instigated by Cicero and supported by Octavian, and was compelled to withdraw from Italy into Gaul, after a battle at Mutina (Modena) which caused the deaths of both consuls and left Octavian virtually in sole charge of Rome. In the east, Cassius proceeded to Syria, but soon afterwards a Caesarian, Publius Cornelius Dolabella, arrived to try to seize the province. This clash so close to their own borders, resulting in urgent appeals from both contestants, faced the Egyptian authorities with the same sort of awkward decision that had confronted them during the civil war between Pompey and Caesar.

Cleopatra's natural reaction was to support Caesar's friend Dolabella – who had proved his loyalty by murdering one of Caesar's assassins – rather than his murderer Cassius. She therefore permitted or encouraged the Roman occupying force which Caesar had left in Alexandria (now increased from three legions to four) to join Dolabella under its commander Allienus. However, Dolabella was worsted by Cassius and cornered inside Laodicea (Lattakia); when the city fell in July 43 BC, he committed suicide. At some stage during these events the legions from Egypt changed sides and went over to Cassius. Cleopatra later assured the Caesarians, perhaps truthfully, that she had planned to send Dolabella a fleet as well, but was prevented from doing so, first by adverse winds, and then by news of his sudden defeat.

Dolabella's downfall subjected the queen, denuded of her Roman garrison, to a very grave threat from Cassius, who was eager to raise funds to pay his large force of legionaries, and showed signs of planning an expedition against Egypt in order to seize its ever-tempting treasures. By now all the other dependent monarchs of the east had declared their allegiance to Brutus and Cassius, and Cleopatra, whose kingdom was by far the wealthiest, would surely be compelled to conform. Moreover, she had assisted Cassius' enemy Dolabella; and her reminder that Allienus' legions had deserted to his side was unlikely to cause Cassius to change his attitude.

Even her own governor of Cyprus, Serapion (who may or may not have been Caesar's envoy to Achillas in 43 BC) had gone over to Cassius; indeed he had actually done so, if the historian Appian can be believed, before Dolabella's suicide.[25] He then sent ships to help Cassius without consulting Cleopatra. This was a particularly worrying development since her hostile half-sister Arsinoe IV was within easy reach of Cyprus from her residence at Ephesus, where the high priest of Artemis was hailing her as queen of Egypt.[26] Serapion's disobedience to Cleopatra probably meant he was backing Arsinoe. If so, he could point out that Caesar himself had once, for a brief period, nominated her as queen of Cyprus. But what Serapion really intended, no doubt, was that Arsinoe should move from Cyprus to Egypt and oust Cleopatra. His defection weakened Cleopatra's position considerably, and meant that Cassius might sponsor this attempt to set Arsinoe on the Egyptian throne. But Cleopatra was narrowly saved from Cassius' invasion when Brutus urgently summoned him to Smyrna. Before the year 43 BC was over, he was in Asia Minor conferring with his colleague.

Their situation had become increasingly serious. For whereas, in the early part of the year, their Caesarian enemies in the west had seemed hopelessly divided, during the summer a reconciliation had been gradually arranged between its three principal leaders, Antony, Octavian, and the man who had succeeded Antony as Caesar's Master of Horse, Lepidus. Finally, in November, the three new masters of the world associated themselves together in a formal pact, the Second Triumvirate, which provided that they should jointly exercise dictatorial powers for five years. The leading role of Antony and Octavian in the pact was sealed by one of the matrimonial arrangements which the Romans considered such important guarantees of a political alliance; it was agreed that Antony's stepdaughter Clodia should marry Octavian.

In preparation for the expected onslaught from the triumvirs, Cassius redoubled his efforts to secure help and money from the eastern kingdoms, and sent a second demand for assistance to Cleopatra.[27] There is no reason to suppose that her hostility to Caesar's assassins had diminished. But certain aspects of the Triumvirate cannot have pleased her. It was disagreeable enough that one of the new dictatorial rulers was Octavian, whose claim to Caesar's heritage was incompatible with her ambitions for her own son Caesarion. But rivalry over the heritage sharpened when the dead Caesar, on 1 January 42 BC, was declared a god by the Roman state. Although at this time, in imitation of eastern models, Rome's leaders were sometimes unofficially spoken of as divine, the Romans, unlike the Egyptians, had never deified them officially during their lifetimes, nor, indeed, were they accustomed to deify them after death. The one exception had been the mythical Romulus, founder of Rome, who was believed to have become the god Quirinus. This precedent was now adapted to the memory of Caesar. Already during his lifetime his statue in the temple of Quirinus implied that he was the second

founder, and the analogy to Quirinus was completed by his formal deification in 42. Cleopatra could have no objection to this. Indeed, she
herself had started building the Caesareum in his lifetime to honour his
divine memory. It was in her interests to do so, since divinization of
Caesar made the divinity of his alleged son Caesarion all the more certain. But official deification of Caesar meant enhancement of the status
of Octavian. Henceforward, as Caesar's legally adopted son, he entitled
himself *Son of Julius the God*, and not long afterwards this designation was
proclaimed to the world on his coins.[28]

In these circumstances it would only be natural for Cleopatra to hesitate before rejecting Cassius' second demand for help – especially as he
and Brutus were so much nearer to her, geographically, than the Triumvirs were. However, she decided not to comply with his request. Three
recent events are likely to have influenced her. The first was the defection of Serapion to Cassius, with its implication that Arsinoe IV was the
rightful queen of Egypt. Secondly, she was gratified by a decree of the
triumvirs that her help to Dolabella against Cassius should be rewarded
by Rome's recognition of Caesarion as her fellow-monarch:[29] aware,
apparently, of her obvious suspicions about Octavian, the Triumvirate
had taken this step to conciliate her. Even if she regarded Octavian as a
grave threat to Ptolemy XV (Caesarion), Octavian cannot have believed
Caesarion to be a serious menace to himself. Or, if he did, he was prepared to ignore any long-term risk in order to guarantee Egyptian
support in the forthcoming struggle against Brutus and Cassius.

To Cassius, Cleopatra gave a third reason: she could not send help because, for the second time in her reign, famine and pestilence had broken
out inside her own country, and she was unable to raise or spare money
or men for external ventures. There is independent evidence of famine
in Egypt during 42 and 41, since in both those years the overflow of the
Nile is known to have been gravely inadequate.[30] The second year has
yielded a joint decree of the queen and Ptolemy XV from Heracleopolis
Magna in Middle Egypt, in which they order that Alexandrians engaged in agricultural work should be protected from unauthorized
emergency measures of local taxation:[31] the agricultural force needed
all the encouragement it could get.

But although Cleopatra used these internal troubles as a pretext for
evading Cassius' demands, he still did not trust her intentions.[32] When
Antony and Octavian transported their legions across the Adriatic to
Macedonia for the final reckoning, Cassius sent one of his admirals,
Lucius Staius Murcus, to Cape Taenarum (Matapan) at the southern
extremity of Greece. Murcus had sixty ships and a legion, and his task
was to prevent Cleopatra from sailing away from Egypt to join Antony
and Octavian.[33] For Cassius had heard that, in spite of her economic

M A C E D O N I A

Dyrrhachium

Philippi

Apollonia
Via Egnatia
Thessalonica

Methone

Samothrace

E p i r u s
T h e s s a l y

Corcyra

Toryne

Pharsalus

AEGEAN
SEA

Gulf of
Ambracia
Actium

Leucas

C.Leucate

Amphissa
Chaeronea

Anticyra

Patrae

Panormus

Achaia

Athens

Corinth

Zacynthus

C y c l a d e s   I s.

IONIAN SEA

Delos
Naxos

Peloponnese

Sparta

C.Taenarum

Greece

0   100km

0   50m

Crete

Cnossus

Gortyna

difficulties, she was preparing a considerable and well-equipped fleet. His information was perfectly correct: and when the fleet was ready, it sailed out of Alexandria harbour, with Cleopatra herself in the flagship. It was the first time for many years that a Hellenistic queen had taken active command of her own navy. However, her presence with the ships may also have been a matter of prudence, because there were probably not enough troops left behind in Alexandria to protect her if internal troubles had arisen in their absence.

It was her intention to join Antony and Octavian, in spite of her suspicions of Octavian, and to run the gauntlet of Murcus' naval blockade. But her voyage was unsuccessful. Only a short distance from the African coast, a storm shattered the Egyptian fleet, and she herself fell ill – probably with the unromantic complaint of seasickness, which was a grave affliction in the relatively small ships of the time. Murcus, in southern Greece, learnt what had happened and saw the wreckage of her ships washed up on to the Greek shore, while Cleopatra sailed back home to Alexandria sorely afflicted by the weather and her health. It has been suggested that the storm and her sickness were merely diplomatic pretexts which enabled her to avoid backing either side in the Roman civil war until the outcome was clearer. But this is unlikely, since if she had remained neutral she would certainly have been in Roman disfavour as soon as the war ended – whichever side eventually won. She had to choose, and it was natural that she should choose the supporters of Caesar against his assassins. Indeed, as she pointed out afterwards, she even made a second attempt to joint the Caesarians, for after her enforced return to Alexandria plans were immediately set on foot to prepare another fleet. But she was too late, for by October 42 BC, the decisive engagements had already been fought.

They were the two successive battles of Philippi in Macedonia. The Caesarians, led by Antony, won an overwhelming victory, and Brutus and Cassius lost their lives. The Triumvirs now had almost the whole Roman world to themselves. The only dissident region was an area of Sicily occupied by Pompey's outlawed son, Sextus Pompeius, a coarse, semi-Republican, semi-piratical figure, to whom some of the surviving Republicans now fled.[34] One member of the Triumvirate, Lepidus, suspected of intriguing with Sextus, was not trusted by his fellow-Triumvirs to govern any territories of his own. Octavian took for himself the entire west, apart from Sextus' Sicilian territories, and Transalpine Gaul which went temporarily to Antony. Antony also assumed control of all the provinces on the far side of the Adriatic.

And it was to these rich eastern lands that he now proceeded to make his way. It was with Antony that Cleopatra would henceforward have to deal.

Part Three

Cleopatra and Antony

6

Cleopatra Summoned
by Antony

When Antony and Octavian were dividing up the Roman world, all Octavian's prestige as the adoptive heir of Caesar could not compensate for Antony's superior advantages. For one thing, Antony was a highly experienced man of forty or forty-one,[1] whereas Octavian was twenty years younger. Although he had made remarkable progress since Caesar's death, there was a measure of truth in Antony's sneer that he was a boy who owed everything to a name. Besides, Octavian had not distinguished himself in the Philippi campaign, partly because of ill health.[2] Indeed, although he lived on for another fifty-seven years, it was believed at the time that his illness, whatever it was, would prove fatal.[3]

Those of the Republicans who surrendered after the catastrophe preferred to surrender to Antony, and some of them took the opportunity to insult Octavian at the same time.[4] When the Triumvirate had first been established in the previous year, the allocation of annual consulships by the Triumvirs down to the year 40 BC had already allowed a preponderance to Antony's supporters; now Philippi confirmed his ascendancy. After the battle, he could probably have taken any region of the empire that he liked. One reason why he selected the east was because of its immense wealth. This had tempted Pompey and numerous others, and Antony urgently needed money for all his troops who were demanding demobilization. Moreover, in Roman eyes, one of the most pressing tasks of the future was to renew the war against the Parthians: it seemed scandalous that their defeat of Crassus in 53 BC had not yet been avenged. Caesar had intended to avenge it by one of the greatest expeditions the world had ever known, and he had been on the very point of undertaking this enterprise when he was murdered. Although disappointed of Caesar's formal heirship, Antony still remained his obvious military heir since he had held large commands and had further enhanced his military prestige at Philippi. To lead the Parthian war which Caesar had planned was a patriotic duty, and it could bring him unprecedented glory. Moreover, Antony's previous experience had given him a wide knowledge of the area.

The eastern provinces he was now called upon to govern were five in number: Macedonia, which included Achaea (Greece); Asia, the extremely rich western region of Asia Minor, including the former kingdom of Pergamum; Bithynia-Pontus to its north and east, Pontus being the former kingdom of Rome's enemy Mithridates VI; Syria, the heavily populated nucleus of the former Seleucid state, and key to the Parthian frontier; and Cilicia, a command area in south-eastern Asia Minor which within the next few years was abolished and, for the most part, merged with Syria.[5] Beyond the provinces, too, Antony possessed many valuable contacts in the dependent or semi-dependent kingdoms which fringed the frontier and played an essential role in its defence. The most important of these states was Cleopatra's Egypt.

After establishing a settlement for ex-soldiers at Philippi itself, named *colonia victrix* to celebrate his recent victories,[6] Antony spent the winter of 42–41 BC in Greece. There he attended literary discussions and religious festivals and ceremonies.[7] In fact, he adopted an amiable phil-Hellenic attitude, which was politically desirable, so as not to invite unfavourable comparison with Brutus, who had behaved in the same way. But it also came much more easily to Antony than to most Romans, since his attachment to the Greek way of life was genuine.

Then, early in 41 BC, he crossed the Aegean and visited the ancient city of Ephesus. Echoing Roman coinages which stressed the alleged Concord between the Triumvirs,[8] the civic mint of Ephesus issued pieces displaying the heads of all three men side by side[9] – a courtesy which no western mint of Octavian's reciprocated. Nevertheless, it was only a courtesy, for Antony was the hero of the day, and in these eastern provinces he reigned supreme.

To express their recognition of his power, the Ephesians and other peoples of Asia made haste to recognize him as the New Dionysus, the characteristic universal god of the Hellenistic age, the deity who stood for eastern conquest.[10] Although living persons were never worshipped at Rome itself, Roman generals, including Pompey and Caesar, had not objected to receiving this sort of veneration in the east. Pompey, celebrating his Triumph over oriental peoples, had allowed all the symbolism of Dionysus to appear at his victorious procession. Like him and Caesar, Antony now exercised wider control in the east than any Hellenistic ruler since Alexander, so that the divine honours seemed to come

to him quite naturally. Besides, he needed to counter Octavian's pro-
clamation that he was the son of a god. So Antony was not just the son
of a god, he *was* a god: Dionysus, the world-conquering provider of
happiness and immortality. 'When, therefore,' recorded Plutarch, 'he
made his entry into Ephesus, women dressed as Bacchantes and men
and boys as satyrs and Pans marched in procession before him. The city
was fitted with wreaths of ivy and ivy-clad wands, the air resounded with
the music of harps, pipes and flutes, and the people hailed him as
Dionysus the Benefactor and the Bringer of Joy.'[11] Ephesian inscriptions, too, proclaimed him God Manifest, son of Ares and Aphrodite
(Mars and Venus), saviour of all mankind.[12]

Antony enacted certain beneficial measures and extended the rights
of asylum of the city's Temple of Artemis[13] – without, so far, laying
hands on Cleopatra's hostile half-sister, Arsinoe, who had been given
sanctuary there. While extorting huge sums of money from the Asian
cities, he pointed out to them that his method of extraction, based on a
sliding system of tithes on their produce, was more humane than the
fixed taxes of the Hellenistic kings. He then left Ephesus and moved
eastwards, raising more money all the time, but also rewarding any
communities which had helped him and his fellow-Triumvirs and
incurred punitive measures from Brutus and Cassius.

Along the frontiers many client-kingdoms needed reform, because
their rulers had compromised themselves with the Republicans, or because they were not strong or loyal enough to play an effective part in
the forthcoming war against Parthia. These, however, were problems
with which for the time being Antony seemed hardly concerned, although one such kingdom, Cappadocia, in the east of the peninsula, may
have received some special, personal attention because its princess
Glaphyra, mother of Archelaus Sisinnes who wanted the local throne,
'struck him as a beautiful woman';[14] it is quite likely that they had an
affair.

Antony's dealings with another monarch, however, could not be postponed, and that was Cleopatra. The position of Egypt in any forthcoming hostilities against the Parthians was vital, since he would need
Egyptian money and other material support. Moreover, the role the
queen had played in the recent Philippi campaign against the assassins
of Caesar seemed ambiguous and obscure – or at least that was what her
enemies informed him. Antony therefore decided that, before extending
his travels any further, he must see Cleopatra. As their meeting-place he
selected Tarsus in Cilicia, one of the cities which had been oppressed by
Brutus and Cassius. His intermediary, ordered to fetch her to Tarsus
from Alexandria, was a certain Quintus Dellius, a man who, although a
scholarly historian, attracted in the course of his varied life a bad

reputation as a homosexual friend of Antony and then his pimp, and a writer of improper letters to Cleopatra.[15] In pursuit of this mission, Dellius now proceeded to Egypt – with letters going before him – and requested the queen to report to Antony. After a suitable delay, designed to show, perhaps, that a divine monarch was not at everyone's beck and call, she obeyed and set out for Tarsus.

*

Antony, whom she already knew well, was a nobleman of famous but impoverished family, the grandson of a great orator and the son of a well-known but easy-going and unsuccessful commander. Antony's own military talents were considerable, though they were displayed to better advantage in the tactical than in the strategic field, and most of all in his capacity to get the very best out of his soldiers, who admired his generosity and endurance. In civilian affairs, he was to prove himself an administrator of large and workable ideas.

If the orient wished to hail him as the New Dionysus, Antony's own fancy was to see himself as another hero-god Heracles (Hercules), whose trophy, the Nemean lion, had already appeared on his coins as the zodiacal sign for the date of his conception.[16] This comparison with Heracles–Hercules had been applied to other Roman generals before Antony. But he, in keeping with the desire of all eminent Roman families to trace divine or mythical ancestors, actually declared (and allowed it to be indicated on contemporary coinage) that he was descended from Hercules himself, through the hero's mythical son Anteon; though this, again, was nothing very unusual, since Cleopatra's family too, in common with other Hellenistic royal houses, was equally ready to claim the same divine ancestor.[17] Hercules had a strong connection with Dionysus, at whose banquets in the Bacchic paradise he was believed to participate.[18] Writers also elevated him into a great unifier of the world, a symbol of concord and reconciliation between the Roman and Greek societies.[19] This was an idea strongly calculated to appeal to Antony's phil-Hellenic instincts. But his enjoyment of Hercules as a model was partly a matter of simple, naive vanity, as Plutarch, in his character-study of Antony, convincingly explains.

There was a noble dignity about Antony's appearance. His beard was well-grown, his forehead broad, his nose aquiline, and these features combined to give him a certain bold and masculine look, which is found in the statues and portraits of Hercules. In fact there was an ancient tradition that the blood of the Heracleidae ran in Antony's family, and Antony liked to believe that his own physique lent force to the legend. He also deliberately cultivated it in his choice of dress, for whenever he was going to appear before a large number of people, he wore his tunic belted low over his hips, a large sword at his side, and a heavy cloak. And indeed it was these same 'Herculean' qualities that the fastidious found so offensive – his swaggering air, his ribald talk, his fondness for carousing in public, sitting down by his men as they ate, or taking his food standing at the common mess-table – which made his own troops delight in his company and almost worship him.[20]

Antony's very considerable intelligence sometimes failed to produce the best results owing to a certain laziness and lack of psychological insight which made him a poor judge of character. It was easy to ignore his failings, however, when confronted with his imposing and somewhat pugilistic looks, bluff natural charm, and strong sense of humour, including a splendidly un-Roman capacity to laugh at himself. Plutarch continues:

He was completely ignorant of much that was done in his name, not merely because he was of an easygoing disposition, but because he was simple enough to trust his subordinates. His character was, in fact, essentially simple and he was slow to perceive the truth. Once he recognized that he was at fault, he was full of repentance and ready to admit his errors to those he had wronged. Whenever he had to punish an offence or right an injustice, he acted on the grand scale, and it was generally considered that he overstepped the bounds far more often in the rewards he bestowed than in the punishments he inflicted. As for the kind of coarse and insolent banter which he liked to exchange, this carried its own remedy with it, for anyone could return his ribaldry with interest and he enjoyed being laughed at quite as much as laughing at others. And in fact it was this quality which often did him harm, for he found it impossible to believe that the real purpose of those who took liberties and cracked jokes with him was to flatter him. He never understood that some men go out of their way to adopt a frank and outspoken manner and use it like a piquant sauce to disguise the cloying taste of flattery. Such men deliberately indulge in bold repartee and an aggressive flow of talk when they are in their cups, so that the obsequious compliance which they show in matters of business does not suggest that they associate with a man merely to please him, but seems to spring from a genuine conviction of his superior wisdom.[21]

Antony's private life was rather disorderly. Cicero, attacking him in the *Philippics* (44–43 BC), made the most of his taste for drink and rowdy parties. Besides, Antony was an insatiable lover of women, and this further resemblance to Hercules, not to speak of Caesar, gave him a reputation which he rather enjoyed. In his youth – if the usual political invective can be believed – he had been notorious for at least one homosexual association, and perhaps more. But those days were long past, and now it was women he pursued, as Plutarch describes:

His weakness for the opposite sex showed an attractive side of his character, and even won him the sympathy of many people, for he often helped others in their love-affairs and always accepted with good humour the jokes they made about his own.... Well versed in the art of putting the best possible face on disreputable actions, he never feared the audit of his copulations, but let nature have her way, and left behind him the foundations of many families.[22]

Nevertheless Antony was married, heavily married. His wife, the beautiful Fulvia, played a very large part in his public life, just as she had already figured prominently in the careers of two remarkable previous husbands, Clodius and Curio. A great heiress, probably descended from the great Fulvian family of Tusculum (Frascati), Fulvia was a masterful and indeed frightening woman, about whom it was said later that there was nothing feminine except her body.[23] Plutarch says of her:

She was a woman who took no interest in spinning or managing a household, nor could she be content to rule a husband who had no ambition for public life: her desire was to govern those who governed or to command a commander-in-chief. And in fact Cleopatra was indebted to Fulvia for teaching Antony to obey a wife's authority, for by the time he met her, he had already been quite broken in and schooled to accept the sway of women. However, Antony did his best by means of practical jokes and other boyish pranks to import a little gaiety into his relationship with her....[24]

Like Fulvia, Antony had been married twice already, but neither of his previous wives had exercised anything like as much influence in public affairs as she did. Cicero (who hated her first husband, Clodius, quite as much as he hated Antony), has ensured that posterity should be provided with a poisonous view of her. Certainly she made mistakes, but she also contributed considerably to the successes of each of her husbands in turn.[25] Indeed, she was a significant phenomenon: a greater political force than any Roman woman had ever been before, and the first wife of a Roman leader and ruler ever to play a really active part in political life.[26]

Fulvia's position as Antony's consort was recognized by an unprecedented official tribute: she seems to have been the first Roman woman ever portrayed on the coinage, in anticipation of many an empress in the centuries to come. The coins were silver pieces (*quinarii*) issued in Antony's name at Lugdunum (Lyon) in 43–42 BC: they bear a head of Victory, with features that have been identified as Fulvia's.[27] The identification has been doubted, on the grounds that the head is not very different from that of an impersonal goddess Victory on another issue forty years earlier.[28] Even if the head of the Lugdunum pieces was not designed to represent Fulvia, it was thought to represent her, since the features and hair-style were closely imitated in local issues of Asian and Syrian cities which were unmistakably intended to depict Fulvia. For example, an identical portrait appears on coins of Eumenia (Işekli) in Phrygia,[29] which actually describe their city of issue not as Eumenia but as 'Fulvia', indicating that Antony, on his way through Asia Minor in 41 BC, gave the little place his wife's name; and hers, clearly, are the features that appear on its coinage. Tripolis in Phoenicia, too, minted with the head of Fulvia as well as Antony.[30] She herself had stayed behind in Italy, to make sure her husband's interests were not neglected by Octavian. But Fulvia's reputation had evidently penetrated to the east.

Cleopatra, then, was well aware that the Mark Antony she was about to meet at Tarsus, although very susceptible to women, possessed a Roman wife whose forcefulness and power were strongly reminiscent of the royal Hellenistic women of her own line. However, being determined, for the sake of her future and Egypt's, to convince him of her own desirability as a queen, Cleopatra appreciated that this probably meant convincing him of her desirability as a woman as well – a campaign she may have begun already during her encounters with Antony at Alexandria or Rome.

And so Cleopatra came from Alexandria to Cilicia, and sailed up a lagoon of the river Cydnus to the ancient city of Tarsus. In Plutarch's description of the scene, in his *Life of Antony*, one cannot suppose that every detail is authentic or unexaggerated, since the dramatic tale had already passed into legend. But his evocation of the event is one of the masterpieces of his vivid biographical method:

She relied above all upon her physical presence and the spell and enchantment which it could create.... She came sailing up the river Cydnus in a barge with a poop of gold, its purple sails billowing in the wind, while her rowers caressed the water with oars of silver which dipped in time to the music of the flute, accompanied by pipes and lutes. Cleopatra herself reclined beneath a canopy of cloth of gold, dressed in the character of Aphrodite (Venus), as we see her in paintings, while on either side to complete the picture stood boys costumed as Cupids who cooled her with their fans. Instead of a crew the barge was lined with the most beautiful of her waiting-women attired as Nereids and Graces, some at the rudders, others at the tackle of the sails, and all the while an indescribably rich perfume, exhaled from innumerable censers, was wafted from the vessel to the river-banks. Great multitudes accompanied this royal progress, some of them following the queen on both sides of the river from its very mouth, while others hurried down from the city of Tarsus to gaze at the sight. Gradually the crowds drifted away from the market-place, where Antony awaited the queen enthroned on his tribunal, until at last he was left sitting quite alone. And the word spread on every side that Aphrodite had come to revel with Dionysus for the happiness of Asia.

Antony then sent a message inviting Cleopatra to dine with him. But she thought it more appropriate that he should come to her, and so, as he wished to show his courtesy and goodwill, he accepted and went. He found the preparations made to receive him magnificent beyond words, but what astonished him most of all was the extraordinary number of lights. So many of these, it is said, were let down from the roof and displayed on all sides at once, and they were arranged and grouped in such ingenious patterns in relation to each other, some in squares and some in circles, that they created as brilliant a spectacle as can ever have been devised to delight the eye.

On the following day Antony returned her hospitality with another banquet. But although he had hoped to surpass her in splendour and elegance he was hopelessly outdone in both, and was the first to make fun of the crude and meagre quality of his entertainment. Cleopatra saw that Antony's humour was broad and gross and belonged to the soldier rather than the courtier, and she quickly adopted the same manner towards him and treated him without the least reserve.[31]

It was Sir Thomas North's translation of this passage which inspired Shakespeare:

> The barge she sat in, like a burnish'd throne,
> Burned on the water; the poop was beaten gold,
> Purple the sails, and so perfumed that
> The winds were love-sick with them; the oars were silver
> Which to the tune of flutes kept stroke and made
> The water which they beat to follow faster,
> As amorous of their strokes. For her own person
> It beggared all description; she did lie
> In her pavilion, cloth-of-gold of tissue,
> O'er-picturing that Venus where we see
> The fancy outwork nature; on each side her
> Stood pretty dimpled boys, like smiling Cupids,
> With divers-coloured fans, whose wind did seem
> To glow the delicate cheeks which they did cool,
> And what they undid did....
>   at the helm
> A seeming mermaid steers: the silken tackle
> Swell with the touches of those flower-soft hands,
> That yarely frame the office. From the barge
> A strange invisible perfume hits the sense
> Of the adjacent wharfs. The city cast
> Her people out upon her; and Antony,
> Enthroned i' th' market-place, did sit alone,
> Whistling to the th' air: which but for vacancy,
> Had gone to gaze on Cleopatra too,
> And made a gap in nature.[32]

Plutarch was not the only ancient writer who dwelt on this historic meeting between Antony and Cleopatra. For the banquets she gave him at Tarsus, which have been depicted by so many painters of later Europe, were also described in luscious terms by a Greek historian, Socrates of Rhodes:

Meeting Antony in Cilicia, Cleopatra arranged in his honour a royal symposium, in which the service was wholly of gold and jewelled vessels made with exquisite art; even the walls were hung with tapestries woven of gold and silver threads. And having spread twelve tables, she invited him and his chosen friends. He was overwhelmed with the richness of the display; but she quietly smiled and said the things he saw were a gift to him. She invited him to come and dine with her again on the morrow, with his friends and his officers. On this occasion she provided an even more sumptuous symposium by far; the vessels used the previous time appeared paltry things; and once again she presented Antony with everything. As for the officers, each was allowed to take away the couch on which he had lain. Even the sideboards, as well as the couch-spreads, were divided among them; and when they went off, she supplied litters for guests of high rank, with bearers, while for the larger number she provided horses with silver-plated harness. For everyone she sent Ethiopian slaves to carry the torches. On the fourth day she distributed fees amounting to a talent for the purchase of roses; the floors of the dining-rooms were strewn with them a cubit deep, in net-like festoons spread over everything.[33]

*

And so Cleopatra, captivating Antony by her personal attractions and royal glamour, became his mistress.

Yet her arrangement of the whole scene, the banqueting and the seduction, was not intended purely for Antony's pleasure, or hers. Plutarch knows what she had in mind when he assures us that '... *the word spread on every side that Aphrodite had come to revel with Dionysus for the happiness of Asia*'. Keenly alive to the feelings of the near eastern peoples, Cleopatra raised the whole occasion far above the level of mere entertainment, and endowed it with the religious significance that would exert the maximum appeal. Antony had entered Asia as the New Dionysus, the conquering, immortalizing god who meant so much to the peoples of these lands. And now Cleopatra, making her entrance at Tarsus, assumed the pose of Aphrodite, surrounded by her train. Aphrodite, too, was a goddess of these times, the mistress of nature, the mother of the Universe, who, in her Roman guise of Venus, had recently inspired the Roman poet Lucretius to utter his heartfelt tribute: 'it is you, who fill rich earth and buoyant sea with your presence! It is through you that every living thing achieves its life.'[34]

Cleopatra's encounter with Antony at Tarsus, stage-managed with her incomparable resourcefulness, did not, of course, comprise a marriage on an earthly plane. But it was an earthly reflection of the Sacred Marriage between two great gods, which seemed profoundly appropriate to all Egyptians, and indeed all inhabitants of the east. For Dionysus was the Egyptian Osiris, and Aphrodite was Osiris' sister-wife, the divine Isis – the true and natural partner of the occupant of the throne. The incarnation of Isis upon earth was Cleopatra herself, and her consequent identification with Aphrodite seemed abundantly right and clear. Innumerable statuettes of the age portrayed a single divine figure as Aphrodite–Isis,[35] Cleopatra's forerunner Arsinoe II had been worshipped simultaneously as each of them, and so was Cleopatra herself.[36] She was Aphrodite consummating a holy union with Dionysus; and she was also re-enacting with Antony the divine, eternal marriage of Isis with Osiris.

The subsequent triumph of Christianity has made it difficult to realize that Isis was the greatest of all the deities of the Greco-Roman world, revered as widely and passionately as Dionysus, and loved with even greater intensity. Her worship had spread beyond the bounds of Egypt on a sensational scale.[37] If the worship of Jesus Christ had not eventually dominated the Mediterranean, then Isis was the only divinity who might have done the same.[38]

She was goddess of Ten Thousand Names, Shelter and Heaven to all mankind, the House of Life, the Word of God, the Great Mother of all the Gods and of Nature. She was the whole of Wisdom and Philosophy. Her magical powers were incomparable. Victorious over Fate, which 'hearkens to her', she shares this victory with her faithful devotees. Among the Mystery cults which consoled and encouraged the disconsolate millions of this age, making their lives seem worth living, giving them strength to endure their days upon earth, purifying their souls by solemn initiations, and finally promising them salvation and immortality, the worship of Isis was the most profoundly satisfying of all.

Under the guidance of a professional priesthood – which none of the Roman deities possessed – elaborate ceremonials, accompanied by music and chanting, took place daily, almost hourly, in the crowded temples of Isis.[39] On feast-days there were sacramental banquets and processions; and the murder of Osiris by Seth, the lamentations and wanderings of his distraught sister-widow Isis, the triumph of her son Horus over Seth, the joy of Isis for Osiris' resurrection, were displayed to the people in a series of ritual dramas exploiting every thrilling, sensational resource of stagecraft and music. In special monastic retreats, the devotees of Isis contemplated the ineffable beauty of her sacred face, and many were the acts of penance and piety that they gladly performed on her behalf. The service of the goddess was a sacred service, entered upon with a soldier's oath of allegiance. But Isis had a welcome for everybody, because she could be identified with any and every other goddess, absorbing all their attributes. She was the divinity of the earth and its fruits,[40] the power of the sea, of the Nile, of the Moon; of love and healing; of the Underworld, and life beyond the grave.

Above all, she exercised a passionate appeal to women. Although women are more inclined to attend religious observations than men, ancient religions tended to shut them out – 'half the human race had been badly off for a friend at the court of heaven'.[41] But the cult of Isis, like Christianity later on, made no such mistake. Sweetly thoughtful, graciously sympathetic, paradoxically both sexual and pure, she taught women how to find pardon and peace. She prevailed by pity and compassion, for she had known sorrow herself: when all other salvations had failed, she still had the power to save. She was the 'Glory of Women',[42] and their champion. She gave them equal power with men.[43] They, in return, rejoiced when she rejoiced, showering gifts of their precious possessions and jewellery upon her effigies,[44] and when she lamented they, too, grovelled in the streets in lamentation.

In Pharaonic times Isis had already been the subject of an extensive Egyptian literature. Then in the Ptolemaic epoch, hymns written in her honour circulated throughout the entire Hellenistic world. One such creed, a strange blend of Greek and Egyptian ideas, has survived in two inscriptions, two poetic paraphrases, and a literary summary:[45]

I am Isis, the Mistress of Every Land, and I was taught by Hermes, and with Hermes I devised Letters, both the Sacred and the Demotic, so that all things might be written with the same letters.

I gave and ordained Laws for men, which no one is able to change.

I am the eldest daughter of Kronos. I am wife and sister of King Osiris. I am she who finds fruits for men. I am mother of King Horus.

I am she that rises in the Dogstar, she who is called Goddess by women. For me was the City of Bubastis built.

I divided the Earth from the Heaven. I showed the Path of the Stars. I ordered the Course of Sun and Moon. I devised the activities of the Sea.

I made man strong. I brought together woman and man. I appointed to women to bring their infants to birth in the tenth month. I ordained that Parents should be loved by Children. I laid punishments on those without natural affection towards their parents.

I made with my brother Osiris an end to the eating of men. I revealed Mysteries to men. I taught men to honour images of the gods. I consecrated the precincts of the gods.

I broke down the governments of tyrants. I made an end to murders. I compelled women to take the love of men. I made the Right stronger than gold and silver. I ordained that the True should be thought good. I devised marriage-contracts.

I assigned to Greeks and Barbarians their languages. I made the beautiful and shameful to be distinguished by nature. I ordained that nothing should be more feared than an oath. I have delivered the plotter of evil against other men into the hands of the one he plotted against. I established penalties for those who practise injustice. I decreed mercy to suppliants. I protect righteous guards. With me the Right prevails.

I am the queen of rivers and winds and the sea. No one is held in honour without my knowing it. I am the queen of war. I am the queen of the thunderbolt. I stir up the sea and I calm it. I am the rays of the Sun.

Whatever I please shall come to an end, it shall end. With me, everything is reasonable. I set free those in bonds. I am the queen of seamanship. I make the navigable unnavigable when it pleases me.

I created walls of cities. I am called the lawgiver. I brought up islands out of the depths into the light. I am lord of rainstorms. I overcome fate. Fate hearkens to me.

Hail, Egypt that nourished me![46]

The goddess Isis made herself manifest upon earth in the person of the queen of Egypt. And so Cleopatra VII, too, was declared the New Isis.[47] When Caesar died, she had to search for a new partner, a new incarnation of Osiris. And now she had found him. For Antony, being Dionysus, was Osiris too.[48] The people of Tarsus understood this clearly enough, for the religion of Osiris and Isis was well known to them. Before long the most eminent theologian Tarsus ever produced, St Paul, would be compelled to wrestle against its power.[49]

At Rome, there had been a guild of the worshippers of Isis for the past forty years. But the Roman authorities had always been nervous of these excitable eastern cults, which seemed to them potential sources of subversion, and in 58 BC the consuls had the altars of Isis on the Capitol destroyed. Then, in 50, the order was given to demolish newly constructed temples of Isis and Sarapis. But no workman dared lay hand on them until one of the consuls himself took off his toga, and drove an axe through the doors.[50]

After the death of Caesar, when emotions and religious feelings were high, the official attitude changed. For in 43 BC one of the first actions of the Triumvirate was to decree the construction of a new shrine to these irresistible Egyptian gods. So Antony, the leading triumvir, came to Tarsus with the reputation of one who favoured Isis. The attentions which he then bestowed upon her earthly reincarnation have become the material of literature, legend and history – though the last is only discernible with difficulty through the distorting mirrors of the other two.

*

For example, there must have been not only all the legendary feasting and love-making at Tarsus, but also a good deal of unromantic negotiation. There must have been hard bargaining, up to the limits which a Ptolemaic monarch could hazard when dealing with the Romans. And Antony, before moving onwards into Syria, was anxious to know how he stood with Egypt. At the moment the country was freer, in practice, than it had been for some time, since the Roman garrison which had departed two years earlier for Syria never returned. It had left in somewhat equivocal circumstances during the civil wars between the Caesarians and Caesar's assassins, and Cleopatra had been summoned to Tarsus partly in order to answer charges that she had assisted the anti-Caesarian side. She was able, however, to explain that she had done nothing of the kind, in spite of severe and repeated pressures from Cassius; and if her Egyptian political enemies cherished any hopes that her civil war record might undermine her position, they miscalculated.

More important were the assurances Antony needed about the material help she could provide for his forthcoming Parthian war. Her agreement was only obtained on certain conditions. First and foremost, she demanded the execution of her half-sister Arsinoe IV, never forgiven for establishing a rival régime in Alexandria in 48 BC. Cleopatra was glad to be able to point out to Antony that, although she herself had not helped Cassius and Brutus, there might well be strong reason to suspect Arsinoe of having done so. On Antony's orders, Arsinoe was torn from her Ephesian sanctuary and executed.

All the other five of the offspring of Cleopatra's father had now perished by violent deaths – three as her enemies, and two of the three through her own personal initiative. The death of Arsinoe, like the death of Ptolemy XIV, must have seemed to Cleopatra an act of self-preservation, since many of the Egyptian ruling class who disliked Cleopatra might have supported her half-sister. Cleopatra also requested Antony to execute the high priest of Artemis at Ephesus, since it was he who had saluted Arsinoe as queen. But an Ephesian deputation came to see Cleopatra, and the priest was spared.[51] On the other hand, her disloyal former governor of Cyprus, Serapion, could not expect mercy. After the downfall of the Republican cause he had taken refuge at Tyre (Sur), in the Phoenician part of the province of Syria. But that city, in disgrace for the support it had given Cassius, had been compelled to surrender him to Antony, and now Serapion was put to death. Yet another enemy was also killed at Cleopatra's request. This was a youth at the Phoenician town of Aradus (Arvad) who claimed to be Cleopatra's older half-brother and husband Ptolemy XIII. After the young king's drowning in the Nile, in mysterious circumstances, Caesar had been afraid that false reports of his survival would get about, and now this person at Aradus had justified these fears by declaring that he himself was the king. So he, too, was executed on Antony's instructions.[52]

In these Syrian territories Antony found that his favour towards Cleopatra had lost him a good deal of support, for the Syrians never forgot that large areas of their country had once been occupied by the Ptolemaic kingdom, and that she was ambitious to re-annex them.

Consequently, the seizure of Serapion at her request must have seemed high-handed to his hosts at Tyre; and there were people at Aradus who resented the execution of the pretender Ptolemy XIII. Indeed, the Aradians showed how they felt soon afterwards, when they revolted against Antony's taxes. A beneficent step which he took, on the other hand, was to restore 'free' (quasi-autonomous) status to the city of Laodicea (Lattakia), which had suffered under Cassius.[53]

Antony also found time, during his short stay in Syria, to deal with the principality of Judaea. In spite of vast Jewish deputations which had to be forcibly dispersed with considerable loss of life, he confirmed the régime of Hyrcanus II, who had come to Egypt in 47 with his minister Antipater to help Caesar. Since then, they had been compelled to aid Cassius.[54] Nevertheless, Antony allowed Hyrcanus to continue as titular ruler. Antipater was now dead, but Antony confirmed that Antipater's able sons Phasael and Herod (later Herod the Great) should rule as Hyrcanus' viceroys in Jerusalem and Galilee, and he granted them princely rank.

With the exception of Judaea, however, Antony still did not tackle the problem of the eastern client kings, many of whose loyalties had been so dubious in the civil war. For his omission, he was retrospectively blamed.[55] His critics declared that he showed an indecent impatience to be with Cleopatra again – and it is true that he now went on to Egypt, to spend the winter of 41–40 BC in her company. But in any case it must have seemed to him that the eve of a major Parthian war was the wrong time for far-reaching revisions in the dependent states. If some of the princes had bad consciences, so much the better; they would be more likely to watch their behaviour now. Besides, Alexandria was not only where Cleopatra lived; it was also, although outside the empire, a reasonable place for his own provisional headquarters, owing to the important part that Egypt was expected to play in the forth-coming campaign.

However, remembering the bad reception Caesar had got in 48 BC when he disembarked with the insignia of a Roman consul and a contingent of troops, Antony was careful to enter the city as a private citizen, unaccompanied by soldiers. He was already popular in Alexandria because fourteen years earlier, when serving with Gabinius, he had prevented a slaughter of Egyptian prisoners. Now he once again created a favourable impression, not only because of his known phil-Hellenic tastes, but also because of his obvious desire to show he was coming as the guest of an independent queen. Roman policy to Egypt had always veered between covetousness and friendship, and although Antony wanted Egyptian aid, he made it clear that he was seeking it as a friend.

The only shadow on the horizon must have been Antony's loyal wife Fulvia, at present representing his interests in Octavian's Italy. Shakespeare[56] liked to think that Cleopatra nagged him ruthlessly about his wife, while complaining, in the same breath, of his failure to suppress Octavian:

Cleopatra: Nay, hear them, Antony:
            Fulvia perchance is angry; or, who knows
            If the scarce-bearded Caesar have not sent
            His powerful mandate to you, 'Do this, or this;
            Take in that kingdom, and enfranchise that;
            Perform't, or else we damn thee.'
Antony: How, my love?
Cleopatra: Perchance? nay, and most like:
            You must not stay here longer, your dismission
            Is come from Caesar: therefore hear it, Antony.
            Where's Fulvia's process? Caesar's, I would say? both?
            Call in the messengers. As I am Egypt's queen,
            Thou blushest, Antony, and that blood of thine
            Is Caesar's homager; else so thy cheek pays shame
            When shrill-tongued Fulvia scolds.

Cleopatra may very well have indicated to Antony that she considered him a better man than Octavian, and she may also have criticized his wife. More probably, however, she concentrated on making his life so pleasant that he would find it better to live with her than with Fulvia. The numerous parties she arranged for him, for example, now and later, are described with imaginative gusto by Plutarch. Then, during the winter, she became pregnant, and there was no doubt that Antony was the father.

*

It was presumably Antony's intention to leave Egypt in the spring of 40 BC and visit his other eastern territories as a prelude to the invasion of Parthia. As it happened, however, his departure was accelerated owing to the receipt, in February or early March,[57] of the gravest possible news. For the Parthians, he now learnt, instead of waiting passively for Rome's expected attack, had themselves launched an ambitious two-pronged invasion of the Roman empire. Their king's son Pacorus descended upon Syria, while a Roman renegade in their service, the ex-Republican Quintus Labienus, advanced rapidly into Asia Minor, accompanied by other Roman Republican refugees like himself. Both columns attracted wide support among Rome's Greek and native subjects.

Antony left Egypt and sailed rapidly north to Tyre, where he heard not only that a number of client-kings had defected, but that his own troops in Syria (many of them former opponents of Caesar) had also gone over to the Parthians; and the governor of the province was reported killed. Antony moved on to Asia Minor. There he received further information, this time from Italy: for news reached him that Fulvia and his brother Lucius Antonius, consul in 41 BC, without receiving any instruction from himself, had launched a rising against Octavian.[58] After a savage campaign, they had been utterly defeated, and Fulvia had fled from Italy towards the east.

Caught between these two disasters, Antony was unable to devote any further time to Cleopatra. The ancient writers' romantic or lubricious emphasis upon the Tarsus meeting, followed by the winter they spent together at Alexandria, tends to divert attention from what happened now. For from this time onwards, they were parted for no less than three and a half years: from the early months of 40 BC until the autumn of 37. Even if, as the writers assure us, he had fallen in love with her at Tarsus, any degree of ascendancy she had established over him was now to be interrupted by a prolonged and continuous separation. Obviously, this separation weakened her influence over his actions. Whether she could ever regain what she had lost, time alone would show.

7

Cleopatra Abandoned by Antony

For Antony, already confronted with a Parthian invasion of the east, the news of his wife's and brother's unsuccessful revolt against Octavian was catastrophic. What happened was that his brother Lucius Antonius had decided, with Fulvia's support, to back the numerous people dispossessed by Octavian's attempt to find land for his 100,000 ex-soldiers. They were acting in what they believed to be Antony's interests, for although Italy, which contained the best land for settling veterans, was supposed to be common ground between the two Triumvirs, Octavian had showed every sign of taking the best plots for his own men, without respecting this agreement between himself and Antony. When Lucius Antonius and Fulvia got engaged in serious fighting against Octavian, there was widespread Italian backing for their cause. Nevertheless, after their downfall in the grim siege of Perusia (Perugia), Octavian was careful to spare Lucius Antonius, and even made him governor of Spain. But Fulvia fled the country for Greece, where she had to explain her actions to her husband.

Her motives for inciting her brother-in-law to violence – for the initiative, apparently, was hers – were variously ascribed to jealousy of Cleopatra, or jealousy of an earlier alleged mistress of Antony, Glaphyra of Cappadocia.[1]

No doubt Fulvia was jealous of both, but so great was the gravity of the Italian political situation that these personal explanations are not necessary. A deputation of ex-soldiers from Italy had been in Alexandria all the winter, attempting in vain to draw Antony's attention to this dangerous crisis that was beginning to develop. But he had known nothing about the actual outbreak of the Perusian war until it was all over. Now, at Athens, he learnt with horror from Fulvia, and from his mother Julia who had left Italy with her, how violently and pointlessly his alliance with Octavian had been compromised. Overwhelming Fulvia with bitter reproaches, Antony left her, and moved on to Italy, in warlike array. She was already ill, and now, at Sicyon, she died.

However, if Cleopatra either wanted Antony to clash openly with Octavian or hoped that Fulvia's death would improve her own position, she was disappointed.

After a period of the sharpest tension, in which fighting actually broke out, Antony and Octavian managed to reconcile their differences, and in October 40 B C, their agreement was incorporated in the Treaty of Brundusium (Brindisi). The Triumvirate was to continue for the remainder of its appointed five years. Lepidus, whom Octavian had provisionally sent to govern north Africa, would be allowed to stay there and retain the post. Octavian was to take the whole of western Europe – but Antony's right to recruit freely in Italy, and to employ its land for the settlement of his veterans, was confirmed. Antony was also to remain the ruler of the Roman east, where his war of revenge and conquest against the Parthians was now to be waged.

Cleopatra, during the autumn of 40 B C, had given birth to Antony's twins, whom she named Alexander and Cleopatra: the boy's name recalled both the glories of her house, which claimed descent from Alexander, and Antony's own desire to become the new Alexander. In view of her perpetual distrust of Octavian, she must have regarded the Treaty of Brundusium with suspicion. But it was nothing like so unwelcome as the further report that Fulvia's death had not, after all, made Antony turn back to Egypt and to herself. For the treaty, she now learnt, was instead to be sealed by his remarriage to Octavian's own sister. This woman, Octavia, was not only young—probably several years younger than Cleopatra – but she was also very beautiful. Her character was said to be flawless. She was also intelligent, indeed intellectual, being a patron of the architectural writer Vitruvius and a supporter of the literary circle of her brother's leading adherent, Maecenas. When Maecenas, a sophisticated and effete Etruscan, praised Octavia's hair for its *naturalness*, he was perhaps being malicious at the expense of Cleopatra, of whose hair-style this would not, in all probability, have been the most accurate description. Octavia was the mother of three children by her first husband, who had recently died – too recently, indeed, for her wedding with Antony to be legally correct, since she had not yet completed the obligatory period of ten months' mourning. But the Senate gave her special permission to marry again immediately, and so they became man and wife.

Cleopatra's displeasure at the marriage was not shared by the Roman world in general, which felt delighted by this apparent guarantee that the harrowing civil wars had at last come to an end. The coinage of the Triumvirs joyfully celebrated the new era of world peace.[2] Moreover, Octavian's wife Scribonia – a relative of Sextus Pompeius, whom he had married while both Triumvirs were speculating on an alliance after Perusia – was pregnant; and Octavia, the wife of Antony, very soon became pregnant too. In this expectant atmosphere the poet Virgil wrote his *Fourth Eclogue*, prophesying the Golden Age which would be created by a child shortly to be born. The poem, as we have it, displays an oracular style which casts deliberate ambiguity over the identity and parentage of this expected Messiah. It is possible, however, that the original version had been more explicit – in favour either of the one expected infant or the other – and that the text which has come down to us represents a revision, perhaps dating from more than twenty years later.[3] But in any case the *Eclogue* expresses, in unforgettable language, the profound desire for peace that prevailed among this whole war-weary generation. At such a moment the dissentient voice of Cleopatra would have been ill received.

Were Antony and Cleopatra – the mother of his recently-born children – writing to each other at this period, apart from official communications? Did the Egyptian court feel obliged to send him a congratulatory message on his wedding? All we know is that Cleopatra kept herself informed of Antony's doings through an Egyptian astrologer attached to his entourage. And she gave this man the additional task of hinting to Antony from time to time that he should win free play for his own noble personality by detaching himself as far as possible from Octavian.

*

When the Parthians overran Syria earlier in 40 BC, they had moved onwards into Judaea, where they arrested and deported Hyrcanus II and replaced him by his nephew Antigonus, a puppet of their own. Hyrcanus' chief administrators, the brothers Phasael and Herod, were also overthrown. Phasael was killed, but Herod managed, with great difficulty, to flee to Egypt. When he reached the eastern frontier station of Pelusium, Cleopatra's admiral there, after some hesitation, sent him on to Alexandria, where he was received by the queen.

She had probably not encountered the thirty-two-year-old Herod before, and at this stage she showed him no enmity. No Ptolemy, it was true, could look favourably upon his Judaean state, because Egyptian monarchs could never forget that less than two centuries earlier it had been a part of the Ptolemaic empire. In the present crisis, however, such considerations were ignored. For the Parthians, after occupying all Syria and Judaea, and setting up their own régimes there, and exterminating such Romans and pro-Romans as they could find, had penetrated as far as the very frontiers of Egypt. But they would not gain any support from Cleopatra: the idea of playing off the great power of the east against the great power of the west did not offer her the slightest attraction. On the contrary, fully accepting her father's pro-Roman policy, she had staked everything on retaining the support of the man to whom the Romans had entrusted so much, namely Antony.[4]

Herod, too, felt the same. And at the present moment what he desired above all was to go to Rome, to seek help in regaining his occupied country. Cleopatra was prepared to give him every assistance. But be-before helping him on his way, she was said to have offered the young man a command in her own Egyptian army.[5] Although the story may have come from Herod's own memoirs – perhaps inserted there to show how she had failed to conquer him with her famous wiles – it is not necessarily untrue. Jewish commanders in the Ptolemaic army were nothing new, and the imminent war against the Parthians meant that she needed all the good officers she could get. Besides, this handsome, charming and plausible man already possessed a reputation for forceful activity in Judaea. His country was in the hands of the Parthian foes, and she had no reason to fear its hostility in the foreseeable future – least of all if she could keep him under her own control. Besides, she was a friend of his mother-in-law Alexandra, who had shared his dramatic escape from Jerusalem and was now lodged for safe-keeping in the fortress of Masada beside the Dead Sea.

If Cleopatra made Herod such an offer, he must have declined. For in spite of the autumn season, when travellers began to avoid the Mediterranean, she gave him a ship which took him as far as Rhodes. From there he proceeded to Rome, where, upon Antony's proposal, the Triumvirs not only made him prince in the kidnapped Hyrcanus' place, but actually gave him the title of king, which Hyrcanus had not been allowed to employ for the past twenty-three years. The Romans were trying to win an ally in the slow struggle to regain the Levant from the Parthians. And indeed, at this point, Cleopatra may perhaps have begun to wonder whether she had been right to welcome Herod so warmly after all. Could it be that, with such unexpectedly vigorous Roman support, he might eventually establish a strong Judaea? That was the last thing she wanted.

Two eminent supporters of Antony, Marcus Valerius Messalla Corvinus and Lucius Sempronius Atratinus, both spoke in favour of Herod in the Roman Senate. They probably did so because they distrusted Cleopatra, and wanted a counter-weight to her authority in the near east. If so, they resembled other leading Romans who, while reluctant to speak openly against Antony's mistress, were most unwilling that Rome's policy for the eastern dependent kingdoms should rely wholly upon a revived and strengthened Egypt. Anticipating the views of many modern statesmen, they felt that it would create a more healthy and prudent balance if there were a strong Jewish state in the region as well.

While Herod fortified his position at Rome, we have no knowledge of what was happening inside the Ptolemaic kingdom. Antony's obvious support for Cleopatra, and his elimination of her sister and other opponents, may have cowed all disaffected elements. And perhaps the alarming presence of Parthian troops not far from the country's borders had rallied opinion behind the queen.

*

Meanwhile, Antony was in the midst of new political complications at Rome. In the spring of 39 BC the Triumvirs felt so seriously inconvenienced by Sextus Pompeius, who had seized Sardinia as well as Sicily and was threatening the grain supply of the city itself, that they decided to reach an agreement with him after all. A pact was concluded at Misenum (Miseno), at the northern extremity of the Bay of Naples.[6] In return for calling off his raids, Sextus was allowed to keep his islands, with Corsica added. Moreover, Antony agreed to hand over the Peloponnese as well[7] – feeling generous because the pact denied Octavian the possibility of a military triumph over Sextus, which would have given him too much of the limelight. At the same time, Antony's own acts, future and past alike, received a heartening confirmation from the Roman Senate, and he himself was made the priest of the deified Caesar's cult.[8] These measures were intended as a reciprocal compliment on the part of the two leading triumvirs: Antony was paying Octavian the honour of becoming the priest of his father – who was shortly to be portrayed on huge western coinages – while the Senate, with Octavian's backing, confirmed Antony's hopes that eastern victories would vindicate him as the true heir of Caesar's military greatness.[9] Shortly afterwards a veteran colony in Antony's dominions, Sinope (Sinop) in northern Asia Minor, issued coins on which the heads of the two men, Caesar and Antony, appeared together.[10] About Cleopatra's claims that the late dictator's true heir was Caesarion nothing was heard, for the moment, outside the frontiers of Egypt.

But the pact of Misenum came to nothing. Antony – this time backed by Octavian – made difficulties about handing over the Peloponnese, and instead ordered one of his commanders, Gaius Sosius, to set up a naval base in the island of Zacynthus (Zante) in the Ionian Sea, in order to ward Sextus Pompeius off.[11] When Sextus, at this point, renewed hostilities, Octavian divorced his relative Scribonia, and in January 38 BC married Livia Drusilla, a lady who was not only a famous beauty, but of highly aristocratic descent. This was an important step towards winning over traditional Republican opinion, which had hitherto tended to favour Antony.

In August or September of the same year, Octavia presented Antony with a child, the elder of her two girls called Antonia. Then, at long last, Antony left Italy, in order to return to his own part of the empire. He was accompanied by Octavia and spent the winter with her at Athens, which remained his headquarters for the next year and a half. There they devoted themselves to a model conjugal and cultural existence. Octavia frequented the company of philosophers, including Nestor, a member of the Platonic Academy, and the Stoic Athenodorus of Tarsus who dedicated one of his books to her. Antony's fondness for Greek costume and habits was widely noted, and he was happy to perform the role of the Athenian gymnasiarch, or minister of education.[12] The Panathenaic Games of August 38 BC were named the Antonieia in his honour, and his identification with the New Dionysus, proclaimed at Ephesus three years previously, was celebrated by special issues of coins on which he and Octavia appear together with various Dionysiac emblems.[13] Their union was further commemorated by a Sacred Marriage which he celebrated with Athena, goddess of the city, whom the citizens identified with Octavia; though when the Athenians offered him Athena he was reputed to have accepted her, with sardonic humour, only on condition that she brought a large dowry with her. Nevertheless, the citizens honoured both him and his wife as 'beneficent gods', and Octavia became the kind of imperial consort that no Roman woman except Fulvia had ever been before. Cleopatra and the Sacred Marriage which she too had hinted at, herself playing the part of Aphrodite, seemed a transient phenomenon of Antony's past.

*

From his capital at Athens, Antony decided that the expulsion of the Parthians from Asia Minor, Syria and Judaea should not be conducted under his own personal direction, but by Roman generals operating under his remote control. This might seem a strange decision for one whose claim to inherit the cloak of Caesar depended so largely on future military triumphs against this very foe. But Antony wished to hold himself in reserve for the eventual great invasion of Parthia itself, postponed for the time being but not for ever; the preliminary glory of sweeping them back across the frontiers could be left to subordinates.

This was by no means how Octavian would have proceeded, even though he was a much less able commander than Antony; at this very moment, he was taking an active part in military operations against Sextus Pompeius, and finding it a painful experience. Nevertheless,

Antony's plan for the vicarious expulsion of the Parthians from Roman territory worked perfectly. It worked because Antony was able to put into the field a certain Publius Ventidius, who happened to be one of the most remarkable generals of the age. First Ventidius drove Labienus out of Asia Minor to his death. Then, in the next year, he defeated and killed the Parthian king's son Pacorus near Mount Gindarus, north-east of Antioch (9 June 38 BC). The Parthians were relying on heavy armoured cavalry instead of horse-archers, and the change of tactics proved a disastrous mistake.

Later in the same year, Antony himself went east (without seeing Cleopatra) and reduced a city which was still proving refractory, Samosata (Samsat) on the Euphrates. The people of Samosata had bribed Ventidius heavily. After his great successes he could not be deprived of his Triumph – the only Triumph a Roman had ever celebrated over the Parthians. But the scandal of the bribery made it impossible for Antony to employ him ever again. This was unfortunate, because at the time Rome possessed only two really first-class commanders. One was Ventidius, and the other was Marcus Agrippa. Agrippa remained exceedingly active, as admiral and general alike. But he also remained in the exclusive service of his friend and schoolfellow, Octavian.

After the Parthian invasion of Asia Minor and Syria, and the revelation of the support the invaders evoked from local inhabitants, the long-expected reorganization of the eastern client kingdoms could wait no longer. Antony was still not ready to produce his final scheme. However, as Asia Minor returned under his firm control, he pointed the way to subsequent solutions by entrusting large tracts of the southern mountains to two Hellenized Asians who had proved their loyalty against the Republicans and Parthians respectively: a Greek with local experience named Amyntas and a rich Greco-Phrygian called Polemo. Contrary to all precedent, these rulers did not come from royal stock, and had not even originated from the territories they were now granted. In Syria Antony rewarded the city of Apamea (Qala'at-el-Mudig), which had likewise tried to resist the Parthians, and then he reduced Aradus, which had caused trouble before and was still proving recalcitrant. Cleopatra, who had reason to dislike the place for supporting the man who claimed to be her half-brother, must have welcomed its downfall.

*

She must also have been pleased – for she still supported Antony in spite of his absence – that whereas 38 BC was proving such a successful year for him, it had started with a disaster for his fellow-Triumvir

Octavian, whose efforts to overthrow Sextus Pompeius were thwarted by crushing storms and defeats. In serious trouble, Octavian asked Antony to join him for a second conference at Brundisium. Antony came, but Octavian, although it was he who had suggested the meeting, failed to put in an appearance. This was because in the meantime his lieutenant, Agrippa, had led a dramatic excursion of Roman troops across the Rhine, as well as dealing successfully with a revolt in southwest Gaul; so Octavian decided that he was after all doing well enough without Antony's help.[15] Antony returned to Athens, and the incident may have made him wonder whether Cleopatra's distrust of Octavian was not justified. Octavia, who always tried to be loyal to her brother and to her husband, must have found it hard to explain Octavian's disconcerting behaviour.

Moreover, history very nearly repeated itself in 37 BC. After suffering a further defeat at the hands of Sextus Pompeius in the previous autumn, Octavian again sought a conference with Antony, this time at Tarentum (Taranto). And once again he himself was late in arriving. But this time Antony waited, perhaps persuaded by Octavia, until her unreliable brother finally appeared. Antony's patience seems singularly long-suffering, especially as his colleague's appeals had delayed his planned operations against Parthia. Yet he had to do everything possible to keep on good terms with Octavian, since in order to raise sufficient good troops for the Parthian campaign it was essential for him to be able to recruit in Italy. With this need in mind, he brought three hundred ships to Tarentum, hoping to exchange some of them for Octavian's soldiers. Meanwhile, however, he took the precaution of maintaining Gaius Sosius' naval post on the island of Zacynthus, strategically located in the Ionian Sea which divided the territories of the two Triumvirs from one another.

Finally, the two men reached agreement once again, and a fresh pact, the Treaty of Tarentum, was duly arranged. Antony gave Octavian 120 ships (2 squadrons) from his fleet, to help defeat Sextus Pompeius, and in return Octavian promised to provide some 20,000 men (4 legions) for the Parthian war. It was said that Octavia's good offices improved the offers made on either side. Moreover, the Triumvirate, which had technically lapsed at the end of 38 BC, was renewed until the end of 33. The pact was sealed by the betrothal of Antony's oldest son by Fulvia, Marcus Antonius (commonly known as Antyllus), to Octavian's daughter Julia; the engaged couple were then aged about nine and two respectively. The commanders of the two squadrons left behind by Antony issued a varied array of bronze coins in his name. These pieces, minted at Tarentum, display Octavia's head with those of Antony and Octavian, or Antony alone.[16] (These facing heads were a novelty for Roman coinage, though Isis and Sarapis were often depicted in this way, and so were Hellenistic monarchs when they wanted to lay particular stress on their conjugal harmony.[17])

When Antony sailed from Italy for the east in the autumn of 37 BC, leaving behind him his ships (though he had not yet been provided with the promised legionaries), he was accompanied on the first stage of the journey by Octavia. But when they reached Corcyra (Corfu), he asked her to return to Italy. This was not the time, he said, for her to come any further. She was pregnant again, and the sea-voyage would be too much for her health; and besides, he was at last embarking on the Parthian campaign, so that her presence in the east would be out of place.

At the time there seemed nothing particularly odd about this. Certainly there was not the dramatic repudiation seen, with hindsight, by the historian Dio Cassius, and accepted by some modern writers. Wives of important Romans were often left behind when their husbands set out for campaigns; and as a result of her and Antony's previous marriages, Octavia had six children to look after at home. She herself saw no finality in the decision to send her away, since she came back to Athens a year later. Meanwhile, she would clearly be of assistance at Rome, where she could try to settle Antony's difficulties with her brother Octavian. It seems strange that she went as far as Corcyra before Antony made his decision. Perhaps, to begin with, they had both intended that she should come further, until her health began to suffer.

It is also quite possible, however, that he willingly seized an opportunity to send her back. For as soon as he reached Syria, he summoned Cleopatra, sending a close friend, Gaius Fonteius Capito, to bring her to Antioch. Thus his summons of 41 BC was repeated, and for somewhat similar reasons. Now that the postponed operations against Parthia once more seemed imminent, the dependent kingdoms were again required to help. As on the previous occasion, the assistance of Egypt was particularly required. This was because of its large resources, and because of its greater stability than the Asian client kingdoms, which were all in a transitional condition. Antony, at long last – this time prompted rather than deterred by the imminence of war – had imposed the sweeping reorganization that was needed. In Asia Minor, beyond the Roman frontiers, vast territories were carved out for trusted rulers: Amyntas and Polemo had their principalities much enlarged to include the central kingdom of Galatia and the northern kingdom of Pontus respectively. East and south of Galatia, extending as far as the Parthian frontier on the Euphrates, stretched the large and ancient state of Cappadocia. This, too, was now placed in the hands of a new dynasty, being entrusted to a learned priest-prince Archelaus Sisinnes, son of

Archelaus, king of Egypt 57–55 BC, and Glaphyra whom Antony had admired. Meanwhile Herod, appointed king of Judaea by the Romans three years earlier at a time when his country was under Parthian occupation, had at last, with the help of Antony's lieutenant, Gaius Sosius, succeeded in establishing himself at Jerusalem, where he founded a new Idumaean dynasty.

Antony's policy of encouraging strong client kingdoms along the frontiers was a sensible one.[18] For weak kingdoms could not stand up against sudden shocks, as the Parthian invasion of 41–40 BC had so clearly shown. Besides, the eastern population, for the most part imperfectly Hellenized, could only be controlled by specialist knowledge, which Roman governors sent out for short terms were never able to muster – and Rome was too suspicious of their ambitions to countenance longer tenures. Moreover, the client kings had their own administrations and tax-collecting machineries, thus saving Rome a task which, in the absence of a civil service of its own, it could never have carried out. And the policy of sponsoring client monarchs was also favourable to the native populations because many Roman governors of the first century BC had displayed such brutal rapacity.

The four kings Antony had now favoured, like the queen of Egypt, were intended to play a key part in his military arrangements against the Parthians – though a less important part than Cleopatra. However, when he now arranged to rejoin her, we need not suppose that military considerations were all that was in his mind: no doubt he was also happy to see her again, and to resume their affair.

He was all the happier because, since the spring, political developments had made the thought of Octavia less attractive. There was still no sign of Octavian's promised four legions, which looked very much as if he was proposing to starve Antony of western manpower. If so, Octavia's endeavours to mediate between her brother and husband had been unsatisfactory. However honest her efforts, they were of no value to Antony – indeed their propaganda effects were positively harmful – if Octavian had no intention of keeping his side of the agreement.

On the other hand these same circumstances made the presence of Cleopatra seem increasingly desirable. If Antony's supplies of manpower from Italy were likely to fail, and Octavian's collaboration was not forthcoming, he needed her resources even more than before. Moreover, with Cleopatra he could relax without the shadow of an unreliable brother-in-law haunting his pleasure.

So Antony spent the winter of 37–36 BC with Cleopatra in Antioch – four years after he had spent his first winter with her at Alexandria. Since then, they had not met. But now they were together again.

8

Cleopatra Revives her Ancestral Kingdom

When Antony and Cleopatra met at Tarsus in 41 BC, she had offered her help in exchange for the removal of her political enemies. Now that their association was renewed she succeeded in driving a much harder bargain. By its terms she was permitted to expand the territory of her kingdom enormously, so that it did not fall far short of the widest boundaries of the Ptolemaic empire two centuries earlier. Antony's concurrence was in keeping with his general policy towards the rulers of loyal client states. In Asia Minor, they had been given much larger kingdoms than had existed in the area for very many years. It was fitting, therefore, that Egypt, the pivot of the whole system, should be treated with equal or even greater generosity. It was all the more fitting because of his personal relations with the queen.

Most of his territorial gifts to Cleopatra seem to date from the last months of the year 37 BC.[1] They form the last and most important stage of the fundamental reorganization of his dependencies that Antony had begun earlier in the same year.

Cleopatra's new acquisitions covered enormous areas of the Levant. One of the most conspicuous gains consisted of a large group of rich, land-owning coastal cities, extending from Mount Carmel up to the River Eleutherus (now the Nahr-el-Kelb, in the Republic of Lebanon) which had formed the original northern frontier of the Syrian domains of Ptolemy I Soter; only Tyre (Sur) and Sidon (Saida) retained their independence. Much of the region had recently been controlled by Rome's governor of Syria, so that Antony was, in fact, alienating Roman provincial territory by giving it to Cleopatra, an action which was later held against him by his Roman critics. In the southern part of the zone, Ptolemais Ace (Acre, Akko, now just inside Israel), which had been the chief centre of Egyptian rule in Phoenicia in the third century BC, resumed its position as the regional Egyptian capital, issuing coins with the head not only of Antony, as general overlord of the whole area, but also of Cleopatra.[2] Their heads likewise appear, singly or together, on the coins of other Phoenician cities, which

inaugurate new eras from their incorporation in Cleopatra's kingdom.[3] These venerable, wealthy communities were an important enrichment of Cleopatra's dominions.

Moreover, in the the hinterland behind the cities, she was permitted to annex an entire state. This was Ituraea, spanning the modern frontier between the Republics of Lebanon and Syria and including the renowned shrine of Zeus Hadad at Heliopolis (Baalbek). For Antony

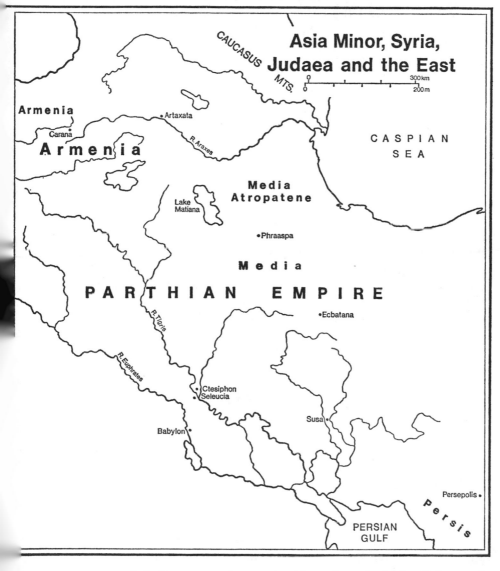

now executed the Ituraean prince-priest Lysanias, who had collaborated with the Parthian invaders in 40 BC, and the country was handed over to Cleopatra.[4] The 'free' city of Damascus, just across the border, was delighted, and placed her head on its coins[5] because the Ituraeans were not only excellent archers but experienced bandits, and Damascus had greatly suffered at their hands.

Farther south, Cleopatra was given part of the Decapolis (Ten Cities), which roughly corresponded with the Biblical Gilead and Bashan and spanned the modern border between Israel and Jordan. Her annexations in this area, though described in a vague and misleading fashion by the ancient authorities,[6] are specifically said to have included the cities of Hippos (or Antiochia ad Hippum, now Susita just inside Israel) and Gadara, a sophisticated outpost of Hellenism (now Umm Keis across the frontier in Jordan). Pompey had detached the ten cities from Judaea so as to form them into a self-governing league, and now Antony assigned its rich northern-most members to Cleopatra, whom they provided with a strip of territory extending eastwards across the River Jordan.

Cleopatra's annexations also extended into Asia Minor, of which extensive portions had once belonged to the early Ptolemies. For Antony now gave her new possessions in Cilicia, the south-eastern coastal zone of the peninsula. When the civilized plainland ('Flat' Cilicia) which formed the eastern part of the region had been united with the Roman province of Syria a few years previously, the mountainous western areas may not have come under direct Roman control.[7] In any case, Antony now proceeded to grant Cleopatra two harbour towns at either extremity of this western region, Elaeusa Sebaste (Ayaş) and Hamaxia (near Alanya). And the gift probably included most of the intervening coast and hinterland.

The fact that these lands were well wooded provides the clue to the purpose behind these four territorial gains. The geographer Strabo, who records Cleopatra's Cilician acquisition, specifically refers to the forests, mainly consisting of cedars, from which the harbour at Hamaxia enabled her to fetch timber – as her Ptolemaic ancestors had done.[8] Moreover, the other three gifts, already mentioned, supplied the same purpose. Phoenicia, with its forests on Mount Lebanon, had been an important source of timber for Pharaohs and Ptolemies alike; Ituraea controlled the timber on the other side of the Lebanon range, and upon Anti-Lebanon as well, while the northern Decapolis enjoyed ready access to the famous oak forests of Gilead. Cyprus too, which already belonged to Cleopatra, served a similar purpose.[9]

Most of the dependent kingdoms were required to find contingents for Antony's army. But Cleopatra's role was to be the construction of ships. Antony could only entrust himself to the land-expanses of the Parthian empire if he left behind him a fleet capable of policing the eastern Mediterranean – and ensuring that Octavian did not attempt any disloyal action in his rear. Since the earlier part of the year Antony's fleet had been seriously weakened because of the two squadrons he had handed over to Octavian. Cleopatra would now make good these losses as a prelude to building a larger fleet still. It was also her duty to produce the rowers from the large Egyptian or Alexandrian population – and Caesar had already noted that they made good seamen.[10] But Egypt could not provide timber, and that is why Antony gave Cleopatra the territories that would make this possible.

*

She also received certain lands and properties at the direct expense of Herod of Judaea. Her relations with him presented Antony with an irritating and delicate problem. For now that Herod was ruling in Jerusalem as king,[11] Cleopatra's friendliness towards him completely vanished, and from this time onwards she became his inexorable enemy.[12] Earlier, he had just been a struggling and homeless prince, but now he seemed all that stood in the way of the restoration of the Ptolemaic empire. It struck her as particularly ironical that she had been given a continuous mass of territory on the further side of Judaea – Phoenicia, Ituraea, the Decapolis – whereas Judaea itself was still beyond her reach. And Herod therefore thought it advisable to rebuild his southern fortresses to provide protection against Egyptian invasion.[13]

Antony, on the other hand, in spite of all his willingness to expand Cleopatra's kingdom, still wished to base his policy for the dependent kingdoms upon a strong Judaea as well as a strong Egypt. In the chain of states which helped the Romans to maintain their frontier in the east, and were intended to be of particular assistance during the forthcoming Parthian war, Judaea was crucial. Antony had taken some trouble to install Herod as king in Jerusalem, and he was not prepared to surrender him to Cleopatra's expansionist ambitions; her arguments, whether backed by vituperation, or pathetic appeals, or diplomacy, still did not succeed in ousting him altogether.

However, it is clear that her persistence severely shook Antony, who told Herod that he must make certain very substantial sacrifices in order to appease her ambitions. In the first place, he was obliged to forgo almost the entire coastline of Judaea. Caesar had allowed the country a harbour of a sort, at Joppa. But now Antony gave this to Cleopatra, as well as all the other coastline cities – removing them from Roman provincial control for the purpose – with the exception of Ascalon which remained free, and Gaza which was left to Herod as his sole means of access to the sea.[14] Almost the entire maritime area, up to the northern extremity of the modern Lebanese Republic, was now Cleopatra's.

Moreover, Herod was also compelled to yield her his extremely lucrative groves near Jericho, not far from the northern end of the Dead Sea. These plantations comprised date palms – the finest grown on a commercial scale anywhere in the world – and balsam shrubs, the 'balm of Gilead' which fetched very high prices as a medicine and a scent. It was arranged, however, that Herod should rent the groves back from Cleopatra for a substantial annual sum. Given the unfortunate circumstances, he was glad enough to do this, because the arrangement at least prevented Egyptian officials from flocking into the area, which was not more than fifteen miles from Jerusalem. Cleopatra took many cuttings of the balsam shrubs, it was said, and planted them in her own country, near Heliopolis (On) in Middle Egypt.

*

Finally, the kingdom of the Nabatean Arabs, on Antony's instructions, made large territorial concessions to Cleopatra. It is doubtful if this was technically a client state, but it certainly depended on Rome, and it was much the largest of the Arabian nations. Based on what is now the kingdom of Jordan, it extended not only far to the south along the Red Sea coast, but also south-westwards to include the Gulf of Elat (Akaba) and the Sinai peninsula which bordered upon Egypt. Not content with her truncation of Judaea, Cleopatra put forward a large expansionist claim against the Nabataeans as well, and Antony conceded it. They may have had to cede her a section of their coast, thus increasing her control of the Red Sea.[15] What is certain, however, is that within their land-borders they handed over to her a most profitable enclave at the southern extremity of the Dead Sea, which carried with it the sole right to exploit the bitumen which rose to the surface of that sea and was used as a medicine, preservative, insecticide and mortar.

Cleopatra arranged that the Nabataeans should, at a price, continue the exploitation of the bitumen they had given her. But now Herod, on the lines of the arrangement he had made about his own groves, seized the opportunity for a political gain to offset his material losses. For he offered to make himself responsible for the sums the Nabataeans were supposed to pay Cleopatra. This was an adroit gesture – almost too adroit, for it would cause him a lot of trouble, as he must have been well aware. But Herod, although linked to the Nabataean monarchs by matrimonial and financial ties, was on very uneasy terms with them, and he hoped that this deal with Cleopatra would enable him to intervene in their affairs. Besides, his offer, by helping to placate Cleopatra, might please Antony.

She accepted Herod's suggestion, since this was an easy way to get money without administrative problems or overheads. She was said to have accumulated great wealth by the end of her life,[16] and no doubt it was because of these annexations in 37 BC that she was able to do so.

*

Nevertheless, if Herod thought he had appeased Cleopatra, he was very much mistaken. She still intended to do everything in her power to eliminate him and his Jewish kingdom from the scene altogether; and this she at once showed by directly interfering in his internal affairs. Herod had married Mariamme (Miriam), a princess of the old Hasmonaean (Maccabee) royal family which he had superseded in 37 BC.[17] His Hasmonaean predecessors had been Jewish high priests as well as monarchs or princes. But after Herod had taken over as king, he himself, being an Idumeaan and without a priestly pedigree, could never become high priest. So he had to find someone else for the job. An obvious candidate, because he belonged to the Hasmonaean family, was Mariamme's brother, Aristobulus. However, Herod, offering the rather good excuse that the boy was only sixteen, made a different choice. The royal mother of Aristobulus and Mariamme, Alexandra, was furious. She wrote at once to her friend Cleopatra sending her letter by hand of a singer.[18] Cleopatra, true to her role as the goddess Isis, found it agreeable to champion the causes of women, and spoke to Antony. Herod gave way, and made Aristobulus high priest after all.

Among her many languages Cleopatra spoke not only Hebrew, but Aramaic – a related language very widely spoken at this time in the near east – as well as Syriac, an eastern Aramaic dialect. She was therefore able to converse in all the main official and unofficial languages spoken in her new domains and spheres of interest. Perhaps she did not learn them as a girl, but mastered them after she had practical reasons for taking an interest in all these territories.

*

Certain Egyptian papyri and Syrian coins, as well as the writings of an ancient chronologist,[19] reveal that at this juncture Cleopatra began to reckon the dates of her current joint reign with her son Ptolemy XV Caesar according to a fresh era, beginning in the year which extended from 1 September 37 BC to 31 August 36. Henceforward this new form of chronological reckoning continued alongside the previous era calculated from her own personal accession (51 BC): so that the 'sixteenth year [37–36] is the first'. The new era surely celebrates her enormous territorial gains,[20] which with the exception of the Aegean lands, and the more conspicuous exception of Judaea nearer home, almost completely restored the Greater Egypt of the first three Ptolemies.

Although this Ptolemaic empire's special task of reinforcing Antony's fleet was clear enough, its status in relation to the Roman empire had become increasingly hard to define. It was dependent upon the Romans, but it could not be described as their 'client', at least not in the sense in which this term had ever been used before. For it was much larger and richer than any client state had ever been; and its queen's relationship with the Roman overlord created a special situation. Egypt was not so much a vassal as an autonomous, allied and protected kingdom, the like of which had not appeared within the Roman orbit before.

*

Since the *de facto* ruler of the kingdom was Cleopatra, nothing much was said, at this stage, about the role of her son and joint monarch Ptolemy xv Caesar. He was still the divine personage whose claim to be Caesar's son over-rode Octavian's pretensions to be Caesar's heir. But there was no mention of him on the coins of Egypt or of its new empire; the time to exploit his alleged paternity had not yet come. Meanwhile all eyes were turned on Cleopatra, the associate of the man whose forthcoming eastern conquests were about to make him a new Julius Caesar and a new Alexander the Great.

Besides, it seemed at this juncture of greater political value for the queen to focus attention upon her children by Antony. These were the twins who had been born in 40 BC, Alexander and Cleopatra. In late 37, when Antony allotted the Ptolemaic kingdom huge additional territories, he apparently acknowledged that he was the two children's father: since Cleopatra declared they were his, it was up to him, having renewed their association, to say the same.

This was probably also the time when the infants Alexander and Cleopatra were given additional names. They were henceforward to be known as Alexander Helios, the Sun, and Cleopatra Selene, the Moon. To the Greeks, the Sun and Moon were themselves regarded as twins, and were hailed as the joint associates and supporters of Victory.[21] The baby Cleopatra's new name was not a surprising one for a Ptolemaic princess, since not only had a previous Cleopatra, the daughter of Ptolemy viii, already been called Selene, but the Moon was identified with Isis, so that the mother of the children, as Isis' living incarnation, was herself the Moon already.[22] But the selection of Helios, the Sun, as the name of her boy, throws special light on the propaganda she was seeking to spread among the near-eastern populations at this time. In the Hellenistic age, which tended to see the old traditional deities as different manifestations of a single, universal god, it was in the form of the Sun that this almost monotheistic divinity seemed to make himself apparent to mortals. Only a generation or so previously, the Greco-

Syrian philosopher Posidonius had declared the Sun to be the burning heart of the world and its intelligent light.[23] It was also the Just God, the Eye of Divine Justice. And in the same way as the supreme deity took the form of the Sun in order to irradiate the physical universe, so the Sun, in its turn, passed on this divine radiation to ruling monarchs, who were godhead made manifest upon earth. Consequently the great imperial governments of the Hellenistic age were very ready to compare and identify the Sun's beneficent sway with the all-seeing, all-pervading, all-quickening justice of their own ruler, who was the very embodiment of animate Law because he was the living incarnation of the Sun itself.

In Egypt these ideas received a readier welcome than anywhere else. There had been a cult of the Sun at Heliopolis since at least the third millennium BC. But the first and most enduring of the Egyptian solar gods was Ra; and the Pharaoh was described as his son. By 1500 BC, however, the Pharaoh himself had assumed the guise of the Sun, and Sun worship was by that time invading the entire ritual of the Egyptian state. The Ptolemies, as might be expected from their readiness to perpetuate Egyptian ideas under Greek forms, maintained the same concept under a fashionable Hellenistic guise. Solar hymns were composed in Alexandria,[24] and Helios was identified not only with ancient Egyptian gods and with the new Greco-Egyptian divinity, Sarapis, but with successive Ptolemies as well. The myth of Osiris and Isis, with whom these monarchs were so closely associated, likewise became adjusted to the solar religion, for Helios was declared to be Isis' own offspring, and her initiates, to celebrate their mystic rebirth, were clothed in the robes of the Sun.[25] The coins of Ptolemy III Euergetes display him crowned with the Sun's rays, and the cornucopia on the reverse is surmounted by a similar diadem.[26]

But above all, the Hellenistic peoples linked the rule of the Sun with the coming of the Golden Age, the Age of Universal Concord (Homonoia), and this association became a commonplace of the literature of the time. It was an apocalyptic hope which inspired not only seditious movements, but a great deal of government propaganda as well, and never more than at this very epoch, when a Golden Age which would at last bring peace was the hope of many millions throughout the Mediterranean world.[27]

Rome itself was highly conscious of the theme. The city had its own ancient cult of the Sun (Sol), and the head of the god had reappeared upon the coinage in recent years. Octavian endeavoured to harness the idea to his own claims by declaring that his own special patron was Apollo, who was identified with the Sun. But Antony, who paid equally careful attention to this popular longing for the Golden Age, had depicted the Sun's radiate head upon his coins. He first introduced the design after the crowning victory of Philippi in 42 B C, and now he deliberately repeated the type at the very time when his son Alexander was given the name of the Sun incarnate, the emblem of the Golden Age which Antony and Cleopatra were going to create.[28]

Such an idea was now particularly apt, when a war against Parthia, the war to end all imperial wars, was imminent. For the king of Parthia called himself 'Brother of the Sun and Moon',[29] so that Antony's coins were claiming in effect that it was he himself, instead, upon whom the Sun's favour rested. Moreover, he may well already have planned (as he certainly did three years later) that when the Parthians had been defeated their new king should be none other than his infant son Alexander Helios. The boy's first name, given him by Cleopatra at his birth, was just as suited to this role as his second, since it was Alexander the Great who had conquered the Persians, the forerunners of Parthia. Antony, like all would-be eastern conquerors, had already shown himself happy to recall memories of Alexander the Great,[30] and now, by linking his son with dreams of world conquest and union, he was making it clear that he had Alexander in mind once again.

1 Ptolemy I Soter, who seized Egypt after the death of Alexander the Great. He wears the diadem of Alexander.

2 Gold coin showing the great central figures of the Ptolemaic cult, on which Cleopatra's régime was based. *Right:* Ptolemy I Soter and his wife Berenice I. *Left:* Ptolemy II Philadelphus and his sister-wife Arsinoe II.

3 Cleopatra's great grandfather Ptolemy VIII Euergetes, who was nicknamed Physcon (fatty), is drastically slimmed on this temple at Ombos (Kom-Ombo), where he is crowned in traditional style by personifications of Upper and Lower Egypt.

4 and 5 Statuette of
Ptolemy XII, nicknamed
Auletes 'the Piper',
wearing a vine wreath as
the New Dionysus: a
complex and much
maligned man, to whose
memory his daughter
Cleopatra was
apparently very loyal.

6 Funeral relief of
Egyptian dance. Romans
and philosophers criticized
Cleopatra's father and
other forebears for their
enjoyment of orgiastic
dances, but these
performances were related
to the identification of the
monarchs with the god
Dionysus.

7 The Temple of Horus at
Apollinopolis Magna
(Edfu) in Upper Egypt,
completed by Cleopatra's
father Ptolemy XII Auletes
who is seen (in ancient
Egyptian style) at either
end smiting his enemies,
while the Egyptian deities
watch.

8 Roman lamp showing the harbour of Alexandria. Behind it, on the left, is the tomb of Cleopatra, in the centre the temple of Alexander the Great, and on the right his tomb. First century AD.

9 Silver plate from Boscoreale, near Pompeii. The figure is probably Africa or Alexandria, or a blend of the goddesses Artemis (Diana) and Isis, whose rattle (low left) and snake are to be seen. This symbolism may well be intended to represent the régime of Cleopatra.

10 (*Right*) Some of the Ptolemies, including especially Cleopatra's father, were keenly interested in Africa beyond their southern borders, and Africans figure prominently in Alexandrian art.

11 (*Below*) Personification of the Nile, on which Cleopatra's great wealth depended. The children (partly restored) stand for the sixteen cubits, which was the maximum annual rise of the water level. From a temple of Isis in Rome. First century AD.

12 (*Above left*) The bull
god Buchis of Hermonthis
(Armant), near Thebes.
Cleopatra apparently
assisted personally in the
installation of a new
animal as one of the first
acts of her reign (51 BC).
Later, Roman emperors
(here Diocletian
AD 284–305) continued to
show reverence to the cult
—and to celebrate it, as
here, in the ancient
Egyptian artistic style.

13 (*Above*) Sarapis, the
god who was invented or
adapted by the Ptolemies
to bridge the gap between
the Egyptian and Greek
religions, and who served
as Ptolemaic Egypt's
divine ambassador in
Greek lands.

14 One of the Ptolemaic queens, whom Cleopatra was brought up to emulate: perhaps Berenice II (*d.* 221 BC), wife of Ptolemy III Euergetes. Like other members of the dynasty, she is represented as the goddess Isis.

15 Arsinoe II Philadelphus (*d.* 270 BC), one of Cleopatra's greatest predecessors. Married to her brother Ptolemy II Philadelphus, who raised the Ptolemaic empire to its zenith, she and he were already deified in their lifetimes, providing models for the deification of Cleopatra.

16 (*Above*) Chalcedony intaglio of Julius Caesar with a garland of flowers; made in Egypt at the time when he was celebrating his victory in the Alexandrian war, in Cleopatra's company.

17 Julius Caesar: one of the few authentic portrait busts dating back to his lifetime.

18 (*Above*) Silver coin (38–37 BC) of the free harbour city of Ascalon (Ashkelon, now in Israel), showing Cleopatra – with whose dynasty Ascalon kept on good terms – at the age of thirty-two, at the time when Antony gave her back the Levantine empire of the Ptolemies.

19 (*Centre*) Bronze coin of Cleopatra issued at Alexandria. The Greek letter *pi* on the reverse, indicating the denomination (80 drachmae), demonstrates the queen's intention that these very debased pieces should be accepted at their official value with profit to herself.

20 (*Left*) Silver coin of Alexandria, showing Cleopatra aged twenty-four during the year in which she arrived in Rome as Julius Caesar's guest (46 BC).

21 Marble head found at
Caesarea (now Cherchel),
the capital of Juba II, of
Mauretania who was
married to Cleopatra
Selene: it has been identified (without certainty) as
her mother, Cleopatra.

22 This young woman has
exactly the hair style of
some of Cleopatra's coins,
but is probably an imitator
of her fashions rather than
Cleopatra herself (as has
sometimes been supposed).

23 The orator Cicero, who was not at his best with women or Greeks, and took a particular dislike to Cleopatra when he met her in Rome in 46–44 BC. She failed to give him a present she had promised.

24 Aerial view of modern Alexandria. This wide isthmus between the city and Pharos island has spread round the site of the ancient mole (Heptastadion), which separated the two principal harbours. Cleopatra's palace lay beyond the eastern harbour on the left.

25 Isis and the Baby Horus: one of the major symbols of this universally popular Graeco-Egyptian cult. The two deities were identified with Cleopatra and her son Caesarion.

26 Ptolemaic priest, in a mystic rapture, from Hermonthis (near Thebes; now Armant), which Cleopatra visited immediately after her accession, and later adorned with a birth-temple for her son Caesarion.

27 The temple of Isis on the island of Philae, one of the many buildings reconstructed by Cleopatra's father Ptolemy XII Auletes. On the right is a Birth Shrine of Isis' son Horus, like the building at Hermonthis where Cleopatra's son Caesarion was worshipped as Horus. The High Dam has made it necessary to move the Philae building elsewhere.

28 The temple of the Egyptian goddess Hathor at Tintyra (now Dendera). On the left is Cleopatra, and in front her son Ptolemy XV Caesar (Caesarion); they are offering incense to the deities of the province. The small figure represented between them is the 'ka' (the soul or double) of Caesarion.

29 (*Above*) This coin, issued in Cyprus, under Ptolemaic rule, shows Cleopatra with an infant at her breast, probably Caesarion (Ptolemy XV Caesar), whom she claimed to be the son of Julius Caesar.

30 (*Right*) Carnelian of Sextus Pompeius, Pompey the Great's son, who held out for seven years against the Second Triumvirate of Antony, Octavian and Lepidus. Signed by Archangelus.

31 Dionysus (Bacchus), the principal god of contemporary Mediterranean cult and mysticism, with whom Cleopatra's father Ptolemy XII Auletes and Antony were both identified. Mosaic from Antioch in Syria, the summer capital of Antony and Cleopatra.

32 On his way through Asia Minor to meet Cleopatra at Tarsus in 41 BC Antony refounded Eumenia (Işekli) under the name of his wife Fulvia, whose portrait, in the guise of Victory, the town depicts on its coins.

33 Painting from Herculaneum showing a white-robed priest of Isis performing the afternoon service, the ceremony of the Nile water, which he holds in a sacred vase inside his robe. A choir of both sexes is ranged in four rows.

34 (*Right*) The meeting of Antony and Cleopatra, by Giovanni Battista Tiepolo (1697–1770).

35 King Orodes II of Parthia,
Rome's formidable enemy whose
armies destroyed Crassus (53 BC)
and overran Syria and Judaea
(41–40).

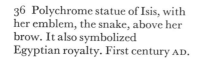

36 Polychrome statue of Isis, with
her emblem, the snake, above her
brow. It also symbolized
Egyptian royalty. First century AD.

37 This bronze coin of Antony, probably issued at Tarentum (Taranto), depicts him with his wife Octavia, whom he married little more than a year after his famous meeting with Cleopatra at Tarsus. The warship celebrates Antony's collaboration with Octavia's brother Octavian to suppress Pompey's son Sextus Pompeius.

38 This head probably represents Antony's wife Octavia.

39 (*Far Left*) Silver coin of Asia Minor showing Antony with his wife Octavia. The symbolism relates to the world-conquering god Dionysus: Antony was hailed as his reincarnation.

40 (*Below*) The triumph of Dionysus, the mythical climax of Dionysiac cult, which figured prominently at the Ptolemaic court, and the model of Antony's triumphal procession at Alexandria in 34 BC. Tomb of the Egyptians, St Peter's, Rome.

41 (*Left*) Alexander the Great, whose inheritors Caesar, Antony and Cleopatra all claimed to be. Roman copy of a bust of the late fourth century BC by Lysippus from Tibur (Tivoli).

42 The jackal-headed god Anubis: seized upon as an emblem of sinister Egyptian exoticism, and associated with Cleopatra, by Roman propagandists.

43 Mosaic of the first century BC from Pompeii. This view of the Nile illustrates the fashionable Italian taste for such Egyptian scenes, which probably originated in the palace of the Ptolemies at Alexandria.

44 (*Left*) A large silver coin of Antony and Cleopatra issued in Syria in *c*. 34 BC. Her description as 'the Younger Goddess' (Thea Notera) is a deliberate claim to emulate Cleopatra 'Thea'; see no. 45.

45 (*Above*) Cleopatra 'Thea' ('the goddess') (d. 121 BC), a Ptolemaic princess whose marriage to three successive Seleucid (Syrian) monarchs, suggesting the eventual unification of the two empires, inspired Cleopatra to call herself 'the Younger Thea'.

46 Official silver *denarius* of Antony (*c.* 34 BC) with Latin inscriptions showing Cleopatra as 'Queen of Kings and of her Sons that are Kings'. This must have confirmed the worst fears of Romans about the major part he intended her to play in his régime.

47 Gold coin on which Antony, as triumvir (III VIR. R.P.C.), depicts not only himself but also Antyllus (M. Antonius M [arci] F [ilius]), his son, by Fulvia. This was an indication that whatever roles Cleopatra and her children might fulfil in the east, his official Roman heir was going to be his son Antyllus.

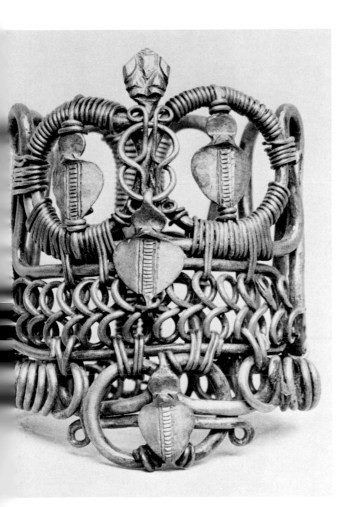

48 (*Left*) The sort of jewellery that was worn by Cleopatra and her predecessors.

49 (*Above*) Pendant worn by a Ptolemaic lady.

50 (*Below*) Terracotta drinking cups from Arretium (Arezzo). Hercules is in woman's clothing and Omphale carries the god's club: the myth told how she made him her slave. This is intended to caricature the relations of Antony and Cleopatra.

51 One of the great series of coins issued just before Actium to honour the legions, other military units and fleets which were about to fight for him and Cleopatra. This gold piece honours his personal bodyguard (CHORTIVM PRAETORIARVM).

52 Marcus Vipsanius Agrippa, to whose superior admiralship, before and during the Actium campaign, the downfall of Antony and Cleopatra was due.

53 (*Left*) Onyx cameo celebrating the victory of Octavian (Augustus) over Antony and Cleopatra at Actium (31 BC).

54 Relief from Praeneste (Palestrina) showing a Roman warship. The crocodile, symbol of Egypt, beneath the prow shows that the ship fought in the battle of Actium against Antony and Cleopatra (31 BC).

55 When Octavian (Augustus) annexed Egypt, his statues replaced Cleopatra's. This is from Arsinoe (Fayum).

56 This gold coin of Augustus in one of the eastern provinces celebrates his annexation of Cleopatra's Egypt

57 The leading priestess
has a snake twined round
her arm. A statue of Isis
with a similar snake car-
ried in Augustus's triumph
after Cleopatra's death
may have originated the
story that she, the in-
carnation of Isis, died of a
snake-bite. Second
century AD.

58 *Cleopatra* by
Michelangelo.

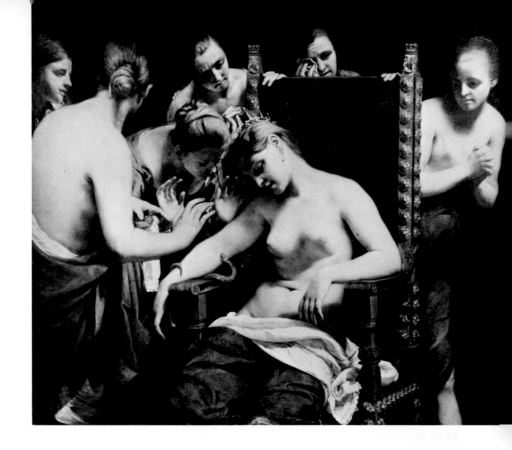

59 *The Death of Cleopatra* by Guido Cagnacci (1601–1681).

60 The only authentic portrait-bust of a descendant of Cleopatra: Ptolemy of Mauretania (AD 23–40), son of her daughter Cleopatra Selene.

9

Cleopatra Receives Antony Back from the Wars

The situation in Parthia gave Antony grounds for encouragement. For the Parthian king Orodes I, distressed by his son Pacorus' death in battle against the Romans in 38 BC, had voluntarily abdicated. His next son and heir Phraates IV, in order to assert his claim to the throne, had then murdered his father and thirty of his brothers. In the resultant confusion, one of the most powerful of the Parthian leaders, Monaeses, fled to Antony, accompanied by a group of other noblemen (37 BC). A Mesopotamian landowner on a huge scale, Monaeses was governor-general of the western frontier areas, and the late king had destined him for the supreme command. When he changed sides, Antony, true to his policy of entrusting extensive territory and even Roman territory to client princes, gave Monaeses a substantial region of the Roman province of Syria, stretching a hundred miles from the Euphrates as far as the Orontes. Antony is also quite likely to have offered an assurance that, once Parthia had been successfully invaded, Monaeses would have the Parthian throne for himself. Even if it had been earmarked for Alexander Helios, the boy was only three, and the crown of Parthia may now have been promised to Monaeses on the understanding that Alexander Helios should succeed him.

History showed what great risks the impending Parthian war involved. Yet it was Antony's supreme opportunity to prove himself the true successor of Caesar, who had planned just such an enterprise in vengeance for Crassus' defeat. Military glory was still the principal ambition of all leading Romans, and Parthia offered Antony an opportunity far outweighing any glory Octavian could acquire in other parts of the world. The suggestion that Cleopatra took a different view is mistaken.[1] She, too, was imbued with the ancient idea that expansion and aggression were noble and desirable aims. Her own policy of restoring the Ptolemaic realm to its former dimensions was based on just that conviction. She was also in agreement with the belief that Parthia was the supreme enemy. Moreover, she had staked everything on Antony, and the most certain way for Antony to improve his position, outshine Octavian, and incidentally lessen the financial pressure on Egypt, was by winning a brilliant victory over Parthia. She herself must have been keenly interested in the area, for in addition to all her other languages she had learnt Parthian, and not only Parthian but another Iranian tongue, namely Median.[2]

Mountainous Media Atropatene, extending from the Caspian to Lake Matiana (Urmia) – nowadays Persia's north-western territory of Azerbaijan[3] – was the country upon which Antony's forthcoming expedition depended. For he planned to carry out Caesar's plan of invading Parthia's Persian homeland, not from the west through Mesopotamia (the scene of Crassus' disastrous attempt) but from the north. Since the break-up of Alexander the Great's empire, Media had remained a separate entity retaining a precarious independence interrupted by subjection to a variety of external suzerains. Its king, Artavasdes, although he possessed a strong force of cavalry and horse-archers, for which his country was famous, depended upon the Parthians. However, Antony could only confront him after passing through another mountainous country, Armenia. The monarch of Armenia was like the Median monarch in three respects. He, too, was strong in cavalry and horse-archers. He, too (inconveniently), was called Artavasdes. And he, too, since the downfall of Crassus, had been a Parthian ally and dependent, though he grandly entitled himself King of Kings.

It was one of the greatest moments in the lives of Antony and Cleopatra when, in mid-May 36 BC, Antony and his army moved off from Zeugma on the Syrian bank of the Euphrates (opposite the modern Birecik) and started on the long march towards Armenia and Media. It was rather late in the season to begin a major operation, not quite so late as Hitler's fatally delayed invasion of Russia on 22 June 1941, but late enough to leave only a small margin for error if victory was to be gained before the extreme rigours of winter; and perhaps too late to make the most of the succession difficulties that had been convulsing the Parthian court.

Subsequently, Antony's alleged infatuation for Cleopatra was blamed for the tardiness of his start.[4] But although she was four or five months pregnant with their third child, neither would have allowed this to prejudice an enterprise of this magnitude. Perhaps laziness, which was inclined on occasion to handicap Antony's plans, played a part. But it is more probable that certain essential diplomatic preliminaries took longer than he had anticipated. For one thing, he had dispatched Monaeses on a mission to king Phraates, who responded with an offer of friendship. Antony decided that the offer was unreliable; but he may have taken a little time to reach the decision. Besides, he was hopeful that the king of Armenia could be induced or forced to change sides. And indeed, this was what happened, but not until he had suffered a military reverse at the hands of Antony's leading general, Publius Canidius Crassus. Antony celebrated the success by depicting the Armenian royal tiara on his coins.[5] He and Canidius imprudently omitted to insist on guarantees in the form of hostages and Roman forces of occupation. But this would have taken longer still to arrange, and might have compelled Antony to put off the expedition for another year. Such a postponement would have been out of the question, after the campaign had been delayed for so many years already. So he started as soon as he could. And meanwhile Canidius, in a further successful campaign, reduced the tribes that lay along Armenia's Caucasus borders, thus effectively encircling its territory.[6]

Proceeding northwards along the Roman bank of the Euphrates, Antony made his way into this supposedly friendly country of Armenia, penetrating deep into the interior as far as the central city of Carana (Erzerum). There he was joined by Canidius, and reviewed his enormous army. It was the finest army of the age, people said, and perhaps of any Roman age; and its soldiers were unsurpassed in their loyalty towards their commander. After the review, Antony led this great host forward once again, on the long trek to Media and its fortified city of Phraaspa (Takht-i-Suleiman), where the national treasure was kept under guard.

But in the open country east of Lake Matiana he found that his numerous baggage waggons, which carried the heavy siege equipment that would be needed at Phraaspa, were seriously retarding progress. So he divided his army into two parts, pushing ahead himself with the main force and letting the baggage train follow behind with two legions. This rearguard, a small force to undertake such a role, was placed under the command of Oppius Statianus, accompanied by king Polemo of Pontus; and an escort of 6,000 cavalry and 7,000 infantry was provided by the Armenian monarch Artavasdes. But suddenly Monaeses, whose friendship now turned out to be a myth, attacked the column with 50,000 horse-archers, including 10,000 Medians, and totally destroyed it, slaughtering the legionaries and their officers and taking Polemo prisoner. Artavasdes, either in treachery or self-protection, fled back to his native land.[7] The baggage train was set on fire, and the entire siege equipment went up in flames.

Without it, Phraaspa could never be captured, and the expedition designed to outdo Alexander the Great was doomed to humiliating failure.[8] Antony lingered on impotently before the walls of the city until October, but then, when winter was already perilously close, he bowed to necessity and set out on the long homeward journey. It took his army twenty-seven terrible days to struggle through to the River Araxes (Aras), the border between Media and Armenia: but not before the ravages of sickness, and losses inflicted by Parthians and Medians in eighteen successive engagements, had cost the Romans more than twenty thousand men. After the survivors finally managed to cross the deep, rapid stream, they marched back as best they could through wintry Armenia, without suffering any further enemy attack. For Antony had felt it advisable to treat the Armenian monarch Artavasdes as a friend, ignoring the suspicion of treachery, and in return the king provided the Romans with supplies. Nevertheless, dense snowstorms in Armenia cost them a further eight thousand Roman lives.

Two-fifths of Antony's army had perished. Indeed, many more would have died had it not been for his leadership, since he was at his best in this time of trouble.[9] However, Napoleonic retreats from Russia, or, as Churchill remarked, British retreats from Dunkirk, are not the way to win wars. Antony had lost a war; and his setback established Parthian invincibility for a hundred and fifty years. His failure to prove himself a military commander of the calibre of Alexander or Caesar was a major disaster for Cleopatra. She had attempted to harness to her ambitions and affections the two greatest Romans of her age. But Caesar had been murdered; and now Antony had failed in the most important enterprise of his life.

*

Furthermore, these same months were producing disquieting evidence that there might, after all, be another Roman who was greater than Antony. For it must have gradually dawned on her that Octavian, however unlikable and cold-blooded, was a man of formidable ability: and perhaps she was even beginning to realize that he was one of the ablest men Rome had ever produced. Octavian maintained, and no doubt genuinely believed, that no one but himself was capable of rescuing the Roman empire from the civil strife which had bedevilled it for generations. It was essential, therefore, that he should obtain complete control of the empire; and with that as his ultimate aim, he proposed to show no more loyalty to Antony or any other colleague than was necessary. As for Cleopatra, the xenophobia which came naturally to him made him see her as merely the foreign, oriental concubine of his potential rival – and a possible point of weakness in that rival's defences.

Antony, not a suspicious man, probably tried to ignore the sinister implications of Octavian's behaviour for as long as he could. Cleopatra, more realistic, saw Octavian and his sister Octavia as direct menaces to her own position, and understood much earlier that reconciliation was impossible. The most comforting feature of the situation hitherto had been Octavian's comparative ineptitude as a military leader, to which Antony's military panache and experience seemed to present a happy contrast. Even in the earlier months of this very year, 36 BC, her hopes had still seemed justified. At the time when Antony was setting off hopefully for Media, fresh naval defeats at the hands of Sextus Pompeius had reduced Octavian almost to the point of suicide. Yet now came a sharp reversal. Antony was a defeated man, yet on 3 September, in a sea-battle off the Sicilian Cape Naulochus (Venetico), Octavian's superb admiral Agrippa had fought Sextus yet again and won a spectacular and conclusive victory; so that Octavian could now proclaim that the civil wars were over.

*

When the remains of Antony's army finally reached winter quarters in Syria, recriminations began among his following, and they spared neither himself nor Cleopatra. Antony was blamed because he had not allowed his exhausted troops to winter in Armenia:[10] but he had calculated that the apparently favourable attitude of the Armenian king could not be relied upon very much longer, so that a prolonged stay in that country might have resulted in even larger loss of life. His enemies inevitably added that he only decided to press on because he could not wait to see Cleopatra again.[11] This was said all the more confidently because Antony sent instructions to Cleopatra to sail from Egypt and join him on the Phoenician coast, and he himself left his army and hurried on to meet her there. It is a measure of his alarm that he chose an insignificant harbour, Leuce Come (White Village), as their rendezvous. For all he knew, invading Parthians might already be occupying the main towns.

But what he wanted from Cleopatra was not only her company, consoling though it would be, but money and clothing for his troops. After some delay, probably in January of 35 BC, she arrived with these supplies. Hostile observers declared that she was slow in order to show her disapproval of the war, and that when in the end she came she brought no money, with the result that Antony had to save face by distributing his own, and pretending it was hers. But if Cleopatra was slow, it was only because she needed time to collect and bring the most substantial aid she could. It was true that, for the time being at least, Antony had failed to become the successful conqueror she required.

But he was still as indispensable as he had been before. Nobody else would be able to fulfil her ambitions. Indeed, nobody else was even likely to allow her to retain what she already had.

Another reason why she was slow in starting may have been because she had just had another baby – her fourth, and her third by Antony. She named the newborn child Ptolemy Philadelphus, after the glorious Ptolemy ii, who had presided over the zenith of the Ptolemaic empire and had come to the throne precisely two hundred and fifty years earlier. So the choice of his name for her new son was a further indication of Cleopatra's essential aims. She wanted to keep what she had already regained, and she wanted more. Antony had suffered a setback, but she must still support him in every way she could. And so she came to Leuce Come, bringing all the funds and provisions she was able to raise.

*

Meanwhile Octavian, after victoriously ending the civil war in Sicily, had found his fellow-Triumvir Lepidus unwilling to accept his supremacy in the west. Lepidus had consequently been dismissed from his triumviral office, and sent into compulsory retirement. This must have been a serious shock to the third member of the junta, Antony, who was not even consulted. For if Octavian was so quick to get rid of one partner, he might well feel inclined, one day, to get rid of the other. But Octavian was not yet ready to clash with Antony. Success against Sextus Pompeius had not been enough to make him into a truly glorious leader, because it was a civil and not a foreign war. However, a convenient foreign war now offered itself, against Illyrian tribes (in what is now Yugoslavia) which threatened the Italian frontier. The Illyrian war would conveniently enable Octavian's troops, who had become restless, to cease inflicting themselves and their feeding requirements upon Italy, and would keep them fully occupied. It also provided a new excuse for not sending Antony the twenty thousand soldiers he was still owed.

So Octavian decided to temporize, and wrote Antony a letter about matters of high policy.[12] We do not know what he said. Possibly he referred to an eventual, mutually agreed, laying down of their triumviral powers, though neither leader can have seriously envisaged retiring into private life. He is also likely to have explained why the treachery of Lepidus had made his deposition inevitable. No doubt he thanked Antony for the naval units which had made a considerable contribution to his success. And he requested Antony's approval of the forthcoming Illyrian war.

Octavian refrained from making any propaganda capital out of

Antony's military failure: instead, the invasion of Media was classified as a victory. Antony himself had sent dispatches to Rome reporting success, and some of his coins displaying trophies may celebrate the same fictitious triumphs. At Octavian's suggestion, the authorities at Rome officially gave thanks for these alleged feats. Such graciousness brought Octavian a useful advantage. For Antony had always insisted on his own right to recruit troops and settle veterans in Italy, and Octavian never had any intention of allowing him to do either. If, therefore, Antony had made such massive gains in the east as he asserted, he could surely henceforward be expected to undertake his own recruitment and settlement in the vast territories he claimed to have conquered there.

In gratitude for the achievements of both Triumvirs, the Senate conferred on each of them an honour which, as far as Antony was concerned, must have seemed malicious. For it was decreed that the two leaders should not only be awarded statues in the Forum and the Temple of Concord, but that they should also be permitted to hold banquets in the same temple – each in the company of his wife and children! The reference to wives and children was the first volley in a propaganda barrage by Octavian. It has been interpreted as an attempt to make public opinion bring pressure on Antony to leave Cleopatra and return to his colleague's sister Octavia. More probably, however, Octavian realized that public opinion could achieve no such thing, and merely wanted to draw as much attention as possible to Antony's liaison with Cleopatra.

Octavian then engineered a second and better opportunity to produce the same result. While Antony was withdrawing through Syria to join Cleopatra, Octavia had, as usual, been spending the winter in her matrimonial home at Athens. But she had returned to Rome at about the end of 36 BC – perhaps at the request of Antony, who may have wanted her to tell the Romans a suitably untruthful version of his disastrous campaign. In the spring of 35, however, Antony, while still in Syria, learnt that she was on her way back from Italy to Athens once again. Like Cleopatra, she was bringing clothing and supplies for his army. She was also bringing the seventy ships that survived from the squadrons her husband had lent Octavian – and two thousand picked soldiers.

Although Romans in general could be induced to see the provision of these troops and ships as a generous gesture, it was in fact, an insult, and that is how Antony must have regarded it.[13] For he was owed not two but twenty thousand men – and after his losses of the previous year, he needed them even more than before. As for the seventy ships, Antony had neither asked for them, nor wanted them; even if their crews came back with them, ships needed legionaries as well as crews if they were to fight battles, and Cleopatra was already building as many ships as there were legionaries available to man them.

At this point an ancient tradition tells of the terrible scenes Cleopatra made to prevent Antony from returning to Octavia.[14] But no such scenes were necessary. He did not want the woman whose brother, though very much younger and less experienced than himself, had treated him so abominably, and had so often proved an untrustworthy collaborator. And now Octavian, taking advantage of Antony's difficulties, accepted Octavia's well-intentioned suggestion that she should go to her husband – but accepted it only in the belief that the derisory smallness of her escort would cause Antony to rebuff her, thus losing him much support in influential circles at Rome.

Octavian's forecast, as so often, proved correct. For when Octavia reached Athens, Antony wrote her a letter from Syria requesting her to send on the troops and supplies, and go home. According to one version, he conveyed this message to her at once. It is more probable, however, that he first wrote instructing her not to move beyond Athens since he was planning a new military expedition, and then later wrote again and told her to go back to Rome.

When she arrived there, Octavian and his friends made the very most of her treatment by Antony. The scene is imagined by Shakespeare:[15]

AGRIPPA: Welcome, lady!
MAECENAS: Welcome, dear madam!
                       Each heart in Rome does love and pity you:
                       Only th' adulterous Antony, most large
                       In his abominations, turns you off;
                       And gives his potent regiment to a trull
                       That noises it against us.
OCTAVIA: Is it so, sir?
OCTAVIAN: Most certain, Sister, welcome! Pray you,
                       Be ever known to patience: my dear'st sister!

In spite of her brother's pleas, however, Octavia refused to leave Antony's Roman house. But Octavian granted her a high personal honour, *sacrosanctitas*, which elevated her to the rank of the Vestals, the most exalted status that a woman could attain; he himself had in the previous year assumed the sacrosanctity of a tribune.

Granted her integrity and good intentions, which have moved modern historians to lyrical praise, she was unable to prevent Octavian from using her as a dupe. It was not her fault that she had disappointed Antony by recently bearing him a second daughter.[16] But when everyone in Rome saw how she was looking after Antony's children, her own and Fulvia's, and interceding for Antony's friends with Octavian, Plutarch was right to conclude that 'she unintentionally did great harm to Antony's reputation, since he was naturally hated for wronging such a woman'.[17]

When Octavian bestowed sacrosanctity upon his sister Octavia, he conferred the same privilege upon his wife Livia, who possessed links with so many of the Roman noblemen, the traditional rulers of the state. This was the class which felt shocked by Antony's ill-treatment of Octavia. It is true that he still retained the support of many of the nobility who had preferred him to Octavian in the days of Philippi. But other leading Romans were beginning to wonder whether Octavian might not be a more useful leader after all. To compensate for these political losses, Antony was obliged to make friends with some less desirable figures merely because they were irreconcilable with Octavian, including two of the shadier of Caesar's assassins, Decimus Turullius and Cassius of Parma. A few people, such as Cicero's old friend Atticus and the historian Pollio, tried not to side with either, but this was becoming an increasingly difficult course to follow.

*

When Cleopatra had been staying in Rome as Caesar's guest, many Romans paid court to her. But now she had been away from the city for nine years, and so had most of her potential supporters. In these circumstances, it was particularly easy to arouse Roman feelings against her by pointing to the pathetic situation of Octavia, who, it was now clear, had been abandoned by Antony in her favour. In the spring of 35 B C, after doing all that could be done for his depleted expeditionary force in its Syrian winter quarters, Antony moved on with Cleopatra to Alexandria. For the next three years his headquarters and capital, like those of certain imperial Pharaohs of the past, were to be alternately in Alexandria and Syrian Antioch, the former usually during the winter and the latter during the summer.[18] He was still, apparently, not Cleopatra's husband, but in future, except during occasional eastern campaigns, he was scarcely ever separated from her again.

Antony's defeat by the Parthians and Medes necessitated even closer links with her kingdom. Immediately after his return from the expedition of 36 B C, he had called upon its resources, and now, in 35, he planned to use them once more. For he had no intention of regarding his failure in Media as final, and still proposed to emulate the conquests of Alexander the Great and Caesar by vanquishing the Parthians. As before, while he marched east with his armies, Cleopatra was to help with supplies and money; and above all she was to employ her fleet, which it was her special mission to create and develop, to secure the Mediterranean home front against Octavian and all others.

This was the third time that Antony had demanded this kind of support, and for the third time she had conditions to impose. Yet again, she demanded the total suppression of Judaea, the sole, infuriating, independent enclave in the otherwise almost wholly Ptolemaic territories of the southern and central Levant. An action taken by Herod at this juncture seemed to give her the opportunity to strike the lethal blow. One of the concessions he had reluctantly made to her was the appointment of his own seventeen-year-old brother-in-law Aristobulus as high priest, because the youth's mother, Alexandra, had appealed to her friend Cleopatra. In order to soothe the two women, Antony, probably before he left for Media in 36, invited Aristobulus to pay him a visit.[19] But Herod, very wisely from his own point of view, declined on the young high priest's behalf. This irritated Alexandra, and her alarm grew when she found herself virtually under house arrest in Jerusalem. After writing a second violent appeal to Cleopatra, she tried, with her son, to escape secretly to Egypt. It was said that he and she were smuggled out of the palace in coffins, and that they were caught in the act.[20] Herod did not dare to punish them openly for their attempted escape, because he was too afraid of Cleopatra. But he now decided that the appointment, which had been forced upon him, of his brother-in-law as high priest was an unworkable mistake that must be rectified as soon as possible – though without the responsibility falling directly on himself.

Herod waited for a holiday occasion, when Aristobulus was the guest of his mother Alexandra at Jericho. And there one day, when the young man was bathing with some friends in one of the royal swimming pools, Herod arranged to have him drowned. Knowing that Antony was safely out of the way in Media, the king brazenly declared that a tragic accident had taken place and a magnificent funeral would be held. But Alexandra wrote a third letter to Cleopatra, demanding revenge in furious, grief-stricken terms.

Such was the position which greeted Antony when he was rejoined by Cleopatra in Phoenicia at the beginning of 35 BC. Herod's crime surely caused her to redouble her demands for his suppression, and the abolition of Judaea. Antony decided that he must give way to the extent of investigating the version offered by Herod, who was therefore summoned to the Syrian town of Laodicea (Lattakia) to give an account of himself. However, Cleopatra again failed to win everything she wanted. Antony still needed Judaea for the renewal of the Parthian war, and he still thought Herod was the right man to govern the country. Whether the king persisted in his assertion that Aristobulus' death was an accident, or claimed he had killed him to forestall a plot, we do not know. At all events his explanation was accepted, and he remained in Antony's high favour. But once more Cleopatra had to be placated – this time with Herod's one remaining port of Gaza. Cleopatra had now succeeded in landlocking him completely: his claims to rule the more or less Hellenized coastal areas were totally superseded by hers. All he retained was the Jewish plateau, from which he derived his troops. And this central region Antony, even now, refused to concede to Cleopatra.

She was reduced, therefore, to undermining operations, by which she tried to stir up a separatist, anti-Jewish movement in Herod's southernmost province, Idumaea. The leader of the secessionists was the provincial governor himself, Costobarus, and he was ready enough to join Cleopatra. But Antony again resisted, and her appeal that this vital portion of Jewish territory should be transferred to her own control was ignored.[21] Nevertheless, Herod, deferring to her special influence over Antony, refrained from punishing Costobarus or the other ringleaders. It seemed enough to ride each successive storm as it came, and to survive.

*

Antony's intention to repair the setback of 36 BC by resuming the Parthian offensive in the following year presumably seemed as essential to Cleopatra as to himself. However, the project had to be delayed owing to an irritating and unexpected distraction.

When Octavian and Agrippa, in the previous year, had finally destroyed the fleet of Sextus Pompeius the defeated Republican (or pirate) had moved eastwards into the Aegean, where he seized the town of Lampsacus (Lapseki) in north-western Asia Minor and raised a little band of followers to the strength of three legions. Sextus sent envoys to Antony, but refused to come to Alexandria, and instead, prompted by Antony's Median defeat, secretly got into touch with the Parthians. Antony discovered this, and sent a strong force under his general Marcus Titius, apparently one of Cleopatra's friends. Titius placed Sextus under arrest (through the good offices of king Amyntas of Galatia), and then put him to death, probably at Miletus.[22]

Octavian congratulated Antony publicly upon the removal of the rebel Sextus. But behind the scenes he allowed this brutal execution to be contrasted with his own lenient treatment of Lepidus, an equally seditious man whom he had nevertheless pardoned, permitting him to withdraw into private life. Whether the order for Sextus' execution was given with Antony's knowledge was disputed. If not, the main suspect was not Titius himself but his uncle, Lucius Munatius Plancus of Tibur (Tivoli), a leading supporter of Antony and, like his nephew, a friend of Cleopatra; he had a reputation as an elegant literary stylist, and a political time-server. Plancus was governor of Syria, and Antony had delegated to him the power to take major decisions. Yet Antony,

Plancus and Titius might all have felt inclined to hesitate before ordering the execution, since Cleopatra was likely to view Sextus with some favour, partly because he was the son of the great man whom her political enemies in Egypt had murdered, but more particularly because he might still turn out to be a useful potential ally against Octavian.[23] However, it is quite possible that she first supported Sextus, but changed her mind when she discovered he was in treasonable communication with Parthia: in which case either Antony or Plancus or Titius could well have felt she would not object if they arranged for his suppression. At Rome, where there was still popular sympathy for Pompey's son, the man blamed for the execution was Titius, who had carried it out.

*

While Sextus Pompeius was still at large in Asia Minor, Antony had not felt it was safe to recommence his activities against the Parthians and their allies. He had therefore lost a year. Octavian, on the other hand, had actively inaugurated his war against the Illyrians, pressing onwards as far as the River Save.

However, Sextus was dead by midsummer, and with hindsight it seems that Antony would have been wise, after his death, to proceed, if not to Parthia, at least to Rome, either before 'or after Octavian arrived back in autumn. This would have given him a good opportunity to hearten and strengthen his political supporters in the city and particularly in the Senate: it was they, in the last resort, whose influence on Octavian was Antony's only hope of recruiting troops and settling veterans in Italy. For, whatever the autocratic authority of the Triumvirate, the Senate was still very powerful. Certainly, Antony had lost some of its members to Octavian, but his adherents remained numerous. It was still uncertain which way many senators would turn, and a personal visit by Antony, supported by a judicious distribution of funds, might have worked wonders.

His failure to make such a visit may have been partly due to preoccupation with the proposed second Parthian campaign. Yet it may also have owed something to a reluctance to accept the inevitable showdown with Octavian. Perhaps the most important deterrent to his journey was the attitude of Cleopatra. The propaganda that she had ensnared Antony in oriental debauchery, and that this was what kept him away from the active life of a Roman, was a lie. All the same, she may well have been reluctant to let him visit Rome. For Rome was now the place where Octavia lived – and Cleopatra remembered that five years earlier, after a whole winter in her own company at Alexandria, Antony had nevertheless returned to Italy and married

Octavia. There seemed to her a very real danger that social pressures, combined with his own inertia, might well draw him back to his Roman house and Roman life, and to the duties of paterfamilias which were suitable to a Roman nobleman of his standing, and would meet with general approval in the capital.

*

At all events, Antony did not go to Rome in 35 BC, and did not fight in the east either. However, a stroke of good fortune almost seemed to justify his inactivity. For without any Roman intervention, Artavasdes of Media now proceeded to quarrel with Phraates of Parthia over the spoils of Antony's expedition in the previous year. Indeed, the Median very soon went over to the Romans and promised to lend them his valuable cavalry and archers for the forthcoming Parthian war.[24]

At this stage Antony also made an attempt to win back the other Artavasdes, king of Armenia. The envoy selected for this mission was the astute Dellius. He carried with him the proposal that the five-year-old son of Antony and Cleopatra, Alexander Helios, should be betrothed to the daughter of the Armenian king. He also invited the king to visit Alexandria, as a token gesture of submission. But Artavasdes did not like the prospect of such a visit, and failed to respond. Subsequently, Antony complained that Octavian had been corresponding secretly with the Armenian and had advised him to turn the offer down, which is not impossible.

After the Median defection, Antony felt free to launch a large army against recalcitrant Armenia. In spring 34, Cleopatra escorted him on the first part of the journey from Alexandria, and they passed northwards together through the Syrian territories she had acquired from him three years earlier. Then they moved on to the Euphrates,[25] where Antony took leave of her, entered Armenia, and marched to the gates of its capital Artaxata. There Artavasdes (the Armenian) came for an interview, and was required to hand over his treasure and fortresses. The Armenian army, however, refused to comply, and gave the crown to the king's eldest son Artaxes, who after initial resistance took refuge with the Parthians. Antony then arrested Artavasdes (by treachery, Octavian later said)[26] and took him back to Alexandria, together with his wife and two younger sons, and much of the portable wealth of Armenia.

Owing to the fog of hostile propaganda which veiled Antony's enterprises, we know little about the campaign. But it had clearly been a conspicuous success. However, it was only a second-class operation, designed as a prelude to the long-expected invasion of Parthia. And now, at long last, this really seemed about to take place. As a preliminary,

Antony left his best general, Canidius Crassus, in Armenia, together with the bulk of the legionary force, in order to complete its reduction to a Roman province. A strip of its territory, however, was presented to Media, and Alexander Helios, rejected as a son-in-law by the Armenian king, was betrothed to his Median colleague's daughter. Then Antony returned triumphantly to Cleopatra.

*

While he had been conquering Armenia, she, too, had spent an active summer, looking after her own diplomatic contacts and resources, and planning the completion of her majestic role in his New Order.

After she had accompanied Antony northwards to the Euphrates, her return journey to Egypt was a glamorous royal progress. First she stopped at one of the greatest self-governing Greek cities of the Roman province of Syria, the fortress of Apamea on the Orontes (Nahr-el-Asi), a leading foundation of the Seleucid monarchs. Then, moving south along the same river, she arrived at the great religious centre of Emesa (Homs), ruled over at this time by a native chieftain whose frontier marched with Cleopatra's own recently annexed Syrian lands. Passing onwards through one of these territories, the former state of Ituraea, she next came to another renowned Seleucid foundation, the free city of Damascus, which welcomed her as its rescuer from Ituraean bandits.

Next, she entered Judaea, and had a strange encounter with Herod. She had last seen him six years earlier, before her obvious desire to obliterate him and his kingdom had ruined their relations. At this second meeting of 34 B C they presumably discussed the humiliating and costly arrangements which Antony had compelled Herod to make with the queen in exchange for an assurance (from Antony, not Cleopatra) that he would not be deprived of this throne. His feelings at having to extend hospitality to this woman, who had deprived him of so many lands and revenues, must have been unspeakably bitter. And yet he had to give her an appropriate welcome, in order to keep the friendship of Antony.

In these conditions the customary exchange of courtesies between Herod and Cleopatra must have rung hollow. Unfortunately we know little or nothing of the external trappings of the visit. We can only imagine the large and resplendent retinue which accompanied her, and the curious blend of cultures she found at Herod's court, which was Greek in all its titles and grades, although Herod himself was outwardly as obedient, as far as he felt was necessary, to the Jewish faith which his Edomite (Idumaean) forebears had been compelled to adopt.[27] The Antonia palace in which he received her at Jerusalem was more fortress-like than her own residence at Alexandria. Indeed, there was the atmosphere of a police-state throughout Herod's recently won dominions. Moreover, in the palace itself there was great tension. Only quite lately, on information received from his own sister, Herod had executed his uncle Joseph; and the drowning of his brother-in-law Aristobulus had, naturally, never been forgiven by the boy's mother Alexandra – who was under Herod's deepest suspicion because of her close friendship with Cleopatra.

The festivities which Herod arranged for Cleopatra must have strained even his well-known charm. His profound hatred of his guest spilt over into two stories which the Jewish historian Josephus derived, at second hand, from the memoirs of Herod himself. The intermediary was Nicolaus, an eminent literary man of Damascus, the city which Cleopatra had just visited. At the time of her meeting with Herod, Nicolaus was the tutor of her children.[28] But later, after Cleopatra was dead, Nicolaus transferred his services to Herod, and became his confidential adviser. He wrote a universal history incorporating passages from Herod's own autobiographical writings, and one of these passages, preserved by Josephus, gives Herod's version of Cleopatra's strange visit to Judaea:

Having Herod's company very often, Cleopatra attempted to have sexual relations with the king, for she was by nature used to enjoying this kind of pleasure without disguise. Perhaps, too, she really felt some measure of passion for him or, what is more probable, she was secretly arranging that any violence which might be done her should be the beginning of a trap for him. In short, she gave the appearance of being overcome by desire. But Herod had for a long while been far from friendly to Cleopatra, knowing how vicious she was to everyone, and at this time he had reason to think her particularly contemptible if it was through lust that she went so far; and if she was making such advances in order to trap him, he would have to hurt her before she could hurt him.

He therefore evaded her proposals, and took counsel with his friends whether he should kill her while he had her in his power. In this way, he said, he would rid of many evils all of those to whom she had already been vicious or was likely to be in the future. At the same time, he argued, this would be a boon to Antony, for not even to him would she show loyalty if some occasion or need should compel him to ask for it. But his friends prevented him from acting upon this plan. In the first place they pointed out that it was not worth his while to incur the very obvious danger of this serious step, and they also urgently begged him not to act impulsively. Antony, they said, would not tolerate such action even though one were to place its advantages before his very eyes. For one thing, his love would flame up the more fiercely if he thought that she had been taken from him by violence and treachery. And for another, no excuse could appear reasonable for making an attempt against a woman who held the greatest position of any living at that time. As for the benefit from it, if any such might be thought to exist, it would be viewed together with his reckless disregard of Antony's attitude. Such a course, it was not hard to see, would bring a host of unending evils upon his throne and his family.... By frightening him with such arguments and making plain to him the danger which would probably result from his attempt, they kept him from carrying it out.[29]

Herod's two main assertions, that Cleopatra had tried to seduce him and that his friends had with difficulty dissuaded him from killing her, are almost certainly both untrue. The principal aim of Herod, as of Cleopatra, was to remain on good terms with Antony, and he would not have retained Antony's confidence by killing the queen any more than she would have done so by seducing him.[30] Later on, however, when Cleopatra was dead, Herod sought to gain credit with her enemy Octavian by saying that, in the end, he had advised Antony to get rid of her. The seduction story is pure malevolence on the part of the king, appropriate to her later reputation as a whore. But both tales are principally interesting because of the lurid light they cast around this impossible relationship between Herod and Cleopatra; and above all because they reveal the detestation she aroused in those whose paths her ambitions had crossed. It was a hatred mixed with deep envy, because of her unique influence over Antony.

At all events, if there were hazards accompanying her remarkable visit to Herod, she survived them. 'Instead of having her murdered,' Josephus continues, 'he plied her with gifts and escorted her on the way to Egypt.' When she arrived there, she made ready to welcome Antony. It was the second time within three years that she had received him back from his eastern wars. This time, he returned as a victor. It was not yet the expected major victory over Parthia; that, he hoped, was still to come, and the success he had just gained in Armenia was only a preparatory step. Nevertheless, it was a very much happier home-coming than his return two years earlier. It also had a highly significant sequel at Alexandria.

10

Cleopatra Queen of Kings

Immediately after his return to Alexandria in the autumn of 34 BC, Antony staged a triumphal procession in the city. He sent his royal Armenian captives ahead of him through the streets, and he himself followed in a chariot to some central place, probably the great temple of Sarapis, where Cleopatra was awaiting him seated on a magnificent throne. The king of Armenia, shackled in chains of gold, refused, out of pride, to do obeisance to her. Yet although he remained under arrest, his life was spared, and the incident was not allowed to damp the rejoicings and banquets that followed, accompanied by free distributions of money and food.

The historian Velleius Paterculus, writing half a century later, correctly indicated the special religious character which Antony gave to the procession: 'He had given orders that he should be called the New Father Liber (Dionysus), and indeed in a procession at Alexandria he had personified Father Liber, his head bound with the ivy wreath, his person enveloped in the saffron robe of gold, holding in his hand the sacred wand, wearing the buskins, and riding in the Bacchic chariot.'[1] It was not, therefore, in his capacity as a Roman general that Antony made his triumphal entry into Alexandria. When he had first arrived there to join Cleopatra seven years earlier, he took great care to avoid displaying himself as a functionary of Rome, and now, once again, it was not as a Roman official that he paraded through the streets of Alexandria. His role, instead, was that of Dionysus, the greatest god of the Hellenistic world, the god of joy and liberation and salvation, and the god, moreover, who was the embodiment of victorious promenades throughout eastern lands. This was a thoroughly familiar concept not only to Antony but to the Alexandrians, for their monarchs had identified themselves with it completely. And now the idea was resuscitated in brilliant and spectacular fashion, at the capital of Cleopatra's revived Ptolemaic empire.

However, when news of these celebrations reached Rome, it aroused shocked comment. For one thing, the people of Rome did not like free distributions which went to the Alexandrians and not to themselves. But most of all, there was anger because Antony seemed to have conducted a Roman Triumph. Yet instead of staging it in Rome, and leading his procession, as was right and proper, to Roman Jupiter's sacred Capitoline temple, he had sacrilegiously held the ceremonies in a foreign city, with the express purpose of conferring greater glory upon his foreign concubine. The misrepresentation was understandable – but it remained a misrepresentation all the same, for this was not intended to be a Roman Triumph at all. If it had been, two writers who incorporated much virulent propaganda against Antony and Cleopatra, namely Livy and Velleius Paterculus, would hardly have failed to mention so damaging a point. Yet they seem not to have heard of it, and Velleius rightly appreciated that Antony instead invested the ceremonies with the religious, Dionysiac character which harmonized with his and Cleopatra's régimes.

*

What robes Cleopatra wore to receive the victorious Antony we do not know. But at another, even more sensational, ceremony a few days later she was dressed in a costume which identified her with the goddess Isis. The events that took place on this occasion are generally described as the Donations of Alexandria. A huge crowd of people assembled in the colonnaded Gymnasium of the city, one of the most splendid and ample buildings in the whole of the Mediterranean world and the very symbol of the Greek, Ptolemaic régime of Egypt – indeed the symbol of the entire Greek system of education, which Cicero and many other Romans so profoundly deplored[2] but which inspired Antony with phil-Hellenic enthusiasm.

There, in the Gymnasium, he and Cleopatra took their places high above the crowd, upon golden thrones set side by side on a platform shining with silver. It was surely not the first time that Cleopatra had worn the robes of Isis, but the identification was particularly noted upon this occasion.[3] And just as she was hailed as the new Isis–Aphrodite, portraits and statues displayed Antony as Osiris–Dionysus, and it was probably in this capacity that Cleopatra, at some time during these years, honoured him with a temple.[4]

At this ceremony of the Donations, there were four other thrones set at a lower level than those of Antony and Cleopatra. One of them was reserved for her thirteen-year-old son and royal colleague Ptolemy XV Caesar (Caesarion). On the other thrones were seated her three children by Antony, the six-year-old Alexander Helios and his twin sister

Cleopatra Selene, and Ptolemy Philadelphus who was only two. When everyone had assembled, Antony rose to his feet and delivered an address. What he proposed to say, he informed them, was in honour of the deified Julius Caesar. Then he announced the conferment of a whole series of titles, territories and overlordships upon Cleopatra and her children.

Nineteen and a half centuries later, the spectacular aspects of the scene stimulated the imagination of an outstanding Alexandrian poet, Constantine Cavafy.[5]

> An Alexandrian crowd collected
> to see the sons of Cleopatra,
> Caesarion and his little brothers
> Alexander and Ptolemy, who for the first
> time were brought to the Gymnasium,
> there to be crowned as kings
> amidst a splendid display of troops.....
> The Alexandrians knew perfectly well
> that all this was words and empty pomp.
> But the day was warm and exquisite,
> the sky clear and blue,
> the Gymnasium and Alexandria a triumph of art,
> the courtiers' apparel magnificent,
> Caesarion full of grace and beauty
> (son of Cleopatra, blood of the Lagidae!)
> and the Alexandrians ran to see the show
> and grew enthusiastic, and applauded
> in Greek, in Egyptian, and some in Hebrew,
> bewitched with the beautiful spectacle,
> though they knew perfectly well how worthless,
> what empty words, were these king-makings.

Yet Cavafy's implication that the whole proceedings were mere empty words and meaningless pomp is misleading. Granted that the atmosphere of Egypt has often lent itself to the weaving of insubstantial verbal fabrics, the Donations were the sketch of a serious design, and a design that possessed real merits. If there seemed to be an element of wishful thinking, it was because Antony had his eye fixed far ahead into the future.

The position envisaged for Alexander Helios illustrates his intentions. Attended by an Armenian bodyguard, and robed in Iranian costume, and wearing the ancient Persian monarchy's high royal cap – swathed in a white turban, and adorned with a peacock feather – the six-year-old boy was declared king of Armenia, and overlord of Media and all territory east of the Euphrates 'as far as India', meaning, particularly,

163

the Parthian empire. One aspect of his new dignity was immediately relevant. Since he was declared king of Armenia, not overlord, it was Antony's intention that he should forthwith succeed the Armenian king who was now a captive in Alexandria, and should supplant that monarch's son who had fled to the Parthians. Armenia, that is to say, was made into a Ptolemaic state. To be entitled overlord of Parthia had no immediate practical significance, for Parthia had not yet been conquered. But when Antony had acknowledged the paternity of Alexander Helios three years earlier he may already have destined the boy for the Parthian throne; and since then a possible alternative candidate, Monaeses, had made himself ineligible by treachery.

But Alexander Helios' new overlordship of Media created a precedent. For Media already possessed a king of its own and a king friendly to the Romans. Hitherto, since his desertion to the Roman side in the previous year, the Median king Artavasdes had presumably regarded himself as a monarch who was in alliance with Rome and more or less its dependant. The betrothal of Alexander Helios to his infant daughter had already conveyed a hint that Alexander, whose names so clearly destined him for an eastern role, would eventually succeed to the throne of Media as well as Parthia. Now, however, it appeared that Alexander Helios was *already* Artavasdes' overlord. This had no immediate application, because he was only six, and there is no evidence that he exercised his titular powers through a Regency Council. But it carried the future implication that the overlord of Media was not going to be a representative of the Roman state, but a boy who, for all his Roman paternity, was nevertheless a monarch of the Ptolemaic house.

*

Antony had now given more emphatic effect than ever to his idea that rule over the east was often better entrusted to easterners than to Romans. Moreover, this concept of Ptolemaic overlords was designed to cover an even wider geographical range, since he applied it to Asia Minor as well.[6] His two-year-old infant Ptolemy Philadelphus, decked out in the miniature costume of a Macedonian king, with purple cloak, diademed bonnet, Macedonian bootees, and a Macedonian bodyguard to match, was not only awarded the kingship of the Syrian territories which had recently been restored to the Ptolemaic realm, but was made the overlord of all the client kings of Asia Minor, westwards from the Euphrates right as far as the Hellespont, the modern Dardanelles.[7] These client monarchs included Antony's three key men, Polemo of Pontus, Amyntas of Galatia and Archelaus of Cappadocia. Once again, there were no immediate practical results, since Ptolemy was only two. But once again there was also the clear implication that these three

Asian monarchs, as well as the various minor princelings around their territories, were ultimately subject to Ptolemaic supremacy. The fact that the infant Ptolemy bore the name of his great ancestor Ptolemy II Philadelphus who had ruled over great possessions in Asia Minor was beginning to assume significance.

About the client principalities of northern Syria and, above all, Judaea, nothing was apparently said in these Donations. Here were complexities best left in the hands of the adjacent Roman province, and what remained of Herod's Judaea must not, in Antony's view, be subjected to the additional humiliation of Ptolemaic overlordship. But the new arrangements modified the status of the Syrian and Palestinian territories acquired by Cleopatra three years earlier. For now their titular rulership was transferred from herself and Caesarion to the same Ptolemy Philadelphus who had been made overlord of the dynasts in Asia Minor. That is to say, these regions remained Ptolemaic, but they were no longer (in name at least) possessions of Ptolemaic Egypt, but of another Ptolemaic kingdom of which this baby was the monarch. In the past, there had often been more than one Ptolemaic state in existence besides Egypt – and now, nominally at least, that situation had been revived.

*

At the same time Cleopatra's six-year-old daughter by Antony, Cleopatra Selene, was made queen of Cyrenaica, that is to say the eastern half of modern Libya, where it borders upon Egypt. Cleopatra's great-uncle Ptolemy Apion had bequeathed Cyrenaica to the Romans in 96 BC, and since 67 BC it had been a joint Roman province with the island of Crete. When Cyrenaica was transferred to Cleopatra Selene, Crete, apart from certain free cities,[8] passed into her hands as well – thus returning to its Ptolemaic status of earlier centuries. Antony had not shrunk from alienating Roman territory three years before, but on this occasion in 34 he earned Octavian's specific disapproval.[9] The new administrative situation is revealed by bronze coinages which were now issued in both parts of the former province by two Romans, Lucius Lollius and then Marcus Licinius Crassus,[10] employing Latin inscriptions in Crete and Greek in Cyrenaica. It is clear, from the appearance of their names on the coins, that the government, or at least the military command, in both territories remained in Roman hands, yet the absence of any Roman title of office – as would have been expected if they had been normal Roman governors – demonstrates their acceptance of the new Ptolemaic sovereignty. The same tactful recognition is indicated by the crocodile which Crassus' coins depict, both in Crete and at a Cyrenaic city – significantly it is Ptolemy III's foundation of

Ptolemais (Barca) [11] – since the crocodile was understood by everyone to be the national emblem of Egypt and the Ptolemies. [12]

In Cyrenaica and Crete, then, there was a curious compromise combining the continued presence of Roman officials with the declaration of Cleopatra Selene's new régime. [13] Whether the same sort of arrangements were installed in the other countries officially transferred to the Ptolemies, we cannot say, nor whether Antony intended that the curious dual system in Cyrenaica and Crete should continue. Perhaps he envisaged the ultimate development of a more or less autonomous kingdom, towards which this was a transitional stage. If so, it was an indispensable stage, because the western approaches of Antony's dominions, and of Egypt, had to be guarded against possible hostile action by Octavian. For five years past, Antony had stationed a naval squadron at Zacynthus, under the command of Gaius Sosius or his deputies, to protect the Ionian Sea against possible incursions from Italy. And now Lollius and Crassus were watching the seas between Greece and north Africa for the same reason.

*

The status of Ptolemy xv Caesar (Caesarion), as redefined by the Donations, was different from that of his half-brothers and half-sister. For while they were Kings and a Queen, he was pronounced King of Kings. [14] The similarity of this title to that of his mother, who at the same time was declared Queen of Kings, was a reminder that they were colleagues in the central Ptolemaic monarchy. But that monarchy had now entered into a new and more glorious phase, and these designations, originally the prerogatives of the ancient throne of Persia, [15] were meant to indicate that their possessors were raised above the other, newly-appointed Ptolemaic monarchs. [16] Just as Alexander Helios and Ptolemy Philadelphus were to be overlords of the dependent kingdoms in the areas under their sway, so they, in turn, were subject to the overlordship of the principal Egyptian Ptolemaic realm, presided over by Cleopatra and Ptolemy xv Caesar.

However, although the two of them were colleagues in this supreme imperial monarchy, they were not equal colleagues. Cleopatra, on her Alexandrian coins, still omitted to portray her thirteen-year-old fellow-monarch, and on the occasion of the Donations, King of Kings though Caesarion was, Antony officially indicated that he was her *junior* partner by placing his throne at a lower level than those of Cleopatra and himself.

Besides, Cleopatra had a role even more important than Queen of Kings. For Antony in his preliminary statement, before announcing the territorial awards, had proclaimed a further doctrine as well. In addition to stating that Caesarion was Caesar's son, he also declared that the boy was his *legitimate* son – in other words that Cleopatra had been Caesar's wife.[17] It is uncertain what subterfuges the lawyers employed in order to achieve this implausible retrospective claim, which ignored the existence of Caesar's last wife Calpurnia. Suggestions that they were thinking of a form of bigamous marriage seem hardly applicable, since the Ptolemies were in full agreement with the general Greek objection to bigamy. Nor does it seem likely that any effort was made to suggest that Caesar's marriage to Calpurnia had been broken or interrupted during his sojourn in non-Roman Egypt, or invalidated by his presence there.

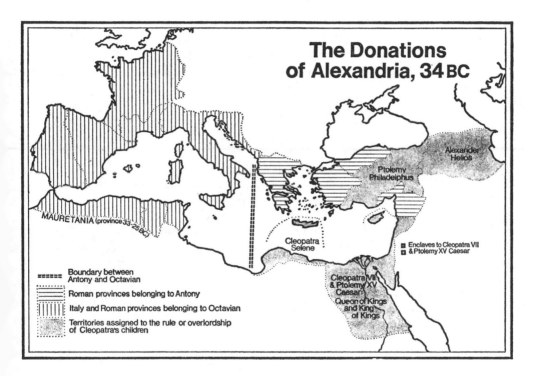

The Donations of Alexandria, 34 BC

Probably the background of Antony's assertion should be related to the divine status both of Caesar and of Cleopatra. The union of Caesar and Cleopatra seemed, in retrospect, a Sacred Marriage between gods, like Cleopatra's present union with Antony. That was the sense, the only sense, in which Caesarion could be described as the legitimate offspring of Caesar. But to say even so much was an unprecedentedly strong move against Octavian, since it suggested that his claim to be Caesar's heir was a mere usurpation. Those eager for peace between the

Triumvirs might point out to him reassuringly that Antony's assertions were only intended for the east. But he was unlikely to regard this as an adequate explanation.

*

The New Order pronounced by Antony had enlarged the scale of Cleopatra's imperial ambitions. Evidence is provided by a large silver coin inscribed in Greek. On one side is the head of Antony, labelled as 'Imperator and Triumvir' (*Antonios Autokrator Trion Andron*). On the other side is a novel and grandiose portrait of Cleopatra (see p. 175) with the inscription 'The Queen Cleopatra, the Younger Goddess' (*Basilissa Cleopatra, Thea Neotera*).[18] The finds of these coins, like their weight and style, prove that they were minted not in Egypt but in Syria, and, more precisely, in the Roman provincial capital of Antioch,[19] which served Antony and Cleopatra as their summer residence. No exact dating is possible, but the latest limit is 33 BC, since they are found over-struck by Parthian coins of that year.[20] An earlier date is unlikely, since all other numismatic descriptions of Cleopatra as *Thea Neotera* belong to a late phase of her reign. Probably, therefore, these impressive pieces were issued to celebrate the Donations of 34; and they constitute a major historical document.

Cleopatra had long been called *Thea*, goddess, just as her father had recalled the hereditary divine pretensions of their line by assuming the official title *Theos*. The term *Neoteros–Neotera* is more unusual. Since it means 'younger', it implies the existence of an 'elder', *Presbytera*.[21] Thus there was a goddess Neotera, who is identifiable with an Egyptian deity Nephthys and was known as *Neotera* because she was born one day after her sister Isis.[22] Now, the reason why Cleopatra is 'the younger Thea' is because there had been an older Ptolemaic queen of that name in Syria before her, namely Cleopatra Thea,[23] the daughter of Ptolemy VI Philometor; residing in Seleucid Syria for twenty-nine years, she had married three successive Seleucid monarchs, and she died in 121 BC.

Contemporaries viewing these coins of Antony and Cleopatra VII would immediately have recognized the allusion to Cleopatra Thea, because she was a famous figure in the history of Syria. She had minted there with her own portrait, and was the only Ptolemaic or Seleucid queen to have called herself Thea on her coins. Moreover, the coins in question had deliberately called attention to a remarkable amalgamation of the Ptolemaic and Seleucid royal houses and traditions: they were Seleucid issues, on Seleucid territory, and yet at the same time they testified to the queen's Ptolemaic origins by displaying the double cornucopiae which were the emblem of Ptolemaic Egypt. And now, a century later, the younger Cleopatra Thea, Cleopatra VII, was reviving these pretensions.

The inclusion of two great Seleucid cities, Apamea and Damascus, in Cleopatra's royal southward progress during the previous year had shown how far she was advancing beyond her earlier ambition of restoring the ancient empire of the Ptolemies. Now, as Queen of Kings and overlord of vast eastern territories, she considered herself the heir not only to the Ptolemaic realm at its greatest extent, but also to the empire of the Seleucids. She had taken over the role of the older Cleopatra Thea as amalgamator of the two greatest Hellenistic kingdoms. Indeed, certain specimens of these Antioch coins depict, behind Antony's portrait, the horse's head which was a well-known Seleucid badge.[24]

The inscriptions of another and even more remarkable coin are in Latin:

ANTONI, ARMENIA DEVICTA (Antonius, after the Conquest of Armenia): bare head of Antony to the right. Behind it, the royal tiara of Armenia.

CLEOPATRAE REGINAE REGVM FILIORVM REGVM (To Cleopatra, Queen of Kings /and/ of her Sons who are Kings): diademed, draped bust of Cleopatra to the right, with jewels in her hair. In front of the portrait, the prow of a ship.[25]

This is an official coin of Antony, a coin of the Roman series belonging to the standard Roman silver denomination, the *denarius*. The place of its mintage is uncertain – it may once again have been Antioch – but this and other *denarii* of Antony were issued in huge numbers and circulated very widely. Once again the issue seems to belong to the occasion of the Alexandrian triumphal procession and the Donations of 34 BC. It might perhaps be just a little later,[26] but the explicit reference to the conquest of Armenia, by inscription and symbol alike, alludes to Antony's victorious campaign of 34. The ship's prow in front of Cleopatra's head celebrates the revived Ptolemaic fleet which was her particular contribution to Antony's system.

But the truly extraordinary feature of the mintage lies in the appearance of Cleopatra's head and name on this standard, Latin-inscribed denomination, issued by a representative of the Roman state for widespread circulation in the Roman world. Only two women, Antony's successive wives Fulvia and Octavia, had ever been portrayed on this sort of official Roman coinage before. Both had been Romans and even so neither had actually been mentioned by name. Yet here we have the unprecedented spectacle of a foreign woman portrayed on a Roman official issue, and not only portrayed but named, and credited with her regal, non-Roman, designations.

The Romans meant people to look at the constantly changing

designs on their coins, and people did. The vast gallery of Roman coin-types throughout the centuries remains for the most part traditional,[27] repeating well-worn themes with minor variations and embroideries. Sometimes we come upon small novelties, representing, often enough, deliberate nuances and innovations of policy. Just very occasionally we may be confronted by a major surprise which stands out strikingly from the conventional character of the series. Here is a surprise of just this kind. Encountering it, the numismatist experiences, in a small degree, the shock the average conservative Roman of the day must have felt when he first saw these coins. For Antony was now announcing the outlines of his proposed system to the Roman world, and here was one of its least familiar and least Roman manifestations. Incidentally, Cleopatra's title here is a little more explicit than writers about the Donations had given us to understand. For she is not only Queen of Kings, but Queen of her Sons who are Kings. Her overlordship of the other Ptolemaic kingdoms, including her superiority to her son and colleague, the King of Kings Ptolemy Caesar, is specified in definite terms.

*

At the apex of the structure, however, towered Antony himself. To Greeks and orientals, he was the incarnation of the god Dionysus–Osiris. To Romans, he was still one of the Triumvirs who had been officially entrusted with the reconstitution of the Roman state, and, unlike his colleague Octavian, who had recently been experimenting with a quasi-imperial use of 'Imperatur',[28] he generally continued to proclaim his triumviral title on his coinage. It was no doubt under this authority that he announced the Donations of Alexandria. If he was Greek god and partner of a Greek goddess and queen, that was for the benefit of the Greek east. On the administrative and military planes he was still Rome's Triumvir, and supreme commander of Rome's armies in the east.

This Roman character of Antony is illustrated by yet another monetary issue, which can again be approximately dated to 34 BC. It is a gold piece (*aureus*) which displays and names not only Antony but also his elder son by his late wife Fulvia, Marcus Antonius junior, commonly known as Antyllus, who was now nine or ten years old.[29] This coin shows unmistakably that, although Antyllus had no place in the Donations, Antony did not forget that he was his eldest son, and his principal personal heir in Roman law. Technically speaking, this was a purely private arrangement, since there could be no question of official powers being inherited. But this sort of distinction had already become heavily blurred ten years earlier, when Octavian had exploited his appointment as Caesar's personal heir so as to inherit as much of Caesar's official status and glory as he could. This coinage on which Antony has placed Antyllus' head shows that a similar attempt at deliberate confusion is once again at work.

Anecdotes circulating in Alexandria illustrated the deference that was being paid to the boy.[30] For Antony, like Octavian, had achieved a status anticipating the Roman emperors of the future – whose imperial positions were not supposed to be heritable in law, yet who also placed the heads of their sons upon their coins. And here is this tradition already being launched. Caesarion, it should be noted, received no such coin-portrait, since he was not destined for any such Roman role. In spite, therefore, of the *denarius* which depicted her as Antony's partner and recounted her new titles in Latin, the child he selects for portrayal is his own oldest son, a son by a Roman mother. Here, then, was a second reservation limiting his willingness to play Cleopatra's game. The first had been his refusal to dismiss Herod. And now came this quite emphatic indication that his son by Fulvia and not by herself was his Roman heir.

It was still Antony who made the decisions. As the representative of the Roman state, he was ruler over the eastern provinces, and patron of the monarchies upon the empire's fringes. Even the gloriously revived Ptolemaic empire still remained dependent upon Antony. And dependent upon him, too, in the last resort, despite all the influence she exerted, was Cleopatra.

*

It is customary to see the Donations of Alexandria as a measure which doomed Antony and Cleopatra to ultimate failure and defeat, and made the victory of the more occidentally-minded Octavian inevitable. Indeed, everything that happened to Antony and Cleopatra during these years can be interpreted in the same light. But to do so is to avail oneself too much of historical hindsight. For a student of Octavian's affairs during this period could equally point to various factors which militated against his ultimate success. His numerous troops were unruly, and needed funds which he was unable to provide. And although he was based upon Italy, he could by no means rely on any appreciable majority in the Senate, where opinion still remained sharply divided. It is true that the Donations, when they became known in Rome, would unmistakably bring Antony disfavour in the Senate, and would handicap his position generally in the west. But he cannot have been unaware of this, and must have concluded that long-term benefits outweighed such disadvantages. Rather than regard these Donations, or other developments of the period, as clouds gathering over the heads of Antony and Cleopatra which would ultimately burst with fatal results, it is better to take the view that up to 34 BC, and for at least another two years thereafter, nothing adverse had befallen them which could not be undone on a single day by the right general or admiral – if such a man could be found.

Nevertheless, the Donations had general, widespread, psychological repercussions which were disquieting to Romans, and may not have been fully anticipated or grasped by Antony himself. Throughout the east, for more than a century past, there had been a great stirring of underground prophetic literature. Its main theme was that the east would eventually prevail, that a great saviour would come out of its territories, and that Rome's end would then be at hand. The new position and renown of Cleopatra meant that this prophetic versification now tended to focus upon herself. She, it seemed, was to be the saviour queen destined to revive the glories of the Hellenic and partially Hellenized east. Already, before 100 BC, a composition known as the Prophecy of the Mad Praetor had foretold that a mighty army would come out of Asia from the Rising of the Sun, for the enslavement of Rome.[31] Then, in the following century, an eastern Greek or Hellenized oriental with the pseudonym Hystaspes, supposedly a Persian sage, once again prophesied the violent passage of power from Rome to a saviour from the east. The Romans forbade the reading of the document on pain of death.[32]

The same subversive trend was strongly apparent in that strange, extensive corpus of Greek prophetic literature which is grouped together under the name of the Sibylline Books. The Roman authorities had long cherished their own selected and doctored versions, of which they produced a new edition in 83 BC. But leaving aside such obviously expurgated collections, the tone of these 'oracles' was anti-Roman.[33] From their places of origin in Syria and many other regions of the east they circulated far and wide, and out of their portentous and cryptic phraseology emerged the comforting message that Roman rule would not last for ever.

Some of these Sibylline Oracles date back to the time when Hellenistic monarchs such as the Seleucid Antiochus IV Epiphanes (175–164 BC) were raising hopes of the downfall of Rome. Other passages speak of the miseries of Greece after it had come under Roman domination (146 BC), or eulogize Rome's enemy Mithridates VI of Pontus (d. 63) in Messianic terms,[34] or gloat over the civil bloodshed in the imperial city. For the Romans, it was insisted, had come to an end of their destiny: a warrior king was not far off, and his destroying sword would prepare the way for the Golden Age.[35]

There are also a number of riddling references to a salvation-bringing Woman, and this Woman is Cleopatra.[36] When her power is at its height, the anonymous seers assure us, then indeed the Day of Judgement and the glorious Millennium will be at hand.

> All the confronting stars fall into the sea,
> many new stars arise in turn, and the star
> of radiance named by men the Comet, a sign
> of emerging troubles, of war and of disaster.
> But when the Tenth Generation goes down to Hades,
> there comes a Woman's great power. By her, God will
> multiply fine things, when royal dignity
> and crown she takes. A whole year then will be
>   prospering eternity.
> Common for all then is life, and all property.
> Earth will be free for all, unwalled, unfenced,
> and bringing forth more fruits than ever before
> it will yield springs of sweet wine, white milk,
>   and honey.... [37]

Moreover, these events will specifically occur at a time when Rome is oppressed by a triumvirate: so that once again the great queen who will come as a rescuer cannot be anyone else but Cleopatra.

> And while Rome will be hesitating over
> the Conquest of Egypt, then the mighty Queen
> of the Immortal King will appear among men....
> Three will subdue Rome with a pitiful fate.
> All men will perish in their private homes
> when a cataract of fire pours down from heaven.
> The Holy Lord, wielding the whole earth's sceptre,
> will come to rule for all the ages to come. [38]

The Woman is sometimes called the Widow, because Cleopatra, after the removal of her brother–husband Ptolemy XIV in 44 BC, had asserted her supremacy by breaking with the Ptolemaic custom of the wedded royal pair.

> And then the whole wide world under a Woman's hand
> ruled and obeying everywhere shall stand,
> and when the Widow shall queen the whole wide world
> and into the sea divine have the gold and silver hurled
> and into the water have hurled the bronzen swords of men,
> those creatures of a day, all the world's elements then
> shall be widowed lorn, and God, who aloft in *aither* is found,
> around shall roll the heavens as a book is turned around.
> And on earth divine and the sea the multitudinous sky
> shall fall, while cataracts the wild fire from on high,
> ceaseless. The earth he'll burn, the sea he'll burn with his
>   curse,

the days and the starry heavens and the whole universe
he'll break up into One, into Purity transmute.
The stars that laugh together as they bring us light shall be
  mute.
There'll be no more night or dawn or the many darts of care,
no spring or summer or winter or autumn anywhere.
Then the Judgement of Mighty God shall come in the midst
  of it all,
in the mighty age to be, when all these things befall.[39]

But then 'you shall no longer be the Widow, you shall mate with the Lion', who is Antony – for the lion was the symbol of his identification with Heracles.[40] This passage, it is true, tells of the past (like many oracles which pretend to predict the future), since it forms part of a story of Cleopatra's fall. However, there is also a long oracle which was evidently written at the height of Cleopatra's power, and casts a vivid light on the ideas that were circulating in her name.

Vast is the wealth of the tribute that Asia has yielded to Rome –
Three times over shall Rome pay it back, to purge her murderous
  pride;
And for every man from Asia's land who's served an Italian lord,
Twenty Italians there shall slave, and thousands on thousands be
  damned.
O delicate gilded voluptuous maiden, O Rome of the Latin race,
Drunk with your hundred lovers' embraces, a slave-bride yet
  you'll be,
Your finery gone and your soft hair shorn by a mistress' stern
  command;
And she in whose hands lies justice and doom will hurl you from
  heaven to earth.
But then she will raise you again from earth to the heights of
  heaven above.
And peace all gentle will come upon Asia, and Europe happy will
  be,
And the air shall grant long life and strength, and food and
  nourishment too,
And the birds and the beasts of the earth shall increase and never
  know storm or hail.
O blessed the man and blessed the woman who live to set eyes on
  that time,
Like peasants who've not seen a palace before, struck dumb at the
  riches displayed.
For one true order and one true law shall descend from the sphere
  of the stars,
And with them shall come to abide among mortals the thing they
  desire above all:

Concord and harmony, trustful and sane, and brotherly love
   between men.
Far from the world shall poverty flee; constraint and chaos shall go;
And envy and blame, with anger and folly, and murderous
   quarrels and strife,
And theft and destruction, and all sort of evil, shall vanish away
   at that day.[41]

Drunken Rome's hair, shorn by the dominant Woman, may be the territory Cleopatra has gained by the Donations. And yet 'this prophecy is unique,' rightly comments John Carter, 'in that it transcends the common motif of revenge and retribution. It promises to the humbled bully, in the end, his share of the blessings and lyrical peace of the world beyond the rainbow that is the prophet's vision.'[42] Here we are given a glimpse of what the Donations of Alexandria seemed to offer to the eastern millions who felt bruised by Rome's rule; and we see also a constructive, generous interpretation of that Concord which was on everyone's lips – promising the true partnership between Romans and Greeks which was conspicuously absent from the ideas of Rome and Octavian, but might have emerged from the New Order of Antony and Cleopatra.

*

The queen's appearance at this time, or at least the image of herself that she wished to impress upon the Levantine populations, is imposingly displayed on the large Greek-inscribed silver piece which was issued at Antioch on the occasion of the Donations. This portrait is strikingly different from her representations on previous issues. The simpler, Hellenistic style has been largely abandoned, and in its place we see an imposing oriental empress, sumptuously arrayed in a fashion anticipating a great series of Syrian portrait busts (from Palmyra) which blend the traditions of east and west. Grace and simplicity have given way to hieratic majesty. The hooked nose the queen inherited from her father has become more strongly pronounced, and in general her face has assumed a formidable and almost menacing look. Instead of the somewhat conventional waves, and large chignon, that had appeared on earlier Alexandrian coins, she now adopted, at least for the purpose of this portrait, an elaborate cluster of curls surrounding her face and descending to a much smaller knot at the nape of her neck. The traditional Greek drapery of the earlier issues has been replaced by a sumptuous robe covered with pearls. The whole front of her royal mantle is embroidered and encrusted with them. She also has pearls in her hair, and the jewels of her necklace and ear-rings may be pearls as well. They were the height of fashion at this time, and exceedingly expensive. Though Egypt produced many precious stones, it imported pearls from the Indian Ocean; Lucan describes Cleopatra attending a banquet loaded with these 'spoils of the Red Sea',[43] and wealthy Romans, too, had formed a similar taste after Pompey's victories over Mithridates. However, like many other costly products of various lands, most of the largest number of pearls found their way to Alexandria and the Ptolemies, and it was not until the Romans had subsequently annexed Egypt that they were able to acquire them more cheaply.[44]

One of the many stories about Cleopatra's extravagance relates to pearls. It was said that she took a specimen of unequalled size and value from one of her ear-rings and dissolved it in vinegar, which she then proceeded to drink so as to show how little the waste of such a valuable object mattered to her.[45] The tale is told of others besides Cleopatra – and scientifically-minded investigators have often demonstrated that it cannot be true, since vinegar does not dissolve pearls. But it is an example of the sort of myth which gathered around her glamorous way of living.

Alexandria was, of course, famous for its luxury – or notorious, as puritanical and politically hostile Romans preferred to say. Its trade was largely a luxury trade, and the greatest luxuries of all were obviously to be found at the royal palace. For one thing, the palace of Cleopatra must have been a remarkably fragrant place, for subtly blended scented essences, perfumes and ointments, which had already been well known in Pharaonic Egypt, were an Alexandrian speciality. The whole perfumery business was one of the state monopolies of the Ptolemies.[46] Cleopatra had already made good use of this expert knowledge when she sailed up the river to Tarsus to meet Antony in 41 BC, 'and all the while an indescribably rich perfume, exhaled from innumerable censers, was wafted from the vessel to the river-banks.' The palace must also have been noteworthy for a special Egyptian kind of mosaic, depicting rich and lively Nile landscapes.[47] There was probably exotic furniture, too, for when Cleopatra's uncle was evicted from Cyprus in 58 BC his extravagances, plundered by Cato for the Roman treasury, included a Babylonian dining-room suite.[48] In the later age of Nero, when similar lavish tastes again came into fashion, the poet Lucan imagines the sort of dinner-party Cleopatra liked to give:[49]

> Great was the bustle as Cleopatra displayed
> a magnificence not yet adopted in Roman ways.
> A temple-size hall, too costly for an age
> corrupted with pleasure-spending. The ceiling-panels
> blazed wealth, the rafters hidden in thick gold.
> Marble the walls shone, not with mere veneers,
> agate in its own right, not just decoration,

and porphyry; on alabaster they trod
throughout the hall. Meroe's ebony
replaced mere wood, not a thin cover of doors;
structural, not for a show. The porch was ivory;
Indian tortoise-shell, hand-coloured, stood,
inlaying doors, with emeralds in its spots.
Gem-gleamed the couches, jasper-tawny cups
loaded the tables, the sofas bright with hues
of coverlets, mostly steeped in Tyrian dye
of many soakings, others richly embroidered
with gold or fiery scarlet in the way
Egyptians mingle leashes in the web.

The hostile gossip of Cleopatra's political enemies at Rome has kept us well supplied with stories about her lavish way of life. Moreover, Plutarch's grandfather Lamprias had heard many tales of this kind from his friend Philotas, who was a student at Alexandria's famous medical school in the days of Antony and Cleopatra, while at the same time acting as personal doctor to Antony's son Antyllus. From this source comes a behind-the-scenes glimpse of the dining arrangements which Lucan had so fancifully described.[50]

Philotas, a physician who lived at Amphissa, used to tell my grandfather that he was studying his profession in Alexandria at this time, and that, having made the acquaintance of one of the royal cooks, he was persuaded, as was natural enough in a young man, to come and see the lavish preparations which were made for a royal dinner. He was introduced into the kitchens of the palace, and, after he had seen the enormous abundance of provisions and watched eight wild boars being roasted, he expressed his astonishment at the size of the company for which this vast hospitality was intended. The cook laughed aloud and explained that this was not a large party, only about a dozen people, but that everything must be cooked and served to perfection, and that the whole effect could be ruined by a moment's delay. It might happen that Antony could call for the meal as soon as the guests had arrived, or a little later he might postpone it and call for a cup of wine, or become absorbed in some conversation. 'So we never prepare one supper', he explained, 'but a whole number of them, as we never know the exact moment when they will be sent for.'

Although the table-ware which Cleopatra personally preferred was a bright, gay pottery from Rhosus (Arsuz) not far from Antioch,[51] her table and court were likely to seem extravagant by Greek or Roman standards. We hear of the orgies she and Antony attended in the famous pleasure resorts of Canopus and Taposiris Magna outside Alexandria.[52] Plutarch's story that they founded a dining-club of Inimitables[53] is confirmed by an inscription of 34 BC, in which the God and Benefactor Antony is hailed as the *Great Inimitable*.[54] The inscription is dedicated by a man who calls himself Parasitos, which is a joking, self-deprecatory term for a cadger at Antony's table, but also contains an implicit reference to the worship of Heracles,[55] with whom Antony liked to identify himself. At one of the parties he and Cleopatra gave, a leading Roman friend of theirs, Plancus, helped to amuse the hosts and guests by amateur theatricals: 'At a banquet he played the role of Glaucus the sea-god, performing a dance in which his naked body was painted blue and his head encircled with reeds, while he wore a fish's tail and crawled upon his knees.'[56] It does not sound the very height of sophisticated debauchery, but graver Romans were deeply shocked that a Roman consul and general should degrade himself in such a fashion.

There was a widespread belief in Rome that Egypt was a country where heavy drinking went on[57] (cabbages were favoured there as a prophylactic against hangovers), and it was thought to be particularly rife at the banquets of Antony and Cleopatra. Horace refers to his or her brain – the context does not make it quite clear which of them he is speaking about[58] – oozing with cheap local wine, and the geographer Strabo declares that Egypt under their régime was soused in a drunken stupor.[59] Stories about Antony's drinking had already been given wide circulation in Cicero's *Philippics* delivered shortly after Caesar's death; but it was also particularly emphasized that Cleopatra drank too much.[60] This may, however, in part at least, have been due to a misunderstanding of a ring in her possession which was inscribed with the word Drunkenness (Methe); in fact this referred to a mystical drunkenness, the philosophical 'mother of virtue', and the stone it was engraved upon was an amethyst, the symbol of sobriety. The device had originated with the 'drunkenness without wine' of the Maenads who were the devotees of Dionysus,[61] and no doubt Cleopatra, in the manner of great Ptolemaic queens before her, was an initiate of this god, of whom both her father and Antony had been declared the Manifest Incarnations.

Cleopatra's enemies also developed the idea that she was a harlot.[62] This is what Herod had intended to suggest in his account of their meeting during the previous year, and the same sort of abuse was subsequently given official currency in the comments of Octavian's historians and poets. Following them, Dante, too, saw her as lascivious and insatiable, and placed her in the second circle of Hell in the company of the lecherous Semiramis and Dido, as well as Helen of Troy to whom poets such as Lucan had already compared her. Such an interpretation came easily to Romans who regarded sensuality as typically Greek, and it seemed readily applicable to a Greek woman who had successively acquired the two most eminent Romans of their day as lovers.

178

Yet, except on the very uncertain assumption that the father of Caesarion was some person unknown, there is no evidence that she ever took any lovers besides Caesar and Antony, and her sexual reputation is based entirely on her liaisons with them. As for Antony, he obviously enjoyed sex, and indeed the man who calls him the Great Inimitable also refers to him as 'Aphrodisios'. This was a term which could refer to his devotion to the goddess Aphrodite, with whom Cleopatra was identified; but it could also mean 'skilled at lovemaking' – a talent of which Antony boasted, as part of his resemblance to Heracles. There was also a somewhat lascivious atmosphere around the court. A man called Chelidon described himself as Antony and Cleopatra's *cinaedus*,[63] which in this context (as in relation to Cleopatra's father) may mean 'performer of improper dances'. Antony also had a taste for sexy talk and jokes, and Cleopatra, according to Plutarch, played up to this.[64]

Who loved the other more, Cleopatra or Antony? Presumably they both felt a measure of love, though doubts have often been expressed about her feelings for him, or indeed her capacity to feel at all. Romans who, for moral or political reasons, disapproved of the liaison declared that Antony was ruined by his infatuation for Cleopatra,[65] and insisted that when he wasted valuable time, in several critical years, this was because she had lured him into a state of inertia. This story partly came about because inertia was regarded as a typical Egyptian vice.[66] But it does not seem to have been one of Cleopatra's faults, and even if she contributed to his dilatory habits by entertaining him so well, she was determined that he should make a success of his public activities. In this context one of Plutarch's stories, in spite of its characteristically anecdotal setting, contains a large element of symbolic truth:[67]

The Alexandrians had a weakness for his buffoonery, and enjoyed taking part in these amusements in their elegant and cultivated way. They liked him personally, and used to say that Antony put on his tragic mask for the Romans, but kept the comic one for them.

Now it would be a great waste of time for me to describe all the details of Antony's childish amusements, but a single instance may serve as an illustration. One day he went out fishing, had no luck with his line, and was all the more enraged because Cleopatra happened to be present. So he ordered some fishermen to dive down and secretly fasten on to his hook a number of fish they had already caught. Then he proceeded to pull up his line two or three times, but the queen discovered the trick. She pretended to admire his success, but then told her friends what had happened and invited them to come and watch the next day. A large party got into the fishing boats, and when Antony had let down his line, Cleopatra ordered one of her own servants to swim immediately to his hook and fix on to it a salted fish from the Black Sea. Antony, believing that he had made a catch, pulled up his line, whereupon the whole company burst out laughing, as was natural, and Cleopatra told him:

'Imperator, you had better give up your rod to us poor rulers of Pharos and Canopus. Your sport is to hunt cities and kingdoms and continents.'

*

The Alexandrian court which amused itself with episodes of the kind was changing. In addition to the Greeks and Greco-Egyptians who were its traditional, picturesquely adorned habitués, it now contained a throng of eminent Romans. On this subject, our information is sparse, because after the deaths of Antony and Cleopatra the survivors of this circle, and their relatives, were eager to forget the whole phase. But the distinguished Romans who occupied governorships and other high posts in Antony's provinces, and who served as senior officers in his army, obviously spent some time, not only at his summer capital of Antioch, but also at his winter capital of Alexandria. In Rome twelve years earlier, Cleopatra had been surrounded by far more numerous admirers than Cicero's sour comments suggest. And now in Alexandria most of the leading Romans in Antony's employment must have been glad to gain her favour – men like Dellius, who had arranged her historic meeting with Antony at Tarsus, and Plancus, who not only painted himself blue to amuse her and her guests but flattered her, so it was said, more shamefully than anyone else, with a lack of self-respect unworthy even of a slave.[68] And her capacity as a ruler impressed Antony's principal general, Canidius Crassus.

Of Cleopatra's own political advisers during these years we are almost totally ignorant. For the first years of her reign the names of Egyptian prime ministers and other state officials are recorded. But by now the ancient historians had shifted their spotlight entirely from the country's internal affairs to the romantic melodrama of the lovers. Nor, as it happens, are papyri any help in filling the gap. All we have to go on is a scornful statement by Octavian, made two years later, that those mainly responsible for the conduct of Egyptian affairs were Mardion the eunuch, a certain Pothinus, Cleopatra's hairdresser Iras, and Charmion, her lady-in-waiting. In the earlier part of the reign the chairman of the Regency Council and prime minister had been called Pothinus; Caesar killed him in 48 BC. Of this second Pothinus of the later 30s BC, we know nothing, but he, too, may have been one of the annually elected prime ministers,[69] and Mardion, who has pride of place in Octavian's list, was probably another. One of her last ministers with financial duties was a man named Seleucus,[70] but the post he occupied is not clear. Another important figure at court was Alexas of Syrian Laodicea, who is credited with greater influence over Antony than any of the other

Greeks or Hellenized easterners of his entourage. He had played a decisive part in luring Antony back to Cleopatra from Octavia.[71] Alexas had been introduced to Antony by Timagenes, who later acquired the reputation of holding virulent anti-Roman views,[72] but was also a learned and famous rhetorician and historian.

The royal palace was devoted to culture as well as business and amusement, as befitted the determined Hellenism of Antony and the erudite tradition of Cleopatra's Alexandria. Antony, dressed in the costume of a Greek official,[73] 'went out to the temples, the schools, and the discussions of the learned, spending his time with Greeks'.[74] About Cleopatra, too, a memorable phrase was used: *that she derived a positively sensuous pleasure from literature.*[75] Philosophy, in particular, absorbed her attention so seriously that some later, unknown, author on the subject assigned her the leading role in a fictitious 'Dialogue between Cleopatra and the philosophers'.[76] Virtually nothing of the Greek philosophy of her own time has survived. But we are able to identify among her courtiers a leading practitioner of the subject named Philostratus, who claimed to be a disciple of the Platonic Academy and had made himself very rich as a skilful extemporaneous orator. Another distinguished figure at her palace, where he tutored her children, was the philosopher and historian Nicolaus of Damascus, whose writings provide our best information about Cleopatra's relations with Herod. Alexandria also continued to boast a famous medical school, not to speak of the world's earliest health service and national medical assistance.[77] Alexandrian doctors of the time included Cleopatra's personal medical adviser Olympus, Athenagoras who presided over an elaborate organization for preserving mummies,[78] and a physician known as Dioscurides the Freckled (Phacas). His voluminous writings included a pioneer treatise on bubonic plague, a disease which may have broken out as a result of the famines of Cleopatra's reign in 48 or 42 BC.[79]

She and Antony also took an interest in the visual arts, of which the Alexandrians had always been important Hellenistic exponents. But to advise in this field Antony imported a Greek from elsewhere, arranging that the sculptor and engraver Gaius Avianius Evander, who had acquired a high reputation at Rome,[80] should be brought from Athens to Alexandria. Information is fragmentary, but Alexandria was still a cultural centre without equal in the Mediterranean world, and the court was unlikely to fall short of traditional achievements and standards.

Part Four

Cleopatra against Rome

11

Cleopatra Declared Rome's Enemy

Antony's increasingly close association with Cleopatra was now harming his position at Rome. In about November 34 BC Octavian, returning from a second laborious, successful Illyrian campaign, learnt about Antony's triumphal procession at Alexandria and the Donations in favour of Cleopatra and her children. When news of Antony's catastrophic expedition two years earlier had reached Rome, every effort was made to be complimentary. But this further disquieting news of the huge territories handed over to Cleopatra's dynasty elicited no such polite response. At first it was received in stony silence. But soon afterwards Octavian, entering upon the consulship on 1 January 33 BC, criticized Antony publicly for the first time. Antony sent him two replies. One was official, and we are not told its contents. But from the other, a private letter, a revealing fragment has been preserved by the biographer Suetonius:

> What's come over you? Is it because I go to bed with the queen? But she isn't my wife, is she (*uxor mea est*). And it isn't as if it's something new, is it? Haven't I been doing it for nine years now? And what about you, is Livia the only woman you go to bed with? I congratulate you, if at the time you read this letter you haven't also had Tertulla or Terentilla or Rufilla or Salvia Titisenia or the whole lot of them. Does it really matter where you get a stand – or who the woman is?[1]

This reference to a wide selection of Octavian's probable mistresses must have been embarrassing, for his record of promiscuity was quite as extensive as Antony's, and contemporaries must have been perfectly capable of identifying the women concerned. But the key section of the letter is its third sentence, *uxor mea est*. As far as the text is concerned, this could mean 'is she my wife?' or 'she is my wife', since the absence of interrogation marks in Latin makes it impossible to distinguish between a question and a statement. But the whole trend of the passage, with the quick fire of questions coming before and after these words, indicates that they, too, are in the form of a question: *she isn't my wife, is she?*[2]

It was impossible for Antony to marry Cleopatra according to Roman law, first because he had a wife already and bigamy was forbidden, and secondly because a Roman could not marry a foreigner.[3] It is true that Antony, at about this very time, flouted this law by arranging for Antonia, the eldest of his daughters (by his cousin Antonia, whom he had married before Fulvia), to be wedded to a Hellenized Asian, Pythodorus of Tralles (Aydin) in Asia Minor. But it would have been an infinitely more serious matter if he himself, a male Roman citizen of the highest position, had done the same: and in this letter he is reminding Octavian that he has not.

The official status of his relations with Cleopatra in Egypt cannot be regarded as equally certain. But since bigamy was anathema to the Greeks as well as the Romans,[4] and Ptolemaic law did not countenance it,[5] they could only have married in Alexandria after a prior declaration by Egyptian jurists that his marriage with Octavia had become null and void in their country. We have no reason to believe, however, that any such step was taken. The ancient authorities would have seized avidly on such a damning development as a 'regular' marriage, if any such thing had occurred. But instead they are singularly vague and inexplicit on the subject. Only two very late writers specifically regarded Antony and Cleopatra as married.[6] Plutarch confusingly refers to a 'marriage' *contrary to the laws*.[7] The summary of Livy, which is all we have of his history about these years, does not say that Antony married her, indicating instead that she was his associate 'in place of a wife' (*uxoris loco*), a phrase used elsewhere for informal domestic association with a foreign concubine.[8] And the tradition of a marriage between Antony and Cleopatra did not reach the historian Dio Cassius at all.

Indeed, as Antony's own letter to Octavian seems to indicate, they were not, in any earthly or legal sense of the word, married at all. Nevertheless, flatterers were always ready, perhaps with official encouragement, to elevate the matter to an other-worldly plane by talking about Sacred Marriages (*hierogamiai*) between Gods. The prototype of such weddings was the original union between Earth and Heaven themselves. But more familiar was the Sacred Marriage between Dionysus and Ariadne (often identified with Aphrodite), and, in Egypt itself, the holy union between Osiris and Isis. For the reincarnations of these deities were the New Dionysus and the New Aphrodite, the New Osiris and the New Isis, namely Antony and Cleopatra themselves. That is the sense in which Caesar and Cleopatra had been married, and that, too, was the only kind of marriage which united Antony and Cleopatra, providing their children with a sort of transcendental legitimacy.

*

In the year 33 BC, a third campaign launched by Octavian in Illyricum not only relieved Italy of its fear of raiders from the north-east, but secured a new Dalmatian recruiting ground for the rowers of his fleet. Although it later turned out that his conquests had not proven very durable, he could at least point to a contrast between all these efforts and the continued inaction of Antony,[9] who, distracted by his deteriorating relations with Octavian, was allowing yet another campaigning season to pass without launching his decisive campaign against the Parthians.

Meanwhile the two men's mutual grievances were piling higher and higher. Propaganda and counter-propaganda proliferated, and both sides, to judge by their perseverance, felt rewarded with a good deal of public response. Moreover, their efforts profoundly influenced historians, biographers and poets, and in consequence have successfully clouded many facts and issues for ever after. The two rival campaigns, with their venomous exchange of accusations, began to approach their maximum strength in the autumn of 33 BC, and continued with undiminished ferocity until the conflict was over. It was the final, foulest breath of the free speech of the old Republic.[10]

For moral, patriotic and xenophobic reasons alike, Antony made a satisfactory scapegoat. Long ago Cicero had implanted the idea that he was a potential overthrower of conventions who kept low company and drank. The rumour was also spread that he had less of the magical charismatic quality of luck than Octavian, whose *daimon* (genius) was said to make Antony afraid.[11] If Antony had to be called Dionysus, then he was not Dionysus the Beneficent, but Dionysus Omestes, the carnivorous, who had arranged to have Sextus Pompeius killed. Even his literary style was criticized as bombastic and un-Roman.[12] The letters Octavian had received from him were read aloud (though the list of their recipient's mistresses was no doubt omitted) and their self-incrimination condemned in pamphlets written by one of Octavian's most distinguished supporters, Marcus Valerius Messalla Corvinus. It was a sign of the times that this former Republican had abandoned Antony's cause for Octavian's; and now, like many others, he was mobilized to contribute to the battle of words.

Although an eminent soldier, orator, statesman and literary patron, Messalla thought fit to declare that Antony, in Alexandria, was using a golden chamber-pot, 'an enormity of which even Cleopatra would have been ashamed'.[13] This was to bring home to the average Roman the dreadful oriental ways into which Antony had been led by the queen. Virgil's *Georgics*, written at this time, conjured up an ideal, Italian simplicity of life, under the patronage of Octavian, which was a total contrast to such extravagances. Antony's enslavement to the foreign woman was emphasized in a hundred ways. It was under her influence, people declared, that he had married his daughter to another foreigner, Pythodorus of Tralles. Antony claimed to be Heracles, but mythology, they pointed out, played him a neat trick here, because it told how Heracles, too, had been bewitched by a woman, Omphale; and so Octavian's friends, pursuing an old joke which had been applied to many others before, pressed home this felicitous comparison.[14] It is even echoed by a relief on an earthenware jar from Arretium (Arezzo), which shows Antony–Heracles in woman's dress, surrounded by attendants bearing a parasol, fan, ball of wool and spindle, while his lionskin and club are taken over by Omphale – who at the same time stretches out her free hand for a bowl of wine.[15] Antony was also said to be a victim of sorcery. On a more serious level, it was declared that this disastrous infatuation had caused him to manage eastern affairs without the slightest authority from the Senate, making scandalous misuse of Roman legionaries who had failed in their proper military tasks and now served under the command of Cleopatra.[16] Worst of all, he had alienated Roman territories and handed them over to foreign monarchs,[17] in sharp contrast to Octavian who was about to do the opposite and convert the kingdom of Mauretania into a Roman province.

What Octavian really achieved was to play successfully upon the Romans' terrified expectation, encouraged by so many anonymous prophecies, that there was going to be a hostile Greco-Asiatic crusade, under Cleopatra's leadership. Antony seemed to be playing perilously with fire, for it was believed that the queen's favourite oath was 'as surely as I shall dispense justice on the Capitol' – and Horace, later on, echoed the conviction that this was what she had in mind.[18] The oath, no doubt, was a propaganda invention, like Kaiser Wilhelm II's alleged declaration that he would eat his 1914 Christmas dinner in Buckingham Palace. But Octavian, in retrospect, felt justified in asserting that the menace with which Cleopatra threatened the Roman state was 'the grimmest of dangers' (*tristissimum periculum*).[19] This seemed almost hysterical language; but it was exaggerations of this kind that prompted an unprecedented outbreak of Roman hatred against Cleopatra.[20]

The charge that she harboured designs upon Rome seemed to be confirmed by the name Caesar that she had given to her eldest son, and by her claim that Julius Caesar was his father – a claim that Antony had now explicitly confirmed. This was one of Octavian's principal complaints against Antony;[21] and a pamphlet by Caesar's friend Gaius Oppius, denying the dictator's paternity, probably belongs to this time.

*

Antony's counter-propaganda included not only plain denials of drunkenness and other accusations, but also an equally varied and violent range of personal attacks upon Octavian. Cleopatra may have contributed helpful hints, but if so it was better that her part should be concealed, so that criticism of Octavian could seem to be coming from purely Roman sources. A good deal of this material has managed to seep anonymously into history, at second- or third-hand. It appears, for example, in the jaundiced picture of Octavian presented by the historian Tacitus; and Plutarch complains indignantly that there were writers who had praised Antony excessively.[22] Since he was the loser in the subsequent conflict, their actual writings have succumbed to the predominant Augustan tradition, and failed to survive. But we are told some of their names,[23] and we know that among his most important spokesmen was Cassius of Parma, one of the conspirators against Caesar, who after serving with Sextus Pompeius had transferred his allegiance to Antony.

Cassius of Parma made much of Octavian's alleged low origins, a telling charge among the snobs of antiquity, and a suitable contrast with Caesarion.[24] He also pointed out, in pursuance of a well-worn theme of invective, that Octavian had only earned Caesar's adoption by submitting to his homosexual desires. Moreover – Cassius went on to say – if Antony had married his daughter to a Greek, Octavian had betrothed his daughter Julia (formerly engaged to Antony's son Antyllus) to an entirely barbarian prince, Coson of the Dacians in what is now Rumania. Indeed Octavian was accused of himself applying for the hand of Coson's daughter – an improbable embroidery on the efforts of both Roman leaders to win support from the rival princes of this rich land.[25] The attacks upon Antony as the cannibal Dionysus Omestes were countered (or preceded) by suggestions that Apollo, whom Octavian hailed as his patron, was Apollo Tortor, the torturer. And Octavian himself was said to have sacrilegiously masqueraded as Apollo at a banquet.[26] Besides, it was added, the less said against Antony's military endeavours the better, since Octavian was completely contemptible as general and fighter. At Philippi he had been a failure, and at Naulochus, while Agrippa was defeating Sextus Pompeius, Octavian had done nothing but sleep all the time in a stupor.[27]

When it came to serious complaints Antony retaliated by putting forward a number of deeply-felt grievances: after taking Sicily from

189

Sextus Pompeius and north Africa from Lepidus, Octavian had given Antony no share of either territory, and no portion of the army of Lepidus – whom he had dismissed entirely on his own initiative. Above ·all, he had failed to give Antony the troops promised in exchange for the naval squadrons. And, finally, he had distributed almost all the land in Italy to his own ex-soldiers, leaving nothing for Antony's veterans.

Who had the better of these exchanges? If we are thinking of legality, fairness and the plighted word, honours are even; or slightly on Antony's side. Certainly he ought to have consulted Octavian and the Senate before making his far-reaching arrangements of 37 and 34 BC involving client-kingdoms and transferring Roman territory to Cleopatra and her family. But Octavian had already behaved unco-operatively towards Antony before 37 or 34. However, legality and the fulfilment of promises were not what really counted. This was a propaganda war, and successful propaganda does not depend on reason, or truth, but thrives on moral, emotional and scandalous issues. Here Octavian had the winning argument. For Cleopatra proved a perfect battle-cry.

*

Nevertheless, Octavian sent Antony a letter answering his specific complaints, and answering them very sharply. He declared, for example, that he would be willing enough to consider dividing Sicily and Africa with Antony – but only after Antony had offered him a share of Armenia in return. And he added the sardonic, wounding postscript that Antony's soldiers surely need not claim any lands in Italy, since 'their rewards lay in Media and Parthia which they had added to the Roman empire by their gallant campaigns under their Imperator'.[28]

This message reached Antony in about October 33 BC, when he was away on the River Araxes, the border between Armenia and Media. Although his preoccupation with Octavian had seemed to make an immediate eastern campaign impossible, he had at least, in response to an urgent request, agreed to meet his Median ally, who believed that a Parthian attack was imminent. Leaving Cleopatra behind in Alexandria, Antony had made the long journey to the Araxes. There he made what plans he could to help the Medes to meet the threat; but when Octavian's letter reached him, he at last realized that he had to return to the west for a possible confrontation. Joined on the way by Cleopatra and her fleet, he set out on the long march to the Aegean, and established his winter headquarters in her company at Ephesus. He took with him only a small force, but ordered Canidius Crassus to follow behind with the bulk of the legions.

It was clear to Antony that the best way to avoid the war with Octavian, or to win it if war proved unavoidable, was to keep the support of the Roman senators, or to regain the support of those whom the events of the past few years had alienated. Somehow or other they must be made to approve the Donations to Cleopatra and her children. So he sent the Senate a dispatch, requesting the ratification of all his proceedings. Among these, of course, the Donations figured prominently, and no doubt he took the opportunity to explain their advantages in terms calculated to overcome senatorial distrust. He also sugared the pill in two ways: he formally announced, and emphasized, his Armenian victory of the previous year; and he offered, not once but twice, to lay down his triumviral powers if Octavian would do the same.[29] However, there was no response, and the propaganda manœuvres and countermanœuvres continued – for example, Octavian made a meticulous show of abandoning his powers when their five-year period concluded at the end of 33.[30] Each accused the other of standing in the way of restoration of the Republic. But the Republic was dead and nothing on earth could have brought about its revival. The choice was not between autocracy and republic: it was between Octavian's version of autocracy, and the version favoured by Antony and Cleopatra.

Nevertheless, for the very last time in Rome's history, a great deal depended upon the consuls who assumed that annual office at the beginning of 32 BC; and a powerful and lurid light fell upon their activities. When the Triumvirs, in their days of relative harmony, had agreed who should hold the consulships for a number of years ahead, it so happened that both of the men they had designated for 32 were leading supporters of Antony – a situation that now proved somewhat perilous for Octavian, who had deliberately declared himself a private citizen.

One of the consuls was Cnaeus Domitius Ahenobarbus, the most reputable member of a notoriously stiff-necked family. Formerly a Republican, he had transferred to Antony's cause, betrothing his son to one of Antony's daughters by Octavia. The other consul was Gaius Sosius. Being an admiral, he took an interest in the aims of Cleopatra and appreciated her material contribution. Ahenobarbus, on the other hand, was exceedingly conscious of the danger she presented to the Antonian cause. Antony had requested the new consuls to read out the dispatch intended to regularize his position, but Ahenobarbus, who was the first to take the chair (consuls presided in alternate months), refrained from reading it, feeling that the references to the Donations would create a disastrous impression. So Octavian, although he thought it best to absent himself from the Senate and from Rome, informed the Senate that Antony's dispatch about his Armenian successes, too, must remain unread.[31]

On 1 February Sosius attacked the absent Octavian, and proposed a motion of censure against him, which was vetoed by a tribune acting for the other side. In mid-February, however, Octavian returned to Rome and delivered stern onslaughts upon Antony and Sosius before the Senate and the Assembly. In the Senate, where he was attended by a bodyguard, he declared a date for a further meeting at which members would be given documentary proof of his case. No one dared attempt a reply, and before the date arrived the consuls and between two and three hundred senators left Rome to join Antony.[32] Octavian seized the opportunity to point out how generous he was to let them go – and anyone else who felt the same way, he added, could go with them and join the other servile adherents of Cleopatra. The prolonged battle between Octavian and Antony to gain favour with the Senate had ended in stalemate. To us, who are provided with most of our history of the period from Octavianic sources, this comes as something of a surprise: if Octavian was so obviously the better man, why did so many senators, not indeed a majority but a substantial proportion, decide against him by fleeing to Antony? Their action reveals that, in the event of war between Antony and Octavian, opinion was divided about who the winner would be.

In May or June of this same year 32 BC, Cleopatra's influence over Antony achieved one of its greatest successes, for he announced that he was divorcing Octavia. This meant a rupture of personal relations between Octavian and Antony: their ostensible former friendship was totally at an end. Yet, however keen the satisfaction the divorce gave Cleopatra, it lost Antony some very useful sympathizers at Rome. It may also have contributed to the desertion of certain eminent supporters to Octavian. The first to go over was Plancus; he was followed soon afterwards by his nephew Marcus Titius. Both men had been friends of Cleopatra,[33] and the reasons why they changed sides at this juncture have been variously explained. Plancus is known to have been hostile to Ahenobarbus; it was also said that Antony had caught him out in financial impropriety. But the truth surely was that, although other senators could not foresee the outcome of the expected war, Plancus and Titius, noting the impact of Antony's divorce upon Roman opinion and weighing up all the other factors involved, had come to the conclusion that he was going to lose. Throughout the civil wars Plancus had shown remarkable skill at changing sides at the right time, and this proved the most inspired decision of his life.

Plancus hastened to Rome, and addressed the Senate. He attacked Antony for such a multitude of crimes that an elderly colleague, Publius Coponius, remarked that Antony seemed to have done a very great deal before Plancus made up his mind to abandon him.[34] Plancus and Titius also disclosed to Octavian that Antony had drawn up a will –

which, according to custom, he had deposited with the Vestal Virgins at Rome. Octavian asked the Chief Vestal if he could see this document, and when she refused he took it by force. After reading it privately, he informed the Senate of three damning clauses. The will announced, he said, that Caesarion was indeed Caesar's son; it provided that the children of Antony and Cleopatra were to receive large legacies; and it requested that when and wherever Antony died, his body should first be carried through the Roman Forum, but was then to be buried in Egypt.

For Antony to say that Caesarion was Caesar's son was nothing new. But the alleged provision about Cleopatra's sons and daughter by Antony could not have been drafted by any Roman lawyer, since these children, as foreigners, could not be heirs or legatees under a Roman citizen's will.[35] It is probable, therefore, that Octavian invented the clause in order to discredit his rival. But the provision on which he laid most emphasis was Antony's insistence upon burial in Egypt.[36] This was just the sort of idea that would cause the maximum emotional hostility in Rome, arousing all the ancient rumours, already current in Caesar's time, that there was a plan to transfer the capital to the east, the homeland of the exotic Cleopatra.

Yet Antony can scarcely have been so stupid as to deposit such an incriminating document at Rome. He would not have supposed that the Vestal Virgins could guarantee its safety. And he was very well aware that political capital could be made out of testamentary documents, since he himself had forged a whole series of papers supposedly found in Caesar's archives after his death. That Antony had deposited a will with the Vestal Virgins is likely enough, because otherwise Octavian's admission that he had taken it from them could too easily have been denied. But the contents were surely not as Octavian specified.[37] Whether Antony really wanted to be buried in Egypt, we cannot tell. He spent the best years of his life there with Cleopatra; but all the same he was a Roman. Probably his will gave no direction about the matter at all. If he was victorious in the forthcoming war, there would be time to think about such matters, and the possibility of defeat was best not considered – especially in a document which could get into Octavian's hands.

*

Meanwhile Antony and Cleopatra were spending the winter of 33–32 BC at Ephesus. For the first time since Alexander the Great, the whole sea-power of the near east was in the hands of one man. In addition to 300 merchant vessels, he had 500 warships, of which Cleopatra contributed 200. She also provided enough money and supplies to see his army through a whole campaigning season. Canidius Crassus had now brought the bulk of it back from Armenia; there were 75,000 legionaries (30 legions), 25,000 light-armed infantry and 12,000 cavalry.[38]

The light-armed infantry and most of the cavalry were easterners. But so were two-thirds of the legionaries, though this was contrary to Roman precedent. For since Antony had been denied his recruiting rights in Italy by Octavian, he was obliged to seek most of his man-power in Syria, Asia Minor, the Black Sea area and Greece.[39] Easterners were not necessarily less brave or less skilful fighters than westerners. But they might prove less loyal to a Roman leader, unless they were con-vinced his interests were the same as their own: and here Antony's manifest phil-Hellenism was a help.

Nevertheless, he considered it essential to demonstrate to the legion-aries and the world that, once enrolled, they were true Romans and soldiers of Rome. And so on a majestic silver and gold coinage, which remained famous for centuries,[40] he called the roll of every one of the thirty legions he commanded, in addition to his praetorian bodyguard and corps of scouts.[41] Each coin displays the Eagle and standards in-dicated by the appropriate number or name, while the other side features a warship of his and Cleopatra's fleet.

*

Ephesus belonged to the Roman province of Asia, but like other cities of the area it possessed strong Ptolemaic connections.[42] Indeed, for a time during the 250s BC it had actually belonged to Ptolemy II Philadel-phus, whose future daughter-in-law Berenice II issued large gold coins at its mint. In the south-western part of the peninsula (Caria) which had likewise formed part of Ptolemy II's empire, Alabanda (Araphisar) had also miscalculated by depicting Octavia on its coins. It now tried to rectify that error by portraying Cleopatra instead.[43]

The building up of army and fleet met various setbacks. A subordin-ate of Antony at Cos, Decimus Turullius (one of Caesar's assassins), earned unpopularity by cutting down the sacred grove of Asclepius (Aesculapius) to get timber for ships. A priest at Tralles (Aydin) was executed by Ahenobarbus for tampering with the sailors' loyalty.[44] And in the circumstances it seemed rather gratuitous that Antony should remove so many statues from principal temples in the area, for presentation to Cleopatra.[45]

She was very much in evidence at headquarters. Wherever there were conferences, law-suits, banquets, she was always at Antony's side; people saw her riding about the city, or reclining in a sumptuous litter. It was now that some of the most damaging stories about her influence were recounted at Rome by Octavian's friends. In these disclosures one of his generals, Gaius Calvisius Sabinus, played a conspicuous part, as Plutarch [46] records:

Calvisius accused Antony of a number of excesses in his behaviour towards Cleopatra: he had presented her with the libraries at Pergamum which contained two hundred thousand scrolls; at a banquet with a large company present he had risen from his place and anointed her feet, apparently to fulfil some compact or wager; he had allowed the Ephesians to salute Cleopatra as their sovereign in his own presence, and on many occasions, while he was seated on the tribunal administering justice to kings and princes, he would receive love-letters from her written on tablets of onyx or crystal, and read them through in public; and on another occasion when Furnius, a man of great distinction and the foremost orator in Rome, was pleading a case, Cleopatra happened to pass through the market-place in her litter, whereupon Antony leapt to his feet from his tribunal, walked out of the trial, and accompanied Cleopatra on her way, hanging on to her litter.

Most people, added Plutarch, thought that Calvisius' stories were often inventions. Nevertheless, they gave some idea of what the atmosphere at Ephesus was like. A particularly awkward situation arose when the consuls arrived there from Rome in early spring. For Ahenobarbus (whose role was subsequently elaborated by Shakespeare) disapproved more and more of the position Cleopatra had established. Although she tried to flatter his vanity by naming a Cilician town, Domitiopolis, after him, he was the only one of Antony's followers who refused to address her as queen, or Queen of Kings, but called her simply Cleopatra.

Other Republicans among his colleagues, who shared his opinions, even thought of setting him up in Antony's place as supreme commander. Ahenobarbus would not commit himself on this point. But he did urge Antony most strongly to send Cleopatra away from headquarters, so as not to alienate the important section of Roman opinion that detested her. However, she still had her own powerful Roman friends. Among them was Canidius Crassus, who pointed out that

it was unjust to refuse a woman who contributed so much to the expenses of the war the privilege of being present at it, and unwise for Antony to depress the spirits of the Egyptians who formed so large a part of their naval force. Besides, there was no indication, as far as he could see, that Cleopatra was inferior in intelligence to any of the kings who were taking part in the expedition. On the contrary, she had for many years ruled a large kingdom by herself and her long association with Antony had taught her many lessons in the management of great affairs. [47]

Although the queen's enemies inevitably said that she had bribed

Canidius to offer this advice, other important members of the staff evidently held the same opinion, since we are told that she still enjoyed considerable support.[48] Antony was said to have felt inclined to send her away, but it was Canidius' view, in the end, that prevailed – and she stayed on. It is generally argued today that her determination not to leave showed her inability to grasp the strength of Roman opposition, and was therefore a political and military mistake. But if the subsequent campaign had happened to go the other way, we might not be saying this at all; and Canidius was probably right to point out that a decisive lowering of Egyptian morale, such as must have resulted from her departure, would have lessened the chances of victory.

In this tense atmosphere, Cleopatra decided that her worst enemy, Herod of Judaea, ought to be kept at a safe distance. Every dependent monarch of the east was expected to be at Antony's side on this decisive occasion, and Herod had hastened to set out, with a strong and well-equipped contingent. But Cleopatra persuaded Antony to halt him, and send him back to the east.[49] Her pretext was the behaviour of the Nabataean Arabs, who were no longer keeping up their rent payments to Cleopatra, which Herod had been supposed to collect[50] – probably they were waiting until one side or other had won the Roman civil war. And so Cleopatra urged that Herod must invade their country, and use force of arms to extract the sums for which he was responsible. But her real reason was to get him out of the way; and in order to make sure he did not gain a permanent ascendancy over the Arabs, she sent an army of her own to the scene, under a general named Athenion. He had always shared Cleopatra's dislike of Herod, and now proceeded (or so the king said) to hamper his operation against the Nabataeans – though it ultimately proved successful.[51]

*

At the end of April, Antony and Cleopatra sailed from Ephesus to the neighbouring island of Samos. This was a 'free' city-state under the general supervision of the Roman governor of Asia, but it had been a member of the federation of Aegean islands formed by Cleopatra's ancestor Ptolemy II Philadelphus. During their two or three weeks' stay upon the island, she and Antony held an ambitious dramatic and musical festival. 'All the theatrical artists,' declares Plutarch, 'were commanded to present themselves at Samos, and while almost the whole world round about was filled with sighs and lamentations at the impending war, this single island echoed for many days with the music of strings and flutes. The theatres were packed, and choirs competed for many days with one another in the magnificence of their gifts and entertainments, until the word went round, "If these people spend so much on festivals just to prepare for war, what will the conquerors do to celebrate a victory?" '52

Although war was imminent, Antony and Cleopatra did not feel that this was a time for austerity, since in pursuance of the custom of the Hellenistic monarchies they were judiciously combining their own and their people's entertainment with religious uplift. All the entertainers who took part in the festival belonged to a corporation of actors, poets, musicians and singers organized under the patronage of Dionysus. The tradition for such gatherings had been established by Antony's model, Alexander the Great, and dramatic and musical performers, led by the poet-priest of the god, were accustomed to march in the processions of the Ptolemaia which were staged every four years at Alexandria 53 and throughout western Asia Minor.

After the Samos festival was over, Antony gave this corporation a new abode at the city of Priene, where they were granted extra-territorial rights. 54

In May, Antony and Cleopatra left Samos for Athens; at the same time their army was being ferried over to join them on the Greek mainland. For it was in Greece, for the third time in less than twenty years, that the fate of Rome was about to be decided. In 48 BC, Caesar had sailed from Italy to fight Pompey at Pharsalus. In 42, Antony himself, with Octavian, had come from Italy to encounter Brutus and Cassius at Philippi. And now Octavian would soon be on his way to confront Antony and Cleopatra. In both previous engagements the invaders had won. But this did not unduly worry Antony and Cleopatra, since, despite problems of recruitment, their financial resources were much larger than Octavian's. In consequence, the stresses and strains that accompanied Antony's preparations were nothing compared to Octavian's. He was obliged to institute a special, comprehensive levy of income-tax in Italy, such as had been imposed only once before (a decade previously), and this caused serious financial discontent throughout the peninsula.

'For this reason,' observes Plutarch, 'Antony's postponement of the war is now considered to have been one of his greatest errors of judgement.'55 Instead of waiting for Octavian to invade Greece in 31 BC, he himself, it was felt, ought to have invaded Italy in 32. According to the poet Horace, the fear that he would do so was very prominent in Italian minds.56 But Antony decided against this course. To accuse him, as people did, of starting the campaign too late in the year 32, is beside the point. It is quite true that he did not complete the transportation of his army across the Aegean until May, when it could no longer have reached Italy in the same summer. But he had already decided not to attempt an invasion of Italy at all – until after the decisive battle had been fought in the Balkans. For one thing, experience had shown that the only adequate south Italian ports, Brundusium and Tarentum, were hard to capture. But the main problem was Cleopatra. If he crossed to Italy and left her behind, the great Egyptian contribution to his navy and supplies could no longer be relied upon. And yet if he took her with him, passionate Italian resistance would be aroused: resistance which could be faced after a victory, but would be a dangerous additional hazard before it had been won.

Besides, Antony thought he had found another, better way of undermining Italy. From his superior financial resources he was pouring money into the country in the shape of bribes, which were causing Octavian grave embarrassment.[57] Indeed, it is even quite likely, however surprising this may seem, that Antony still possessed a mint at his disposal in Italy. Servius, the commentator on Virgil, declares that he did, and specifically locates it at the central Italian town of Anagnia (Anagni).[58] He also adds that its products included a coin 'in the name of Cleopatra'. This can only refer to the *denarius*, already mentioned, which portrayed her with her royal titles in Latin. Now, we have no idea whatever where any of Antony's gold or silver coins with Latin inscriptions were minted during this period, and it would therefore be unwise to reject Servius' curiously explicit statement out of hand.[59] Although the dies were probably designed and cut at Antioch or Ephesus or Athens, they are quite likely to have been circulated to various other centres for minting, to avoid the transportation of large quantities of actual coins.[60] And one of these centres could well have been an Italian town. Such a mint may still have existed in 33–32 BC, playing an important part in Antony's financial campaign.[61]

As the scene, then, of the coming clash of armies and navies, Antony rejected Italy in favour of the Balkans. Earlier commanders who, like Antony, wanted to move to that region from Asia Minor, such as the Persian king Xerxes in the fifth century BC, had selected the northward route round the head of the Aegean, thus securing Macedonia as a prelude to the operations in Greece. Within recent years, too, the campaigns preceding the battles of Pharsalus and Philippi had centred round the main Roman road, the Via Egnatia, which spanned Macedonia on its way from the Ionian Sea to Byzantium and the east. Antony, however, decided to adopt a new strategy, leaving Macedonia and the Via Egnatia out of account and concentrating entirely on the more southerly shores and waters of the Ionian Sea. And so in May 32 BC, while he and Cleopatra sailed to Athens, his fleet, after ferrying the army across the Aegean, sailed onwards round the Peloponnese and took up a chain of positions well to the south of the Via Egnatia.

This might seem a surprising decision, since it deliberately sacrificed the principal artery between the Adriatic and the east. It was also a strategy which offered fuel to the critics of Cleopatra, since it looked as though Antony was adopting this southward stance in order to protect Egypt. And so he was; but this was a justifiable enough policy in military terms, since his indispensable supply route from that country had to be secured. However, Antony's main purpose was to make Octavian's sea journey as long as possible: he would now have to sail a very long way towards the south, and the perils involved in lengthy voyages were enormous. But above all, this long crossing would take up a great deal of time, and Antony, convinced that Octavian lacked the money for a prolonged war, believed that time was on his own side.

*

Antony and Cleopatra stayed in Athens throughout the summer of 32 BC. A city which traditionally favoured the Ptolemies, it had habitually celebrated their festival the Ptolemaia, and received rich benefactions from Egyptian monarchs.[62] Cleopatra herself may have been there with her father when she was a young girl. Nevertheless, the place had painful personal memories for her, because it had been the home of Antony and his wife Octavia, who enjoyed great success with the Athenians. Now, they did all they could to erase this memory in favour of Cleopatra. They were able to applaud the fact that she was the first Egyptian queen who had ever visited the city. They also set up her statue upon the Acropolis itself, dressed in the robes of the goddess Isis; and Antony, too, was honoured by statues. Already during his earlier period of residence he had entered into Athenian customs with great gusto, and now he himself headed an Athenian deputation to Cleopatra, loading her with abundant compliments.

This triumphant reception at Athens encouraged her determination to play a leading part in the war, although it was becoming clearer all the time that her active participation was harming Antony's cause in Italy. This had flourished when his distribution of bribes presented such a pleasant contrast to Octavian's taxes. But now discontent over the taxation had died down,[63] and the propaganda against Cleopatra was taking effect. So Antony's friends in Italy dispatched a special envoy to him in Greece, urging that she should leave his headquarters.

They sent one of their number named Gaius Geminius to urge Antony not to sit and allow himself to be voted out of authority and declared an enemy of Rome. But as soon as Geminius landed in Greece, he was suspected by Cleopatra of being an agent working for Octavia, and she arranged that he should be humiliated by being seated in the least distinguished place at the dinner table and having practical jokes played upon him.

Geminius endured these insults with great patience and waited for an opportunity to speak to Antony. But when he was called upon to explain the reason for his presence, they were seated at dinner, and so Geminius answered that he would keep the rest of his message for a more sober occasion, but that he had one thing to say, sober or drunk, and this was that all would go well if Cleopatra were sent back to Egypt.

Antony was furious at this reply, but Cleopatra put in, 'You have done well, Geminius, to confess the truth without being put to torture!' Geminius escaped a few days later and returned to Rome.[64]

Plutarch's source may have invented the picturesque details, as an illustration of the insobriety of Antony's and Cleopatra's table, and above all as an indication of Cleopatra's insufferable arrogance in threatening a Roman citizen with torture – a punishment from which his free birth ought to have exempted him. But there is no reason to doubt that an emissary of such a kind, indeed perhaps more than one, came from Rome to implore Antony to send the queen away.

It is also likely enough that even Antony's decision to divorce Octavia had not completely relieved Cleopatra's suspicions of her possible influence. And such fears may have been reinforced by the arrival from Rome of Antyllus, Antony's teen-age son by Fulvia, with the news that Octavia, who had looked after him until she left Antony's house, always treated him with the utmost kindness. The boy's presence in Athens did not make Cleopatra's position any easier, since it was Antyllus, and not one of her own children, who remained Antony's personal heir.

*

In the late autumn of 32 BC both the rival leaders made a supreme claim upon the loyalty of their subjects by administering oaths to as many of them as they could round up in the limited time available. The oaths Octavian extracted from the Italians have earned reverent attention from posterity because he himself, retrospectively, invested them with profound significance, claiming, with dubious accuracy, that they had been entirely spontaneous.[65] But less attention has been devoted to the similar oaths sworn in favour of Antony – whether before or after Octavian's we do not know – by the inhabitants of the provinces and client kingdoms in his own sphere.[66] On receiving these promises of allegiance, Antony himself made a solemn assertion to his own soldiers, swearing that when the time came he would fight on *without reconciliation*.[67] This provision, the ancient equivalent of insistence upon unconditional surrender, was intended to discourage the desertions which were such a frequent feature of the civil strife at this time. Nevertheless, neither side yet issued a declaration of war.

The decisive steps in this direction were taken by Octavian, shortly before this same year 32 BC came to an end. First of all, he arranged for Antony to be deprived of his triumviral office and all his other official powers, including the consulship he was due to hold in the following year. Henceforward, in the eyes of Octavian's supporters, he was just a private citizen, an ex-official whose proceedings had not yet been sanctioned, and above all an adventurer in the service of an alien queen.

Yet war was not declared against Antony, either now or at any time before Actium. This absence of a formal Roman enemy meant that Octavian did not have to go back on his assurance, proclaimed five years earlier after his victory over Sextus Pompeius, that the civil wars were at last over. Octavian was also able to suggest that this tactful handling gave Antony a chance to change his mind, and abandon his foreign concubine.[68] Antony obviously had no intention of doing anything of the sort. But what Octavian really meant was that Antony's Roman followers still had an opportunity to change *their* minds.

However, war was declared against Cleopatra – and with all possible solemnity. As a member of the long-obsolete priesthood of the Fetiales, who in antique times had presided over the magical rites accompanying declarations that Rome was at war, Octavian walked in ceremonious procession to the Campus Martius, brandishing a lance dipped in fresh blood from the temple of the war goddess, Bellona. And Dio Cassius is probably right in supposing that a speech he delivered at this time concentrated its virulence entirely upon her.[69]

She was the ideal national foe, the oriental woman who had ensnared the Roman leader in her evil luxury, the harlot who had seized Roman territories, until even Rome itself was not safe from her degenerate alien hordes. Later on, every poet who supported Octavian looked back upon the conflict in the same tones of ghoulish, excited abuse. Virgil dwells on the weird and barbarous monstrosities of Egyptian religion; Horace twice tells of the despicable oriental eunuchs who thronged her court; and the elegist Propertius, too, though contemporary patriotic subjects did not suit his gifts very well, was accustomed to write eloquently about whores, and chose this alleged aspect of Cleopatra to dwell upon:[70]

> What of that woman, she whose charms
> Brought scandal on the Roman arms,
> And, strumpet to her very thralls,
> Aspired to pass the Roman walls
> And rule our Senate, as the fee
> Due from her lover's lechery?
> Cursed Alexandria, Memphis curst,
> Thou land in cunning deeply versed,

How often on thy noisome silt
Has Roman blood been freely spilt....
To think that courtesan obscene,
Incestuous Canopus' queen,
That worst of stigmas branded on
The royal race of Macedon,
Dared pit against our Jupiter
Her god Anubis, half a cur;
Compel our Tiber for a while
To bear defiance from the Nile!
Aside the Roman trumpet set
For Egypt's clattering castanet! ...
How could that Rome at whose command
The fasces broke in Tarquin's hand,
Alike by name and nature proud,
Before a woman now have bowed?

These sentiments of Propertius, though expressed after the event, faithfully represented the verbal onslaught upon Cleopatra which had reached its crescendo in 32 BC. In reply Antony, ignoring the official cancellation of his powers, published a statement that he would lay them down within six months after victory, restoring the fullest authority to the Senate and people of Rome. Yet in comparison with the feverish outpourings of his enemies, this concrete assurance lacked credibility and made no impact. For Cleopatra had lost him the propaganda battle, the first engagement of the campaign.

That did not necessarily matter, if only the second and real engagement, the naval and military battle, could be won. Until that had taken place, the issue remained open.

12

Cleopatra's Escape from Actium

Antony's northernmost base on the Ionian Sea was at Corcyra (Corfu), a hundred miles south of the Macedonian highway. From Corcyra downwards, as far as the coast of north Africa, he had established a chain of further stations: first Actium, at the entrance to the Gulf of Ambracia (Arta); then the island of Leucas, almost joined to the mainland; Patrae (Patras), within the entrance to the Corinthian Gulf; the island of Zacynthus (Zante), where Gaius Sosius, Antony's principal admiral, was still in command of the naval post he had established seven years earlier;[1] Methone at the south-western tip of Greece, placed under the command of King Bogud, exiled from western Mauretania; Cape Taenarum (Matapan), the central prong of the three southern extremities of the Greek mainland; and finally bases in Crete and Cyrenaica, territories which were officially in the domains of Cleopatra Selene but contained Roman garrisons.

In September or October 32 BC Antony and Cleopatra transferred their headquarters westwards from Athens and moved into residence for the winter at Patrae, which occupied a key position in the midst of these naval stations. Patrae was a city that had risen rapidly to importance after Rome's destruction of Corinth in 146 BC. It belonged to the Roman province of Macedonia–Achaea. Yet its local authorities now issued a coinage portraying Cleopatra and describing her as queen; also to be seen is the sacred rattle of the goddess Isis, of whom she was the earthly incarnation.[2] Here was a reminder that the Ptolemies had once been powerful as far afield as Greece: and Greece was already halfway from Egypt to Rome.

As the following spring approached, Antony looked out westwards across the waters where the fleet of Octavian, now consul once again with the aristocratic Messalla, would surely soon appear. Even if he failed to stop the invaders en route, he was confident that he could deal with them thereafter, either at sea or on land. He also felt pleasantly certain that Octavian's lack of funds would compel him to act boldly and rashly.

And indeed the course of action now adopted by Octavian, or rather by his admiral Agrippa, was extremely bold. But it was also brilliantly successful. For in the early days of March, when the milder weather had barely begun, Agrippa, taking a considerable part of Octavian's fleet, sailed across the Ionian Sea, not taking the direct passage but a long, diagonal route which brought him to the south-western extremity of Greece. There he captured Antony's naval station Methone. In the fifteenth century AD the Venetians defended Methone against the Turks for forty years. But now the strongpoint fell to Agrippa immediately; its Antonian commander Bogud was killed, and Agrippa garrisoned the place with a force of occupation.

This downfall of one of his most secure, and most important, harbour-fortresses came as a complete surprise to Antony. It also produced immediate and alarming results. For from this admirably situated base, Agrippa at once began to harass Antony's other coastal stations, thus drawing off his warships to defend them. He also threatened the sea-route by which Cleopatra's supply ships had to travel in order to reach Antony's harbours, so that, henceforward, their arrival became extremely problematical. The queen cannot have been pleased to hear Dellius, who had once so greatly admired her, remarking at dinner that the wine they were now obliged to drink seemed very sour, whereas at Rome a page at Octavian's court, Sarmentus, was able to get the best Italian vintages.[3] More serious still was the non-arrival of Egyptian grain. As a result, it had to be extorted from infertile Greece, and Plutarch's great-grandfather, Nicarchus, described how all the citizens of his hometown Chaeronea were forced to march down to the Corinthian gulf at Anticyra, carrying on their backs a load of wheat for Antony's soldiers and crews, while overseers kept them moving with lashes of the whip.[4]

The seizure of Methone had other serious repercussions as well. It was only thirty miles from the leading autonomous city-state of the Peloponnese, Sparta. The supreme Spartan official, Eurycles, cherished a grudge against Antony, who had executed his father as a pirate; and at this point Eurycles went over to Octavian. Sparta had been issuing coins with the head and name of the Antonian general Atratinus, who was probably in command of a detachment of troops there.[5] But now, with masterly economy, the Spartans altered ATR (*atinus*) on the coins to AGR (*ippa*), a change which, in Greek, only involves the erasure of half a horizontal stroke.[6] As for Atratinus, we know that he, too, went over to Octavian at some stage – and it was probably now.[7]

Later on the Augustan tradition sought to build up the battle of Actium itself as the decisive turning-point, since Octavian personally took part. But the historian Velleius Paterculus expressed the view that Actium had really been decided long before it was ever fought.[8] He was referring to a long chain of events, but the capture of Methone in itself meant that the war was half lost already. It also underlined the painful and inescapable fact that Agrippa, although the nobles on Octavian's side did not care for him personally, was a superb admiral, perhaps the only Roman who ever really understood naval strategy and tactics. This unique ability, combined with the long, hard experience he had gained in the Sicilian fighting against Sextus Pompeius, presented Antony and Cleopatra with far their most serious problem, in comparison with which all the torrents of propaganda on either side, all the moral and constitutional rights and wrongs, were meaningless and insubstantial.

Very soon after the capture of Methone, Octavian transported the main part of his army across the Ionian Sea by the short northern route, landing between the Via Egnatia and Corcyra – probably at the small port of Panormus. Antony's naval squadron at Corcyra failed to intercept it or give warning of its approach, because the squadron was no longer there; it had been drawn off to help protect his other bases against raids from Methone. Seizing Corcyra, Octavian moved rapidly southwards by land and sea. When Cleopatra learnt that he had already got as far as a place called Toryne ('ladle') she tried to combat the consternation by a pun which, it is to be hoped, sounded funnier in ancient Greek than it does in English: she remarked that it surely was not such a terrible catastrophe if Octavian chose to sit in a ladle.[9]

But Octavian still pressed on, and was soon in sight of Antony's next fleet-station, Actium, situated on the southern side of the half-mile-wide opening of the Ambracian Gulf. Two or three days later, Antony and Cleopatra themselves arrived at Actium, and established a new headquarters there; henceforward she lived with him in the camp. On their arrival, they found that Octavian had fortified a base on the north side of the opening. He also launched a surprise attack on Antony's ships, but the attempt failed, an occasion which may have inspired the celebration of a victory on Antony's coins.[10] However, Agrippa, based now on Corcyra as well as Methone, soon afterwards fought two victorious engagements at sea, and captured both Leucas and Patrae.[11] In consequence, Plutarch's forbears at Chaeronea were spared a second journey carrying grain to the Corinthian Gulf, since these waters were no longer under Antony's control.

Indeed, his fleet was shut inside the Gulf of Ambracia. His cosmopolitan crews, lacking the discipline the Sicilian War had given Octavian's, began to grow restless, and the unhealthy climate of the area gave them malaria or dysentery or both, so that a shortage of rowers soon left serious cause for concern.[12] Time was no longer on Antony's side. His enemies possessed an uninterrupted supply route to Italy; and he was soon compelled to take the initiative. So he crossed over to the north bank of the strait, took up a position next to Octavian's camp, and offered battle. But Octavian refused to fight. Antony also failed to cut him off from a local stream which provided his troops with water, suffering a cavalry defeat in which an Asian client prince went over to the enemy.[13]

Worst of all, Ahenobarbus, long discontented with the presence of Cleopatra, finally reached the conclusion that the future of the Republic under Antony's leadership was hopeless. And so he too decided to desert. Gravely ill though he was – probably infected by the epidemics that were attacking the soldiers and sailors – he took a small boat, and had himself rowed across to Octavian's headquarters. Against Cleopatra's wishes, Antony courteously sent his baggage on after him, making light of his desertion and joking that he evidently could not wait to be in the arms of his mistress at Rome.[14] But Ahenobarbus never reached her, for a few days after joining Octavian he died. Other important desertions followed, among senior officers and client kings alike.[15] Finally Antony was moved to disciplinary action: when he heard that yet another Roman senator and client prince were about to abandon him, they were executed as a warning to others.[16]

*

In early August Antony made a serious attempt to break out. First, he dispatched a land force northwards under the joint command of his friend Dellius and one of the leading Asian client monarchs, Amyntas of Galatia; and then he himself went off and joined them. The ostensible aims of the mission were to seek reinforcements from Macedonia and Thrace, and to contact his trans-Danubian allies in Dacia – in competition with Octavian, who had also sent detachments towards those regions. But Antony's real purpose was to draw off the enemy's attention while his fleet, under Gaius Sosius, tried to break out of the Gulf of Ambracia into the open sea. Either Cleopatra and her ships were with Sosius, or they stayed behind with the intention of following once he had broken through the gap. However, Sosius' attempt failed, and in one of the most important engagements of the war he was driven back inside the gulf.[17] Antony, Dellius and Amyntas now returned and Antony made a further attempt to break the blockade, this time by forcing a cavalry engagement. But that too was unsuccessful, for Amyntas deserted to Octavian, taking with him two thousand horsemen, the best in the whole of the near east. His loyalty, and that of the other Asian princes, had been seriously strained three years earlier when the Donations placed their kingdoms under the titular overlordship of one of Cleopatra's small sons. But their main reason for deserting was that they had decided Octavian was going to win the war.

These abortive Antonian endeavours to smash the blockade were justly singled out for celebration by Horace, in lines of his *Ninth Epode* which were written, or made to look as if they had been written, at this very time. 'Twice a thousand Gauls (Galatians) chanting the name of Caesar (Octavian), turned their snorting steeds towards us; and the ships of the foe, having backed in a leftward direction, lurk hidden inside the harbour.'[18] The same poem refers to Crete, indicating that it was still in Antonian hands, or rather in the titular possession of Cleopatra Selene, just as it had been for the past three years. But soon afterwards the island, or at least portions of it, deserted Antony's cause. For two towns in the north-west, nearest to Greece, are expressly stated to have gone over to Octavian, and Marcus Licinius Crassus, who commanded the Antonian garrison in Crete and Cyrenaica, probably went over at the same time.[19] Crete seems, for the most part, to have passed into the hands of a Greek called Cydas,[20] presumably representing Octavian, but Antony's four legions in Cyrenaica, which still remained loyal to him although abandoned by their commander, were placed under the orders of Lucius Pinarius Scarpus, a relative of Julius Caesar. Scarpus at once began issuing silver coins honouring one of the legions under his command, crediting Antony with his current consulship (of which Octavian had sought to deprive him), and celebrating the most recent victory to which the Antonian side could lay claim.[21]

As the hot month of August wore on, and the blockade at Actium passed into its sixteenth week, Antony's setbacks began to weigh heavily upon him. The health and morale of his men were bad, his shortage of rowers had forced him into numerical inferiority, and the failure of the Egyptian grain supplies was proving impossible to repair. And so at the end of the month he called a decisive Council of War.

Once more, an attempt had to be made to break out. But this time should it be by land or sea? Antony's principal land commander, Canidius Crassus, had previously been in favour of retaining Cleopatra at headquarters, which meant, in effect, that he wanted to settle the war at sea and not on land. But now the deterioration of Antony's naval position had made him change his mind. He urged Antony to withdraw his army northwards, and trust to a land-battle in Macedonia or Thrace to decide the issue. His assurance that Antony's Dacian allies would bring help from the other bank of the Danube was not, perhaps, very convincing.

But he also had other strong arguments to offer. 'There would be no disgrace,' he urged, 'in giving up the control of the sea to Octavian, since his forces had been trained in naval operations during the Sicilian campaign against Sextus Pompeius. On the other hand, it would be absurd for Antony, who was as experienced in fighting on land as any man living, not to take advantage of the superior numbers and equipments of his legions, but to distribute his fighting men among the ships and so fritter away his strength.'[22]

But such a decision would mean abandoning the fleet. And that, in turn, meant abandoning Cleopatra: which Canidius now urged. Either she must try to break out with the rest of the fleet at the head of her own squadron, and share the grave hazards of an attempted escape, or she must depart by land and relinquish her ships. Both these courses were obviously intolerable to her. Both signified that she would lose most of her precious ships; and above all she would, in either case, be separated from Antony upon whom all her fortunes depended. She therefore urged with the utmost insistence that the decision should be sought at sea. If a sea-battle was to be fought, she would fight in it with Antony and her fleet, and her Ptolemaic realm would play its part in the engagement as a sovereign state.

Cleopatra's arguments and pleas prevailed. What the military result would have been if Antony had decided in favour of a land engagement instead, we cannot, of course, tell: though the precedents of Pharsalus and Philippi were scarcely encouraging, and he might well have continued to find it difficult to bring Octavian to battle. But in any case the decision could not be taken on military grounds alone, since it involved political and personal considerations which affected the very survival of Cleopatra and all she stood for. Antony's close relation with her left him no option. He had no illusions about a sea-fight; the very most that he could hope for was to extricate himself and his fleet from an intolerable position, so that he could then continue the fight elsewhere.[23] The Pompeians had several times achieved such extrications in their wars against Caesar, and Antony himself, in the past, had succeeded in bringing off similar manœuvres. Moreover, even now, in spite of desertions, he still had great regions of the wealthy east to fall back upon.

And so the instructions he issued for the forthcoming battle included an order that sails should be taken aboard the ships. In ordinary sea-battles it was not customary to carry sails, because of their bulk and weight; and Antony's order, though he cheerfully explained that it was to facilitate pursuit of the defeated enemy,[24] could not fail to damage the already weakened morale of his men because it suggested, rightly, that he was thinking in terms not of victory, but of escape.

Ancient square-rigged Mediterranean ships found it almost impossible to make headway against a wind. But Antony knew that on this shore, every afternoon, a brisk sailing breeze, the Maestro, rises from the west-north-west. Once it had begun to blow, he and Cleopatra proposed to use it in order to get away. They would sail down the coast of Greece, and then onwards round the south of the Peloponnese. Their destination was to be Egypt, which had often protected the Ptolemies against their foes, and would be the best base for their own future operations. Meanwhile the legions under Canidius Crassus would move eastwards by land, proceeding along the head of the Aegean into Asia Minor. And Canidius was secretly directed to set off as soon as he saw that Antony and Cleopatra had broken out and were on their way.

However, the decisions taken at the Council of War were reported to Octavian soon afterwards, because one of its members deserted and told him all about Antony's situation and decisions.[25] The deserter was Dellius. He was in peril from Cleopatra's anger, he said, because of that tactless joke he had made about her failure to bring in supplies of decent wine; and he declared that an informant, a doctor, had told him she was planning his assassination. He also seized the opportunity to publish intimate letters he claimed to have written her in the past. But his real reason for changing sides was because he believed, like others before him, that Antony could no longer win the war. Dellius had already deserted two successive leaders in the civil wars since Caesar's death, and had been right both times; the decision to escape by sea had convinced him the time was ripe to change sides once again.

Antony did not dispose of nearly enough rowers to man all his ships, and those he could not man he burnt, leaving himself only 230 vessels in face of Octavian's 400. Sixty of these belonged to Cleopatra; they were the remains of her original 200. The tradition grew up that Octavian's ships were much lighter and faster than Antony's,[26] but whether there was any significant difference in size or speed is open to question. In any case, both sides intended to employ the tactics that had served Octavian and Agrippa so well in their decisive victory over Sextus Pompeius five years earlier. On that occasion they had lain alongside the enemy ships and let the infantry board them. With the intention of repeating these methods now – Octavian in order to fight and win, Antony in order to fight his way through and flee – each fleet made abundant use of massive iron-bound timbers to resist ramming, and many legionaries were taken aboard: 20,000, apparently, on Antony's ships,[27] and perhaps 37,000 on Octavian's more numerous vessels. The legionaries were accompanied by archers and slingers – on Antony's side they numbered 2,000 – and towers were constructed for them at bow and stern.

And so, on 2 September 31 BC, the day of the battle of Actium dawned. It began with the spectacle, witnessed by both land armies

from the shore, of the whole fleet of Antony and Cleopatra being rowed out in file through the narrow opening of the Ambracian Gulf. Octavian's first plan had been to let their ships get through and away, believing he could then overtake them and fall on their rear, whereupon many Antonians would desert.[28] But after Dellius had reported that sails would be on board, Agrippa advised against these tactics, since he doubted whether he could ever catch the fugitives. When, therefore, Antony's vessels got outside the gulf and fanned out in a great half-moon, he found Octavian's larger fleet ranged against him in similar formation.[29] Consequently his own ships came to a stop, at a distance of about a mile from their enemies. The centres of both fleets were comparatively weak, and the most senior commanders were elsewhere. On Antony's side, Sosius commanded the left wing, and Antony himself, as commander-in-chief, was with Gellius Publicola on the right. To the rear of his centre was Cleopatra's squadron of sixty ships, with a number of merchantmen in their company. She also had the treasure on board; anxious care had to be taken of her flagship, the *Antonias*, which carried not only her own person, but enormous quantities of gold and silver coin, as well as bars of the same precious metals, and jewels, and other valuables. Octavian's right wing, opposite Sosius, was under his own command, though he gave himself a roving commission. His left, opposite Antony and Publicola, was under the orders of Agrippa, who was entrusted with the supreme direction.[30]

Octavian's tactics were to lure Antony's ships out into the open water and force them to spread out, so that they could then be outflanked and outnumbered by his own much more numerous craft. Antony, who had to get through the line of enemy ships, must forestall this tactic by forcing his foes to come to grips before open water was reached. But Octavian held off. This meant that Antony had only two courses of action: either he must return to harbour, or he must move further out, in order to be able to engage in battle. Since the former course would obviously be disastrous, he had to go on; and at about midday, his rowers started forward again, with Sosius and his left wing in the lead. Octavian, opposite Sosius, was delighted,[31] and backed water so as to lure him as far out to sea as he could. Meanwhile Agrippa, on Octavian's left wing, had extended his line outwards, and Publicola, facing him, moved outwards too, so as not to be outflanked.

This, then, was the position when the two fleets clashed and grappled. However, owing to the preceding manœuvres their already weak centres had thinned considerably, and, as these central vessels became locked in an even fight, Cleopatra's squadron, led by herself in her flagship, suddenly pressed forward, passed through first Antony's centre and then Octavian's, and with the help of the afternoon breeze[32] set off southwards through the open sea. At one moment the two entire fleets were locked in battle; at the next Cleopatra had moved through them and disengaged. For her the battle was over.

Contrary to the reports later spread by her numerous detractors, the plan had surely been prearranged with Antony; and so far it had gone well. Moreover, Antony himself, after a hazardous moment, was equally successful in carrying out the second stage of the plan, which involved his own disengagement and departure. For this he now managed to achieve, though he was obliged to abandon his heavily-engaged flagship for another vessel, taking only Alexander the Syrian and Scellius in his company. But thereafter the plan began to break down. It had been the intention that the other first-line craft, when they saw Antony escape, should immediately get away and follow. But very few of them were able to achieve this since Octavian's numerical superiority told so severely that, after 30 or 40 of the Antonian ships had been sunk, the others were compelled to surrender. Some capitulated during the battle itself, but a greater number backed into the gulf and were blockaded there by Octavian, who remained at sea all night to make sure they did not get away. In the morning they bowed to the inevitable, and gave in.[33] Perhaps the total number that surrendered was 130 or 140.[34] The number of Antony's soldiers who were killed did not exceed 5,000, though casualties among crews must have been higher.

Meanwhile, at sea, Antony and Cleopatra had shaken off a damaging attack by the Spartan princeling Eurycles – and were well away heading towards the south. It took them three days to reach the naval station at Cape Taenarum, the southern point of the Peloponnese, which, although not far from Methone, had hitherto remained in Antony's hands. During the voyage he may not have been so melodramatically dejected as Plutarch likes to record. He had fought the battle not to win but to escape with Cleopatra, and that was what they had succeeded in doing. True, nearly three-quarters of the fleet was captured or destroyed, but 'to save even sixty ships out of two hundred and thirty was a creditable achievement for a man embayed on a lee shore and vastly outnumbered'.[35] A battle was lost, but not necessarily the war, which could be renewed in other lands or waters.

When they called in at Taenarum, they learned nothing to contradict this view. For Canidius Crassus' large land army still seemed intact. And so, after taking leave of a number of his associates and sending instructions to Corinth which he believed to be loyal,[36] Antony sailed on with Cleopatra towards north Africa, in the belief that the army was withdrawing to Asia to await his instructions. It was during this further voyage that he discovered his hopes were illusory.[37] Canidius' force had duly struggled off towards Macedonia, but when a column sent by Octavian caught up with them they halted, and their leading centurions decided to negotiate. Octavian offered highly favourable terms, which, in the end, they accepted. It was not so much that the soldiers disliked Cleopatra – though no doubt many of their officers did. But the men wanted their traditional piece of land, preferably in Italy, and any prospect that Antony could provide this had receded into the indefinite distance. The surrender of this great land force converted the naval battle of Actium, in retrospect, into a more decisive engagement than it had seemed at the time. Canidius and his fellow-generals, abandoned by their troops, fled secretly by night to Antony. But Octavian was happy not only to give the Antonian soldiers good terms, but to save their faces as well; and he therefore spread the myth that they had bravely gone on fighting until Canidius fled and betrayed them.[38]

This was only one of a number of myths spread by the victors in the

Actium campaign. The most poisonous of these stories, and the most suitable for Roman consumption, was the report that Cleopatra's flight from the battle, far from conforming to a plan prearranged with Antony, had taken place without his knowledge or approval: she had betrayed him in order to save herself, as might be expected of the degenerate foreign queen who had been solemnly declared the enemy of Rome.[39] The Augustan poets, however, prefer a second myth, which tells how Antony deserted his troops and seamen and fled after Cleopatra, because he was so hopelessly infatuated.[40]

> How infamous a love was she
> Who bade him turn his ships and flee
> On earth's remotest bounds to live
> Defeated and a fugitive!

'He thus proved,' adds Plutarch, 'the truth of the saying which was once uttered as a jest, namely that a lover's soul dwells in the body of another, and he allowed himself to be dragged along after the woman, as if he had become a part of her flesh and must go wherever she led him.'[41]

A third myth that similarly established itself has a certain amount of truth in it: namely, the Augustan tradition that Actium was a great battle which decided the supremacy of the West over the East. This was true to the extent that the result of the battle *did* cause Octavian's conception of empire, based on the supremacy of Italy, to prevail over Antony's and Cleopatra's, based on a more or less equal partnership of Romans and Greeks. In that sense all the pro-western propaganda about Actium, although it deliberately deformed Cleopatra's Hellenism into a monstrous and degraded oriental luxury, was true. Yet in order to load this message with all the force it could command, Actium also had to be converted, retrospectively, into a great naval engagement. To see it as it really was – a blockade-breaking attempt that was only partially foiled – was not nearly dramatic enough. Nothing much could be said, therefore, of Agrippa's preceding patient months of successful strategy and tactics. Instead, the whole glory must be vested in the climactic clash, the naval battle to end all naval battles; all the most resplendent language of Augustan poetry was mobilized to secure acceptance of this version. It is immortalized by Horace:[42]

> Today is the day to drink and dance on. Dance, then,
> Merrily, friends, till the earth shakes. Now let us
>   Rival the priests of Mars
> With feasts to deck the couches of the gods.

213

Not long ago it would have been high treason
To fetch the Caecuban from family store-rooms,
    When the wild Queen was still
Plotting destruction to our Capitol

And ruin to the Empire with her squalid
Pack of diseased half-men – mad, wishful grandeur,
    Tipsy with sweet good luck!
But all her fleet burnt, scarcely one ship saved –

That tamed her rage; and Caesar, when his galleys
Chased her from Italy, soon brought her, dreaming
    And drugged with native wine,
Back to the hard realities of fear.

As swiftly as the hawk follows the feeble
Dove, or in snowy Thessaly the hunter
    The hare, so he sailed forth
To bind this fatal prodigy in chains.

And Virgil, too, devotes to the historic and fateful scene, prophetically engraved upon the shield of Julius's ancestor Aeneas, one of the most solemn passages of the entire *Aeneid*:[43]

Between these scenes on a broad swathe there swept
A golden semblance of the swelling sea,
Its blue billows flecked with whitening wave crests,
And all about it dolphins silver bright
Threaded, and thrashed the surface with their tails.
Then you could see as centrepiece the battle.
All Leucate was clear as it throbbed with warwork,
And the waves gleamed with gold. There was Augustus
Leading the Italians into battle, the whole Senate
And people behind him, and the small household Gods,
And the Great of Heaven – he stood on the high stern:
Twin flames played round his joyous brow, the Star
Of his Father dawned above his head. Elsewhere
Agrippa, with the aid of winds and gods,
Towering led his line, and on his brows,
A proud war-emblem, gleamed the naval crown
Embellished with its replicas of ships' rams.
Opposing them was Antony backed by the riches
Of all East and various nations' arms,
A conqueror from the far East and the shores
Of the red sea, enlisting with him Egypt
And the strength of the Orient and the farthest limits
Of Bactria and – shame! – his Egyptian spouse.
The navies closed at speed and the whole sea

Boiled with oar-strokes and the three-pronged rams.
They sought the open sea and you would think
The Cyclades uprooted were afloat,
Or that high mountains crashed against high mountains.
So bulked the embattled poops on which the warriors mustered;
Wads of blazing tow and a whirl of steel
From every hand came hurling, and Neptune's fields
Were newly incarnadined. In the midst the Queen
Rallied her forces with her native timbrel:
Nor did she give us yet a glance at the pair
Of asps in wait for her. Here were her gods,
Monsters of every kind, to the baying doghead Anubis,
With weapons poised against Neptune, against Venus,
Against Minerva. In the thick of the fray
Raged Mars, picked out in iron, and from the sky
Loomed the grim Furies; Discord swept along
Rejoicing, her mantle rent, and Bellona followed her
With a bloody knout. Apollo of Actium,
Seeing all this from above, was drawing his bow,
In dread of which every Egyptian,
Indian, and Arab, every Sabaean there
Was turning his back for flight. The Queen herself
Was shown as she whistled for the wind of flight,
And setting sail she was shaking loose the sheets.
The Master of Fire had printed upon her the pallor
Of her approaching death, as she forged ahead
Cleaving the slaughter, with following wind and tide.

13

Cleopatra's Death

When Antony and Cleopatra fled from Actium, poetic licence spoke of Octavian's hot pursuit.[1] Yet in fact he did not immediately attempt to follow them, but paused to consolidate his gains. First, he proceeded to Athens, where he displayed a pious phil-Hellenism intended to outbid Antony's, and sought initiation in the Mysteries of Demeter at Eleusis. Then, since Asia Minor as well as Greece had gone over to his side, he crossed the Aegean to Samos and established his winter quarters there.

At Samos, however, he received disquieting news from Italy. While he was away fighting the Actium campaign, a young man named Marcus Lepidus, son of the Triumvir dismissed five years earlier, had been caught in an alleged conspiracy at Rome, and Octavian's representative in Italy, Maecenas, put him to death. Learning of the tension the incident had caused, Octavian promptly sent Agrippa home to reinforce the authority of Maecenas. But when Agrippa arrived in Italy, he was at once confronted with a far more serious outburst of discontent. It arose among the very numerous soldiers who had been fighting for Octavian in his various campaigns, or had been taken over from his defeated enemies. They were demanding release, rewards and land. Before long, Octavian himself had to hasten back across the Ionian Sea to Brundusium, where official congratulations for Actium were soured by the rudeness of the veterans.

He calmed them as well as he could. But one thing had become abundantly clear. They would not be content for any length of time unless he could lay hands on Cleopatra's ancestral treasure, the treasure which she had restored to something like its ancient dimensions – the last great accumulation of Mediterranean wealth that still remained outside the grasp of Rome. The seizure of the Ptolemaic treasure had become essential, since there was no other way of paying the soldiers off. So the losing side in the war might still win the peace, if they could only keep the riches of Egypt out of Octavian's hands.

*

As Antony and Cleopatra approached north Africa in their flight, messengers informed them that their land army in northern Greece had surrendered; and it became clear that their general in Cyrenaica, Scarpus, had also gone over to Octavian, whose name now replaces Antony's on his coinage.[2] So Antony felt it wise to stop for some weeks at the Greek town of Paraetonium, just inside Egypt, in case Scarpus tried to sail past towards Alexandria. The stone quay where he landed is still to be seen. 'Only those,' remarked Arthur Weigall, 'who have visited these regions in the summer time can realize the strange melancholy, the complete loneliness, of this sun-scorched outpost.'[3] Cleopatra did not stay with Antony at Paraetonium, for it seemed best that she should sail straight back to her country. Her arrival might well have been the signal for a revolt among her political enemies, but she faced her supreme crisis with resolution.

Cleopatra had hastened to Egypt, for fear that her subjects would begin a revolt if they heard of the disaster before her arrival. And in order to make her approach safe she crowned her prows with garlands as if she had actually won a victory, and had songs of triumph chanted to the accompaniment of pipes. But as soon as she had reached safety, she slew many of the foremost men, since they had always been displeased with her and were now elated over her disaster; and she proceeded to gather vast wealth from her estates and from various other sources, both profane and sacred, sparing not even the most holy shrines, and also to fit out her forces and to look about for allies.[4]

Antony, on the other hand, when he finally rejoined her in Alexandria, sat in despair in a tower in the harbour, which he named the Timonium after the misanthrope Timon of Athens. Finally he returned to the palace, where the royal dining club of the Inimitables was renamed, with similar desperate bravado, 'Those who are going to die together'.[5]

Cleopatra was busy with every scheme she could think of to perpetuate the rule of her dynasty, whatever might happen to herself. A great show, almost comparable to the Donations four years earlier, was laid on to stimulate the loyalty of the Alexandrians. It celebrated the coming of age both of her son, the King of Kings, Ptolemy xv Caesar (Caesarion), and of Antony's eldest son and personal heir Antyllus. Caesarion, aged sixteen, was enrolled in the ephebate, the youth organization which was one of the most characteristic institutions of the Hellenistic and Ptolemaic world. Antyllus, who was about fourteen, was invested with the *toga virilis*, which enrolled him as a Roman adult.

Cleopatra staged the ceremony for Caesarion, we are told, because she wanted to show the Egyptians that they now had a grown man capable of acting as their king.[6] She may have been encouraged by alleged assurances from certain Egyptians, perhaps including her friends who were priests in Upper Egypt, that they were ready to take up arms in her cause.[7] Yet she should have realized that to the victorious Octavian, Caesarion and Antyllus would seem a greater potential danger as adults than if they remained minors.

Before long, she apparently came to appreciate this herself, since she decided to send Caesarion away.[8] Accompanied by his tutor Rhodon and part of the royal treasure, he travelled up the Nile to Coptos (Kuft), with the intention of reaching the port of Berenice across the regular desert camel-track. From there he proposed to sail to India, with which Egypt had trading relations.

Cleopatra, too, began to plan her own emigration to the east, where her resources would enable her to found a new oriental kingdom, as other Hellenistic rulers, the Indo-Greeks, had done before her. At one time she thought of going to Spain instead,[9] but Caesarion's dispatch towards the Indies was a sign that she also was preparing to move east. First, she took steps to safeguard her alliance with the king of Media, whose infant daughter Iotape, betrothed to her son Alexander Helios, was still in Egypt. Media was alarmed, not for the first time, by the prospect of an imminent invasion from the Parthians, who were ready to take advantage of Rome's preoccupation with its civil war. And Cleopatra now offered them a demonstration of her goodwill by executing her prisoner, the king of Armenia, whom the Median monarch (called Artavasdes, like himself) hated because of his friendship with Parthia. She may also have sent Alexander Helios to Media for his safety.[10]

As for herself, she decided that the best escape route was provided by the Red Sea, to which she arranged to have ships transferred from the Nile. She did not, however, use the Ptolemaic canal from river to sea, either because it was out of order or because its channel was too small for warships. Instead she transported her vessels overland to Heroonpolis (Tell Mashkutah) which stood on a sort of inlet of the Gulf of Suez. We have no details of this remarkable enterprise, which presumably involved the raising of the ships on to wooden frames borne on solid wheels or rollers, so that a labour force could then pull them along, perhaps for more than twenty miles. However, when the ships had safely arrived at their destination, Malchus, the monarch of the Nabataean Arab kingdom, fell upon them and burnt them; and at the same time he may have destroyed other ships Cleopatra was building there.[11] This seemed ungrateful, since it was only a year or two since Cleopatra had intervened to prevent Malchus from being crushed by Herod. But the Arab could never forget that Cleopatra had persuaded Antony to give her the revenue of his Dead Sea bitumen deposits, and probably a strip of the Arabian Red Sea coast as well. Cleopatra, according to one source, revenged herself for the destruction of her fleet by having Malchus murdered.[12] But she had to give up her idea of leaving Egypt; and later she expressed understandable regret that she had not managed to get away.

*

Such protection as may have been offered Malchus by Quintus Didius, the Roman governor of Syria-Cilicia, had not availed to save him. Yet it was Didius who had instigated the burning of Cleopatra's ships. For the governor, like almost everyone else in the eastern world, was now aware of the menacing presence of Octavian, and was seeking to fall in with his wishes. Leaving Italy at the earliest possible moment of the new year 30 BC, Octavian was soon back in Samos. From there he proceeded east. When the Syrians learnt of his approach, their loyalty to Antony and Cleopatra – still intact on official coinages of 31 and on city-coinages even of 30[13]–sharply declined, and the scramble to change sides was led by the governor of Syria himself. It is possible that Didius was not the first holder of this post to desert, but that his predecessor had already gone over to Octavian.[14] At any rate, Didius not only persuaded Malchus to burn Cleopatra's Red Sea fleet, but arranged for the interception of a party of gladiators, who were marching from Cyzicus (Bal Kiz) in north-western Asia Minor to Antony's assistance. At Didius' request, they were stopped by King Herod.[15]

For Herod too had made his peace with the victor. When Octavian moved on from Samos to Rhodes, Herod came there to visit him; and, according to his own account preserved in the pages of Josephus, he made a frank and dignified statement indicating that he had been loyal to Antony and would be loyal to Octavian as well. He added an assurance that, after Actium, he had urged Antony to kill Cleopatra; this is certainly possible, since at that stage she could not have retaliated. Octavian accepted Herod's plea, because, like Antony, he believed that a dependent kingdom in Judaea was useful to Rome, and that Herod was the best man to run it. But the king was less successful when he attempted to secure pardon for a leading friend and adviser of Antony and Cleopatra, Alexas of Laodicea. Alexas had been sent to urge Herod not to desert, but instead he had deserted himself. Octavian refused to spare Alexas, because it was he who had taken the lead in persuading Antony to abandon Octavia.[16]

Herod's defection, though it should not have surprised Cleopatra after the way she had treated him, made a deep impression upon her. Later, according to one reading of Josephus, she cried out that she wished she had slaughtered the Jews with her own hand, because then all would have been well.[17] She was surely referring, at least in part, to Herod and his Judaea. Antony had never allowed her to suppress the kingdom, and consequently Herod had gone over to Octavian, who was now able to make his way unhindered as far as the very gates of Egypt itself: and it may well be that the Egyptian Jews had helped him.

*

Nevertheless, Cleopatra's determination held firm; as long as she possessed her royal treasure, her soldiers were more likely to be paid than Octavian's. She must keep the treasure at all costs, and he at all costs must come and take it.

In the course of the summer Octavian disembarked at Ptolemais Ace in Phoenicia. But either before or after he had reached this stage of his journey, he received no less than three envoys from Alexandria, making various suggestions intended to ensure the survival of the Ptolemaic house.[18] The first messenger brought Cleopatra's royal insignia, which, in imitation of Herod, she placed at his disposal. She herself was prepared to abdicate, she said, but she asked that her children should be allowed to inherit the Egyptian throne. Octavian kept the insignia, but gave an evasive reply.

The second envoy had been sent by Antony, and was his own son Antyllus, who had once been engaged to Octavian's daughter. He now handed over a large sum of money, and announced that his father was willing to retire into private life. Arrangements were also made, shamefully, to hand over Decimus Turullius, as one of Caesar's last surviving assassins, against whom Octavian had sworn revenge. Octavian had Turullius executed at Cos, where he was unpopular because he had plundered the sacred grove of Asclepius for timber. But to Antony's offer of retirement he gave no answer. Then, finally, Cleopatra sent a tutor of her children, Euphronius, with a further large bribe, in order to reiterate the plea that they should be allowed to succeed to her kingdom. Once again there was no positive reaction.

*

Octavian's forces were now closing in on Egypt. The poet Cornelius Gallus, a friend of Virgil, came east from the province of Africa to replace Scarpus in Cyrenaica, and started to sail on towards Egypt. Antony went to stop him with forty ships, but lost the frontier-post Paraetonium and the ships as well; and before long Gallus' flotilla had moved onwards past the Egyptian frontier. Meanwhile, from the eastern desert, with the assistance of Herod, Octavian in person approached the delta, and took Pelusium by storm. Cleopatra put the wife and children of its unsuccessful commander, Seleucus, to death. Statements that she deliberately arranged for the place to be betrayed, like other rumours of her alleged treacheries to Antony at this time, are probably groundless, belonging to the same hostile tradition which asserted that she had betrayed Antony at Actium: even the Augustan poets do not favour this kind of report.[19] But as Octavian came nearer and nearer, she apparently ceased any diplomatic approaches and concentrated instead, on her chief concern: the retention and protection of her treasure somewhere beyond his reach. For this purpose, she chose the mausoleum she had constructed for herself in the royal cemetery of the Ptolemies beside the tomb of Alexander the Great. As Plutarch wrote:

Not long before, she had built for herself a number of high monuments and tombs of great beauty near the Temple of Isis, and she now collected here all the most precious items of the royal treasures, gold, silver, emeralds, pearls, ebony, ivory, and cinnamon – and also a great quantity of firewood and tinder. Octavian became alarmed at these preparations, and as he drew nearer to the city with his army he continued to send her messages and hints of generous treatment, for he was afraid that Cleopatra might set fire to all this wealth in a fit of despair.[20]

One such letter was conveyed to her by a clever and attractive young freedman called Thyrsus.[21] But Antony had him flogged, and then returned him, saying that Octavian was at liberty to retaliate by flogging a former freedman of Antony named Hipparchus, one of his supporters who had changed sides. At about this time, too, Antony sent a message to Octavian saying that he was prepared to kill himself if this would save Cleopatra. But once again no answer was forthcoming.

Octavian had now penetrated to Alexandria's eastern suburb Canopus, the favourite pleasure resort of Antony and Cleopatra. As the invaders encamped near the hippodrome, Antony fell upon their advance cavalry and put them to flight. 'And then,' Plutarch continues, 'elated by his victory, he marched back in triumph to the city, entered the palace, embraced Cleopatra just as he was in full armour, and presented to her one of his soldiers who had fought particularly well. Cleopatra gave the man a golden breastplate and helmet as a reward for his valour. He accepted them – and the very same night deserted to Octavian.'[22] Nevertheless, Antony tried to win over the advancing legionaries by shooting arrows carrying financial promises into their camp. These were rejected, and so was Antony's proposal that he and Octavian should settle the issue by single combat, to which Octavian merely replied that there were all sorts of other ways in which Antony could get rid of himself quite easily.

When Antony read this message he knew that the time had come for the final, fateful battle by sea and land. That evening he dined particularly well, in the knowledge that the very next day would bring an end, one way or the other.

There was a familiar legend that the gods abandon a city before its fall. They had abandoned doomed Troy, and Athens, and Jerusalem.[23] And that night, it was said, Dionysus was heard leaving Alexandria.

About the hour of midnight, so the story goes, when all was hushed and a mood of dejection and fear of its impending fate brooded over the whole city, suddenly a marvellous sound of music was heard, which seemed to come from a consort of instruments of every kind, and voices chanting in harmony, and at the same time the shouting of a crowd in which the cry of Bacchanals and the ecstatic leaping of satyrs were mingled, as if a troop of revellers were leaving the city, shouting and singing as they went. The procession seemed to follow a course through the middle of the city towards the outer gate, which led to the enemy's camp, and at this point the sounds reached their climax and then died away. Those who tried to discover a meaning for this prodigy concluded that the god Dionysus, with whom Antony claimed kinship and whom he sought above all to imitate, was now abandoning him.[24]

The story moved the Alexandrian poet, Cavafy, to a poem about this solemn moment in the life of his city, the city where Antony and Cleopatra had lived:[25]

> When suddenly there is heard at midnight
> A company passing invisible
> With wonderful music, with voices,
> Your fortune giving way now, your works
> All turned illusions, do not mourn uselessly.
> As one prepared long since, courageously,
> Say farewell to her, to Alexandria who is leaving.
> Above all do not be tricked, never say it was
> All a dream, and that your hearing was deceived;
> Do not stoop to such vain hopes as these.
> As one prepared long since, courageously,
> As becomes one worthy as you were of such a city,
> Firmly draw near the window,
> And listen with emotion, but not
> With the complainings and entreaties of cowards,
> Listen, your last enjoyment, to the sounds,
> The wonderful instruments of the mystic company,
> And say farewell, farewell to Alexandria you are losing.

*

On the next day, 1 August, Antony's fleet sailed eastwards out of Alexandria to engage the enemy's ships, while his army, such as it was, stood drawn up on rising ground between the hippodrome and the walls. But his fleet surrendered without a fight, and his cavalry did the same; and then the infantry force precipitately fled. Antony was heard crying out that Cleopatra had betrayed him. In this hour of final defeat and disappointment, it is possible that some such words passed his lips.

But, if so, his inference that Cleopatra was a traitress was unjustified. At this late and hopeless hour, no persuasion from her had been needed to show the soldiers and sailors the wisdom of desertion.

Octavian entered the city, and in spite of the anti-climax of the battle, the first of August was ever afterwards celebrated as a public holiday. For this, it was declared, was the day 'when Imperator Caesar rescued the state from the grimmest peril'.[26] And for the same reason the conqueror chose this month, rather than September in which he had been born, as the month that should bear his later name Augustus. These were imposing testimonials to the fears Cleopatra had inspired.

After the battle, she fled inside her mausoleum, and barricaded herself with her treasure, accompanied only by Iras her hairdresser, Charmion her lady-in-waiting, and a eunuch.[27] A report came to Antony that she had committed suicide. She was said to have sent the news herself in order to persuade him to do likewise, but perhaps she had dispatched some other incoherent message which was misunderstood. At all events Antony believed that she was dead, and ordered his servant Eros to kill him too. But Eros turned the blade upon himself: so Antony took another sword, and plunged it into his own body.

As he lay dying, Cleopatra's secretary Diomedes came to tell him that she was still alive, and that she wanted him to come to her. Two slaves carried him to the mausoleum, but since the doors were sealed he had to be hoisted through a window in the uncompleted upper storey of the building. When, with the utmost difficulty, the queen and her attendants brought him in, Antony called for a glass of wine. Then, it was said, he 'begged her not to grieve over this wretched change in his fortunes, but to count him happy for the glories he had won and to remember that he had attained the greatest fame and power of any man in the world, so that now it was no dishonour to die a Roman, conquered only by a Roman.'[28] But this wording, in all probability, goes back to one of his Roman admirers, who wanted to minimize the phil-Hellenic policies to which he had been so attached.

Soon afterwards he died. One of his bodyguard hastened to Octavian with the news, taking the dead man's bloodstained sword as proof. During the last moments of his life, Antony told Cleopatra to put her trust in a Roman knight on Octavian's staff called Gaius Proculeius, the brother-in-law of Maecenas. She must have followed his advice very quickly, for it was not long before Proculeius appeared in front of the mausoleum, with orders from Octavian to capture Cleopatra alive, if he could, and above all to prevent her from setting fire to her treasure. Proculeius stood in front of the barricaded door, and spoke to her through a grating. Nothing conclusive was said, but Proculeius noticed the open window on the upper floor, through which the dying Antony had been brought in. He returned to report to Octavian, but was soon back again, accompanied by Cornelius Gallus (who had led the invading fleet from Cyrenaica). This time it was Gallus who walked up to the door and spoke with the queen. But meanwhile, out of sight, Proculeius placed a ladder beneath the window, climbed up rapidly with two servants, and burst into the building. Once inside, he rushed down the stairs, and seized hold of Cleopatra as she stood talking to Gallus. She grasped a dagger inside her dress, but Proculeius disarmed her, and she was taken prisoner.[29]

Octavian's anxieties were at an end, for he had gained possession not only of the queen but of her treasure. When news of its acquisition reached Rome, and various financial measures had been taken, the standard rate of interest fell from twelve to four per cent. At last he could satisfy his veterans. His new riches enabled him to buy land for many thousands of them, and to issue coinages of unprecedented size.

Proculeius left his freedman Epaphroditus in the mausoleum, to keep guard over Cleopatra.[30] Very soon afterwards, however, with Octavian's authorization, she left the building in order to arrange for Antony's body to be embalmed with appropriate rites. But his death and her own capture had shattered her spirit and she fell ill. Octavian had her moved to the palace. It was said that he wanted to keep her alive for his Triumph at Rome. But this was a fate, she told her attendants, that she would never accept.[31] Shakespeare, reading of her refusal, imagined her elaborating on the theme:[32]

> Now, Iras, what think'st thou?
> Thou, an Egyptian puppet, shall be shown
> In Rome, as well as I: mechanic slaves
> With greasy aprons, rules and hammers, shall
> Uplift us to the view: in their thick breaths,
> Rank of gross diet, shall we be enclosed
> And forced to drink their vapour ...
> Nay, 'tis most certain, Iras: saucy lictors
> Will catch at us like strumpets, and scald rhymers
> Ballad us out o'tune: the quick comedians
> Extemporally will stage us and present
> Our Alexandrian revels; Antony
> Shall be brought drunken forth, and I shall see
> Some squeaking Cleopatra boy my greatness
> I'th' posture of a whore ...
> Shall they hoist me up
> And show me to the shouting varletry
> Of censuring Rome? Rather a ditch in Egypt
> Be gentle grave unto me! Rather on Nilus' mud
> Lay me stark nak'd, and let the water-flies

> Blow me into abhorring! Rather make
> My country's high pyramids my gibbet,
> And hang me up in chains!

But the report that Octavian wanted Cleopatra to figure in his Roman Triumph is unlikely to be true. He remembered that the presence of her half-sister Arsinoe at the Triumph of Caesar, sixteen years previously, had caused a revulsion of popular sympathy in her favour, and he was anxious that all his propaganda depicting Cleopatra as the devil incarnate should not be undermined by any similar reversal of opinion. Besides, her appearance in a Triumph might well be interpreted as an insult to the memory of Caesar, who had placed her statue in the Temple of Venus Genetrix. Most intractable of all was the problem of what to do with her once the Triumph was over. To execute a woman would greatly damage his reputation. Yet he would by no means feel safe with the continuing presence of Cleopatra on some Aegean rock, writing her memoirs.[33]

It would therefore be much better if she died. But he did not want to seem responsible for her death. He is said to have visited her at the palace. But all the details given of the interview bear the marks of romantic fiction or propaganda, and it is more than doubtful if it ever took place.[34] To the biographers it seemed a necessary and symbolic climax,[35] but to Octavian it could have served no conceivable purpose. Instead, he arranged for her to be visited by a young and aristocratic member of his entourage, Publius Cornelius Dolabella, whom he knew to have been on friendly terms with her.[36] Dolabella's mission was to inform her privately that Octavian was leaving for Rome, and he was instructed to pretend that she and her children were also to be sent there, in order to appear in his Triumph; they were leaving in three days' time. Cleopatra sought permission, which was granted, to pour a last libation at Antony's tomb, on the ostensible grounds that she wanted to pay a final tribute to his remains before leaving on the long journey to Italy. But Octavian was well aware that she would rather die than go. For Cleopatra, the end had come.

> Finish, good lady, the bright day is done.
> And we are for the dark.[37]

Her guard, Epaphroditus, was told by Octavian that if he learnt of any plans for her suicide he was to turn a blind eye – though, in order to spare Octavian from any imputation of complicity, the story had to be spread later that her apparently cheerful attitude had entirely deceived them both.[38] On about 12 August, she asked Epaphroditus to convey a sealed letter to Octavian, and he duly sent the messenger she requested. The letter contained a request that she should be buried beside Antony;

225

and Octavian knew that this meant she had put an end to her life. He sent men to the palace, and they found her lying upon a golden couch, dressed in her royal robes. She was already dead, and Iras lay dying at her feet. Charmion, also at the point of death, was trying to adjust the diadem on the brow of her mistress. One of the guards cried out 'Charmion, was this right?' And Charmion's last words were the epitaph for a whole epoch: 'It is entirely right,' she managed to say, 'and fitting for a queen descended from so many kings.'[39]

Cleopatra had poisoned herself. The Alexandrian School of Medicine, including no doubt her own personal doctor Olympus, were well informed about poisons of every kind. But how she did the deed was the subject of a great deal of speculation which has continued in later centuries; and the answer was never known. The ancient writers, usually so ready with the fictitious explanations required by propaganda or romance, report this uncertainty categorically. Strabo, who died in the twenties AD, knew of at least two contradictory accounts, and hesitated between the venom of a snake and a poisonous ointment.[40] The second-century physician Galen refers to a belief that Cleopatra bit herself and poured snake poison into the wound.[41] 'But no one knows clearly how she died,' says Dio Cassius, 'for the only marks on her body were slight pricks upon the arm.'[42] Some told, he added, of a snake brought in hidden inside a water jar or among flowers, while others believed she had scratched her arm with a poisoned hair-pin. Plutarch marshals an even greater variety of stories, with equally inconclusive results. According to one:[43]

A snake was carried in to her with figs by an Egyptian peasant, and lay hidden under the leaves in his basket, for Cleopatra had given orders that the snake should settle on her without her being aware of it, so the story goes, and said, 'So there it is', and, baring her arm, she held it out to be bitten. Others say it was carefully shut up inside a jug and that Cleopatra provoked it by pricking it with a golden spindle, until it sprang out and fastened itself upon her arm. But the real truth nobody knows, for there is another story that she carried poison about with her in a hollow comb, which she kept hidden in her hair, and yet no inflammation nor any other symptom of poison broke out on her body.

And indeed the snake was never discovered inside the monument, although some marks which might have been its trail are said to have been noticed on the beach on that side where the windows of the chamber looked out towards the sea. Some people also say that two faint, barely visible punctures were found on Cleopatra's arm. And Octavian himself seems to have believed this, for when he celebrated his Triumph he had a figure of Cleopatra with the snake clinging to her carried in the procession.

The story that she died of a snake-bite was the version that finally prevailed, though this legend perhaps gained currency because a snake often appeared upon statues of the goddess Isis,[44] including some that have been found at Rome.[45] The statue 'of Cleopatra' which figured in the Triumph (Propertius saw it with his own eyes),[46] may well have been an effigy of Isis, or of Cleopatra as Isis; and this, probably, inspired onlookers at the Triumph to draw the conclusion that a snake had caused Cleopatra's mysterious death.[47]

The blackish or brown-and-yellow Egyptian cobra, personified by the cobra goddess in the marshes of the delta,[48] had been the special protector of the Pharaohs, and its image, threatening their enemies, took pride of place in the insignia upon their brows. The same snake-diadem continued to be employed during the Ptolemaic era. In this period, as earlier, it sometimes took the form of two snakes instead of one; and knowledge that this was so created a tradition that Cleopatra's death was caused not by one snake, but two.[49] That is why Propertius referred to them in the plural:[50]

> I've seen the sacred adders' fang
> Upon her bosom close and hang,
> And her whole body slowly creep
> On the dark road to endless sleep.

Horace likewise speaks not of a snake but of snakes, while Virgil explicitly refers to '*the pair* of asps in wait for her' – not the only passage in which he sees twin snakes as a sign of death.[51] There was also an Egyptian idea that death by snake-bite conferred immortality.[52] But neither the Pharaohs nor the Ptolemies needed any such additional conferment, since they were already immortal in their lifetimes. The story of Cleopatra's snake-bite was intended only to show that she had died a queenly death, by the poison of the snake which was the royal crown itself.[53]

Capital punishment in Alexandria was sometimes inflicted by the bite of a cobra, since this was considered the most painless and humane method of execution.[54] But the anti-Cleopatran tradition at Rome developed a legend that the queen, before choosing to die in this way, had tested out various ways of dying upon criminals in the Alexandrian market-place, callously scrutinizing their death-agonies.[55] Surprisingly enough, Octavian did not echo this hostile version. For now that his enemy was dead, and he himself was going to occupy the throne of the Ptolemies, he could afford to be generous. With his usual deliberation, he began to display a measure of belated respect for the memory of the queen. In the first place, he let it be understood that the instant he learnt of her suicidal act he had summoned snake-charmers, known as Psylli, and had ordered them to suck the poison from the wound.[56] No doubt the report that he had summoned them was true, for to invent such an assertion would too easily lay him open to a charge of lying. But of course they arrived too late – which did not surprise or disappoint him. Secondly, he allowed Cleopatra to be buried with royal honours beside Antony, giving orders that the construction of her mausoleum should be completed for the purpose, and that Iras and Charmion should be buried with their mistress. And thirdly Octavian, though he had so greatly detested Cleopatra when she was alive, allowed himself to be heard expressing admiration of the lofty spirit with which she died. Virgil, too, for all his abhorrence of everything she stood for, writes with profound feeling of the sorrowing god of the Nile who received her as she fled back to Egypt, with the pallor of approaching death already printed upon her countenance:[57]

> Before her was the Nile, his mighty length
> One throe of grief, opening all his breast
> And with his whole raiment summoning the defeated
> To the lap of his blue stream, his harbouring waters.

Octavian's calculated conflict of sentiments, weighing Cleopatra's noble end against her evil life, was even more openly echoed by Horace, to whom the paradox strongly appealed. After he has finished telling of her degraded court, her insane ambition to rule over Rome, her blessed downfall at Actium, and her flight with Octavian close behind her, his tone entirely changes. For she died, it seemed to him, gloriously, and his verses commemorating her death are the finest of her epitaphs:[58]

> Yet she preferred a finer style of dying:
> She did not, like a woman, shirk the dagger
>   Or seek by speed at sea
> To change her Egypt for obscurer shores,
>
> But gazing on her desolated palace
> With a calm smile, unflinchingly laid hands on
>   The angry asps until
> Her veins had drunk the deadly poison deep:
>
> And, death-determined, fiercer then than ever,
> Perished. Was she to grace a haughty triumph,
>   Dethroned, paraded by
> The rude Liburnians? Not Cleopatra.

14

Cleopatra's Conqueror
in Egypt

Before Cleopatra was dead, Octavian had already installed himself in Alexandria. Proceeding to the Gymnasium, the scene of Antony's Donations, he delivered a speech to the people, informing them that he proposed to be lenient because their city was so splendid, because Alexander was its founder, and because he wanted to please his teacher and adviser on Egyptian affairs, the Alexandrian philosopher Areius.[1] Then he visited the tomb of Alexander (part of whose nose he reportedly broke off by mistake). But he declined a proposed visit to Egyptian temples, saying that he revered gods not bulls, and he also refused to see the tombs of the Ptolemies, indicating that he found corpses of no interest. For he did not want to associate himself too openly with the Ptolemaic régime – at least not for the moment.

Alleged profiteers of Cleopatra's time were tried and put to death.[2] He also killed her son, Ptolemy xv Caesar or Caesarion, who was the reputed son of Caesar, and the eldest son of Antony and Fulvia, Antyllus. The recent coming-of-age of the two boys had done nothing to help their chances, but even without these ceremonies they could scarcely have hoped to survive. As Caesarion fled southwards in the hope of reaching the Red Sea, his tutor Rhodon betrayed him, and he was overtaken on the road and murdered, or perhaps lured back to his death in Alexandria.[3] In this miserable fashion, before her own death or just after it, Cleopatra's supreme dynastic hope was brought to an end. Octavian's motive in removing Caesarion was admirably summed up by Areius, who remarked, parodying a verse of the *Iliad*, that 'it is bad to have too many Caesars'.[4]

To us it is clear that the Roman civil wars were at last over, and that, under the immensely skilled leadership of the new ruler, a historic period of prolonged if not entirely happy stability, the Pax Augusta, had begun. To Octavian, only just emerging from the internecine strife that had continued since before he was born, this cannot have seemed so certain. Nor can he have felt entirely sure that the resurgence of an independent Egypt was out of the question. For such a movement, Caesarion would have been an ideal leader or figurehead. So his life could not be spared.

Antyllus met his death at about the same time. He had sought sanctuary beside a statue of Caesar – probably in the Caesareum which Cleopatra had begun to erect in Caesar's memory – but was dragged from this refuge and beheaded.[5] He, too, had been betrayed by his tutor. But this individual, Theodorus, then found himself accused of stealing a precious stone that his charge had worn round his neck, and was likewise put to death, by crucifixion. Antyllus had paid the penalty for the special signs of honour he had received as Antony's heir. Indeed, Octavian may very well have considered him a greater danger than Caesarion, who, as the son of an Egyptian queen, was never likely to impress the Roman people, whereas Antyllus, already eminent enough to have his head engraved on coins, could easily have given his name to a rebellious movement.

There were also other casualties. In addition to the last two surviving assassins of Caesar, Cassius of Parma and Turullius, the senator who had managed Cleopatra's wool-mill, Quintus Ovinius, was singled out for execution. A further set of Antonians, too, was put to death, including Canidius Crassus. It was with questionable accuracy, therefore, that Octavian afterwards recorded that he had spared all Roman citizens who survived the war and 'asked for pardon'.[6]

All the same, his clemency, even if only relative, was still sufficiently noteworthy for it to be said that his entire circle of intimates were now drawn from Antonians.[7] Moreover, once Antyllus had been removed, he spared all Antony's remaining children, regardless of who their mothers were. His eldest daughter Antonia (by a mother of the same name) had perhaps predeceased her father, but in spite of official Roman disapprobation of her marriage to a foreigner their daughter Pythodoris married successively two of Antony's Asian monarchs, whom Augustus retained, Polemo of Pontus and Archelaus of Cappadocia. Fulvia's younger son Iullus Antonius, the brother of Antyllus, survived under the care of his stepmother Octavia and enjoyed her imperial brother's favour. But twenty-eight years later he was forced to commit suicide for adultery with the emperor's daughter, Julia, since this crime, or the suspicion of it, seemed to augur that very same sinister revival of the Antonian name which had been feared in connection with his elder brother Antyllus.[8] Iullus Antonius had two sons, but when the second and last of them perished in exile, the family died out. Of Antony's daughters by Octavia, the elder became the grandmother of the emperor Nero, and the younger was the grandmother of Caligula and mother of Claudius.

The children of Antony and Cleopatra were not harmed.[9] Their daughter Cleopatra Selene was carried in Octavian's subsequent Triumph at Rome, and then given in marriage to a phenomenally learned Numidian prince Juba II, who obtained the gift of the client kingdom Mauretania in 25 BC, only eight years after Octavian had annexed it to the Roman empire.[10] Their son, whom they ventured to call Ptolemy, succeeded his father in AD 23 and ruled until 40, when he was executed by his cousin Caligula. Alexander Helios was seized – perhaps he had to be fetched back from Media for the purpose – and marched with his sister Cleopatra Selene in Octavian's Triumph. But then he and his small brother Ptolemy Philadelphus were spared and 'given' to Selene and her husband Juba. The subsequent histories of the two boys are entirely unknown, but it is probable that they, too, went to Mauretania, and lived a cautious life that evoked no perilous memories.

*

Egypt was now annexed by Rome. The last great Successor Kingdom of Alexander had finally succumbed, after a life-span of a little less than three centuries. But when the new ruler later declared, 'I added Egypt to the empire of the Roman people',[11] he was, as often, telling something less than the entire truth. For unlike every other major province, the country was placed, not under a senator appointed by the state in the course of his official career, but under a knight (that is to say a man ineligible for such a career) selected personally by the emperor himself; and it was the duty of that knight to make sure that the ultimate control of the country remained directly in the emperor's own hands. Julius Caesar, when he left a garrison in Egypt seventeen years earlier, had decided he could not entrust its command to a senator, and now Octavian came to the same decision about the governorship. This post was first held by the poet and general Cornelius Gallus, previously mentioned as one of the kidnappers of Cleopatra. For the first three years of his tenure, he held only a military rank.[12] After that he was still not called proconsul or *legatus* like the governors of other important provinces, but bore the title of *praefectus* such as was also employed for certain other territories depending directly upon the emperor, though none was as important as Egypt. Gallus had to crush rebellions at Hernoopolis and in Upper Egypt, a region with which Cleopatra had maintained particularly close ties. But he also followed up the active southern policy of her father by advancing beyond the frontier at the First Cataract, creating a buffer state which extended as far as the Second Cataract and establishing a loose suzerainty over Ethiopia. However, Gallus then displayed such arrogant conceit that he was recalled and forced to commit suicide (26 BC), thus confirming Rome's worst suspicions of how officials left in Egypt were likely to behave. Nevertheless, the government of the country by *praefecti* continued.

They extorted work and produce from the Egyptians in much the same way as the Ptolemies had. Indeed, the extortions of the Roman administrators were so effective that before long the country was supplying Rome with enough grain to feed the entire city for four months of every year. On the whole, Roman imperial rule was not as beneficent in Egypt as in certain other parts of the world. Indeed, the new order compared unfavourably with the Ptolemaic régime.[13] But the emperors sought to draw a veil over these shortcomings by entering formally into the heritage of the Pharaohs and allowing themselves to be depicted on temple walls with Pharaonic insignia and titles. Before Octavian left Egypt in 30 BC he had already appointed a new high priest at Memphis, Psenemon, now described as 'the prophet of Caesar', that is to say, of the reigning emperor himself.[14]

Moreover Octavian, after only the briefest hesitation, had decided that donning the Pharaonic mantle involved acceptance of the Ptolemaic calendar, too, and a papyrus duly links him with the immediate past by equating his first year with Cleopatra's last.[15] He also celebrated his Triumph by founding Victory-towns named Nicopolis, not only beside the site of his camp across the strait from Actium,[16] but also on the eastern outskirts of Alexandria itself. He may well, at first, have considered making this foundation his new capital of Egypt in Alexandria's place, but if so he changed his mind, and it became a grandiose Alexandrian suburb (now Ramle) equipped with amphitheatre, stadium and five-yearly Victory Games.[17]

15

Cleopatra's Position in History

Although Cleopatra, not Antony, had been Octavian's declared foe, all his statues at Alexandria were torn down, but hers were allowed to stand, because one of her friends, Archibius, gave the victor two thousand talents to save them from destruction.[1] For a generation to come she was still spoken of as *the* queen, like Arsinoe II before her,[2] and a 'Cleopatreion' mentioned in AD 4–5 at Rosetta (Rashid), like other similar buildings in different parts of the country, appears to have been a shrine erected in her honour.[3] Sixty years after her death an Alexandrian grammarian named Apion, hated by Josephus, championed her memory.[4] Her statue in the Temple of Venus Genetrix at Rome, set up by Julius Caesar, was still standing there in the third century AD, and the cult of Cleopatra Aphrodite remained alive more than one hundred years later still.[5] It was said that another powerful empress Zenobia (Bat Zabbi), ruling in the Syrian desert city of Palmyra (AD 269–73), claimed descent from Cleopatra and made a collection of her drinking cups,[6] and although the story may be fictitious it illustrates the continuing power of the Egyptian queen's name. The historian Ammianus Marcellinus (*c.* AD 330–95) suggests that the Egyptians were still flattering her memory to a scandalous extent,[7] and a Coptic bishop of the seventh century AD, John of Nikiu, declared that it was impossible to think of any monarch or woman who had ever surpassed her. Many of Alexandria's greatest monuments and architectural masterpieces, including the palace and Pharos lighthouse, were believed to have been her work. Alone of Alexander the Great's successors she became a legend, like Alexander himself.[8]

*

Most historians, ancient and modern alike, see a total inevitability in the defeat of Antony and Cleopatra at Octavian's hands.[9] But their defeat was only inevitable because Agrippa was a better admiral than Antony or any of his lieutenants. To contrast the faults of their régime with the merits of that of Octavian, the later Augustus, and to conclude that the Augustan system was bound to win is an unjustifiable procedure. There were many faults and merits on both sides, and if Antony and Cleopatra had been victorious in the Actium campaigns, it would not have been their failings but Octavian's which posterity would have emphasized. The particular brand of Roman empire that he established turned out, in its own way, to be one of the great, durable success stories of history. But it has meant that all appreciation – apart from the sympathies attaching to personal melodrama – has been withheld from the losers, and that their aspirations have been lost sight of.

During the last hundred years and more there has been lively discussion about the qualities, first of the successful Julius Caesar, and then of the successful Augustus, and both their personalities have come under a sharper and colder process of inspection than before. But the cases of Caesar and Augustus are different. The trouble about withholding all sympathy from Caesar is that his 'Republican' opponents were for the most part so very unpleasant. There is a movement today, from praiseworthy motives, to get away from the cult of success, and this has even led to a certain veneration for failure, as exhibited, for example, in the downfall and death of Che Guevara. But to make similar anti-heroes out of Julius Caesar's adversaries is absurd. Caesar possessed extremely distasteful qualities, but to be ruled by him might well have appeared the lesser evil.

A comparison between Augustus and *his* opponents, Antony and Cleopatra, ought to yield a different result. As the historian Tacitus explains in his sour preface to the *Annals*,[10] Augustus was a cold-blooded and ruthless man. Without that ruthlessness he could never have carried through the unparalleled achievements and reorganizations of his forty-five-year reign that followed Actium. But his enemies were very different from the enemies of Julius Caesar. Between the nobility who hated Caesar, and Antony and Cleopatra who fought against his heir, there is little in common. The record of the anti-Caesarian nobility is negative and brutal, especially in their later years. But Antony and Cleopatra had plans to provide a much more positive and constructive policy. Its existence has not, in general, been admitted, though W. W. Tarn in *The Cambridge Ancient History* (1934) was not unsympathetic, while Ronald Syme, in his *Roman Revolution* (1939) pointed to the wisdom of many of Antony's administrative arrangements.

But why is it that so few other historians have appreciated that Antony and Cleopatra had a serious, valid point of view? If devotees of the cult of failure can even muster sympathy for Caesar's opponents, one might have expected them to find more promising scope here. There are two main reasons why this has not been so. In the first place, the story of the lovers offers such unexampled opportunities for romantic senti-ment that attention has constantly been distracted from matters of policy. Secondly, their conflict with Octavian is seen as part of the historic feud between east and west – and we are westerners. The countries of western Europe, and the United States of America, are the direct heirs of the occidental victor of Actium, and of the tradition which he deliberately implanted. Indeed, this very assertion, that Actium was part of the clash between east and west, is itself a direct echo of his propaganda – propaganda which, because of Octavian's naval victory, prevailed.

However, like so much of the best propaganda, it contains an element of truth. Many lies were told on both sides, but Actium *was* a clash between eastern and western ideologies. There is less truth, on the other hand, in the further statement, endlessly repeated, that Antony and Cleopatra stood for the queer, outlandish tribes and fetishes of the remote orient. What they really stood for was Hellenism – or rather, a partnership between Hellenism and *Romanità*. How they envisaged the shape of this partnership was suggested, in broad outline, by the terri-torial gifts of 37 BC, and the Donations of Alexandria in 34. Although a Roman was to remain in supreme charge, Antony and Cleopatra saw the Romans who occupied the western part of the empire, and the Greeks and Hellenized orientals who lived in the eastern provinces and client kingdoms, as more or less equal partners. This was how they interpreted the Concord between Peoples (Homonoia) which was one of the most vigorous ideals of the age, and the Sibylline Oracles and other anonymous contemporary writings showed the enthusiasm evoked by such concepts among eastern peoples.

Augustus felt otherwise. It is true that the elaborate, rather super-ficial apparatus of phil-Hellenism which accompanied his religious and cultural policy provided a certain mild corrective to the anti-Hellenic sentiments of his compatriots. Nevertheless, he was ultimately the heir of Roman imperialism: the Italians were unmistakably intended to be top dogs. Certainly, there was to be a great reconciliation between east and west, and it is expressed with extraordinary brilliance and subtlety by Virgil. But the prophetic words the poet ascribes to Aeneas' father Anchises reflect Augustus' belief that it must be a reconciliation presided over by Rome, which would still reign supreme over the Greeks:[11]

There are others, assuredly I believe,
Shall work in bronze more sensitively, moulding
Breathing images, or carving from the marble

235

More lifelike features: some shall plead more eloquently,
Or gauging with instruments the sky's motion
Forecast the rising of the constellations:
But yours, my Roman, is the gift of government,
That is your bent – to impose upon the nations
The code of peace; to be clement to the conquered,
But utterly to crush the intransigent.[12]

That is unforgettably said, but in terms of politics it is very one-sided. The Greeks and Hellenized easterners, according to Virgil, were to be excluded from the heights of government – which is precisely what continued to happen. But it was the antithesis of the intentions of Antony and Cleopatra. Under their guidance, great areas of the east were to be under the administration and overlordship of Greek monarchies, led by a nexus of Ptolemaic kingdoms. The official coinages link Antony and Cleopatra together, not only as gods united in a divine union, but as human leaders of this partnership between Romans and Greeks.

The partnership never materialized, because Agrippa proved too good an admiral. But that does not mean it was impossible.[13] W.W. Tarn's somewhat reluctant conclusion that the Hellenistic world had already fallen victim to itself before it fell victim to Rome[14] is the product of hindsight. It is true that the age of wholly independent Hellenistic monarchies was at an end, because their continued existence was incompatible with Rome. But the idea of great Hellenistic kingdoms in intimate and honourable association with the Romans was a novel one and the relatively high status it conceded the Greeks was by no means an unrealistic dream. That is conclusively proved by the condition of the Roman world three or four centuries later, in which the Greeks had risen to the political surface once again – with the result that the subsequent Byzantine empire was not Roman but Greek. If the events of 31 BC had gone the other way it is difficult to believe that this same sort of development would not have occurred, or at least begun to occur, three hundred years sooner.

In the foregoing discussion Antony and Cleopatra have been bracketed together, as a single political entity. This identification of their attitudes must not be carried too far, since there were certain political differences between them – for example, their disagreement about King Herod of Judaea. But the grand design belonged to them both, and both of them believed in it. Antony's methods of government, both inside and outside the Ptolemaic sphere, show a wide philhellenic sympathy for the concept of Greek ruling Greek. Nevertheless, it is only right to ascribe the main initiative to Cleopatra. For one thing she was Greek herself. And secondly, Antony, for all his very considerable gifts, was her inferior in drive, energy and ambition.[15]

Josephus sums up her character in a statement which seems to mean: 'if she lacked one single thing that she desired, she imagined that she lacked everything'.[16] She was a woman of single-minded determination. Moreover, as Canidius Crassus pointed out to Antony before Actium, she was a ruler of outstanding ability and experience.

The question of what might have happened if Actium had gone the other way raises one special, inflammable problem, which must have been constantly in Cleopatra's mind, even if Antony tried not to think of it too often. The problem is this. Once the campaign was won, what would have been her political position in the new order?

During the immediately preceding years, Antony's official Latin coinage, with unprecedented explicitness and emphasis, had declared her to be his honoured partner. If they had been victorious in 31 BC, she would have been his partner in the rulership of the entire Roman empire. The propaganda of the other side, which declared that she intended to dispense justice from the sacred Capitol itself, was surely right in supposing that she would have gone to Rome. For that is where Antony would have gone, and she would never have stayed behind permanently in Alexandria. Modern historians usually dismiss the idea of her going to Rome as an utter impossibility on the grounds that the Roman ruling class would never have tolerated such a thing. Yet her Roman supporters, though they had decreased in number, still remained fairly numerous – a fact of which little was heard, naturally enough, once she had been defeated and was dead. Moreover, after Antony had victoriously entered Rome, the opposition would have been cowed, just as the surviving Antonians were cowed after the issue went the other way.[17] To discuss how long she might have lasted at Rome would be taking historical might-have-beens too far.

Another obscure but all-important question is the nature of the constitutional relationship which would then, following the victory, have existed between Cleopatra and Antony.[18] Probably they would then, at last, have married, no longer merely in the theological sense of a union between gods, but as man and wife. Once Antony had become autocrat over the whole Roman world, he could have twisted Roman law to his needs – as the victorious Octavian, too, in his own way, was ready enough to give it a twist or two. In Italy, the Antonian régime would have encountered greater difficulties than the Augustan régime ever did. But Antony, on the other hand, would have received far greater and keener support from the rich and numerous populations of the east – which would thus have become a more potent political force than his opponent ever allowed them to be.

Actium set the scene for three centuries of western supremacy. If the losers had won, there would instead have been some sort of partnership between the two great populations of the empire, the Romans represented by Antony (who would have remained the supreme overlord), and the Greeks led by Cleopatra. She would never have tried to rule without Roman support, for she was faithful to her father's realistic recognition that Egypt could do no such thing. She preferred a theme of partnership. If we can forget the sentiments of occidentalism, whether conscious or unconscious, that her enemy Octavian has implanted in our hearts, Cleopatra's plan was not necessarily a less noble or even a less practicable plan than his. But she was born before her time, and her plan had to wait, as it turned out, for three hundred years.

Bibliography

A. ANCIENT SOURCES

The only contemporary historians from whom a few references to Cleopatra have come down to us are Julius Caesar and one of his officers, both writing in Latin, and the tutor of her children Nicolaus of Damascus, writing in Greek. Julius Caesar in his *Civil War* touches briefly, and with a characteristic mixture of accuracy and disingenuousness, upon the initial stages of his visit to Alexandria in the autumn of 48 BC;[1] and a member of his staff narrates the ensuing *Alexandrian War* which continued early in the following year.[2] But they tell us nothing about Caesar's personal relations with Cleopatra. The voluminous compositions of Nicolaus of Damascus, who taught Cleopatra's children before entering the service of Herod, are represented only by six excerpts from his autobiography and two sections of his eulogistic account of the youth of Octavian. However, a good deal more of his work has come down to us at second hand in the pages of Josephus.

Apart from these allusions, almost all contemporary literary evidence for the life and reign of Cleopatra is lost. With the exception, for example, of papyrus fragments of an Octavianic epic poem on the Actian War,[3] the torrents of Octavian's and Antony's propaganda are only preserved in echoes of later writers. But most unfortunate of all is the disappearance of the significant *History* of Gaius Asinius Pollio (75 BC–AD 4), a supporter of Antony who turned neutral before Actium but did not warm to Octavian.[4] This work, which dealt with events down to 42 BC and perhaps as far as 36–35, does not survive at all except in a number of facts and opinions paraded by later writers. But, even so, this tradition forms a valuable corrective to the generally pro-Augustan nature of our evidence.

Nor are we given the opportunity to read any of Livy's writings about this decisive age. It is lamentable that we are only in a position to judge him by his treatment of earlier historical and mythical periods, and not by the contemporary history that made his name. For out of his 142 'books' (shorter than modern volumes), the 35 that still exist are not concerned with the first century BC. The missing books have only been preserved in the form of brief epitomes or summaries (*Periochae*).[5] These show that he dealt with the period between Pharsalus (48 BC) and the death of Augustus' stepson Drusus the elder in 9 BC (his terminal point) in no less than 31 books, so that he must

239

have written about the period in great detail. Livy was willing enough to take a romantic Republican line, when the occasion demanded; Augustus even described him, fortunately without complete seriousness, as a 'Pompeian'. But Livy showed uncompromising hostility to Antony, whose envoys his home-town Patavium (Padua) had refused to admit when the Senate declared Antony a public enemy in 43 BC. Cleopatra also received severe treatment from Livy, though if the surviving summary can be trusted he lost interest in her activities after Actium.[6] He was evidently a very important source for later ancient historians of the period.

One of these was an officer of the emperor Tiberius, a third-rate writer named Velleius Paterculus. His extant history, completed in AD 30, contains a brief account (14 pages in the Loeb edition) of the period of Antony and Cleopatra. Adulatory of Octavian, Velleius declares Antony to have been wrong almost from start to finish – and responsible for any and every action of the civil war period which did not suit the Augustan régime. Cleopatra is presented as the evil temptress who first besotted Antony, and then betrayed him at Actium. However, he admitted that she died 'untouched by a woman's fears'.[7]

An item or two of background can be added from the Sicilian historian Diodorus and the geographer–historian Strabo. Other than these writers, none of whom deal with more than an exceedingly small proportion of the events of Cleopatra's life, there is no surviving information about her dating from her lifetime or from the first hundred years after her death. Then comes the Jewish historian Josephus, whose *Jewish War* (written in *c.* AD 74–79, about the rebellion of 67–73) and *Jewish Antiquities* contain a good deal of material about her relations with Herod. But Josephus' chronology cannot be trusted, and besides, since he depended on Herod's own memoirs, and to an even larger extent on the history of Nicolaus who transferred from Cleopatra's service to Herod's, he is savagely biased against the queen. Later, in his pamphlet *Against Apion*, he refutes an Alexandrian grammarian of that name, living in the second quarter of the first century AD, who had praised Cleopatra and criticized the Jews.[8]

*

Our first major surviving source is another Greek writer from Alexandria, Appian. After experiencing the Jewish rebellion of AD 116 in his native city, and holding office there, Appian moved to Rome where he occupied a legal post under the sponsorship of the emperor Antoninus Pius (AD 138–161). Appian's *Roman History*, written in Greek, sacrificed continuity and chronology by following a regional and ethnological arrangement according to Rome's campaigns and conquests. Eleven of his twenty-four books survive, including five (13–17) on the Civil Wars, down to 35 BC. The following four volumes relating to Octavian's conquest of Egypt are lost.

Mainly interested in warfare, Appian provides valuable military facts and figures. He is a loyal supporter of Roman government and imperialism. Nevertheless, Antony secures relatively impartial treatment; his ruin is attributed to Cleopatra's greater cleverness and power of intrigue. Appian seems to rely a good deal upon Pollio – for example in his unfavourable references to Plancus, whom Pollio disliked. He also draws on Livy, and shows he has read Octavian's own autobiography, and perhaps the works of Nicolaus of Damascus as well. Such writers, however, were probably only known to him through an intermediary, who may have been some historian of the first century AD.[9] Appian's shaky knowledge of the constitutional and political history of earlier times, notably the age of Cleopatra, left him at the mercy of his sources, and sometimes he made no attempt to decide between contradictory versions, so that he gives us, for example, three separate, irreconcilable points of view about the events following Caesar's death. To us, three such accounts are more valuable than one; and Appian's work, in spite of all its deficiencies, remains indispensable – chiefly because it tells us so much, indirectly, about the authorities he used, whose own works have failed to survive.

Perhaps the most important single source for Cleopatra that we possess, and far the most alluring – although its historical shortcomings are greater still – is Plutarch's *Life of Antony*. Lucius (?) Mestrius Plutarchus of Chaeronea in Greece, who was born before AD 50 and died after 120, spent the later part of his life at his home town. But before that he lived for a time at Athens, and lectured and taught in Rome. He wrote very extensively in his native Greek, and many of his philosophical, moralistic, religious and biographical works have come down to us. Forty-six of his forty-eight surviving biographies are arranged in 'parallel' pairs according to a common practice of the rhetorical schools. Brief comparisons between the selected personages are appended. Each pair comprises a Greek and a Roman, in order to illustrate Plutarch's conception of a partnership and compatibility between Greece, the educator, and Rome, the great power – though Plutarch did not believe Antony's and Cleopatra's dreams of an almost *equal* partnership to be practicable.[10]

Antony, the last Roman of the series in point of chronology, is paired with the Macedonian Demetrius I Poliorcetes (the Besieger) who died in 283 BC. Plutarch is a tremendous moralist, and most of his biographies are object lessons in a particular virtue – the 'pasturage of great souls' as Madame Roland called them. A few of them, however, present an innovation, 'for perhaps,' he says, 'I may as well introduce one or two pairs of personages *of a worse type* into my *Lives*'.[11] His prize examples of this category are Demetrius and Antony: though Plutarch adds that both men possessed good points as well, thus illustrating the thesis that great natures produce great vices as well as great virtues. Plutarch, on the whole, belonged to the ancient school of thought which believed that a man's vices and virtues were implanted in him from the start, so that only acquired characteristics could be altered.[12] But Plutarch, true to his classical conception of biography as something altogether less pretentious than history, is quite happy to sacrifice public life and political significance to romance and glamour; and the unforgettable picture of Antony's seductress Cleopatra which emerges from his narrative has been referred to again and again in these pages.

Although he had read a great deal of Greek, and a fair amount of Latin,[13] Plutarch's interpretation of all these sources is undistinguished. Yet his *Life of Antony* possesses a special quality because of the personal sources it employs. Many of his splendid anecdotes (not all of them historically unreliable) are derived from his own grandfather Lamprias. Lamprias had heard them from Philotas, a doctor of Amphissa who was at Alexandria in Cleopatra's time. Another story, concerning the chores that fell upon the population of Greece before Actium, came from Plutarch's great-grandfather, Nicarchus, who had himself been one of the sufferers. For the last phase of Cleopatra's life, Plutarch drew upon the writings of her doctor Olympus. But he had also been to Egypt himself – it was the first country he had visited on his travels – and his *Antony* is full of touches of personal reminiscence which help to raise it above the level of his other biographies.

Because of Plutarch, Boccaccio launched the long line of Renaissance writings about Cleopatra in 1473.[14] The years between 1540 and 1905 witnessed no less than 127 dramatic productions concerned with Cleopatra: 77 plays, 45 operas and 5 ballets.[15] The earliest French tragedy on the subject was Étienne Jodelle's *Cléopatre* (1552), and the Countess of Pembroke, sister of the versatile Elizabethan, Sir Philip Sidney, launched the theme on the English stage in 1592. Meanwhile Jacques Amyot had translated Plutarch's *Antony* into French (1559), and Amyot's version had been rendered in English (1592) by Sir Thomas North. North's Plutarch was the source of Shakespeare's *Antony and Cleopatra* (1606–07). It is one of the miracles of literary history that the comparatively modest essay of Plutarch, read at third-hand, could be so utterly transfigured: perhaps his effort cannot have been so modest after all, if he inspired this soaring, imaginative creation.[16]

Shakespeare is undazzled by empire, and conscious of its resplendent hollowness. The grand poetry is reserved for the lovers:

> The nobleness of life
> Is to do thus, when such a mutual pair
> And such a twain can do't.

Antony's great-heartedness is true greatness. Yet he is brought down to destruction, because he has been torn apart between the enchantment of Egypt and the honour of Rome:

> He was disposed to mirth, but on the sudden
> A Roman thought had struck him.

Cleopatra 'dreamt there was an emperor Antony', a world-ruling colossus:

> Realms and islands were
> As plates dropped from his pocket.

But his weaknesses have been gradually emerging ever since the beginning of the play. They are discernible through a strange aura of jewelled corruption, revealing itself in continual hints of sterile, luxuriant, Alexandrian revelry. And out of this cloying and hallucinatory atmosphere comes the desperate conclusion that all things, even things that, at first sight, seem more solid and enduring than palace banquets, are ultimately just magical, insubstantial unreality.

As for Cleopatra, a Victorian spectator of the play was indeed right to declare, 'How unlike the home life of our own dear Queen!' For Shakespeare's Cleopatra is the incarnation of primeval energy and sexual passion. Yet by insisting upon its own terms, her sensuality thwarts the very fulfilment it is seeking. And so Shakespeare resembles his model Plutarch in one respect at least: for they both dwell at length upon the deaths of Antony and Cleopatra. To Shakespeare, death brings an enhanced perception of life, supplying the only possible resolution of the deep, sombre, frustrating ambivalence that pervades this unequalled play.

Plutarch's younger contemporary Suetonius was born in about AD 69, and held palace appointments under Trajan and Hadrian. He too, though in Latin not in Greek, was a biographer of quite another kind. Plutarch had adopted a mainly chronological arrangement, but Suetonius classified his material by topics; Plutarch had been a moralist, but Suetonius had no intention of adopting a moral tone.

In his *Lives of the Twelve Caesars*, he collects a host of varied materials and displays them all with a drily indiscriminate astringency, perfectly prepared (in this resembling Appian) to admit contradictions. Thus his biography of Caesar presents conflicting reports of his relations with Cleopatra and of Caesarion's paternity; and a long chapter in his *Augustus* about the last year of the queen's life once again incorporates, without integration, propaganda from both sides.[17]

Dio Cassius Cocceianus (*c.* 155/163–235) was a Greek from Nicaea (Iznik) in north-western Asia Minor, who became a Roman senator and held two consulships. He also wrote an eighty-book Roman History, of which Books 36–54, relating to the years 68–10 BC, are fully preserved. Despite their late date and numerous faults, they provide an indispensable chronological framework, and without them we should be much further adrift than we are.

Nevertheless, like so many ancient historians, Dio avoids precision and detail, since he does not want to inhibit the easy flow of his narrative – and, like Plutarch, what he really enjoys is citing examples of good and evil moral qualities. Besides, although interested in the second Triumvirate as a prelude to the imperial system which he himself served, he finds it difficult to think his way out of the totally different conditions of his own time. But when he has practical affairs to discuss, his own experiences help him achieve a surer tread, and he feels especially at home whenever the methods of autocratic government are his theme. However, the workings of cause and effect often defeat him, and accuracy frequently goes by the board. His account of Actium, for instance, is a useless conventional battle-picture, and his narrative of Cleopatra's last months is full of elaborate and melodramatic sentimentalities – far removed from the austere precedent of Thucydides, although Dio was proud to have given him careful study.

Dio's sources are as problematical as those of his predecessors. He is inclined to be anti-Antonian. Yet he is also aware of the tradition that Antony was let down by Cleopatra, for he quotes several of these alleged acts of treachery. A considerable part of his account is based on Livy, or on the writers Livy had used.[18] But he also employs at least one secondary Augustan authority, who remains unidentifiable.

There are also certain literary sources for Cleopatra besides the historians and biographers. One of them is Cicero, whose *Letters to Atticus* of the year 44 BC refer to her a number of times.

More abundant, however, are the allusions of the Augustan Latin poets Virgil, Horace and Propertius. Their estimates of the Actium campaign and the death of Cleopatra have been indicated. Gone, fortunately, are the days when anyone could consider poets of this calibre as nothing better than tools of Augustan propaganda. Yet, ready though they may have been to see a certain grandeur in Cleopatra's death, they were wholeheartedly of the opinion that Augustus was right and Antony and Cleopatra wrong. For these writers were Italians, and the policy of Antony and Cleopatra would have meant the end of Italy's complete supremacy over the Greek east. It is true that all three of these poets had declined suggestions from Augustus, or his minister Maecenas, that they might turn their hand to contemporary epics in honour of the régime; for they found that the artistic, political and social problems of such an enterprise were too great.[19] Nevertheless, their poetry always contained 'a rich undercurrent of topical application – the Augustans rarely wrote without consciousness of the present'.[20] So each of them was ready enough to celebrate the crowning mercy of Actium, and each of them did so, in his own poetically memorable and historically misleading fashion.

*

Our first extant account of the affair between Julius Caesar and Cleopatra comes from the Latin poet Lucan who died in AD 65. His epic on the Civil War between Caesar and Pompey remained unfinished; perhaps he intended to carry it on until the death of Caesar. But the last book which he wrote, the tenth, describes Caesar's presence with Cleopatra in Alexandria. This is not history but rhetorical epic, casting a lurid illumination upon selected episodes. Yet Lucan has moments of penetrating insight into the greatest melodrama of the age. As the poem proceeded, and especially after his own estrangement from the emperor Nero who later put him to death, Lucan displayed an increasingly strong bias against Caesar. He is likely to have drawn heavily upon Livy,[21] but was far more 'Pompeian', or at least opposed to autocracy, than Livy had ever been.

*

We also rely on several categories of non-literary evidence. In the first place, there are many coins extant, some with Latin and some with Greek inscriptions. Although much work on the subject still remains to be done, this numismatic material is revealing not only (rather disconcertingly) about Cleopatra's physical appearance, but also about her political position and 'image'.[22] Two coins of *c.* 34 BC bearing the heads of Antony and Cleopatra are as replete with historical information as any other documents of the age.

The topography of Alexandria will be more informative than it is at present after the publication of a comprehensive forthcoming book.[23] As for papyri, the first century BC is not one of the richest periods of ancient history.

Yet there are several of these documents which cast a unique, though fitful and enigmatic, light upon the internal situation of Egypt. And a good many others provide varying royal headings and other pieces of evidence which, after careful scrutiny, offer at least a little guidance through the disturbed last years of Auletes' reign, and the initial phases of his daughter Cleopatra's.[24]

A number of Greek and Latin inscriptions add their quota of evidence. And, finally, there is the valuable but cryptic Egyptological material, including various shrines illustrating the building activity of Auletes, the Bucheum stele apparently describing a visit by Cleopatra to Hermonthis immediately after her accession, and the politically significant reliefs on the birth temple of Caesarion at the same centre. These reliefs display the Pharaonic trends which still persisted in Egyptian art, though other works of art of the period blend native and Egyptian features in varying proportions.

All these sources only add up to a tantalizingly inadequate total, and while making the best use of them that we can, we have to concede that it still remains impossible to penetrate all the mists. We can only hope that, in the future, further research and discoveries will throw new light on Cleopatra's profoundly significant career.

B. MODERN SOURCES (BOOKS)*

I. Becher, *Das Bild der Kleopatra in der griechischen und lateinischen Literatur*, Deutsche Akademie der Wissenschaften, Schriften der Sektion für Altertumwissenschaft, LI, Berlin, 1966†

H. Idris Bell, *Egypt from Alexander the Great to the Arab Conquest*, Oxford, 1948 (with bibliography of papyrus collections)

E. Bevan, *A History of Egypt under the Ptolemaic Dynasty*, Methuen, London, 1927 (reprinted, Amsterdam, 1967)

E. Bloedow, *Beiträge zur Geschichte des Ptolemäus XII*, Würzburg dissertation, 1963

A. Bouché-Leclercq, *L'Histoire des Lagides*, II, Paris, 1904

E. Bradford, *Cleopatra*, Hodder and Stoughton, 1971 (background illustrations)

B.R. Brown, *Ptolemaic Paintings and Mosaics*, Cambridge, Massachusetts, 1957

H. Buchheim, *Die Orientpolitik des Triumvirs Marcus Antonius*, Abhandlungen der Heidelberger Akademie der Wissenschaften, philosophisch-historische Klasse, Heidelberg, 1960 (fundamental)

Cambridge Ancient History, Vol. IX, 1932, and Vol. X, 1934 (see also Tarn)

J.M. Carter, *The Battle of Actium*, Hamish Hamilton, London, 1970 (authoritative account of events)

L. Cerfaux and J. Tondriau, *Le culte des souverains dans la civilisation gréco-romaine*, Bibliothèque de la Théologie, III, 5, Tournai, 1957

L. Craven, *Antony's Oriental Policy*, University of Missouri Studies, III, 2, 1920

P.G. Elgood, *The Ptolemies of Egypt*, Arrowsmith, London, 1938

E.M. Forster, *Alexandria: A History and Guide*, Alexandria, 1922 (new ed., Anchor Books, New York, 1961)

P.M. Fraser, *Ptolemaic Alexandria*, Oxford University Press, 1972 (forthcoming)

M. Grant, *From Imperium to Auctoritas*, Cambridge University Press, 2nd ed., 1971 (on bronze coins)

M. Grant, *Herod the Great*, Weidenfeld & Nicolson, London, and the American Heritage Press, New York, 1971

H.A. Grueber, *Coins of the Roman Republic in the British Museum*, London, 1910 (chronology superseded)

H. Heinen, *Rom und Ägypten von 51 bis 47 v. Chr.*, Tübingen dissertation, 1966 (new conclusions)

A.H.M. Jones, *Cities of the Eastern Roman Provinces*, 2nd ed., Oxford University Press, 1971

P. Jouguet, *L'Égypte ptolemaique*, in *Histoire de la nation égyptienne* (ed. Hanotaux), Vol. III, Paris, 1933

Jacqueline Leroux, *Les problèmes stratégiques de la bataille d'Actium*, Recherches de philologie et de linguistique, Faculté de Lettres, de l'Université de Louvain, Section de philologie classique, II, Louvain, 1968

J. Lindsay, *Cleopatra*, Constable, London, and Coward McCann and Geoghegan, New York, 1971 (extensive collections of material)

G.H. Macurdy, *Hellenistic Queens*, London, 1932

* For relevant articles in journals, which are extremely numerous, see citations in the Notes.
† Reviewed by G. W. Bowersock in *American Journal of Philology*, 1969, pp. 252 ff.

J. Marlowe, *The Golden Age of Alexandria*, Gollancz, London, 1971

A. Momigliano, *The Development of Greek Biography*, Oxford University Press, 1972 (forthcoming)

I. Noshy, *The Arts in Ptolemaic Egypt*, Oxford University Press, 1937

E. Olshausen, *Rom und Ägypten von 116 bis 51 v. Chr.*, Erlangen-Nuremberg dissertation, 1963

R.S. Poole, *The Ptolemies*, Catalogue of Greek Coins in the British Museum, 1883 (chronology superseded)

F.R. Rossi, *Marco Antonio nella lotta politica della tarda republica romana*, Facoltà di Lettere e Filosofia, Trieste, 1959

M. Rostovtzeff, *Social and Economic History of the Hellenistic World*, Oxford University Press, 1941 (fundamental)

A.E. Samuel, *Greek and Roman Chronology*, Handbücher der Altertumswissenschaft, Munich, 1971

T.C. Skeat, *The Reigns of the Ptolemies*, 2nd ed., Münchner Beiträge zur Papyrusforschung und antiken Rechtsgeschichte, XXXIX, Munich, 1969

F. Stähelin, *Kleopatra VII*, in Pauly-Wissowa-Kroll-Mittelhaus, *Realencyclopädie der classischen Altertumswissenschaft*, Vol. XI, 1921 (columns 550–581)

J.N. Svoronos, *The Coins of the Ptolemaic Kingdom* (in Greek), Vols. I–III, 1904 (German translation of Vol. I, 1908), and Vol. IV, 1908 (chronology superseded)

E.A. Sydenham, *The Coinage of the Roman Republic*, Spink, London, 1952

R. Syme, *The Roman Revolution*, Oxford University Press, 1939 (reprinted 1960) (indispensable)

W.W. Tarn and M.P. Charlesworth, *Octavian, Antony and Cleopatra*, Cambridge, 1965 (reprint of *Cambridge Ancient History*, Chapters 2–4) (very valuable)

H. Thierfelder, *Die Geschwisterehe in hellenistischen-römischen Ägypten*, Münster, 1960

H. Volkmann, *Cleopatra*, Elek, London, 1958 (revised translation, by T.J. Cadoux, of *Kleopatra*, Munich, 1953) (excellent)

L. Widman, *Isis und Sarapis bei den Griechen und Römern*, Religionsgeschichtliche Versuche und Vorarbeiten, XXIX, 1970

R.E. Witt, *Isis in the Graeco-Roman World*, Thames & Hudson, London and New York, 1971

Of the innumerable older biographies and fictional biographies of Cleopatra, O. von Wertheimer's *Cleopatra: A Royal Voluptuary* (English ed., Harrap, 1931), M. Maffii's *Cleopatra contro Roma* (Florence, 3rd ed., 1939) and R. Pernoud's *Cléopatre* (Paris, 1963) are relatively faithful to the ancient literary sources; A. Weigall's *Life and Times of Cleopatra Queen of Egypt* (Thornton Butterworth, 1914, revised ed. 1923) benefits from the author's knowledge of Egypt (though it is not so good as his *Nero*); C. Ferval's *Private Life of Cleopatra* (English ed., Heinemann, 1930) is somewhat gushing; and H. Rider Haggard's *Cleopatra* (1889, Hodder & Stoughton paperback) is almost uninhibited fantasy. What the Russians make of Cleopatra (V. Stucevskij, *Voprosy Istorii*, X, 1965, pp. 210 ff.) I should very much like to know.

List of Abbreviations Used
in Notes

AJ	Josephus, *Antiquitates Judaicae* (*Jewish Antiquities*)
AJA	*American Journal of Archaeology*
Bevan	E. Bevan, *A History of Egypt under the Ptolemaic Dynasty*
BGU	*Ägyptische Urkunden aus den Staatlichen Museen zu Berlin* (*Griechische Urkunden*), Berlin, 1895 etc.
BJ	Josephus, *Bellum Judaicum* (*Jewish War*)
BMC	British Museum Catalogues (coins)
BMCR	*Catalogue of Coins of the Roman Republic in the British Museum*
Bouché-Leclercq II	A. Bouché-Leclercq, *L'Histoire des Lagides*
Buchheim	H. Buchheim, *Die Orientpolitik des Triumvirs M. Antonius*
CAH	*Cambridge Ancient History*
Carter	J.M. Carter, *The Battle of Actium*
CIG	Boeckh, *Corpus Inscriptionum Graecarum*
CIL	*Corpus Inscriptionum Latinarum*
CR	*Classical Review*
FGH	F. Jacoby, *Die Fragmente der griechischen Historiker*
FITA	M. Grant, *From Imperium to Auctoritas*
Heinen	H. Heinen, *Rom und Ägypten von 51 bis 47 v. Chr.*
HG	M. Grant, *Herod the Great*
IG	*Inscriptiones Graecae*
IGRR	*Inscriptiones Graecae ad Res Romanas pertinentes*
ILS	H. Dessau, *Inscriptiones Latinae Selectae*
JEA	*Journal of Egyptian Archaeology*
JHS	*Journal of Hellenic Studies*
JRS	*Journal of Roman Studies*
Leroux	Jacqueline Leroux, *Les Problèmes stratégiques de la bataille d'Actium*

NC	*Numismatic Chronicle*
Noshy	I. Noshy, *The Arts in Ptolemaic Egypt*
OGIS	W. Dittenberger, *Orientis Graeci Inscriptiones Selectae*
P. Berl.	S. Möller, *Griechische Papyri aus dem Berliner Museum*, Gothenburg, 1929
P. Cairo Zen.	C. C. Edgar, *Catalogue général des antiquités égyptiennes du Musée du Caire: Zenon Papyri*, Cairo, 1925–31
P. Fay	B.P. Grenfell, A.S. Hunt and D.C. Hogarth, *Fayûm Towns and their Papyri*, London, 1900
P. Grenf. II	B.P. Grenfell and A.S. Hunt, *New Classical Fragments and other Greek and Latin Papyri*, Oxford, 1897
P. Hib. II	E.G. Turner, *The Hibeh Papyri*, Part II, 1955
P. Lond.	F.G. Kenyon and H.I. Bell, *Greek Papyri in the British Museum*, London, 1893–1917
P. Oxy.	B.P. Grenfell, A.S. Hunt, etc., *The Oxyrhynchus Papyri*, 1898–
PSI	G. Vitelli, M. Norsa, etc., *Papiri greci e latini*, Florence, 1912–
P. Tebt.	B.P. Grenfell, A. S. Hunt, etc., *The Tebtunis Papyri*, London, 1902–38
RE	Pauly-Wissowa-Kroll-Mittelhaus, *Realencyclopädie der classischen Altertumswissenschaft*, 1893–
SEHHW	M. Rostovtzeff, *Social and Economic History of the Hellenistic World*
SEHRE	Id., *Social and Economic History of the Roman Empire*
S	E.A. Sydenham, *The Coinage of the Roman Republic*
*SIG*³	W. Dittenberger, *Sylloge Inscriptionum Graecarum*, 3rd ed., 1924
Volkmann,	H. Volkmann, *Cleopatra*, Elek, London, 1958
Witt	R. E. Witt, *Isis in the Graeco-Roman World*

Notes

FOREWORD

1. Shakespeare, *Antony and Cleopatra*, Act II, Scene 2.
2. W. W. Tarn, *Cambridge Ancient History*, Vol. IX (1932), p. 98.

PART ONE: CLEOPATRA'S FIRST TWENTY-ONE YEARS

CHAPTER 1   CLEOPATRA'S FATHER

1. Sources in Stähelin, *RE*, XI (1921), col. 749.
2. Cf. discussion in Bevan, pp. 348 f.
3. Strabo, XVII, 796. He wrongly says Auletes had three daughters.
4. Thracian, Illyrian, Greek; cf. C. Habicht, *Ancient Macedonia* (1970); A. Dascalakis, *The Hellenism of the Ancient Macedonians* (1965); M. Grant, *The Ancient Mediterranean* (1969), p. 211.
5. Theocritus, XVII, 103, cf. note by A. S. F. Gow, ed., II, p. 342.
6. E.g. Seleucus I had married a Persian, Apama.
7. Didyme, mistress of Ptolemy II Philadelphus; cf. Bevan, p. 77.
8. Robert Greene, *Ciceronis Amor* (1589) (ed. Grosart), VII, 142.
9. Shakespeare, *Romeo and Juliet*, Act II, Scene 4.
10. The idea is traceable back to a fictitious will of Alexander the Great, W. Schmitthenner, *Saeculum*, XIX, 1968, pp. 31 ff.
11. Lepsius, *Denkmäler*, II, 136H.
12. Callimachus, *Hymn IV*, to Delos.
13. E. M. Forster, *Alexandria* (1922, new ed. 1961), p. 28. The sites of the Museum and Library are disputed, cf. J. Marlowe, *The Golden Age of Alexandria* (1971), pp. 57, 333, but they were probably inside the Palace Quarter.
14. Cf. coin of *c*. 70 BC, *S*, p. 137, no. 831, *BMCR*, I, no. 3648 (M. Aemilius Lepidus).
15. Though Livy, XLV, 13, 7, now uses the term 'client' for Egypt.
16. Rome's annexation of the former kingdom of Macedonia in 146 BC had been an ominous blow to the monarchs of the other successor states, Plutarch, *On the Oracles of the Pythia*, 11.

17. Pseudo-Plutarch, *Apophthegmata of Scipio the younger*, 13.
18. Polybius, XXXI, 10, 7 treats Roman policy on Egypt in the second century BC as typical of Rome's exploitation of the mistakes of others in order to strengthen its own position.
19. P. Tebt., I, 33.
20. The will, if it existed, was made by Ptolemy x Alexander I (d. 88 BC) not Ptolemy XI Alexander II (d. 80 BC); cf. E. Badian, *Rheinisches Museum*, 1967, pp. 178 ff.
21. Especially *On the Alexandrian Kings* (65 BC; only fragments survive); cf. *On the Agrarian Law* (Against Rullus) (63 BC), I, 1; II, 44.
22. Varro in Pliny the elder, *Natural History*, XXXIII, 136.
23. Diodorus Siculus, I, 83.
24. Volkmann, p. 53, places the application to Rabirius in 58-57. His father was Gaius Curtius.
25. Plutarch, *Cato the younger*, 35; cf. Oost, *Classical Philology*, 1955, p. 111, n. 4. Cato's accounts got lost on the way home, and he had to persuade the Senate they were not lost on purpose, Dio, XXXIX, 23.
26. Cf. Bouché-Leclercq, II, p. 145, Stähelin, *RE*, XI, 749 f., against Bevan, p. 354, n. 2, identifies her with the mother of Cleopatra VI Tryphaena, i.e. Cleopatra V Tryphaena (who had disappeared from view over a decade previously). Cf. Porphyry, *FGH*, 260.
27. A. Wilhelm, *Mélanges Bidez*, Brussels, 1934, p. 1007.
28. Strabo, XVII, 1, 11, and Cicero, *For Caelius*, X, 23.
29. Cicero, *For Rabirius Postumus*, VIII, 20.
30. P. Grenf., II, 38.
31. Heinen, p. 39 and n. 2; cf. the European Commission appointed in the 1870s to handle all Egypt's funds in order to pay off the ruler's private debts.
32. Cicero, *For Rabirius Postumus*, XIV, 40.
33. Caesar, *Civil War*, 110 (trans. Jane F. Mitchell).
34. Cf. E. Badian, *JRS*, 1968, p. 258.
35. Cf. A. B. Brett, *AJA*, XLI, 1937, p. 460 and fig. 6.
36. H. Seyrig, *Revue archéologique*, 1968, pp. 252 ff.
37. *CIG*, 4926 (Tryphon, Nicolaus, Strothein [?Strouthon]); cf. P. Tebt., 208 (1). See also Chapter 10, n. 73.
38. Athenaeus, XII, 550b.
39. Cf. M. Gelzer, *Caesar* (1968), p. 40, n. 3.
40. E.g. Cicero, *Tusculans*, I, 4, *Laws*, II, 38; cf. M. Grant, *Nero*, p. 101.
41. Athenaeus, V, 206d.
42. M. Rostovtzeff, *SEHHW*, II, pl. CXI, 2.
43. Aristotle, *Politics*, III, 13, 1284a.
44. Pliny the elder, *Natural History*, II, 7, 18.
45. 'Epiphanes' first, apparently, for Ariarathes IV of Cappadocia (220–162 BC): E. Kornemann, *Klio*, I, 1910, p. 83.
46. Cf. A. D. Nock, *JHS*, 1925, pp. 93 f., n. 84; *ibid.*, 1928, pp. 30 ff. Gods and goddesses, too, could be worshipped with this designation, e.g. Isis as *Nea* at Patmos (Oxyrhynchus Litany, P. Oxy., 1380). Cf., in general, J.

Tondriau, *Le culte des souverains*, Louvain, 1956; F.K. Kiechle, *Historia*, XIX, 1970, pp. 259 ff.

47. G. Posener, *De la divinité du Pharaon*, Paris, 1960, seems to qualify this excessively.

48. Bevan, pp. 49 f.

49. K. Regling, *Zeitschrift für Numismatik*, XXV, 1906, p. 393; Kahrstedt, *Klio*, X, 1910, pp. 275 ff.

50. For the early date of this deification see P. Hib. II, 199.

51. Bevan, p. 50: though god-titles were omitted from royal decrees and, except on one issue of Ptolemy vi, from coins, Kornemann, *Klio*, I, 1901, p. 78. Coins with the heads of Ptolemy i and Ptolemy ii and their wives, inscribed *Theoi Adelphoi*, were issued by Ptolemy iii, cf. *American Numismatic Society Museum Notes*, V, p. 7.

52. *OGIS*, 741.

53. *CIG*, 4926, etc.

54. Cf. especially E.R. Dodds, *The Greeks and the Irrational* (1968 ed.), pp. 64 ff.

55. M. Grant, *Cities of Vesuvius*, pp. 103 ff.

56. As Boyancé, *Rendiconti della Pontificia Accademia*, 1965–66, pp. 79 ff. For Semele cf. C. Bérard, *Pro Aventico*, XIX, 1967, pp. 57 ff. (Avenches bronze vase).

57. H. Jeanmaire, *Dionysus*, pp. 417 ff. and 500 ff.

58. A.D. Nock, *JHS*, 1928, pp. 22 ff.; cf. R. Vallois, *Revue des études anciennes*, XXXIV, 1932, pp. 79 f.: e.g. an epic by a certain Dionysius with Indian expedition as theme, D.L. Page, *Greek Literary Papyri*, 1950, p. 534; cf. the *Bassarica* of Nonnus of Panopolis (fifth century AD).

59. M.J. Price, *NC*, 1968, p. 5; cf. in general, K. Scott, *Classical Philology*, 1929, p. 133. The Seleucids devoted to Dionysus included Antiochus vi and xii.

60. Ptolemy i's mother Arsinoe was alleged to be descended from Deianira, daughter of Dionysus (and wife of Heracles, cf. below Chapter 6, n. 17).

61. Athenaeus v, 198B (Philiscus).

62. Dio Chrysostom, *Discourse* XXXII (*To the People of Alexandria*), 55 f.

63. Athenaeus, V, 196; cf. M. Rostovtzeff, *SEHHW*, pl. CXXXVI, no. 2, T.B.L. Webster, *Hellenistic Art*, p. 67, Noshy, p. 55.

64. Cf. Roussel, *Comptes-rendus del'Acadèmie des Inscriptions*, 1919, p. 237. Coins with ivy-wreathed bust and Dionysiac wand (thyrsus) on shoulder (*BMC Ptolemies*, p. 63, no. 16) may belong to this reign.

65. *OGIS*, 50, 51; Rostovtzeff, *SEHHW*, II, p. 1085, III, p. 1586.

66. Aristides, iv, p. 49 (ed. Dindorf).

67. *Rheinisches Museum*, XXXVIII, 1883, p. 391.

68. Diodorus Siculus, I, 11 f., gives an account of Osiris' doings on earth.

69. Le Corsu, *Revue archéologique*, 1967, pp. 239 ff.; the Casa del Cubiculo Floreale.

70. Cf. Mary as the 'sister, mother and consort' of Christ, *Gospel of Philip*, 107, 10; Witt, pp. 36 ff.

71. F.E. Adcock, *Greek and Macedonian Kingship*, 1953, p. 171.

72. E.g. Euripides, *Andromache*, 175. Attic law (though not Roman law) allowed marriage between the children of the same father, but not the same mother. For the custom in other cultures (which led Kornemann to deny Egyptian origin for the Ptolemaic custom) cf. H. Thierfelder, *Die Geschwisterehe in hellenistisch-römischen Ägypten*, Münster, 1960, p. 12. The wife of the Seleucid Antiochus II, Laodice, may have been his full sister.

73. Arsinoe II was probably already called Philadelphus in her lifetime: *OGIS*, I, p. 648; cf. Wilcken, *Archiv für Papyruskunde*, III, p. 318 (against Bouché-Leclercq). According to the scholiast on Theocritus, XVII, 61, Ptolemy I's wife Berenice I was his half-sister; cf. F.M. Heichelheim, *Oxford Classical Dictionary*, 2nd ed. (1970), p. 165. Or was this a fabrication to give a precedent for Ptolemy II's marriage?

74. J. U. Powell, *Collectanea Alexandrina* (1925), fragment I; Athenaeus, XIV, 620f.

75. Theocritus, XVII, 130. Among ordinary Egyptian people the custom of brother–sister marriage only became common in the Roman period (though it was forbidden for Romans in Egypt).

76. The last Inca ruler of Peru was the product of fourteen incestuous unions, Thierfelder, *op. cit.*, p. 95 and n. 2.

77. Caesar, *Civil War*, III, 108.

78. H. de Meulenaare, *Chronique d'Égypte*, XLII, 1967, pp. 297 f.; cf. A.E. Samuel, *ibid.*, 1965, pp. 376 ff. (who sees such double eras as representing the eras of two monarchs), against Volkmann, p. 11 (reversing his former view), and T. C. Skeat, *JEA*, 1960, pp. 91 ff.

CHAPTER 2   CLEOPATRA GAINS AND LOSES THE THRONE

1. *BGU*, 1829; cf. *OGI*, 190; Stähelin, *RE*, XI (1921), col. 750; Heinen, p. 28, n. 2; H. de Meulenaare, *Chronique d'Égypte*, XLII, 1967, p. 304, prefers the earlier date.

2. *BGU*, 1827; cf. A. E. Samuel, *Chronique d'Égypte*, XL, 1965, pp. 349 f.; E. Badian, *JRS*, 1968, p. 259.

3. Cicero, *Letters to Friends*, VIII, 4, 5, from Marcus Caelius Rufus. Caelius was one of those suspected of murdering members of the deputation who had come to Italy in 58 BC to protest against Auletes.

4. H.S. Smith, *JEA*, LIV, 1968, pp. 209 ff.

5. Perhaps Ptolemy XIII only assumed the title Philadelphus in 50 BC: Heinen p. 180 and n. 4.

6. *PSI*, X, 1098b, 23; Heinen, pp. 179 f.

7. The name Cleopatra goes back to the wife of Perdiccas, King of Macedonia, in the fifth century BC (Plato, *Gorgias*, 471C). There was also a sister of Alexander the Great of the same name – and various Cleopatras in mythology. 'Cleopatra', in its Egyptian form, was the first Egyptian word to be successfully translated from hieroglyphics (by W.J. Banks, on the obelisk from Philae, 1821).

8. A.B. Brett, *AJA*, 1937, XLI, p. 461; *FITA*, p. 372 (era of 81–80 BC).

9. There were also smaller Greek settlements along the Canopic branch, e.g.

Archandroupolis; Anthylla (where the best wine came from); Taposiris Magna lay west of Alexandria, on the strip between Lake Mareotis and the sea.

10. P. Berl., 130405, line 26.
11. Egypt had long been a centre of glass-making, Rostovtzeff, *SEHHW*, III, p. 1553, n. 198. But glass-blowing may perhaps have originated in Syria.
12. Orosius, VI, 19.
13. He held office from at least 78 to 51 BC; Bevan, p. 362.
14. Cosmas, III, 169.
15. Strabo, XVII, 798.
16. Volkmann, p. 23.
17. P. Cairo Zen. passim (Zeno, steward of Apollonius); cf. Bevan, pp. 132 ff.
18. U. Wilcken, *Urkunden der Ptolemäerzeit*, No. 14 (Apollonius, a Macedonian, at Memphis).
19. Bevan, p. 139.
20. P. Tebt., I, 5; cf. Bevan, pp. 315 ff; Lindsay, p. 318.
21. Rostovtzeff, *SEHHW*, II, p. 894.
22. Theocritus, XVII, 77 ff. Yet the average breadth of the cultivated area was only 9 miles in Middle Egypt, 1–2 miles in Upper Egypt.
23. Josephus, *BJ*, II, 386.
24. Arsinoe II after her death was called 'Locris', after Locri Epizephyrii, the chief base for Ptolemaic trade in south Italy.
25. Oertel, *CAH*, X, p. 398.
26. Diodorus Siculus, I, 83; Cicero in Strabo, XVII, 797; cf. Bevan, p. 352 and n. 1.
27. Josephus, *AJ*, XV, 90 f.
28. Giesecke, *Das Ptolemäergeld*, pp. 71 ff.
29. Reinach, *Revue des études grecques*, 1941, pp. 28 and 181 ff.
30. Hultsch, *Metrologicorum Scriptorum Reliquiae*, I, pp. 233 ff.
31. F.S. Taylor, *JHS*, L, 1930, p. 116. It was said to be 'learnt from the philosopher Comarius'.
32. The distinction tended to be blurred; even the kings sometimes abandoned their Macedonian dialect: Plutarch, *Antony*, 27, 4.
33. Philo, *Against Flaccus*, 78, probably referring to the bastinado (and going back to Ptolemaic times).
34. Livy, XXXI, 29, 15.
35. Papyri of second or third century AD, perhaps re-edited from an early Hellenistic document: R. MacMullen, *Aegyptus*, 1964, p. 184.
36. Cf. the story that the last fourth-century Pharaoh, Nekht-nebf (Nectanebes) II, had, as Amon, become the father of Alexander the Great.
37. P. Lond., I, p. 48, no. 43 (second century BC).
38. O. Brendel, *AJA*, LXXI, 1967, pp. 407 ff.; Noshy, pp. 138 ff. on sculpture. L. Guerrini, *Oriens Antiquus*, VI, 1967, pp. 135 ff., points to an element of social protest in the 'popular-Pharaonic' style. For architecture cf. A. Boethius–J.B. Ward-Perkins, *Etruscan and Roman Architecture* (1970), pp. 458 ff., and for the rock-tombs, J. Marlowe, *The Golden Age of Alexandria* (1971), pp. 325 ff.; Noshy, pp. 24 ff.

39. W. Perelmans, *Festschrift F. Oertel* (1964), pp. 49 ff.
40. A. Boethius–J. B. Ward-Perkins, *op. cit.*, p. 458.
41. Cf. M. A. Korostovcev, *Vestnik Drevnej Istorii*, 95, 1966, pp. 40 ff. (Upper Egypt). The ancient Egyptian language revived as Coptic. Juvenal, *Satires*, XV, 31 ff. and 51 ff., regarded Egyptian villagers as extremely violent.
42. Plutarch, *Antony*, 27, 4 (she spoke Egyptian, Ethiopian, Trogodyte, Hebrew, Aramaic, Syriac, Median and Parthian). This description of Cleopatra's linguistic abilities has been considered a fictitious echo of similar eulogies of Mithridates VI, but without justification since the two accounts are quite different (see H. Reinach, *Mithridate Eupator*, 1890, p. 282, n. 1).
43. P. M. Fraser, *Opuscula Atheniensia*, VII, 1967, pp. 23 ff., against C. B. Welles, *Historia*, XI, 1962, pp. 271 ff., XII, 1963, p. 512 (cult found at Rhacotis); R. Stiehl, *History of Religions*, III, 1963–64, pp. 21 ff. (Sinope and Babylon connections). See also L. Vidman, *Isis und Sarapis bei den Griechen und Römern*, 1971.
44. P. Jumilhac, 18n.
45. Stele in British Museum, translated by S. R. K. Glanville, in Bevan, pp. 347 ff. Perhaps he was succeeded by Achoreus (Lucan, *Civil War*, VIII, 475, X, 194), whose real name may have been Anchoreus (*nh-Hr*).
46. Apollinopolis Magna (Edfu) (finished temple of Horus); Tintyra (Dendera) (temple of Hathor); Coptos (walls); Ombos (Kom-Ombo) (pylon and pronaos), Thebes (Karnak); Philae (near Aswan); Senmet (Biggeh beside Philae). Noshy, pp. 68 ff., ignores Auletes' contributions.
47. Bouché-Leclercq, II, p. 223, believed that there was jealousy between the priests of Thebes and Hermonthis. There is a statuette of a mild and mystic priest of Hermonthis in the Louvre, Rostovtzeff, *SEHHW*, II, pl. CXI, no. 1.
48. Witt, p. 13.
49. Mond and Myers, *The Bucheum*, II, 1934, p. 12.
50. Heinen, p. 26, n. 1; cf. W. W. Tarn, *JRS.*, 1936, pp. 187 ff., against H. de Meulenaare, *Chronique d'Egypte*, XLII, 1967, p. 303, etc. There seems no need to disbelieve in Cleopatra's presence on the grounds that she had too little time for her preparations, as T. C. Skeat, *Mizraim*, VI, 1937, p. 39.
51. Volkmann, p. 60, unjustifiably assumes that Ptolemy XIII was at Hermonthis (against Skeat, *op. cit.*).
52. *PSI*, X, 1098b; cf. documents of 6 July and 12 August.
53. U. Kahrstedt, *Klio*, X, 1910, pp. 261 ff.
54. Berenice II and Arsinoe III exceptionally appeared alone outside Egypt (Ephesus and ?Cyprus).
55. Cf. Bevan, p. 360.
56. Diodorus Siculus, XIX, 67; cf. G. H. Macurdy, *Hellenistic Queens* (1932), pp. 1, 3 ff.
57. Cf. Athenaeus, XI, 497B.
58. Cf. Catullus, LXVI, 25 f.
59. Valerius Maximus, IV, 1.

60. Heinen, p. 38.
61. *BGU*, VIII, 1835.
62. *Ibid.*, 1843.
63. *Ibid.*, 1730. Wrongly attributed to 79 BC by P. G. Elgood, *The Ptolemies of Egypt*, 1938, p. 175.
64. Cf. Heinen, pp. 27 ff. against Skeat, *JEA*, XLVIII, 1962, pp. 100 ff. (who believes the boy's brother Ptolemy XIV was temporarily promoted). It has also sometimes been considered that the queen is Cleopatra's half-sister Arsinoe.
65. Cleopatra's first year extended from her succession until 4 September 51 BC (end of Egyptian year); her second, September 51–September 50; her third, September 50–September 49.
66. P. Berl., Inv. 16277 (Abusir-el-Malaq); P. Lond., 827 (Bacchias).
67. Caesar, *Civil War*, III, 103.
68. Skeat, *op. cit.*, Heinen, p. 28 and n. 1.
69. Plutarch, *Antony*, 25, 3, suggests that Cleopatra exercised her charms upon Cnaeus Pompeius.
70. Heinen, pp. 57 ff., E. Badian, *JRS*, 1968, p. 259, against Volkmann, *op. cit.*
71. J. Briscoe, *CR*, 1969, p. 323.
72. Heinen, p. 17, n. 4.
73. P. Lond., 827, P. Fay., 151 (June), H. Brügsch, *Zeitschrift für die Ägyptische Sprache*, XXIV, 1886, p. 38, no. 54 (sole name); cf. P. Berl., 16876, perhaps of 28/1/48, Heinen, p. 27, n. 3.
74. Malalas, *Chronica*, 10 init.
75. Appian, *Civil Wars*, II, 84, speaks of 'the region around Syria'.
76. *BMC, Palestine*, pp. 107 f., A. B. Brett, *AJA*, XLI, 1937, pp. 452 ff.; cf. *FITA*, p. 372. The issue was repeated in 38–37 BC.
77. *HG*, pp. 24 ff.
78. Caesar, *Civil War*, III, 103.
79. There also developed a category of 'Equals in Honour' to kinsmen (*isotimoi*). L. Mooren, *Antidorum W. Perelmans*, Louvain, 1968, pp. 161 ff., discusses whether there was a link between title and function.
80. Horace, *Epodes* IX, 15; *Odes* I, 37, 7.
81. M. Dothan, *Israel Exploration Journal*, XVII, 1967, pp. 279 f.
82. Badian, *JRS*, 1968, p. 259, against Heinen, pp. 41 ff.
83. Cicero, *Letters to Atticus*, XI, 6, 5.
84. Pliny the elder, *Natural History*, V, 58.
85. Lucan, *Civil War*, VIII, 480 f.

PART TWO: CLEOPATRA AND CAESAR

CHAPTER 3   CLEOPATRA AND CAESAR IN EGYPT

1. Florus, IV, 2, 60, attributes to Theodotus a leading part in the Alexandrian War.
2. Lucan, *Civil War*, X, 170.
3. Cf. R. MacMullen, *Aegyptus*, XLIV, 1964, pp. 179 ff.

4. Diodorus Siculus, I, 83 (60 BC): 300,000 (citizens?).
5. Cf. R.A. Todd, *Popular Violence and Internal Security in Hellenistic Alexandria*, Berkeley dissertation, 1963.
6. Dio, XLII, 34, 4 f.
7. Lucan, X, 57.
8. Plutarch, *Caesar*, 48 f.
9. The assumption of E. Bradford, *Cleopatra*, 1971, p. 13, that she spoke fluent Latin seems unproved.
10. Cf. Seel, *Cicero*, pp. 245 f.
11. A. Boethius – J.B. Ward-Perkins, *Etruscan and Roman Architecture*, p. 461.
12. For references see H. Fuchs, *Der geistige Widerstand gegen Rom in der antiken Welt* (1938), G.W. Bowersock, *Augustus and the Greek World* (1965), pp. 1 ff.
13. G.W. Bowersock, *ibid.*, pp. 109 ff.
14. Plutarch, *Antony*, 27, 2 f.
15. J. Dover Wilson, ed. Shakespeare, *Antony and Cleopatra*, p. xxxvi.
16. Volkmann, p. 222 (references), add A.B. Brett, *AJA*, XLI, 1937, p. 463.
17. *BMC, Ptolemies*, p. 122, no. 1. A somewhat similar early portrait appears at Ascalon, Chapter 2, n. 77. (A.B. Brett, *op. cit.*, p. 459; cf. A. Mamroth, *Berliner Numismatische Zeitschrift*, 1951, pp. 161 ff.) The theory that the bad portraits are enemy propaganda comes from Woerl, *Bericht über eine Anzahl im Jahr 1849 aufgefundener römischer Münzen*. A. Stahr, *Cleopatra* (1864), pp. 290 f., was also dismayed by her coin-portraits.
18. Diodorus Siculus, IV, 3.
19. Cf. terracotta statuettes in Alexandria Museum, Bevan, p. 97, fig. 23.
20. Priscian, X, p. 536 (ed. Hertz).
21. Galen in Hultsch, *Metrologicorum Scriptorum Reliquiae*, I, pp. 108 f.; cf. n. 233 (note by Gilbert Murray) at end of Bernard Shaw's *Caesar and Cleopatra*: he does not know what 'vine-rag' is.
22. Dio, XLII, 36, 3 f.
23. Lucan, *Civil War*, X, 109 ff.
24. Cf. Oost, *Classical Philology*, 1955, pp. 105 ff. Brutus' role was particularly oppressive.
25. E. Bradford, *Cleopatra* (1971), p. 49.
26. E.M. Forster, *Alexandria*, p. 17; see forthcoming P.M. Fraser, *Ptolemaic Alexandria* (1972).
27. Vanderpool, *AJA*, LXI, 1957, pp. 284 f. Ptolemy II's pavilion had possessed colonnades on three sides, Noshy, p. 55.
28. Caesar, *Civil War*, III, 109; cf. scholiast on Lucan, *Civil War*, X, 468.
29. Caesar, *Civil War*, *loc. cit.*, Dio XLII, 36 f.
30. Perhaps the harbour is shown on a mosaic of the second century AD from Lepcis Magna, M. Rostovtzeff, *SEHHW*, pl. XL. The island is now under water.
31. M. Gelzer, *Julius Caesar* (1968), p. 249, n. 7.
32. Caesar, *Civil War*, III, 112 (trans. J.F. Mitchell).
33. Anon., *Alexandrian War*, 9.
34. Gelzer, *op. cit.*, p. 250, n. 7.
35. Anon., *Alexandrian War*, 21 (trans. J.F. Mitchell).

36. Plutarch, *Caesar*, 38 (trans. Rex Warner).
37. Sources in Gelzer, *loc. cit.*
38. Anon., *Alexandrian War*, 21.
39. Gelzer, *op. cit.*, p. 251, and n. 1.
40. Josephus, *BJ*, I, 187, *AJ*, XIV, 129 f.
41. Cf. R. de Vaux, *Revue biblique*, LXXV, 1968, pp. 188 ff. The high priest was Onias IV.
42. For this friction see S.W. Baron, *Social and Religious History of the Jews*, I, 2nd ed., 1952, pp. 190 ff., 381 ff.
43. Apion in Josephus, *Against Apion*, II, 56, 60.
44. *OGIS*, 742: synagogue built on behalf of Cleopatra and Ptolemy XV Caesar by Alypus.
45. Plutarch, *Antony*, 27, 4; cf. above, p. 256, n. 42.
46. Herodotus, II, 90; cf. Mustafa el Amir, *JEA*, 1951, pp. 81 ff., W. den Boer, *Mnemosyne*, VIII, 1955, p. 137.
47. Anon., *Alexandrian War*, 33.
48. Suetonius, *Divus Julius*, 35.
49. P. Oxy., XIV, 629; cf. Heinen, pp. 177 f.
50. M. Gelzer, *Caesar*, p. 258 and n. 3, *HG*, p. 36. But Hyrcanus II was still not allowed to call himself king.
51. Josephus, *AJ*, XIV, 188, *Against Apion*, II, 37, doubted by F.E. Adcock, *CAH*, IX, p. 694, n. 1.
52. Anon., *Alexandrian War*, 33 (trans. J.F. Mitchell).
53. J. Briscoe, *CR*, 1969, p. 322.
54. Heinen, pp. 142 ff., Badian, *JRS*, 1968, p. 259, against Lord, *JRS*, 1938, pp. 19 f., Balsdon, *Julius Caesar and Rome*, p. 140.
55. Appian, *Civil Wars*, II, 90; Suetonius, *Divus Julius*, 52.
56. H. Seyrig, *Revue numismatique*, XI, 1969, pp. 53 f. (chalcedony).
57. Athenaeus, V, 37; cf. M. Rostovtzeff, *History of the Ancient World: Orient and Greece*, p. 393, fig. 36, Noshy, p. 56.
58. Appian, Civil Wars, II, 90.
59. Heinen, pp. 156 ff. He left by land, not sea (*Alexandrian War*, 33, 5, against *CAH*, IX, p. 677).
60. A. Boethius – J.B. Ward-Perkins, *Etruscan and Roman Architecture*, pp. 459 f. The Caesareum was on the sea-front between the Emporium and Antony's villa. Thothmes III's obelisk ('Cleopatra's Needle', now on the Thames Embankment in London) was one of a pair of obelisks placed in front of the Caesareum.
61. Pseudo-Philo of Byzantium, *De Septem Mundi Miraculis*, ed. Hercher, 1858.

CHAPTER 4   CLEOPATRA AND CAESAR IN ROME

1. Born in Caesar's lifetime: Suetonius, *Divus Julius*, 52, 2, Plutarch, *Caesar*, 49, 10. Born after Caesar's death: Plutarch, *Antony*, 54, 6. Volkmann, p. 75, Heinen, *Historia*, 1969, pp. 181 ff., 203, support the former view, and J.P.V.D. Balsdon, *CR*, 1960, p. 70, tends to favour the latter.
2. Suetonius, *op. cit.*

3. V. and E. Revillout, *Revue égyptologique*, VII, 1896, p. 168.

4. Balsdon, *op. cit.*, p. 71.

5. Cf. T.J. Cadoux, *Oxford Classical Dictionary*, 2nd ed. (1970), p. 191.

6. The earliest report of Caesar's alleged intention to recognize Caesarion appears in Nicolaus of Damascus, *Life of Augustus*, 20, who contradicts it, declaring that Caesar repudiated him in his will: cf. Balsdon, *Historia*, 1958, p. 85, n. 32. There was also a rumour that a will in favour of Caesarion was suppressed by Calpurnia.

7. Suetonius, *Divus Julius*, 52. For such denials cf. Dio, XLVII, 31, 5.

8. Though a Gaul, Julius Sabinus boasted in AD 70 that he was descended from Caesar through his great-grandmother; Tacitus, *Histories*, IV, 55, Dio, LXVI, 3, 1, and 16, 1.

9. The theory of Carcopino, *Passion et Politique chez les Césars*, 1958, that Antony was Caesarion's father is purely conjectural: Heinen, *Historia*, 1969, p. 203.

10. *BMC, Ptolemies*, p. 122, no. 1; cf. Heinen, p. 145, n. 1.

11. From Democritus (5th cent. BC)? M. Grant, *Julius Caesar* (1969), p. 206.

12. Dio, XLIII, 20, 2.

13. Scholiast on Lucan, *Civil War*, X, 521: accepted by A. Weigall, *The Life and Times of Cleopatra Queen of Egypt* (1914), p. 114 (against Bouché-Leclercq).

14. Dio, XLIII, 27, 3.

15. Porphyrion on Horace, *Satires*, I, 2; cf. III, 3.

16. Cf. A.D. Nock, *Harvard Studies in Classical Philology*, XLI, 1930, pp. 1 ff.

17. E.g. F.E. Adcock, *CAH*, IX, pp. 718 ff.

18. Dio, XLIII, 27, 3, Appian, *Civil Wars*, III, 154, stresses the debts Caesar owed to his Alexandrian stay.

19. Servius on Virgil, *Eclogues*, V, 29, referring to 'Liber', whose name is used to represent the Alexandrian version of Dionysus (Velleius Paterculus, II, 82, 4). I owe a valuable note on this subject to Dr T.J. Cadoux.

20. Cf. Volkmann, p. 87.

21. J.H. Collins, *Historia*, IV, 1955, pp. 462 ff.

22. Cf. M. Grant, *Julius Caesar*, pp. 224 f.

23. Callippus, a friend of Aristotle with whom he stayed at Athens, modified the theory of concentric spheres of Eudoxus of Cnidus, whom Lucan (*Civil Wars*, X, 187) mentions as Sosigenes' superseded predecessor.

24. A.E. Samuel, *Ptolemaic Chronology* (1962), E.J. Bickerman, *Chronology of the Ancient World*, pp. 40 ff., 101, n. 36, R.A. Parker, *The Calendars of Ancient Egypt* (1950). In the second century BC Hipparchus of Nicaea postulated a year of $365\frac{1}{4} - \frac{1}{100}$ days.

25. Cf. M. Grant, *Roman Imperial Money*, pp. 180 f., *Roman Anniversary Issues*, pp. 4, 120.

26. Cicero, *Letters to Atticus*, XV, 15, 2.

27. Suetonius, *Divus Julius*, 52, 1.

28. First in Nicolaus of Damascus, *Life of Augustus*, 28.

29. Suetonius, *Divus Julius*, 52, 3.

30. Against J.H. Collins, *Historia*, IV, 1955, p. 463 and n. 86.

CHAPTER 5   CLEOPATRA AFTER CAESAR'S DEATH

1. Cicero, *Letters to Atticus*, XIV, 8, 1.
2. *Ibid.*, XIV, 20, 2 – not amending *illo* (that) to *filio* (son).
3. Cf. J.H. Collins, *American Journal of Philology*, LXXX, 1959, p. 127 and n. 35.
4. Lucan, *Civil War*, X, 76 (or poetic licence?).
5. Cicero, *Letters to Atticus*, XV, 1, 5.
6. *Ibid.*, XV, 4, 4.
7. *Ibid.*, XV, 15, 2 (trans. L.P. Wilkinson). Sara, though a male name, is not the same as Serapion, Shackleton-Bailey (ed.), *Letters to Atticus, loc. cit.*, against Münzer.
8. M. Grant (ed.), *Cicero: On the Good Life*, p. 174.
9. Was he, perhaps, Cleopatra's prime minister, or had she left that official behind in Egypt? Cicero, *Letters to Friends*, I, 1, 1, mentions a Hammonius who had been an envoy of Auletes (p. 16).
10. P. Oxy., XIV, 1629; cf. Heinen, p. 178.
11. Porphyry, *FGH*, 260.
12. Josephus, *Against Apion*, II, 58, *AJ*, XV, 39.
13. *HG*, pp. 231 f.
14. Dio, XLVII, 31, 5.
15. Lefebvre, *Annales du Service des Antiquités de l'Égypte*, 1908, 241, and *Mélanges Holleaux*, 1913, pp. 103 ff., P. Tebt., V, 57–61.
16. Porphyry, *FGH*, 260.
17. Witt, pp. 28, 30, 55, etc.
18. Volkmann, p. 77. Mut was a local goddess of Thebes (Karnak), where her temple was linked with Amon's by an avenue of stone rams.
19. E.g. Philae, Apollinopolis Magna, Tintyra (later). They are called by the Coptic term Mammisi. Cf. F. Daumas, *Les Mammisis des temples égyptiens* (1958).
20. Witt, pp. 210 f. Cf. M. Rostovtzeff, *SEHHW*, II, p. 886 no. 2, for Egyptian-robed bust of Horus, probably of the early first centuries BC. There is no evidence for an actual performance of birth-rituals by the Ptolemies.
21. Cf. the Heroonpolis (Pithom) stele of Ptolemy IV Philopator, translated in Bevan, pp. 388 f, and B. H. Stricker, *Ex Oriente Lux*, XIV, 1963.
22. Witt, pp. 40, 50, 215 f.
23. It may have been now that Hermonthis became the capital of its *nome* or province (formerly the Pathyrite), Bouché-Leclercq, II, p. 217, n. 1.
24. *OGI*, 194; cf. R. Hutmacher, *Das Ehrendekret für den Strategen Kallimachos* (Beiträge zur klassischen Philologie, 17), Meisenheim am Glan, 1965, Museo Egizio, Turin. The god is Amon-Ra-Sonther, Amon king of the gods.
25. Appian, *Civil Wars*, IV, 61; cf. V, 8, IV, 63.
26. Appian, *Civil Wars*, V, 9.
27. Appian, *Civil Wars*, V, 8.
28. *S*, p. 184, nos. 1125 ff., *BMCR*, I, nos. 4313 ff.

29. Dio, XLVII, 31, 5.
30. Seneca the younger, *Naturales Quaestiones*, IV, 2; cf. Pliny the elder, *Natural History*, V. 58. Appian, *Civil Wars*, IV, 61, places the famine earlier, in 43 BC; this may be a mistake, or there may have been a succession of famines.
31. P. Tebt., V, 57-61 (13/4/41).
32. Appian, *Civil Wars*, IV, 74.
33. *Ibid.*, IV, 82; V, 8.
34. For his motives see M. Hadas, *Sextus Pompey*, New York, 1930.

PART THREE: CLEOPATRA AND ANTONY

CHAPTER 6   CLEOPATRA SUMMONED BY ANTONY

1. For Antony's birthday, 14 January (82 or 81 BC), see Heinen, p. 190.
2. First Octavian had to be left behind at Dyrrhachium; then in the first battle of Philippi his camp had been stormed by Brutus, and, in the second, his health was still so bad that he had to delegate the command of his camp.
3. Plutarch, *Antony*, 23.
4. Suetonius, *Augustus*, 13 (M. Favonius).
5. R. Syme, *The Roman Revolution*, pp. 260, 271 f.
6. *FITA*, p. 274.
7. Plutarch, *Antony*, 23, 2.
8. *S*, p. 181, no. 1092, *BMCR*, I, no. 4236: the type contains overtones of a more general sort of Concord as well.
9. *FITA*, pl. XI, no. 51; Octavian also appears at Thessalonica (Salonica), *ibid.*, p. 369.
10. K. Scott, *Classical Philology*, 1929, pp. 133 ff., H. Jeanmaire, *Revue archéologique*, 1924, pp. 241 ff.
11. Plutarch, *Antony*, 24, 3. Octavian was developing the cult of Apollo.
12. *SIG*³, 760.
13. Strabo, XIV, 23. The occasion is uncertain.
14. Appian, *Civil Wars*, V, 7.
15. Dio, XLIV, 39, 2; Seneca, *Suasoriae*, I, 7.
16. *S*, p. 189, nos. 1160, 1163, *BMCR*, II, p. 394, no. 40, and p. 396, no. 48; cf. D. Michel, *Alexander als Vorbild für Pompeius, Caesar and Marcus Antonius* (Collection Latomus, XCIV, 1967), J.M.C. Toynbee, *CR*, 1970, p. 84.
17. Anteon appears on L. Regulus' coinage for Antony, *S*, p. 182, no. 1103, *BMCR*, I, no. 4255. The Ptolemies claimed descent from Heracles through Ptolemy I Soter's mother Arsinoe; Satyrus, fragment 21; cf. Ptolemy III Euergetes, *OGIS*, 54 (Adulis).
18. Turcan, *Mémoires de l'Ecole Française de Rome*, LXXIV, 1962, p. 602.
19. M. Grant, *Roman Myths*, p. 55.
20. Plutarch, *Antony*, 4 (trans. Ian Scott-Kilvert); cf. M.A. Levi, *Ottaviano Capoparte*, II, p. 99, n. 5. Tarn, *CAH*, X, p. 52 (on coins): 'his strange disharmonic face, too long between eyes and mouth, reflected the discontinuity of his life'.

21. Plutarch, *Antony*, 24, 6–8 (trans. Ian Scott-Kilvert).
22. *Ibid.*, 4, 3, and 36, 4 (trans. Ian Scott-Kilvert).
23. Velleius, II, 74.
24. Plutarch, *Antony*, 10, 3–4 (trans. Ian Scott-Kilvert). His previous wives were Fadia and his cousin Antonia.
25. C.L. Babcock, *Historia*, 1965, p. 32.
26. J.P.V.D. Balsdon, *Roman Women* (1962), p. 50.
27. See above, n. 15. H. Mattingly, *Roman Coins*, 2nd ed., p. 72, n. 2, doubts the attribution; but cf. nn. 29, 30, and Balsdon, *op. cit.*, pp. 294 f., n. 13. For the iconography of Fulvia, see H. Bartel, *Studien zum Frauenporträt der augusteischen Zeit*, Munich, 1967.
28. *S*, p. 120, no. 747, *BMCR*, II, p. 388, nos. 1 ff.
29. *BMC, Phrygia*, p. 213, nos. 20 f.; cf. *FITA*, pl. XI, 52; cf. p. 350.
30. H. Seyrig, *Syria*, XXVII, 1950, pp. 40 ff.; cf. G.F. Hill, *BMC, Phoenicia*, pp. cxvii f., *FITA*. p. 368, nn. 6, 7.
31. Plutarch, *Antony*, 25, 4–27, 1 (trans. Ian Scott-Kilvert).
32. Shakespeare, *Antony and Cleopatra*, Act II, Scene 2.
33. Socrates of Rhodes in Athenaeus IV, 147 f. (trans. C.B. Gulick).
34. Lucretius, I, 3 f.; cf. M. Grant, *Cities of Vesuvius*, pp. 93 ff. Cleopatra's links with Aphrodite could be thought of as a challenge to Octavian's claim, through Caesar, to be descended from Venus.
35. J. Charbonneaux, *Mélanges A. Piganiol* (1966), pp. 407 ff.
36. P. Oxy., 1629: Cleopatra as Aphrodite. For her as Isis, see below, n. 47.
37. Witt, pp. 46 ff., cf. L. Vidman, *Isis und Sarapis bei den Griechen und Römern* (1971).
38. For the reasons why the religion of Isis did not conquer the world, see Witt, pp. 139 f.
39. For these see T. Szentléleky, *Acta Antiqua Scientiarum Hungaricae*, XV, 1967, pp. 457 ff.
40. The character and rites of Isis were much influenced by Demeter: sources in Witt, pp. 16, 67, 121, 125, 146, 224.
41. W.W. Tarn and G.T. Griffith, *Hellenistic Civilisation* (University paperback ed., Methuen, 1966) p. 359.
42. P. Oxy., 1380, line 30.
43. Diodorus, I, 27, 2.
44. *ILS*, 4422.
45. Sources in Witt, pp. 106 f.
46. Cyme version (trans. J. Lindsay); cf. J. Bergman, *Acta Universitatis Upsaliensis, Hist. Relig.* III (1968). The Greek text is reproduced by P.G. Walsh, *The Roman Novel*, C.U.P. (1970), pp. 252 f.
47. Plutarch, *Antony*, 54, 6 (this does not imply Cleopatra VII was never called Isis before 34 BC). But the head of Isis or Hathor at Tintyra (Dendera) (Bevan, p. 367, fig. 62) is not Cleopatra, since her cartouche has only been added in modern times, Maspero, *Comptes-rendus de l'Académie des Inscriptions*, 1899, p. 133. For a second-century BC queen as Isis, cf. M. Rostovtzeff, *SEHHW*, II, p. 872.
48. Dio, L, 5, 3.

49. Witt, p. 257 and n. 11.
50. Valerius Maximus, III, 4 (L. Aemilius Paullus).
51. Josephus, *AJ*, XV, 89.
52. Appian, *Civil Wars*, V, 9. Dio, XIVIII, 27, implies the pretender *was* Ptolemy XIII. He also tells a strange story of Cleopatra's 'brothers' being dragged from the Ephesus temple, XLVIII, 24, 2.
53. Appian, *Civil Wars*, V, 7. Some of these measures had already been taken, or at least hoped for, in advance of Antony's arrival: e.g. Rhosus dates its new era back to 42 BC.
54. *HG*, p. 44.
55. Josephus, *BJ*, I, 243; *AJ*, XIV, 324.
56. Shakespeare, *Antony and Cleopatra*, Act I, Scene 1.
57. Or perhaps Antony heard the bad news late in 41 BC: Buchheim, p. 118, n. 188.
58. For the Perusian War, see now W.V. Harris, *Rome in Etruria and Umbria* (1971), p. 300.

CHAPTER 7   CLEOPATRA ABANDONED BY ANTONY

1. Appian, *Civil Wars*, V, 29, 75 (cf. V, 66); Augustus in Martial, *Epigrams*, XI, 20, lines 3 ff.
2. *S*, p. 192, no. 1189, *BMCR*, II, p. 495, no. 114 (winged caduceus and double cornucopiae emblems of prosperity); cf. slightly earlier, *S*, p. 184, no. 118, *BMCR*, I, no. 4276.
3. H. Mattingly, *CR*, 1934, p. 161; G. Williams, *The Nature of Roman Poetry* (1970), pp. 60 f. The children of Scribonia and Octavia both turned out to be girls. Later, Gaius Asinius Gallus, son of the historian Pollio (consul 40 BC), claimed that he himself had been the child Virgil was referring to. In 20 BC Gaius Caesar (the grandson of Augustus) was born.
4. Ascalon revived its silver coinage with Cleopatra's head in 38–37 BC as a hostile gesture to the pro-Parthian Antigonus in Judaea, *FITA*, p. 372, n. 6; A.B. Brett, *AJA*, 1937, pp. 452, 455.
5. Josephus, *BJ*, I, 279, *AJ*, XIV, 14, 2; cf. *HG*, pp. 48 ff.
6. Appian, *Civil Wars*, V, 73, Plutarch, *Antony*, 32.
7. 'Achaea' according to Velleius, II, 72.
8. Deutsch, *University of California Publications in Classical Philology*, IX, 6, 1928, pp. 186 f.; cf. *FITA*, p. 370.
9. *FITA*, p. 353.
10. *S*, p. 199, no. 1271, *BMCR*, II, p. 504, no. 138, *FITA*, p. 41 (*c.* 39 BC).
11. Appian, *Civil Wars*, V, 76, Plutarch, *Antony*, 33.
12. *S*, p. 193, nos. 1197 f., *BMCR*, II, p. 502, nos. 133 ff., A.M. Woodward, *Essays to H. Mattingly*, p. 151; cf. Bacchus on other coins of *c.* 39–38 BC, *S*, p. 185, no. 1136, *BMCR*, I, no. 4299 (C. Vibius Varus); and other portraits of Octavia, *S*, p. 193, no. 1196, *BMCR*, II, p. 499 (40 BC, unique), *S*, p. 193, no. 1200, *BMCR*, II, p. 507, nos. 144 f. (38–37 BC).
13. Dio, XLVIII, 39, 2, Seneca the elder, *Suasoriae*, I, 6.
14. Dio, XLIX, 22.

15. Or was Octavian merely late? Subsequently he reproached Antony for not waiting, Appian, *Civil Wars*, X, 80.
16. *S*, p. 197, nos. 1254 f., *BMCR*, II, pp. 510 ff: no less than six denominations.
17. Tran Tam Tinh, *Revue archéologique*, 1970, p. 170 and n. 2.
18. Cf. R. Syme, *The Roman Revolution*, p. 272.

CHAPTER 8   CLEOPATRA REVIVES HER ANCESTRAL KINGDOM

1. The descriptions given by the ancient writers are confused and contradictory. There is a full discussion in A. Schalit, *König Herodes*, 1969, pp. 772 ff; cf. *HG*, pp. 77 ff.
2. P. Lederer, *Numismatic Chronicle*, 1938, pp. 65 ff., *FITA*, p. 371.
3. Tripolis (H. Seyrig, *Syria*, XXVII, 1950, p. 40, Aradus, Balanea (Leucas on the Chrysoroas), (Seyrig, *op. cit.*, pp. 22 ff., etc., *FITA*, p. 371), Berytus (Seyrig, *op. cit.*, p. 44 and fig. 1; cf. A.B. Brett, *AJA*, XLI, 1937, p. 460), Orthosia (Seyrig, *op. cit.*, p. 44, no. 3).
4. Josephus, *BJ*, I, 440, *AJ*, XV, 92. Josephus' report that a prince Zenodorus leased the kingdom probably refers to the time of Augustus (Tarn, *CAH*, X, p. 67; cf. Seyrig, *op. cit.*, p. 47), not Cleopatra (Jones, *CERP*, ed. 2, p. 271).
5. *FITA*, p. 371. Damascus also introduced a dating formula borrowed from the Ptolemies. Seyrig, *Numismatic Notes and Monographs*, XIX, 1950, p. 32 and n. 42.
6. E.g. as 'Coelesyria' (*sic*); cf. Buchheim, pp. 100 f., n. 28.
7. Carter, p. 157, regards this as the only one of the gifts which did represent an alienation of (short-lived) Roman control, but the client prince Polemo had briefly controlled at least part of the territory earlier. The province of Cilicia in Cicero's time had consisted neither of Flat nor of Rough Cilicia but of areas to their west and north-west.
8. Strabo, XIV, 669, 671 (later Hamaxia was in the province of Pamphylia).
9. H.U. Instinsky, *Studies to D.M. Robinson*, II, pp. 975 ff. For Cyprus cf. M. Rostovtzeff, *SEHHW*, III, p. 1612, n. 113. Strabo, XIV, 665, is wrong in saying that Antony gave it to Cleopatra 'and her sister Arsinoe'. Caesar had already returned it to the Egyptian crown.
10. Caesar, *Civil War*, III, 12.
11. Trophy on coin of Sosius at Zacynthus: *S*, p. 199, no. 1272, *BMCR*, II, p. 508, no. 146.
12. Josephus, *BJ*, I, 359 ff.
13. Josephus, *BJ*, VII, 300.
14. *HG*, p. 78.
15. Volkmann, p. 125; cf. Josephus, *BJ*, I, 360.
16. Dio, LI, 15, 4.
17. *HG*, pp. 76 ff.
18. Josephus, *AJ*, XV. 24.

19. Porphyry, *FGH*, 260, F. 2, 17.
20. D. Magie, *Roman Rule in Asia Minor* (1950, reprinted 1966), II, p. 1287, n. 29, H. Seyrig, *Syria*, XXVII, 1950, pp. 43 f., Volkmann, *Gnomon*, XXXI, 1959, p. 179. As Heinen, *Historia*, XVIII, 1969, pp. 188 f., sees, the double era has nothing to do with the rule of Caesarion (against A.E. Samuel, *Études de papyrologie*, IX, 1964, pp. 73 ff., cf. Piganiol). Nor should it be described as a joint era of Cleopatra and Antony. Chersonesus Taurica (near Sevastopol) started an era in 36 BC.
21. *CIL*, III, Suppl. 2, 143, 86 d, from Heliopolis (Baalbek). Perhaps of the first century AD.
22. Dio, L, 5, 3 and 25; 3; cf. Witt, p. 147.
23. Cf. Cicero, *Republic*, VI, 17, 17.
24. E.g. *Homeric Hymns*, XXXI.
25. Proclus, I, 30D, etc.; cf. Witt, p. 36.
26. *BMC, Ptolemies*, p. 56, no. 103.
27. Sources in W.W. Tarn, *JRS*, 1932, pp. 144 ff.
28. *S*, p. 193, no. 1199, *BMCR*, II, p. 506, no. 141.
29. Tarn, *CAH*, X, p. 68; cf. Cumont, *Comptes-rendus de l'Académie des Inscriptiones*, 1930, pp. 216 ff.
30. J.M.C. Toynbee, *CR*, 1970, p. 84. The lion, sign of Antony's conception (see above, Chapter 6, n. 16), was also the symbol of Alexander, cf. Tarn, *JRS*, 1932, p. 144, n. 3.

CHAPTER 9   CLEOPATRA RECEIVES ANTONY BACK
FROM THE WARS

1. As Tarn, *CAH*, X, p. 75.
2. Plutarch, *Antony*, 27, 3.
3. Henceforward described as 'Media' – though there is also another Media (which does not come into this story), i.e. Media proper, with its capital Ecbatana (Hamadan), which since the middle of the second century BC had at most times formed an integral part of the feudal Parthian realm.
4. Plutarch, *Antony*, 37, 4, confusingly says Antony began the war too *early* in order to get back to Cleopatra.
5. *S*, p. 194, no. 1202, *BMCR*, II, p. 520, no. 172. For the date cf. Buchheim, p. 120, n. 205, and Tarn against Sydenham and Mattingly (35 BC). At about the same date Antony coined with a trophy (though see Chapter 8, n. 11 above), *S*, p. 194, no. 1202, *BMCR*, II, p. 509, no. 147 (the portrait was imitated on a local issue of Byzantium, *BMC*, 60, *FITA*, p. 369).
6. Plutarch, *Antony*, 34, 6.
7. Although, says Plutarch (*ibid.*, 39, 1) rather unfairly, he was the 'prime mover' of the war.
8. Tarn, *CAH*, X, p. 73.
9. Plutarch, *Antony*, 17, 2.
10. Dio, XLIX, 31, 3, wrongly implies that Antony's troops did winter in Armenia.
11. Livy, *Epitome*, CXXX.

12. Appian, *Civil Wars*, V, 132.
13. Cf. Rice-Holmes, *The Architect of the Roman Empire*, I, pp. 138 f, n. 6.
14. Plutarch, *Antony*, 53, 2, against Dio, XLIX, 33, 1.
15. Shakespeare, *Antony and Cleopatra*, Act III, Scene 7.
16. Cf. B. Doer, *Altertum*, XIV, 1968, pp. 20 ff.
17. Plutarch, *Antony*, 54, 2.
18. Antioch placed Antony's head on its local silver coinage, *BMC*, *Syria*, p. 157, no. 52, Lederer, *NC*, 1938, p. 69.
19. It is uncertain whether Antony invited Aristobulus before or after the latter became high priest, *HG*, p. 80 and n. 2.
20. Josephus, *AJ*, XV, 46 ff.
21. *Ibid.*, 256.
22. Appian, *Civil Wars*, V, 144. Sextus may have died at Midaeum, not Miletus.
23. Dio, XLIX, 18, 4: Antony did not order Sextus' death. Velleius, II, 79: he did. Appian, *op. cit.*, gives the various views.
24. Plutarch, *Antony*, 52, 1–2. The captive Polemo was returned and was promised Lesser Armenia.
25. Josephus, *BJ*, I, 362, *AJ*, XV, 96.
26. Velleius, II, 82.
27. *HG*, pp. 21 ff., 117 ff.
28. Nicolaus, *FGH*, ii A, 90. For the date, cf. G.W. Bowersock, *Augustus and the Greek World* (1965), p. 135.
29. Josephus, *AJ*, XV, 97–103 (trans. R. Marcus).
30. The idea that the queen might have planned to ruin Herod by putting the blame on him is novelettish. See *HG*, pp. 84 f.

CHAPTER 10   CLEOPATRA QUEEN OF KINGS

1. Velleius, II, 82.
2. Cicero, *Republic*, IV, 3, etc.; cf. Pliny the younger, *Letters*, X, 40, 2.
3. Plutarch, *Antony*, 54, 6. Cleopatra 'assumed' the robe of Isis (imperfect tense): some new modification of the role seems to be implied.
4. Dio, LI, 15, 5 (temple); cf. Velleius, II, 82, Heinen, *Klio*, XI, 1911, p. 138. A sketch on a jar from the Ibis cemetery at Abydos (Arabet-el-Madfuneh) seems to show Antony and Cleopatra in these capacities, J.G. Milne, *JEA*, I, 1914, p. 99.
5. C.P. Cavafy in E.M. Forster, *Pharos and Pharillon* (1923), p. 95 (trans. George Valassopoulo).
6. Tarn, *CAH*, X, p. 80.
7. Probably this definition of the infant Ptolemy Philadelphus' overlordship (Dio, XLIX, 41) limits it to Asia Minor; cf. Carter, p. 176, M.A. Levi, *Ottaviano Capoparte* (1933), p. 146.
8. But not, probably, a new Roman colony at Cnossus, as *FITA*, p. 261, n. 7, and p. 55, since this does not seem to have been founded until after 31 BC, A.E. Chapman, *NC*, 1968, p. 14, n. 1, G. Perl, *Klio*, 1970, pp. 342, 345.

9. *Res Gestae Divi Augusti*, 27.
10. Not P. Canidius Crassus: *FITA*, p. 56; cf. Chapman, Perl, *op. cit.*
11. E.S.G. Robinson, *BMC, Cyrenaica*, pp. 119 n., ccvi, no. 25 bis (a), ccix n., Chapman, *op. cit.*, p. 15.
12. Sacred crocodiles were mummified at Ombos (Kom Ombo) and the gods Iqu and Sebek (Souchos) took their form. Ptolemy x Alexander i dedicated a temple to Sebek at Socnopaeus (97–95 BC), and a Fayum Greek declared Caesarion to be the great-grandson of the crocodile deity (Lefèbre, *Annales du Service des Antiquités de l'Egypte*, 1908, p. 241). On imperial Roman coins the crocodile was still the emblem of Egypt (*BMC, Empire*, I, p. 106, no. 650, M. Grant, *The Six Main Aes Coinages of Augustus*, pp. 11, 119); see relief from Praeneste (Palestrina), L. Casson, *The Ancient Mariners* (1960), pl. 10a. Cf. Juvenal, *Satires*, XV, 2. The Romans imported men from Tintyra to look after their crocodiles.
13. Because of this evident link Lollius and Crassus are probably later than *c.* 39 BC (Alföldi, *Mélanges Carcopino*, p. 30) or *c.* 37–36 (A.E. Chapman, *op. cit.*, for Crassus).
14. Plutarch, *Antony*, 54, 4, mistakenly makes Antony grant the title of King of Kings also to Alexander Helios and Ptolemy Philadelphus. How Caesarion was dressed at the Donations we do not know: Cavafy, *op. cit.*, imagines for him a resplendent bejewelled uniform.
15. Though the title of King of Kings had lately become devalued; e.g. Pompey allowed it unofficially, and contrary to custom, to Tigranes i of Armenia as a Seleucid (Dio, XXXVII, 6, 2), and it was employed by Pharnaces ii in the Crimean (Cimmerian) Bosphorus.
16. O. von Wertheimer, *Cleopatra: A Royal Voluptuary* (1931), p. 259, is wrong in saying that Caesarion received this precedence (and no specific territory in the east) because a special sphere had been reserved for him in the west.
17. Dio, XLIX, 41, 2.
18. *BMC, Syria*, p. 158, no. 53. Numerous dies: cf. A.M. Woodward, *Roman Coinage: Essays to H. Mattingly* (1956), p. 152. The coin is a tetradrachm (four drachma piece); see Note on Money.
19. E.g. H. Seyrig, *Revue archéologique*, 1968, p. 256, on Derik find against T. Buttrey, *American Numismatic Society Museum Notes*, VI, 1954, p. 105. The issuing authority was therefore the Roman governor, either Lucius Munatius Plancus or Lucius Calpurnius Bibulus, who succeeded him in about 34 BC and was the brother of the youths whose murderers Cleopatra had handed over to justice in 51 BC.
20. P. Lederer, *NC*, 1938, p. 67.
21. E.g. Titus (Vespasianus junior) in contrast to his father and senior colleague Vespasian, J.R. Jones, *NC*, 1966, pp. 61 ff.
22. Moretti, *Aegyptus*, XXXVIII, 1938, pp. 203 ff. Osiris is often shown standing between his sisters; for Nephthys see also Witt, pp. 16, 18, 31, 36, 39, 143. At Eleusis, too, Kore is *Neotera* in comparison with her mother Demeter. *IG*, 1672, 3546, 3585.
23. T. Buttrey, *op. cit.*, pp. 95 ff., wrongly rejected by Moretti, *op. cit.*
24. Lederer, *NC*, 1938, pp. 67 ff.; cf. coins of Seleucus i and Antiochus i.

25. *S*, p. 194, no. 1210, *BMCR*, II, p. 525, no. 179. *Cleopatrae* probably means 'to Cleopatra', not 'of Cleopatra'.
26. Cf. G.F. Hill, *Historical Roman Coins*, p. 132, against H. Mattingly, *Roman Coins*, 2nd ed., p. XX, no. 16 (*c.* 32 BC).
27. M. Grant, *Roman History from Coins* (1958), p. 15; cf. p. 13.
28. After *S*, p. 208, no. 1337, *BMCR*, II p. 580, no. 32. But *S*, p. 208, no. 1334, *BMCR*, II, p. 415, no. 116, might be later in the same year (36 BC).
29. *S*, p. 194, no. 1206, *BMCR*, II p. 521, no. 173.
30. Plutarch, *Antony*, 28, 4 ff.
31. Phlegon, *Mirabilia*, 32.
32. R. MacMullen, *Enemies of the Roman Order* (1967), pp. 130, 148, 329 f. It is possible, however, that 'Hystaspes' may not be pre-Augustan.
33. *Id.*, *Aegyptus*, 1964, p. 180.
34. E.g. Athenaeus, V, 213B: a comet blazed for seventy days at his birth.
35. *Oracula Sibyllina*, III, 520; cf., III, 464 ff., VIII, 148 ff., III, 652 ff. *Ibid.*, XIV, 284 ff.: gold, the cause of quarrels, will be abolished.
36. Tarn, *JRS*, 1932, pp. 135 ff.
37. *Oracula Sibyllina*, VIII (trans. Jack Lindsay); Tarn, *op. cit.*, does not refer this particular prophecy to Cleopatra.
38. *Ibid.*, III, 46 ff. (trans. Jack Lindsay). For the reference to the Triumvirate, Tarn, *op. cit.*, p. 141, n. 7. The prophecy may be Jewish, *ibid.*, p. 142, but this is not certain.
39. *Ibid.*, III, 75 ff. (trans. Jack Lindsay; cf. his *Cleopatra*, p. 364). *Aither*: heaven.
40. *Ibid.*, XI, 290 ff.; cf. Tarn, *op. cit.*, p. 150.
41. *Ibid.*, III, 350–61, 367–80 (trans. J.M. Carter).
42. Carter, pp. 182 ff. agrees with Tarn, *op. cit.*, p. 138 and H.I. Bell, *Egypt from Alexander the Great to the Arab Conquest* (1948) (against Fuchs) that the reference is to Cleopatra. The reference to the drunkenness of Rome may be a retort to the charge that Cleopatra drank, see below, n. 58.
43. Lucan, *Civil War*, X, 139. 'Red sea' was also a term used for the Indian Ocean.
44. Pliny the elder, *Natural History*, IX, 59, 123; cf. XXXVII, 6, 12, IX, 54, 106.
45. *Ibid.*, IX, 58, 117–22.
46. P. Lond., Inv. 859A; cf. T.C. Skeat, *JEA*, LII, 1966, pp. 179 f.
47. A. Boethius – J.B. Ward-Perkins, *Etruscan and Roman Architecture*, p. 461 (Barberini mosaic, Palestrina). This sort of scene goes back to the landscapes of the Alexandrian painter Demetrius, of the second century BC.
48. Pliny the elder, *Natural History*, XXIX, 96, VIII, 196.
49. Lucan, *Civil War*, 109 ff. (trans. Jack Lindsay). Meroe was the capital of Ethiopia (Napata).
50. Plutarch, *Antony*, 28, 2 f. (trans. Ian Scott-Kilvert).
51. Athenaeus, VI, 229 BC.
52. Plutarch, *Comparison between Demetrius and Antony*, 3, Dio, L, 27, 2.
53. Plutarch, *Antony*, 28, 2.
54. *OGIS*, 195 (28/12/34); Greco-Roman Museum, Alexandria.

55. Athenaeus, VI, 234D–235F. Antony also fancied the antics of a pet dwarf Sisyphus, who was less than two feet high, Scholiast on Horace, *Satires* I, 3, 44 ff. Octavian had a similar dwarf Lucius, of good family and stentorian voice, weighing 17 pounds.

56. Velleius, II, 83, 2. It was also Plancus who allegedly prevented Cleopatra from swallowing a *second* earring in vinegar, n. 45 above.

57. Philo, *On the Contemplative Life*, 5, Juvenal, *Satires*, xv, 45 ff.

58. Horace, *Odes*, I, 37, 14; cf. N.E. Collinge, *The Structure of Horace's Odes* (1961), p. 84 and n. 1.

59. Strabo, XVII, 797, Juvenal, *Satires*, XV, 44 ff.

60. Propertius, III, 11, 56; also suggested by Plutarch, *Antony*, 29, 1.

61. Plutarch, *Roman Questions*, 112, *Moralia*, 291A, elaborated by Philo; cf. Tarn, *CAH*, X, pp. 38 ff.

62. Propertius, III, 11, 30, Dio, LI, 15, 4.

63. Seneca the younger, *Moral Letters*, 87, 16.

64. Plutarch, *Antony*, 27, 1; cf. Bevan, p. 360: 'She was not above quickening her talk with lubricity, when it was a case of ensnaring the coarse, masterful Roman.' See p. 116.

65. Livy, *Epitome*, CXXX, Seneca the younger, *Moral Letters*, 83, 25, etc.

66. Cf. Polybius, XXVIII, 21, 5.

67. Plutarch, *Antony*, 29, 2–4 (trans. Ian Scott-Kilvert).

68. Velleius, II, 83, 1.

69. There is no need to suppose that this is a rhetorical reference to the first Pothinus (d. 48 BC, Chapter 3), as B. Perrin, Plutarch, *Lives*, IX (Loeb ed.), p. 617 s.v.

70. Plutarch, *Antony*, 83, 3.

71. *Ibid.*, 72, 2.

72. Seneca the younger, *Moral Letters*, 91, 13.

73. Gymnasiarch: Dio, L, 5, 1 (he had also acted as Athenian gymnasiarch).

74. Appian, V, 11, 'out of deference for Cleopatra'. He is speaking of Antony's earlier visit to Egypt in 41 BC.

75. Flavius Philostratus (born *c.* AD 170), *Lives of the Sophists*, I, 4, 486.

76. F.S. Taylor, *JHS*, L, 1930, p. 116.

77. Plutarch, *Antony*, 82, 2.

78. A.S. Hunt and C.C. Edgar, *Select Papyri*, 104; uncertain date in first century BC.

79. Galen, XIX, 63. There were two physicians called Dioscurides. It is uncertain if either of them was Caesar's envoy (if he survived).

80. Scholiast on Horace, *Satires*, I, 91; Cicero, *Letters to Friends*, VII, 23, XIII, 2, Pliny the elder, *Natural History*, XXXVI, 5, 32.

PART FOUR: CLEOPATRA AGAINST ROME

CHAPTER 11   CLEOPATRA DECLARED ROME'S ENEMY

1. Suetonius, *Augustus*, 69, 2. Uncertain date: between spring or summer 33 and May or June 32. Here the earlier date is preferred.

2. Cf. K. Kraft, *Hermes*, XLV, 1967, pp. 496 ff., Carter, p. 177, against Volkmann, Jones, Tarn.

3. Justinian, *Institutes*, I, 10: marriage with a *peregrina* (i.e., not possessing *conubium*), fails to be *iustum matrimonium*.

4. Cf. Euripides, *Andromache*, 177 f.

5. Ptolemy VIII Euergetes II (Physcon), who married Cleopatra III (142 BC) without apparently being able to divorce Cleopatra II, is exceptional and irregular.

6. Eutropius, VII, 6, 2, Orosius, VI, 19, 4.

7. Plutarch, *Comparison between Demetrius and Antony*, 4.

8. Cf. Terence, *Woman of Andros*, 146.

9. Appian, *Illyrian Wars*, 16.

10. Dio, L. 1, 2–5, Carter, p. 184.

11. Plutarch, *Antony*, 33, 2 f.; cf. H.J. Rose, *Annals of Archaeology and Anthropology*, XI, 1924, pp. 25 ff., K. Scott, *Classical Philology*, 1929, p. 135.

12. Suetonius, *Augustus*, 86, 2.

13. Pliny the elder, *Natural History*, XXXIII, 50.

14. Cf. Plutarch, *Comparison between Demetrius and Antony*, 3, Propertius, III, 11, 17 ff. The same comparison was applied to Pericles and Aspasia, and to Alexander and Roxana.

15. A. Oxé, *Bonner Jahrbücher*, CXXXVIII, 1933, pp. 81 ff., Volkmann p. 139 and Plate VII. Cf. also M. della Corte, *Antonio e Ottaviano nelle allegorie storico-umoristiche delle argenterie del tesoro di Boscoreale*, 1951.

16. Dio, L, 5, Horace, *Epodes*, IX, 11 ff. But Cleopatra's bodyguard seems to have been Galatian, Josephus, *BJ*, I, 397, *AJ*, XV, 217.

17. Dio, L, 1, 4 f.

18. Dio, L, 5, 4, Horace, *Odes*, I, 37, 6.

19. *CIL*, I², pp. 214, 244.

20. Tarn and Charlesworth, *CAH*, X, p. 98.

21. Dio, L, 1, 5.

22. Plutarch, *Quomodo Adulator*, *Moralia*, I, p. 50E; cf. Charlesworth, *Classical Quarterly*, 1933, pp. 177 ff.

23. Aquilius Niger and Julius Saturninus were among these anti-Augustan writers.

24. Cf. K. Scott, *Memoirs of the American Academy at Rome*, XI, 1933, pp. 13 ff.

25. For the name Coson (Cotiso in Horace and Florus), see A. Alföldi, *CAH*, XI, p. 83, n. 4, Daicoviciu, *Acta Musei Napocensis* (Cluj), II, 1965 (1966), pp. 107 ff. For his coins, M. von Bahrfeldt, *Über die Goldmünzen des Daker-königs Koson*. The rival, pro-Antonian, prince was Dicomes in Moldavia (M. Chitescu, *Studii si Cercetari de Istorie Veche*, XIX, 4, 1968, pp. 655 ff. Coins: *Dacia*, LXXXIII, 1969, p. 33). A third prince, who wanted peace, was Sermylo. Confusion is caused by the descriptions of these rulers as 'Getic'. The Augustan poets expressed awed respect for the power and wealth of Dacia.

26. K. Scott, *Classical Philology*, 1929, p. 140, Charlesworth, *Classical Quarterly*, 1933, p. 175.

27. Suetonius, *Augustus*, 16.

28. Plutarch, *Antony*, 55, 2.
29. Dio, XLIX, 41, 6, indicates that Antony repeated this offer.
30. *Res Gestae Divi Augusti*, 7.
31. Dio, L, 2, 3 f.
32. Cf. T.J. Cadoux, *JRS*, 1956, pp. 168 f. There was a precedent from 49 BC, when Pompey, forced to abandon Rome and then Italy to Caesar, had declared that the legitimate government was wherever the consuls and Senate were. But the consuls of 32 BC could be technically faulted because their departure had not been ratified by a law.
33. Cleopatra had apparently named a Cilician town, Titiopolis, after him, cf. R. Syme in A.H.M. Jones, *Cities of the Eastern Roman Provinces*, 2nd ed. (1970), p. 438, n. 30, cf. p. 209.
34. Velleius, II, 83, 3. For the story of Plancus' financial irregularities, *ibid.*, 83, 2.
35. J.A. Crook, *JRS*, 1957, p. 36.
36. Plutarch, *Antony*, 58, 4.
37. Syme, *The Roman Revolution*, p. 45, against Charlesworth, *Proceedings of the Cambridge Philological Society*, CLI-CLIII, 1932 (1933), p. 7. But Dio, L, 20, 7, suggests that Antony admitted he had deposited a will.
38. Carter, p. 188 and n.: she provided 20,000 talents; a legion cost 40 to 50 talents a year to maintain.
39. There are Greek or Hellenized officers with C. Julius Papeius when he visits the shrine of Isis at Philae in 32 BC *OGIS*, 196, *IGRR*, I, 1300.
40. E.g. the coinage was recalled on its bicentenary, M. Grant, *Roman Imperial Money*, pp. 200, 290, n. 207; cf. Bristol hoard of Severan times, H. Mattingly and J.W.E. Pearce, *NC*, 1938, pp. 86, 98.
41. *S*, p. 195, nos. 1212 f., *BMCR*, II, p. 526, nos. 183 ff.
42. *OGIS*, 193 from Didyma: Auletes covered the great door of the temple with ivory.
43. *FITA*, pp. 369, 373. Alabanda also used a Ptolemaic dating sign, H. Seyrig, *Numismatic Notes and Monographs*, CXIX, 1950, p. 34, n. 48.
44. Strabo, XIV, 649 (Menodorus).
45. *Ibid.*, 637; cf. XIII, 595, *Res Gestae, Divi Augusti*, 24. Messalla wrote a pamphlet *On Antony's Statues*.
46. Plutarch, *Antony*, 58 (trans. Ian Scott-Kilvert).
47. Plutarch, *Antony*, 56, 2-3 (trans. Ian Scott-Kilvert).
48. Dio, L, 5, 3; e.g. her friend Marcus Junius Silanus, *S*, 194, no. 1208, *BMCR*, II, p. 522, no. 175 (*quaestor proconsule*), may be a garrison commander in Greece; cf. *SIG*³ 767.
49. Josephus, *AJ*, XV, 110. There is no reason to suppose that he came as far as Ephesus, as Tarn, *CAH*, X, p. 95.
50. At least two payments had been made, Josephus, *AJ*, XV, 107.
51. *HG*, pp. 86 ff.
52. Plutarch, *Antony*, 56, 5.
53. Athenaeus, V, 198B; cf. M. Rostovtzeff, *SEHHW*, II, p. 1085, III, p. 1586.

54. Sources in D. Magie, *Roman Rule in Asia Minor* (1950, reprinted 1966), II, p. 1633, s.v. Priene was a 'free' city.
55. Plutarch, *Antony*, 58, 2.
56. Horace, *Odes*, I, 37, 16.
57. Dio, L, 7, 9.
58. Servius on Virgil, *Aeneid*, VII, 684 f.
59. H. Mattingly, *NC*, 1946, pp. 91 ff.
60. Cf. C.H.V. Sutherland, *NC*, 1952, p. 145, *JRS*, 1953, pp. 200 f.; cf. M. Grant, *The Six Main Aes Coinages of Augustus* (1953), p. 84.
61. But the mint had surely ceased to operate by 31 BC; M. Grant, *The Six Main Aes Coinages of Augustus*, p. 154, n. 3, against Mattingly, *NC*, 1946, p. 95.
62. Arsinoe II had induced Ptolemy II Philadelphus to intervene to the advantage of Athens. For a statue of Ptolemy VI Philometor see M. Thompson, *American Numismatic Society Museum Notes*, X, 1964, pp. 119 ff. Ptolemy IX Soter (Lathyrus) was a benefactor. The Athenian magistrate Aphrodisius placed the Ptolemaic cornucopiae on his coins.
63. Plutarch, *Antony*, 58, 2.
64. *Ibid.*, 59, 1–3 (trans. Ian Scott-Kilvert).
65. *Res Gestae Divi Augusti*, 25. Octavian virtuously excused Bononia (Bologna), because it owed clientship to Antony.
66. Dio, L, 6, 6; cf. A. von Premerstein, *Vom Werden und Wesen des Prinzipats* (1937), p. 45, P. Herrmann, *Der Römische Kaisereid* (Hypomnemata, XX, 1969). A reconstruction of Antony's oath can be based on suggested reconstructions of Octavian's (Volkmann, p. 173).
67. Dio, L, 7, 1.
68. Dio, L, 26, 4.
69. Dio, L, 5, 6.
70. Propertius, III, 11, 29 ff., 38 ff., 47 ff. (trans. S.G. Tremenheere).

CHAPTER 12   CLEOPATRA'S ESCAPE FROM ACTIUM

1. *S*, p. 199, no. 1274, *BMCR*, II, p. 524, no. 178, *FITA*, p. 41, 32 BC. Presumably Sosius had now returned to Zacynthus in person.
2. *BMC, Peloponnese*, no. 15, *FITA*, p. 374.
3. Plutarch, *Antony*, 59, 4.
4. *Ibid.*, 68, 4 f.
5. *BMCR*, II, p. 50, n. 1 (*c.* 32). *FITA*, p. 382 is probably wrong to date Atratinus' issue earlier.
6. *FITA*, *op. cit.*
7. Syme, *The Roman Revolution*, p. 282.
8. Velleius, II, 84, 1.
9. Plutarch, *Antony*, 62, 3.
10. Dio L, 11, 1, and 12, 1; cf. *S*, p. 195, no. 1211, *BMCR*, II, p. 531, no. 227 (Dec. Turullius, 31 BC–IMP. IIII.) But it is possible that this refers to a victory in Cyrenaican waters, see below, n. 21.

11. Velleius, II, 84. He also reports that Corinth was taken, but this must have been only temporary, cf. Plutarch, *Antony*, 67, 7, and n. 36 below.
12. Plutarch, *Antony*, 62. There were many ex-Antonians in Octavian's fleet, Dio, L, 11, 2 ff.
13. Deiotarus Philadelphus of Paphlagonia, Dio, L, 13, 5.
14. Servilia Nais, Suetonius, *Nero*, 3. For Ahenobarbus' grievance against Cleopatra, Dio, L. 13, 6.
15. E.g. M. Junius Silanus (Chapter II, n. 48), and King Rhoemetacles of Thrace.
16. Q. Postumius and Prince Iamblichus of Emesa (Homs).
17. Dio, L, 14, 2. King Tarcondimotus I Philantonius of the Amanus (Nur, E. Cilicia) was killed.
18. Horace, *Epodes*, IX, 17–20 (reading '*at huc*'); cf. A.E. Housman, *Journal of Philosophy*, 1882, p. 193, E. Wistrand, *Göteborgs Universitets Årsskrift*, LXIV, 1958, pp. 21 ff., 24 ff., 34. For Horace's wish to give the impression that these lines were written before Actium, cf. L.P. Wilkinson, *CR*, 1933, p. 4. I.e. the latter clause does *not* refer to Actium itself, as Tarn, *CAH*, X, p. 105 and n. 1. 'The left' means ill-omen for them: Wurzel, *Hermes*, LXXIII, 1938, pp. 361 ff.
19. For Marcus Licinius Crassus' desertion at some stage or other; cf. Syme, *The Roman Revolution*, p. 296, n. 2.
20. A.E. Chapman, *NC*, 1968, p. 31, G. Perl, *Klio*, 1970, p. 348: but Cydas was not necessarily a Cretarch of the same name who had coined earlier at Gortyna. The coins of Crassus are found overstruck by designs bearing his name, *FITA*, p. 55 and n. 15.
21. *S*, p. 200, nos. 1279 ff., *BMCR*, II, p. 583, nos. 1 ff. Or was this victory (IMP .1111) a local one (cf. above, note 10)?
22. Plutarch, *Antony*, 63, 4 (trans. Ian Scott-Kilvert).
23. Carter, pp. 213 ff., T.J. Cadoux, *JRS*, XLVI, 1956, p. 169; cf. G.W. Richardson (*JRS*, 1937, pp. 153 ff.), Kromayer, Leroux, Syme, against Tarn, *JRS*, 1931, pp. 173 ff., 1938, pp. 165 ff., who believed that Antony intended a decisive action and was let down by misunderstanding or treachery among his men. For the difficulty of bringing Octavian to a land-battle, cf. Leroux, p. 30.
24. Plutarch, *Antony*, 64, 2.
25. For the chronology see Carter, p. 214.
26. Volkmann, p. 185 (cf. Dio), against Carter, p. 215. For the numbers, cf. Leroux, pp. 37–43.
27. This is the explanation of the figure in Plutarch, *Antony*, 64, 1, Carter, p. 216, against Tarn, *CAH*, X, pp. 215 f. The legionaries did not serve as crews: Cadoux, *JRS*, 1956, p. 169.
28. Dio, L, 31, 1.
29. Propertius, IV, 6, 25.
30. Octavian's centre was commanded by L. Arruntius, and Antony's by M. Insteius and M. Octavius. Under Octavian, on his right wing, was M. Lurius.
31. Virgil, *Aeneid*, VIII, 710.

32. Plutarch, *Antony*, 65, 5. Perhaps Agrippa, in spite of the north-west breeze, pretended to be fleeing; cf. Servius on Virgil, *Aeneid*, VIII, 682.
33. Orosius, VI, 19, 11 makes the battle continue until the next morning.
34. Octavian's reference to the capture of 300 ships (Plutarch, *Antony*, 68, 1) probably refers to the whole campaign (he claimed to have captured 600 during his career, *Res Gestae, Divi Augusti*, 3).
35. Carter, p. 224.
36. Dio, LI, 5, 3.
37. It is uncertain when or where Antony received this news, T. J. Cadoux, *JRS*, 1956, p. 169.
38. Plutarch, *Antony*, 68, 3, Velleius, II, 85, 5 f.
39. Velleius, II, 85, 3, Dio, L, 33, 2; cf. Plutarch, *Antony*, 66, 3 (apparently using an eye-witness source hostile to Cleopatra and/or to the plan for a sea-battle).
40. Propertius, II, 16, 38 f. (trans. S. G. Tremenheere).
41. Plutarch, *Antony*, 66, 4 (trans. Ian Scott-Kilvert). Antony was 'a deserter', Velleius, *op. cit.* Feeble pro-Antonian propaganda maintained he only had to transfer ship because sucking-fish had immobilized his own, Pliny the elder, *Natural History*, XXXII, 1, 1; cf. Leroux, pp. 45 f.
42. Horace, *Odes*, I, 37, 1 ff. (trans. James Michie). Caecuban was a famous wine from southern Latium. 'All her fleet burnt' was an inaccurate observation by Horace. It would not even have been true of Antony's fleet. For Horace about Actium see also Leroux, pp. 37–43, 57–61, and B. Hanslik, *Horace and Actium* (Serta Philologica Aenipontana, 1962, pp. 355 ff.). See also above, p. 178 and n. 58.
43. Virgil, *Aeneid*, VIII, 671 ff. (trans. Patric Dickinson). Leucate (Ducato) is the south-west cape of the island of Leucas. Star of his Father: i.e. of the deified Julius Caesar (I have amended the translation from 'Fathers'). Bectria: N. Afghanistan, S. Uzbekistan and Tadjikstan. Sabaeans: south-west Arabia.

CHAPTER 13 CLEOPATRA'S DEATH

1. Horace, *Odes*, I, 37, 17.
2. *BMC, Empire*, I, p. 111, nos. 686 ff. (rightly eliminating *S*, p. 201, no. 1285; cf. *BMCR*, II, p. 584).
3. A. Weigall, *The Life and Times of Cleopatra of Egypt* (revised ed., 1923), pp. 368 f. But it was not just 'a few mud huts and a little fort', and even if Antony only had two friends with him (Aristocrates and Lucilius), he was not in complete solitude (as Plutarch, *Antony*, 69, 1) – for one thing he surely retained some troops.
4. Dio, LI, 5, 3 ff. (trans. E. Cary). T. R. S. Broughton, *American Journal of Philology*, LXIII, 1942, pp. 328 ff., is probably right in accepting this story of Cleopatra's fund-raising, against Tarn, *CAH*, X, p. 36.
5. Plutarch, *Antony*, 71, 3 – the title of a Greek comedy.
6. Dio, LI, 6, 1 f.
7. Pseudo-Acro on Horace, *Odes*, I, 37, 23; cf. Tarn, *CAH*, X, p. 36 and n. 3,

rejected by Broughton, *American Journal of Philology*, LXIII, 1942, p. 328.

8. Plutarch, *Antony*, 81, 1, Orosius, VI, 19, 13.
9. Dio, LI, 10, 4, places this plan to emigrate to Spain later, at the time of the last sea-battle. But all Cleopatra's post-Actian plans are dismissed as mere malicious gossip by F. Wurzel, *Der Krieg gegen Antonius and Kleopatra in der Darstellung der augusteischen Dichter*, Diss. Borna-Leipzig, 1941, p. 20.
10. A. Weigall, *op. cit.* (see above, n. 3), pp. 273 f.
11. Dio, LI, 7, 1, refers to locally-built ships.
12. Josephus, *BJ*, I, 440.
13. Official coinages: – *FITA*, pp. 64 f. (inscriptions of Antony and Cleopatra; no designs). But Cleopatra's title *Thea Neotera* (cf. at Chalcis beneath Lebanon, H. Seyrig, *Syria*, XXVII, 1950, pp. 44 f.) suggests a territory with Seleucid connections (see also the silver tetradrachm, Chapter 10, n. 18), not Patrae. Local coinages: e.g. Ptolemais Ace, A. Kindler, *Alan Hahevra Hanumismatit Le' Israel*, IV, 2, 1969, pp. 21 ff.
14. Q. Oppius: *FITA*, pp. 63 f., against Alföldi, *Mélanges Carcopino*, 1966, p. 34 (Cyrene 41–40 BC).
15. Josephus, *AJ*, XV, 195.
16. *Ibid.*, 197; cf. Plutarch, *Antony*, 72, 2.
17. Josephus, *Against Apion*, II, 60, rejected by H. St J. Thackeray, Loeb ed., p. 316, n. 2, E. M. Smallwood (ed.), *Philo: Embassy to Gaius*, p. 11.
18. Dio, LI, 6, 4 and 8, 1 and 8, 2 f: telescoped by Plutarch, *Antony*, I, 72; cf. Rice-Holmes, *The Architect of the Roman Empire*, 1, p. 166. Carter, p. 231, disbelieves in Antony's message.
19. Tarn, *JRS*, 1931, p. 196 on Dio, LI, 9, 5, Plutarch, *Antony*, 74, 1, etc.
20. Plutarch, *Antony*, 74, 2.
21. Plutarch, *Antony*, 73, 2. Dio, *op. cit.*, confuses chronology by stating that Cleopatra betrayed Pelusium because she believed Octavian's message that he loved her.
22. Plutarch, *Antony*, 74, 3 (trans. Ian Scott-Kilvert).
23. Tarn, *CAH*, X, p. 108, n. 1.
24. Plutarch, *Antony*, 75, 3 f. (trans. Ian Scott-Kilvert). H. J. Rose, *Annals of Archaeology and Anthropology*, XI, p. 25, saw the story as Octavianic propaganda, to kill the godhead of Antony.
25. C. P. Cavafy (trans. J. Mavrogordato, *Poems by C.P. Cavafy*, paperback ed., 1971, p. 41, no. 26). The same passage in Plutarch had inspired Shakespeare's 'music under the earth' scene, in *Antony and Cleopatra*, Act IV, Scene 3.
26. The date corresponds with 3 August of the Julian calendar, which did not, however, reach its final form for another thirty-eight years. For the chronology of these days see T. C. Skeat, *JRS*, 1953, pp. 98 ff.
27. Dio, LI, 14, 3, adds the eunuch. Plutarch, *Antony*, 76, 2, believes she shut herself in to escape injury from Antony; cf. Volkmann, p. 198.
28. Plutarch, *Antony*, 77, 4.
29. *Ibid.*, 79, 3, Horace, *Odes*, I, 37, 23.
30. Dio, LI, 11, 4 implies that Epaphroditus had been sent with Proculeius.

31. Livy in Pseudo-Acro on Horace, *Odes*, I, 37, 30; cf. Suetonius, *Augustus*, 17, 4, Plutarch, *Antony*, 78, 3 for his intention.
32. Shakespeare, *Antony and Cleopatra*, Act V, Scene 2.
33. Tarn, *CAH*. X, p. 109, Carter, p. 233; cf. Stähelin, Groag, against Rice-Holmes, Jones. Detailed analysis by W.R. Johnson, *Arion*, 1967, pp. 393 f. *Id.*, p. 401, n. 19: Roman devotees of Isis would have been shocked at her execution. For the theory that Octavian had her killed, *ibid.*, p. 393, n. 16. Her statue was still standing in the third century AD, cf. Chapter 15, note 5; but possibly Octavian temporarily removed it.
34. Cf. Johnson, *op. cit.*, p. 394, on Plutarch, *Antony*, 83, etc. For the fictional character of accounts of the interview, cf. Tarn, *CAH*, X, p. 110, and Carter, p. 233.
35. E.g. Dio, LI, 15, 4; 'she captured the two greatest Romans of the day, and because of the third she destroyed herself'; Tarn, *op. cit.*, p. 109: 'two civilizations, soon to be fused, stood face to face in their persons'.
36. Plutarch, *Antony*, 84, 1. This may be the Dolabella who became consul in AD 10 – or his father. Cleopatra had rendered a service to their kinsman of the same name who was consul in 44 BC.
37. Shakespeare, *Antony and Cleopatra*, Act V, Scene 2.
38. Dio, LI, 13, 4.
39. Plutarch, *Antony*, 85, 4.
40. Strabo, XVII, 296. Livy, *Epitome*, CXXXIII, merely says she died *voluntaria morte*.
41. Galen, XIV, 237 Kühn.
42. Dio, LI, 14, 1.
43. Plutarch, *Antony*, 86, 1–3 (trans. Ian Scott-Kilvert). Shakespeare makes the 'asp' bite her breast, not her arm.
44. E. Herrmann, *Philologische Wochenschrift*, 5/9/31, pp. 1100 ff.; cf. W.R. Johnson, *Arion*, 1967, pp. 394, 401, n. 19.
45. J.G. Griffiths, *JEA*, XLVII, 1961, p. 114, n. 2; cf. wall-paintings at Pompeii, Witt, pl. 24, 27.
46. Propertius, III, 11, 53. Cf. below, n. 50.
47. The head, accompanied by a snake, on a silver plate from Boscoreale in the Louvre, interpreted as Cleopatra by M. della Corte, *Cleopatra, Marco Antonio e Ottaviano* (1951), pp. 35 ff., cf. J.G. Griffiths, *op. cit.*, is better interpreted as Africa or Alexandria or Isis-Artemis or all of them combined; cf. *SEHRE*, pl. XL, no. 1, Witt, p. 150.
48. V. Seton-Williams, *Archaeology*, XIX, 1966, pp. 208 ff. (Buto, the modern Tel-el-Farain). The snake is the *Naja haje* or *Naja nigricolus*, not the horned viper as Spiegelberg, *Sitzungsberichte München*, 1925, pp. 3 ff.
49. J.G. Griffiths, *op. cit.*, pp. 116 ff.
50. Propertius, III, 11, 51–54 (trans. S.G. Tremenheere: wrongly printed as 'adder's').
51. Virgil, *Aeneid*, VIII, 697; cf. II, 203 f. (Laocoon), XII, 845 ff. (Turnus); cf. Griffiths, *op. cit.*, B. Baldwin, *ibid.*, 1964, pp. 181 ff.
52. Josephus, *Against Apion*, II, 86.
53. Griffiths, *op. cit.*, pp. 115 ff., against Spiegelberg, *op. cit.*, Tarn, *CAH*, X,

p. 110. M.A. Levi, *La Parola del Passato*, 1954, pp. 293 ff., detects an additional intention to prevent Octavian from succeeding to the Egyptian throne.

54. Galen, *De Theriacis ad Pisonem*, 7.
55. Anon., *Carmen de Bello Actiaco* (Bibliography, n. 3); cf. Tarn, *loc. cit.*, n. 3.
56. Suetonius, *Augustus*, 17, 4. For Octavian's 'generosity' cf. Johnson, *op. cit.*, pp. 394 ff.
57. Virgil, *Aeneid*, VIII, 711–13 (trans. Patric Dickinson).
58. Horace, *Odes*, I, 21 ff. (trans. James Michie). The Liburnians were a form of light warship adopted by Octavian from the Illyrian people of that name, and used at Actium. For the details of Horace's sympathetic hints see A.T. Davis, *Greece and Rome*, 1969, p. 93.

CHAPTER 14   CLEOPATRA'S CONQUEROR IN EGYPT

1. Plutarch, *Antony*, 80, 1, Dio, LI, 16, 4, adds that he was also motivated by respect for Sarapis. Octavian proposed to give Areius a leading post in Egypt, but he refused, Julian, *Letter to Themistius*, 343 f. Hertlein. The post was probably the financial office of *idios logos*, G.W. Bowersock, *Augustus and the Greek World*, p. 41; cf. p. 33.
2. Dio, LI, 17, 6. But Philostratus, the rich philosopher-friend of Cleopatra, appealed to Areius and was spared, Plutarch, *Antony*, 80, 3, Bowersock, *op. cit.*, p. 33.
3. Plutarch, *Antony*, 81, 2, Dio, LI, 15, 5.
4. Plutarch, *op. cit.*, Homer, *Iliad*, II, 204.
5. Suetonius, *Augustus*, 17, 5.
6. *Res Gestae Divi Augusti*, 6; cf. Syme, *The Roman Revolution*, pp. 229 f.
7. Seneca the younger, *On Clemency*, I, 10, 1.
8. Syme, *Tacitus*, pp. 313, 368, 379, 382, 404, K.M.T. Atkinson, *Historia*, 1958, p. 337.
9. But their alleged eighteen-day reign (Clement of Alexandria, *Stromateis*, XXI, 129, 1 f., Stähelin) is a pure fiction designed to adjust the chronology of Cleopatra's and Octavian's reigns, T.C. Skeat, *JRS*, 1953, p. 100.
10. Dio, LI, 15, 6; cf. Bevan, p. 384. It is possible that Juba II was first given Numidia (Africa Nova), and then transferred to Mauretania in 25. Cleopatra Selene's head appears on Juba II's coinage; B.V Head, *Historia Numorum*, 2nd ed., 1911, p. 888, fig. 339; cf. J. Baradez, *Bulletin d'archaeologie marocaine*, IV, 1960, pp. 117 ff.
11. *Res Gestae Divi Augusti*, 27.
12. *Praefectus fabrum*: G. Guadagno, *Opuscula Romana*, VI, 1968, pp. 21 ff.
13. J.G. Milne, *JRS*, 1927, pp. 1 ff., emphasizes Egypt's deterioration under the Romans. But for Octavian's efforts to win favour see L. Kákosy, *Antik Tanulmányok*, XIV, 1967, pp. 307 ff.
14. U. Wilcken, *ibid.*, 1937, p. 142.
15. P. Oxy., 1453, trans. J. Lindsay, *Cleopatra* (1971), pp. 485 f.
16. N.G.L Hammond, *Epirus* (1967), p. 62; cf. Carter, pp. 235 f. For the

trophy and its inscription, see J.H. Oliver, *American Journal of Philology*, 1969, p. 180.

17. Cf. J. Marlowe, *The Golden Age of Alexandria* (1971), p. 208.

CHAPTER 15 CLEOPATRA'S POSITION IN HISTORY

1. Plutarch, *Antony*, 86, 5.
2. *BGU*, 1182; cf. Tarn, *CAH*, X, p. 38 and n. 1.
3. Sources in Stähelin, *RE*, XI (1921), column 780.
4. Sources in Tarn, *op. cit.*, p. 38 and n. 2.
5. Statue: Dio, LI, 22–3. Cult: A.D. Nock, *JHS*, 1928, p. 36.
6. *Scriptores Historiae Augustae, Triginta Tyranni*, 27, 1.
7. Ammianus Marcellinus, XXVIII, 4, 6.
8. Tarn, *op. cit.*, p. 38.
9. O. Spengler, *Der Untergang des Abendlandes* (1918), p. 230, took the reverse view.
10. Tacitus; *Annals*, I, 2; cf. Timagenes (friend of the Antonian Alexas), Seneca the younger, *Moral Letters*, XCI, 13.
11. Cf. M. Grant, *Proceedings of the Virgil Society*, III, 1963–64, pp. 1 ff.
12. Virgil, *Aeneid*, VI, 847 ff. (trans. Patric Dickinson).
13. Tarn, *CAH*, X, p. 83, maintained (rather unwillingly) that unification *had to be* achieved from the west, by a Roman through Romans: in *JRS*, 1932, pp. 141 ff., he had taken a less western attitude.
14. Tarn, *CAH*, VII, p. 700. His conclusion followed Burckhardt against Beloch; cf. A. Momigliano, *JHS*, 1943, p. 116.
15. F.E. Adcock, *CAH*, IX, p. 740, says of Antony: 'A spark of Caesar glowed smokily in him and was extinguished.'
16. Josephus, *AJ*, XV, 91. Syme and Carter somewhat minimize Cleopatra's role.
17. Tacitus, *Annals*, I, 2.
18. The position of Antony's personal heir Antyllus was a special problem.

BIBLIOGRAPHY

1. Cf. M. Grant, *Julius Caesar* (1969), pp. 94 f., on Caesar's brand of veracity. The author of the *Alexandrian War* may perhaps have been his officer Aulus Hirtius; cf. M. Gelzer, *Caesar*, p. 251, n. 1.
2. *HG*, pp. 236 f.
3. The *Bellum Actiacum* (or *Aegyptiacum* or *Alexandrinum*) from Herculaneum, J. Garuti (ed.), *Studi dell' Istituto di Filologia Classica dell' Università di Bologna*, V, 1958.
4. J. André, *La vie et l'œuvre d'Asinius Pollion* (1949); cf. A.H. McDonald, *Fifty Years (and Twelve) of Classical Scholarship* (1968), p. 476.
5. They may include additional data of a chronological, antiquarian and anecdotal nature. Cf. C.M. Begbie, *Classical Quarterly*, 1967, pp. 332 ff.
6. Livy, *Epitome*, CXXX.

7. Velleius, II, 87, 1: nothing else about her post-Actian activities. For his sources see Dihle, *RE*, VIII.A.1 (1955), columns 637 ff.
8. *HG*, pp. 235 ff.
9. For these cf. M. Grant, *The Ancient Historians* (1970), pp. 293 f., 453, n. 44.
10. *Ibid.*, pp. 312 f.
11. Plutarch, *Demetrius*, 1.
12. *The Ancient Historians, op. cit.*, pp. 317 f., 431, n. 46. But Plutarch's sources vary in their attitudes to Octavian, cf. C.P. Jones, *Plutarch and Rome* (1971), p. 102.
13. Cf. A.J. Gossage, *Latin Biography* (ed. T.A. Dorey), p. 71.
14. Cf. M. Finlay, *Listener*, 17 September 1970, p. 375. And in Chaucer's *Legend of Good Women* Cleopatra had been the faithful wife who followed her husband even in death.
15. Volkmann, p. 228.
16. Shakespeare, *Antony and Cleopatra*, Act I, Scenes 1 and 2. Cf. now J. Ingledew, *Shakespeare: Antony and Cleopatra*, pp. xxxv ff. (pointing out the differences between Plutarch's and Shakespeare's Antony), R. Lee, *Shakespeare: Antony and Cleopatra* (1971), pp. 56 f. Shakespeare's greatest departure from Plutarch is in the character of Enobarbus (Ahenobarbus), *ibid.*, pp. 16 f., 39 ff., cf. T.J.B. Spencer (ed.) *Shakespeare's Plutarch* (Penguin ed., 1968), pp. 15 f. See also Ingledew, *op. cit.*, pp. xlviii ff.
17. Another Hadrianic writer, Florus, who deals briefly with Cleopatra (II, 14–21), follows an abridgment of Livy and subscribes wholly to the hostile and melodramatic tradition, cf. Volkmann, p. 226.
18. F.G.B. Millar, *A Study of Cassius Dio* (1964); cf. G.B. Townend, *JRS*, 1965, pp. 306 f., A.H. McDonald, *CR*, 1966, pp. 318 ff.
19. K. Quinn, *Virgil's Aeneid* (1968), pp. 27–40. For the relation of Virgil's Dido to Cleopatra, as a symbol of eastern allurements, *ibid.*, p. 55, R.D. Williams, *CR*, 1954, pp. 34 f., and M. Grant, *Roman Myths* (1971), p. 86.
20. L.P. Wilkinson, *Horace and his Lyric Poetry* (1946), p. 69.
21. Emphasized (perhaps too much) by R. Pichon, *Les Sources de Lucain* (1912).
22. See numismatic works in List of Abbreviations above – including British Museum Catalogues of Greek as well as Roman coins – and research on Syrian coinage by H. Seyrig, notably in *Syria*, XXVII, 1950, pp. 5 ff., and by A.B. Brett, *AJA*, XLI, 1937, pp. 447 ff. Numerous other articles have been referred to in these notes.
23. P.M. Fraser, *Ptolemaic Alexandria* (1972). See also J. Marlowe, *The Golden Age of Alexandria* (1971), pp. 54 ff., E. Badian, *History Today*, 1960, pp. 779 ff., S. Handler, *AJA*, LXXI, 1967, p. 188.
24. Mostly collected in *BGU*, VIII. Cf. also n. 3 above.

Note on Money

T.J. Cadoux, in the prefatory note (p. 9) to his translation of H. Volkmann's *Cleopatra*, expresses the situation as follows:– 'The unit of wealth in the Hellenistic East was the talent, a sum of money equal to a weight of silver which varied somewhat from state to state; the Attic talent most commonly in use weighed about 57 lb. Large sums were paid in gold, the value of which was about twelve times that of silver. The talent was divided into 6,000 drachmas. The Roman *denarius* (4 = *sestertii*) was generally regarded as equivalent in value to the Greek drachma.' To this it should be added that both the *denarius* and the drachma were normally silver coins; but after a series of debasements, during previous reigns and her own, the coinage issued by Cleopatra for local use in Egypt included bronze pieces officially valued at 40 and 80 drachmas each.

Table of Dates

BC

323 Death of Alexander the Great: Ptolemy I Soter takes over Egypt (becomes king in 305)*

80 Ptolemy XII Neos Dionysos Aulete, father of Cleopatra VII (the Cleopatra of this book), becomes king of Egypt

End of 70 or beginning of 69.   Birth of Cleopatra VII

70/68 Death or disappearance of Cleopatra V Tryphaena (sister–wife of Ptolemy XII and probably Cleopatra's mother)

68/65, 61, 59 Births of Cleopatra's half-sister Arsinoe IV and half-brothers Ptolemy XIII and XIV

59 Ptolemy XII recognized as Friend and Ally of the Roman people by Caesar and Pompey

58 Cyprus annexed by Rome: its king Ptolemy, brother of Ptolemy XII, commits suicide

58 Ptolemy XII, ejected from Alexandria, flees to Rome: his daughters Cleopatra VI Tryphaena and Berenice IV appointed queens of Egypt

57 Archelaus and Berenice IV monarchs of Egypt

55 Aulus Gabinius, assisted by Mark Antony, restores Ptolemy XII to the throne

51 Possible brief joint reign of Ptolemy XII and Cleopatra VII

51 Death of Ptolemy XII, temporarily concealed

51 Joint reign of Cleopatra VII and her brother Ptolemy XIII: Cleopatra in effect sole ruler

51 Cleopatra attends installation of sacred bull Buchis at Hermonthis

50 Probable resumption of joint reign: Ptolemy XIII's Regency Council effectively in charge

49 Visit of Cnaeus Pompeius the younger to Alexandria

49 Cleopatra probably withdraws to Upper Egypt

* For Ptolemies I–XI see Genealogical Table No. I

48 Cleopatra driven out across eastern border of Egypt

48 Caesar arrives and is joined by Cleopatra. Caesar grants Cyprus to Ptolemy xiv and Arsinoe iv. Alexandrian War begins. Deaths of Pothinus and Achillas. Arsinoe iv and Ptolemy xiii leave palace and join fight against Caesar

47 Ptolemy xiii defeated and drowned. Caesar grants Egyptian throne to Cleopatra and Ptolemy xiv and gives them Cyprus.

47 Birth of Caesarion (Ptolemy Caesar)

46 Arsinoe iv carried in Caesar's Triumph at Rome

46 Cleopatra and Ptolemy xiv arrive in Rome

44 Murder of Ptolemy xiv. Joint reign of Cleopatra and Caesarion (Ptolemy xv Caesar) begins

43 Cleopatra supports Dolabella in Syria against Caesar's assassins (Brutus and Cassius), but he is defeated and killed

42 Cleopatra takes fleet to help Triumvirs (Antony, Octavian, Lepidus) against Brutus and Cassius, but turns back

42 After victory at Philippi, Antony takes over eastern provinces

41 Cleopatra meets Antony at Tarsus and spends the winter with him at Alexandria

40 Parthian invasion of Syria and Asia Minor

40 Antony's brother Lucius Antonius capitulates to Octavian at Perusia and his wife Fulvia flees to Greece and dies

40 Treaty of Brundusium between Antony and Octavian. Antony marries Octavian's sister Octavia

40 Birth of Cleopatra's twins by Antony, Alexander (Helios) and Cleopatra (Selene)

40 Cleopatra receives Herod at Alexandria

39 Treaty of Misenum (Puteoli) between the Triumvirs and Sextus Pompeius

39 Antony and Octavia take up residence at Athens

39–38 Parthians driven out of Roman territory

37 Treaty of Tarentum between Antony and Octavian. Triumvirate renewed for five years

37 Antony sends Octavia back to Italy and rejoins Cleopatra at Antioch

37 Antony grants Cleopatra large extensions of territory and revenue

36 Failure of Antony's expedition into Media Atropatene

36 Birth of Cleopatra's son by Antony, Ptolemy (Philadelphus)

36 Agrippa, Octavian's admiral, defeats Sextus Pompeius off Cape Naulochus

36 Lepidus deposed from the Triumvirate by Octavian

35–33 Octavian's campaign in Dalmatia, Illyricum and Pannonia

35 Sextus Pompeius killed in Asia Minor by Antony's general Marcus Titius

34 Antony invades and annexes Armenia and captures its king

34 Antony's victory procession at Alexandria

34 Antony's Donations of Alexandria granting titles, territories and overlordships to Cleopatra and her children

33–32 Propaganda war between supporters of Octavian and of Antony and Cleopatra

33–32 Antony and Cleopatra winter at Ephesus.

32 The consuls and more than two hundred senators leave Italy to join Antony

32 Antony divorces Octavia

32 Octavian seizes Antony's will and publishes its alleged contents

32 Octavian declares war against Cleopatra

32–31 Antony and Cleopatra winter at Patrae

31 Agrippa crosses the Ionian Sea and storms Methone. Octavian crosses to Epirus. Antony and Cleopatra move to Actium, and his fleet and army fail to break out. The battle of Actium. Antony and Cleopatra escape to Egypt

30 Octavian conquers and annexes Egypt. Suicide of Antony and Cleopatra. Execution of Caesarion and of Antony's eldest son Antyllus

Genealogical Tables

1. THE ANCESTORS OF CLEOPATRA

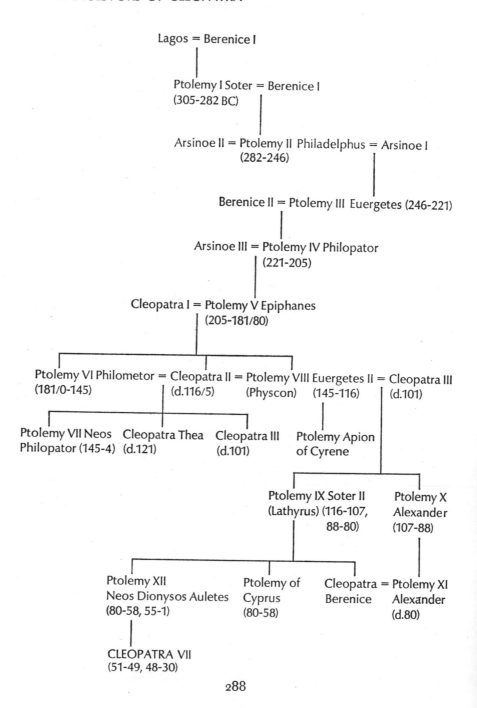

Lagos = Berenice I

Ptolemy I Soter = Berenice I
(305-282 BC)

Arsinoe II = Ptolemy II Philadelphus = Arsinoe I
(282-246)

Berenice II = Ptolemy III Euergetes (246-221)

Arsinoe III = Ptolemy IV Philopator
(221-205)

Cleopatra I = Ptolemy V Epiphanes
(205-181/80)

Ptolemy VI Philometor = Cleopatra II = Ptolemy VIII Euergetes II = Cleopatra III
(181/0-145)   (d.116/5)   (Physcon) (145-116)   (d.101)

Ptolemy VII Neos   Cleopatra Thea   Cleopatra III   Ptolemy Apion
Philopator (145-4)   (d.121)   (d.101)   of Cyrene

Ptolemy IX Soter II   Ptolemy X
(Lathyrus) (116-107,   Alexander
88-80)   (107-88)

Ptolemy XII   Ptolemy of   Cleopatra = Ptolemy XI
Neos Dionysos Auletes   Cyprus   Berenice   Alexander
(80-58, 55-1)   (80-58)   (d.80)

CLEOPATRA VII
(51-49, 48-30)

2. CLEOPATRA'S BROTHER'S AND SISTERS

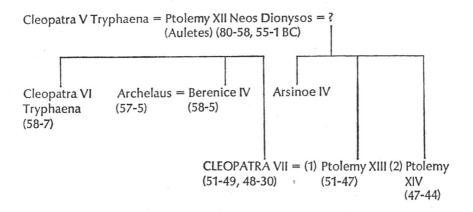

Cleopatra V Tryphaena = Ptolemy XII Neos Dionysos = ?
(Auletes) (80-58, 55-1 BC)

Cleopatra VI   Archelaus = Berenice IV   Arsinoe IV
Tryphaena   (57-5)   (58-5)
(58-7)

CLEOPATRA VII = (1) Ptolemy XIII (2) Ptolemy
(51-49, 48-30)   (51-47)   XIV
                                     (47-44)

3. THE DESCENDANTS OF ANTONY AND CLEOPATRA

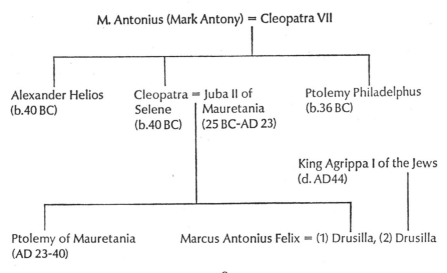

M. Antonius (Mark Antony) = Cleopatra VII

Alexander Helios   Cleopatra = Juba II of   Ptolemy Philadelphus
(b.40 BC)   Selene   Mauretania   (b.36 BC)
                      (b.40 BC) (25 BC-AD 23)

King Agrippa I of the Jews
(d. AD44)

Ptolemy of Mauretania   Marcus Antonius Felix = (1) Drusilla, (2) Drusilla
(AD 23-40)

289

4. THE FAMILY OF ANTONY BY HIS ROMAN WIVES

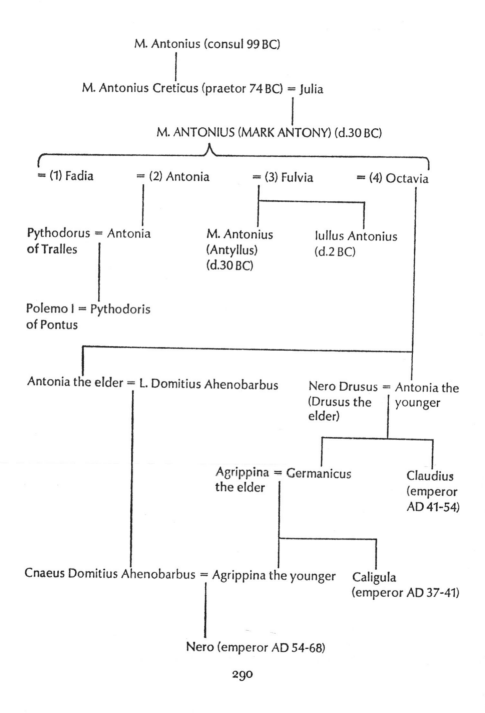

M. Antonius (consul 99 BC)

M. Antonius Creticus (praetor 74 BC) = Julia

M. ANTONIUS (MARK ANTONY) (d.30 BC)

= (1) Fadia   = (2) Antonia   = (3) Fulvia   = (4) Octavia

Pythodorus = Antonia
of Tralles

M. Antonius   Iullus Antonius
(Antyllus)   (d.2 BC)
(d.30 BC)

Polemo I = Pythodoris
of Pontus

Antonia the elder = L. Domitius Ahenobarbus   Nero Drusus = Antonia the
                                                   (Drusus the   younger
                                                   elder)

Agrippina = Germanicus   Claudius
the elder   (emperor
                              AD 41-54)

Cnaeus Domitius Ahenobarbus = Agrippina the younger   Caligula
                                                           (emperor AD 37-41)

Nero (emperor AD 54-68)

Index

Aahmes, see Amasis
Abu, see Elephantine
Abydos 267
Ace, see Ptolemais Ace
Achillas 57, 70ff., 85, 101
Acoreus, see Anchoreus
Actium xvii, 203, 205, 207, 209–13, 215f.,
 219, 221, 228, 232, 234f., 237, 239f.,
 242, 244, 274ff., 278f.
Adulis 262
Aemilius, see Lepidus, Paullus
Aeneas 87, 214, 235
Aeon, see Aion
Aesculapius, see Asclepius
Afghanistan 5
Africa (Roman province) (Tunisia) 36,
 78, 85, 90, 126, 190, 277
Africa Nova, see Numidia
Agrippa, Marcus Vipsanius xviii, 131f.,
 149, 155, 204f., 210f., 213f., 216, 234,
 236, 275
Ahenobarbus, Lucius Domitius 191f.,
 195, 206, 274, 280
Alabanda 194, 272
Alban Hills 16
Alexander Helios 126, 142, 144f., 157f.,
 162ff., 166, 218, 231, 268
Alexander the Great 5, 7, 12, 22, 24, 31,
 44, 63, 66, 69, 81, 89, 92, 110, 126, 142,
 144, 146, 148, 193, 197, 221, 229, 231,
 233, 254f., 266, 271
Alexander the Syrian 211
Alexandra 128, 141, 154, 159
Alexandria xvif., 7, 10f., 15f., 18–22, 24,
 29, 31ff., 38, 40–4, 46, 49, 52ff., 61–4,
 66–78, 84f., 87–90, 92f., 105, 111, 115,
 121f., 134, 139, 143, 153, 155f., 158,
 160–4, 169ff., 175ff., 179ff., 185ff.,
 190, 197–201, 217, 222, 224, 227, 232f.,

235, 237, 239f., 242, 244, 251, 255, 257,
 260, 269, 277, 279
Alexas 180f., 219, 279
Allienus 101
Amanus 274
Amasis (Aahmes) 8
Ambracia, Gulf of 203, 205, 210
Ammianus Marcellinus 233
Ammon, see Amon, Jupiter
Ammonius, Hammonius (agent of Au-
 letes) 16, 261
Ammonius, Hammonius (minister of
 Cleopatra) 96f.
Amon 45, 47, 99, 255, 261
Amphissa 177, 242
Amyntas 131, 133, 155, 164, 206
Amyot, Jacques 242
Anagnia 198
Anchises 235
Anchoreus (Achoreus) 58, 256
Anteon 262
Anthylla 255
Anticyra 204
Antigonids 7, 65
Antigonus (of Judaea) 127, 264
Anti-Lebanon, Mount 138
Antioch (capital of Syria) 131, 133f., 153,
 168f., 177, 180, 198, 267
Antiochia ad Hippum, see Hippos
Antiochus I 268
Antiochus II 254
Antiochus III the Great 64
Antiochus IV Epiphanes 9, 172
Antiochus VI 253
Antiochus XII 253
Antipater 75, 77, 79, 122
Antirrhodus 71
Antonia (daughter of Antony and An-
 tonia) 186, 231

Antonia (elder daughter of Antony and Octavia) 130, 191
Antonia (second wife of Antony) 186, 230, 263
Antonia (younger daughter of Antony and Octavia) 231
Antonia (palace) 158
Antonias (ship) 211
Antoninus Pius 240
Antonius, Iullus 230
Antonius, Lucius 124f.
Antonius, Marcus, senior (Mark Antony) xv–xviii, 3, 17, 83f., 87, 93, 97, 101–244, 262, 264–8, 270–7
Antonius Marcus, junior (Antyllus) 132, 170f., 177, 189, 200, 217, 220, 229f., 279
Anubis 43, 202
Apama 251
Apamea (in Syria) 131, 158, 168
Aphrodisius 273
Aphrodite (Venus) 14, 82, 85, 87f., 111, 115–18, 130, 162, 179, 186, 225, 233, 263
Apion 76, 233, 240
Apis 43, 46
Apollinopolis Magna (Edfu) 15, 256, 261
Apollo 143, 189, 215, 262
Apollodorus 63
Apollonia 97
Apollonius (Macedonian) 25
Apollonius (minister) 255
Appian 81f., 101, 240f., 243, 260, 262, 265
Aquilius (Aquillius) Niger 271
Arabia 34, 42, 74, 215; see also Himyarites, Nabataeans, Sabaeans
Aradus 121f., 131, 265
Aramaic 141, 256
Araxes, River 148, 190
Archandroupolis 255
Archelaus (King of Egypt) 17, 134
Archelaus Sisinnes (King of Cappadocia) 111, 133f., 164, 230
Archibius 233
Areius 229, 278
Ares (Mars) 111, 213, 215
Ariadne 23, 186
Ariarathes IV Epiphanes 252
Aristobulus 141, 154, 159, 267
Aristocrates 275
Aristonicus 55

Aristotle 260
Armenia, Greater 92, 146–9, 160f., 163f., 169, 190f., 194, 218, 266, 268
Armenia, Lesser 267
Arretium 188
Arruntius, Lucius 274
Arsinoe II Philadelphus 21, 24, 26, 48, 118, 233, 254ff., 273
Arsinoe III 66
Arsinoe IV (half-sister of Cleopatra) 3, 28, 68, 71f., 74, 79, 85f., 102, 111, 121, 225, 257, 265
Arsinoe (mother of Ptolemy I) 7, 253, 262
Artavasdes (king of Armenia) 146ff., 157, 218
Artavasdes (king of Media Atropatene) 146, 157, 164, 190, 218
Artaxata 157
Artemis (Diana) 16, 86, 102, 111, 121, 277
Ascalon 53, 74ff., 139, 258, 264
Asclepius (Aesculapius) 194, 220
Asia (Roman province) 110f., 114, 196f.
Asia Minor, see Asia (province), Armenia (Lesser), Bithynia, Cappadocia, Cilicia, Galatia, Pamphylia, Paphlagonia, Phrygia, Pisidia, Pontus; and names of towns
Asinius Gallus, Gaius, see Asinius
asp, see cobra
Aspasia 271
Athena 130; see also Minerva
Athenagoras 181
Athenion 196
Athenodorus 130
Athens 15f., 41, 125, 132f., 151, 181, 197–200, 203, 217, 222, 260, 270, 273
Atratinus, Lucius Sempronius 128, 204f., 273
Atticus, Titus Pomponius 95f., 153, 244
Augustus, see Octavian
Auletes, see Ptolemy XII
Aventicum 253
Avianius Evander, Gaius 181

Babylon 176, 256; see also Mesopotamia
Bacchae, Bacchanals, Bacchants, see Maenads
Bacchus, see Dionysus
Bactria 214, 275
Bakis, see Buchis

Balanea (Leucas on the Chrysorrhoas) 265

Balbus, Lucius Cornelius 93

Bambyce, see Hierapolis

Bashan 138

Bast, see Bubastis

Bellona 201, 215

Berenice I 22, 254

Berenice II 194, 256

Berenice IV (sister of Cleopatra) 3f., 15, 17

Berenice (town on Red Sea) 218

Berytus 31, 265

Bibulus, Lucius Calpernius 268

Bibulus, Marcus Calpurnius 48f., 53, 55, 268

Biggeh, see Senmet

Bithynia 110

Bitter Lakes 90

Black Sea 8, 179, 194

Boccaccio 242

Bogud I 87, 91, 203f.

Bononia 273

Boscoreale 277

Bosphorus, Cimmerian 8, 36, 268

brother–sister marriages 4, 26f., 254

Brucheion 69

Brundusium 126, 132, 198, 216

Brutus, Marcus Junius (Quintus Caepio) 93ff., 101ff., 105, 110 f., 121, 197, 258, 262

Bubastis 119

Buchis, Bucheum 46f., 245

Buto 277

Byzantium xviii, 82, 198, 236, 266

Caecuban wine 214, 275

Caelius Rufus, Marcus 47, 254

Caesar, Gaius Julius (dictator) xvff., 3, 12–16, 18f., 28f., 48, 51–4, 57, 61–103, 109ff., 120, 129, 142, 145f., 148, 163, 167, 170, 178f., 187ff., 193, 207, 214, 225, 231, 233ff., 239, 244, 259f., 263, 265, 270, 272, 275, 279

Caesar Octavianus, Gaius Julius, see Octavian

Caesareum 82, 103, 230, 259

Caesarion (Ptolemy XV) 83–8, 92, 95–100, 102f., 129, 141f., 162, 165ff., 170f., 179, 189, 193, 217, 229f., 243, 245, 259f., 266, 268

Caligula (Gaius) 231

Callimachus (governor-general of Thebaid) 34, 100

Callimachus (governor of Thebes) 100

Callimachus (poet) 8, 48

Callippus 89, 260

Calpurnia 87, 167, 259

Calpurnius Bibulus, see Bibulus

Calvisius Sabinus, Gaius 195

Canidius Crassus, Publius 147, 158, 180, 190, 194ff., 207ff., 212, 230, 237, 268

Canopic branch of Nile 254

Canopus 177, 180, 202, 221

Canopus Street 33

Capito, see Fonteius

Capitol 43, 120, 162, 188, 214, 237

Cappadocia 111, 125, 133, 164

Carana 147

Caria 194

Carmel, Mount 135

Carrhae 48

Carthage 31, 90

Casca Longus, Publius Servilius 93f.

Cassius Dio Cocceianus, see Dio Cassius

Cassius Longinus, Lucius 93ff., 101ff., 105, 111, 121, 197

Cassius of Parma 153, 189, 230

Cato, Marcus Porcius 14f., 252

Caucasus, Mount 147

Cavafy, C. P. 163, 222

Ceres, see Demeter

Chaeronea 204f., 241

Chalcis beneath Lebanon (capital of Ituraea) 276

Charmion 180, 223, 226, 228

Chaucer 280

Chelidon 179

Chersonesus Taurica 266

Chios 61

Christ, Christianity 118f., 253

Cicero, Marcus Tullius 3, 12, 18, 47, 58, 64f., 91, 95ff., 114, 162, 178, 180, 187, 244, 265

Cilicia 19, 110, 117, 138, 195, 219, 265, 272

Cimber, see Tillius

Cimmerian Bosphorus, see Bosphorus

Cinna, see Helvius

Claudius (emperor) 231

Claudius, see Clodius, Marcellus

Clement of Alexandria 278

Cleopatra I 5, 48

Cleopatra II 48
Cleopatra III 76, 271
Cleopatra IV 53
Cleopatra V Tryphaena (probably mother of Cleopatra) 4, 252
Cleopatra VI Tryphaena (half-sister of Cleopatra) 3f., 15, 17, 252
Cleopatra VII, passim; see also languages
Cleopatra (sister of Alexander the Great) 254
Cleopatra Selene (daughter of Cleopatra) 126, 142, 163, 165f., 203, 207, 231
Cleopatra Selene (daughter of Ptolemy VIII) 11, 142
Cleopatra Thea 168
Cleopatreion 233
Clodia 102
Clodius Pulcher, Publius 14, 114
Cnidus 89, 260
Cnossus 267
cobra (asp) 226f., 277
Coelesyria 265
Comarius 255
Concordia, see Homonoia
Coponius, Publius 192
Coptic 256
Coptos 218, 256
Corcyra 133, 203, 205
Corduba 91
Corinth, Corinthian Gulf 89f., 203ff., 274
Cornelius, see Balbus, Dolabella, Gallus, Scipio, Sulla
Corsica 129
Cos 194, 220
Coson, Cotiso 189, 271
Costobarus 155
Crassus, Marcus Licinius (consul 30 BC) 165f., 268, 274
Crassus, Marcus Licinius (triumvir) 12f., 48, 92, 109, 145f., 207
Crassus, see also Canidius
Crete 165f., 203, 207
Crimea, see Bosphorus, Cimmerian
Curio, Gaius Scribonius 114
Curtius, Gaius 252
Cyclades 215
Cydas 207, 274
Cydnus, River 115
Cyme 263
Cyprus 8, 14f., 68, 71, 79, 102, 121, 138, 176, 256, 265

Cyrenaica, Libya 8, 10, 15, 165f., 203, 207, 217, 220, 224, 273f.
Cyzicus 34, 219

Dacia, Dacians 189, 206f., 271
Dalmatia 187
Damascus 137f., 158f., 168, 181, 265
Dante 178
Darius I 90
Dead Sea 128, 140, 218
Decapolis 138f.
Deianira 253
Deiotarus Philadelphus 274
Dellius, Quintus 111f., 157, 180,204,206, 209f.
Delos 38
Demeter (Ceres) 216, 263, 268
Demetrius I Poliorcetes 241
Demetrius (artist) 269
Demetrius (philosopher) 20f.
Dendera, see Tintyra
Diana, see Artemis
Dicomes 271
Didius, Quintus 219
Dido 178, 280
Didyma 272
Didyme 251
Dinocrates 33
Dio (Egyptian envoy) 16
Dio Cassius Cocceianus 70, 133, 186, 201, 226, 243, 272, 274, 276f.
Dio Chrysostom 24
Diodorus Siculus 25, 240, 258
Dionysius 253
Dionysus (Bacchus, Liber) 22–6, 57, 66, 71, 82, 88, 110ff., 115, 117f., 130, 161f., 170, 178, 186f., 189, 197, 222, 253, 260, 264
Dioscurides (doctor, envoy) 70, 270
Dioscurides Phacas (doctor) 181, 270
Dioscuridou Nesos 34
Discordia 215
Dolabella, Publius Cornelius (consul 44 BC) 101
Dolabella, Publius Cornelius (friend of Cleopatra) 225, 277
Domitiopolis 195
Domitius Ahenobarbus, see Ahenobarbus
Donations of Alexandria 162–75, 185, 191, 268
Drusus the elder (Nero Drusus) 239
Dyrrhachium 51, 262

Ecbatana 266
Edfu, see Apollinopolis Magna
Egypt, Lower, see Map p. 39
Egypt, Middle, see Map p. 39
Egypt, Upper, see Thebaid
Elaeusa Sebaste 138
Elephantine 75
Eleusis 216, 268
Eleutherus, River 135
Emesa 158, 274
Enobarbus, see Ahenobarbus
Epaphroditus 224f., 276
Ephesus 16, 86, 110f., 121, 130, 190, 193–196, 198, 256, 264, 272
Eros (Cupid) 85
Eros (servant of Antony) 223
Ethiopia (Napata) 33f., 232, 269
Eudoxus 34, 260
Eumenia 114
Eunoe 87, 91
Eunostos harbour 33
Euphranor 73
Euphrates, River 9, 133, 145, 157f., 163
Euphronius 220
Euripides 23
Eurycles 204, 212
Evander, see Avianius

Fadia 263
Fayum (Moeris) 15, 19, 35, 268
Fetiales 201
Florus 271, 280
Fonteius Capito, Gaius 133
Forster, E.M. 9
Forum Julium 87
Forum Romanum 87, 193
Frederick the Great 20
Fulvia 114f., 123–6, 130, 132, 152, 169ff., 186, 200, 229f., 263
Furies 215
Furnius 195

Gabinians 18f., 49, 51, 53, 57, 70, 77, 80
Gabinius, Aulus 16–19, 49, 57, 122
Gadara 138
Gaius Caesar 264
Gaius, see Caligula
Galatia, Galatians, 6, 133, 155, 164, 206f., 271
Galen 226
Galilee 122
Gallic Wars, see Gaul

Gallus, Gaius Asinius 264
Gallus, Cornelius 220, 224, 231f.
Ganymedes 72, 74, 85f.
Gaul, Gauls 6, 18, 28, 105, 132
Gaza 139, 155
Gellius Publicola 210f.
Geminius, Gaius 199f.
Georgica, Georgics 40, 188
Germany, Germans (across Rhine) 18, 132
Getae, see Dacians
Gilead 138, 140
Gindarus, Mount 131
Glaphyra 111, 125, 134
Glaucus 178
Gortyna 274
Graces 115
Greene, Robert 5

Hadad 137
Hadrian 243, 280
Hamaxia 138, 265
Hammonius, see Ammonius
Hasmonaeans (Maccabees) 12, 75, 141
Hathor 99, 256, 269
Hebrew, see Jews, languages of Cleopatra
Helen 178
Heliopolis (Baalbek) 137, 266
Heliopolis (On) 140, 143
Helios, see Alexander, Sun
Helvius Cinna 92
Hephaestion 55
Hephaestus (Vulcan) 215
Heptastadion mole 32, 73
Hera (Juno) 27
Heracleopolis Magna 17, 103
Heracles (Hercules) 112f., 174, 178f., 188, 253
Herculaneum 279
Hermogenes, Marcus Tigellius 87
Hermonthis 46f., 52, 99f., 245, 256, 261
Herod the Great 122, 127ff., 134, 139ff., 154, 158, 160, 165, 171, 181, 196, 218ff., 236, 239f., 267
Herodotus 25, 42, 55
Heroonpolis 218, 231, 261
Hiera Nesos 49
Himyarites 34
Hindu Kush, see India
Hipparchus (freedman of Antony) 221
Hipparchus of Nicaea 260
Hippodamus 33

Hippos 138
Hirtius, Aulus 73
Hispania, see Spain
Homer 229
Homonoia (Concordia) 143, 235, 262
Horace 55, 188, 197, 201, 207, 213, 227f., 244, 271, 274f., 278
Horus 85, 99f., 118f., 256, 261
Hyrcanus II 75, 77, 79, 122, 127f., 259
Hystaspes 172, 269

Iamblichus 274
Idumaea 75, 134, 141, 155, 158
Iliad, see Homer
Ilium, see Troy
Illyricum 150, 156, 185, 187, 278
Incas 254
India, Indian Ocean 5, 9, 34, 81, 163, 176, 215, 218, 269
Indo–Greeks 218
Insteius, Marcus 274
Iotape 218
Iqu 268
Iranians, see Armenia, Parthia, Media, Media Atropatene, Persia
Iras 180, 223f., 226, 228
Isis 26f., 43, 85, 88, 99f., 117–20, 133, 141, 143, 162, 168, 186, 203, 221, 227, 252, 263, 267, 272, 277
Israel, see Judaea
Ituraea 137ff., 158

Jaffa, see Joppa
Janiculum 87
Jericho 140, 154
Jerusalem 75, 122, 134, 139f., 154, 158, 222
Jesus, see Christ
Jews, Judaea, 6, 12, 17, 33, 75ff., 79, 122, 127–30, 134, 138f., 141, 154f., 158f., 165, 196, 219f., 236, 240, 264, 269
Jodelle, Etienne 242
John of Nikiu 233
Joppa 79, 139
Jordan, River 138, 140
Joseph 159
Josephus 159f., 219, 233, 237, 239f., 265, 272
Juba II 231, 278
Judaea, see Jews
Julia (daughter of Caesar) 84

Julia (daughter of Octavian) 132, 189, 220, 230
Julia (mother of Antony) 125
Julius Caesar, see Caesar
Julius Papeius, see Papeius
Julius Sabinus, see Sabinus
Julius Saturninus, see Saturninus
Junius Brutus, see Brutus
Junius Silanus, see Silanus
Juno, see Hera
Jupiter 11, 31, 43, 162; see also Zeus
Juvenal 256

Karnak, see Thebes
Kom Ombo, see Ombos
Kore (Persephone, Proserpina) 268
Kronos 119

Labienus, Quintus 123
Lagos 7
Lamprias 177, 242
Lampsacus 155
languages of Cleopatra 20, 34, 42f., 63, 76, 141, 146, 256, 258
Laocoon 277
Laodice 254
Laodicea (in Syria) 101, 122, 154, 180, 219
Lathyrus, see Ptolemy IX
Lavicum 91
Lebanon, Mount 138
Leontopolis 76f.
Lepcis Magna 258
Lepidus, Marcus Aemilius (moneyer) 251
Lepidus, Marcus Aemilius (triumvir) 93, 102, 105, 126, 150, 155, 190, 216
Lepidus, Marcus Aemilius (triumvir's son) 216
Lesser Armenia, see Armenia, Lesser
Leucas (island) 203, 205, 275
Leucas on the Chrysorrhoas, see Balanea
Leucate, Cape 214, 275
Leuce Come 150
Liber, see Dionysus
Library (Alexandria) 8f., 69, 71, 90, 251
Library (Rome) 90
Liburnians 228, 278
Libya, see Cyrenaica
Licinius Crassus, see Crassus
Livia Drusilla 129f., 153, 185
Livineius Regulus, see Regulus

Livy 162, 186, 239ff., 243f., 277, 280
Lochias, Cape 69
Locri Epizephyrii 255
Lollius, Lucius 165f., 268
Lucan 58, 61, 63, 68, 96, 176ff., 244, 260
Lucilius 275
Lucius 270
Lucretius 117
Lugdunum 114
Luna, see Moon
Lurius, Marcus 274
Luxor, see Thebes
Lysanias 137

Maccabees, see Hasmonaeans
Macedonia, Macedonians 3, 5, 7, 11f., 18, 40, 54, 69, 103, 105, 110, 164, 198, 202f., 206f., 212, 251, 254f.
Mad Praetor, Prophecy of 172
Maecenas, Gaius 66, 126, 216, 223, 244
Maenads (Bacchants) 111, 178, 222
Malalas 52
Malchus 218f.
Mammisi 261
Mardion 180
Mareotis, Lake 31, 33, 43, 77, 255
Mariamme I 141
Mars, see Ares
Mary, Virgin 253
Masada 128
Master of Fire, see Hephaestus
Matapan, Cape, see Taenarum
Matiana, Lake 146
Mauretania 87, 188, 203, 231, 278
Media, Median 146, 256, 266
Media Atropatene 146–50, 153ff., 157f., 163f., 190, 218, 231, 266
Memmius, Lucius 10
Memphis 4, 35, 40, 43–6, 58, 76, 83, 201, 232, 255
Menedemus 96
Menodorus 272
Meroe 177, 269
Meson Pedion, see Canopus street
Mesopotamia 92, 145; see also Babylon
Messalla Corvinus, Marcus Valerius 128, 187, 204, 272
Methe 178
Methone 203ff., 212
Midaeum 267
Miletus 155
Minerva (Athena) 215

Miriam, see Mariamme
Misenum 129
Mithridates VI 12, 17, 24, 38, 65, 74, 85f., 110, 172, 176, 256
Mithridates of Pergamum 74, 76f.
Moeris, Lake, see Fayum
Mole, see Heptastadion
Monaeses 145, 147, 164
Moon (Selene, Luna) 118, 142, 144
Munda 91
Murcus, Lucius Staius 103, 105
Murray, Gilbert 258
Museum (Alexandria) 8f., 69, 89f., 251
Mut 99, 261
Mutina 101

Nabataeans 53, 140, 196, 218
Nais, Servilia 274
naja haje, naja nigricolus, see cobra
Napata, see Meroe
Napoleon 81
Naucratis 31
Naulochus, Cape 149, 189
Naxos 23
Nectanebes (Nekht-Nebf) II 255
Nemea 112
Neotera 168
Nephthys 168
Neptune, see Poseidon
Nereids 115
Nero 176, 231, 244
Nero Drusus, see Drusus the elder
Nestor 130
Nicaea 243, 260
Nicarchus 204, 242
Nicolaus (*cinaedus*) 252
Nicolaus of Damascus 159, 181, 239ff., 259
Nicopolis (Egypt) 232
Nicopolis (Epirus) 232
Niger, Aquilius, see Auilitius
Nile, River 25, 31ff., 36f., 58, 77, 81, 85, 90, 103, 118, 121, 176, 202, 218, 224, 228; see also Canopic, Pelusiac branches
No-Amon, see Amon
Nonnus 253
North, Sir Thomas 66, 242
Numidia (Africa Nova) 231, 278

Octavia 66f., 126f., 130, 132ff., 149, 151ff., 156, 169, 181, 186, 191f., 194, 199f., 230f., 264

Octavian (Augustus) xviif., 81, 84, 89, 92, 97, 99, 101ff., 105, 109ff., 123–7, 129–34, 142, 145, 148–53, 155ff., 160, 166f., 170, 175, 180, 185–95, 197, 199–241, 262–5, 269, 273–8
Octavius, Gaius, see Octavian
Octavius, Marcus 274
Olympus 181, 226, 242
Ombos 256, 268
Omphale 188
Onias IV 259
Oppius, Gaius 84, 93, 189
Oppius, Quintus 276
Oppius Statianus 147
Orodes I 145
Orontes, River 145, 158
Orthosia 265
Osiris 25f., 43, 77, 99, 117–20, 143, 162, 170, 186, 253
Osor-Hapi, see Apis
Ovinius, Quintus 33, 230
Oxyrhynchus 19

Pacorus 123, 131, 145
Pakis, see Buchis
Palatitza 69
Palestine, see Jews
Palestrina, see Praeneste
Pallas, see Athena
Palmyra 175, 233
Pamphylia 265
Pan 25, 111
Panopolis 253
Paos 41
Papeius, Gaius Julius 272
Paphos 14
Paphlagonia 274
Paraetonium 31, 217, 220
Parasitos 178
Parma 153, 189
Parthia 48f., 74, 92, 98, 109ff., 121–34, 137ff., 144–9, 153–7, 160, 164, 168, 187, 190, 218, 256, 264, 266
Pascal, Blaise 66
Patavium 240
Pathyrite name (province) 261
Patmos 252
Patrae 203, 205, 276
Paul, St. 86, 120
Paullus, Marcus Aemilius 264
Peloponnese 129, 198, 204, 209, 212
Pelusiac branch of Nile 90

Pelusium 17, 53, 90, 127, 220, 276
Pembroke, Countess of 242
Perdiccas 254
Pergamum 74, 110, 195
Pericles 271
Persephone, see Kore
Persia 5, 44, 55, 144, 163, 166; see also Media
Peru 254
Perusia 125, 127, 264
Petra 53
Pharnaces II 85, 268
Pharos 8, 32f., 71, 73, 85, 180, 233
Pharsalus 57f., 197f., 208, 239
Phasael 122, 127
Philadelphus, see Arsinoe II, Deiotarus, Ptolemy II, Ptolemy (son of Antony and Cleopatra)
Philae 20, 256, 261, 272
Philip II (of Macedonia) 7
Philippi 105, 109ff., 144, 153, 189, 197f., 208, 262
Philostratus 181, 270, 278
Philotas 177, 242
Phoenicia 31, 115, 121, 135f., 138f., 149, 154, 220
Phraaspa 147
Phraates IV 145, 147, 157
Phrygia 114, 131
Physcon, see Ptolemy VIII
Pinarius Scarpus, Lucius, see Scarpus
Pithom, see Heroonpolis
Plancus, Lucius Munatius 155f., 178, 180, 192, 241, 268, 272
Plato 181
Plautus 64
Pliny the elder 275
Plutarch xvi, 42, 65f., 73, 76, 83, 111–15, 123, 152, 177, 179, 186, 189, 195ff., 200, 204, 212f., 221, 226, 241ff., 266, 274ff., 280
Polemo 131, 133, 147, 164, 230, 265, 267
Pollio, Gaius Asinius 153, 239, 241, 264
Polybius 42, 252
Pompeii 23, 25, 38, 277
Pompeius, Cnaeus (son of Cnaeus Pompeius Magnus) 51, 62, 85, 90, 257
Pompeius, Sextus 85, 90, 105, 127, 129f., 132, 149, 187, 189f., 201, 205, 208f., 262, 267
Pompeius Magnus, Cnaeus (Pompey the Great) 12ff., 16f., 28f. 48, 51ff., 57f.,

61f., 70, 75, 78, 85f., 93f., 105, 109f., 138, 155, 176, 197, 240, 244, 268, 272

Pontine Marshes 89

Pontus 12, 17, 24, 38, 65, 85, 110, 133, 164, 172, 230

Popilius Laenas, Gaius 9

Porcius Cato, Marcus, see Cato

Poseidon (Neptune) 215

Postumius, Quintus 274

Postumus, Gaius Rabirius, see Rabirius

Pothinus (minister of Ptolemy XIII) 55, 57f., 62, 64f., 68ff., 72, 85, 180, 270

Pothinus (official of Cleopatra) 180, 270

Potter's Prophecy 40

Praeneste 268f.

Priene 197, 273

Proculeius, Gaius 223f., 276

Propertius 201, 227, 244

Proserpina, see Kore

Protarchus 49, 55

Psenemon 232

Pshereniptah 45

Psylli 227

Ptolemaeus (*dioecetes*) 55, 57

Ptolemaia 24, 41, 197, 199

Ptolemais Ace 135, 220, 276

Ptolemais (in Cyrenaica) 166

Ptolemais (in Egypt) 31

Ptolemy I Soter 7f., 21f., 31, 34, 43–6, 63, 75, 90, 135, 141, 253f., 262

Ptolemy II Philadelphus 5, 8f., 24, 26ff., 33f., 44, 46, 54, 90f., 141, 150, 165, 194, 196, 251, 253f., 258, 273

Ptolemy III Euergetes 9, 21f., 33f., 48, 141, 143, 165, 253, 262

Ptolemy IV Philopator 9, 24, 30, 41, 46, 66, 82, 261

Ptolemy V Epiphanes 5, 9, 21f., 41, 45f., 48, 54

Ptolemy VI Philometor 9, 22, 27, 37, 48, 76, 168, 273

Ptolemy VII Neos Philopator 22, 30

Ptolemy VIII Euergetes II (Physcon) 9, 18, 27, 34, 38, 41, 142, 271

Ptolemy IX Soter II (Lathyrus) 10f., 46, 53, 273

Ptolemy X Alexander I 10f., 14, 20, 27, 252, 268

Ptolemy XI Alexander II 11, 252

Ptolemy XII Neos Dionysos 'Auletes' (father of Cleopatra) xvf., 3–31, 45ff., 49ff., 54, 57, 61, 70, 78f., 100, 245, 251, 254, 256, 261, 272

Ptolemy XIII (half-brother of Cleopatra) 3f., 28, 30, 47, 49ff., 52ff., 57, 61–4, 67–70, 72, 74, 256, 264

Ptolemy XIV (half-brother of Cleopatra) 3f., 28, 68, 78ff., 85, 87, 97f., 121, 173, 257

Ptolemy XV Caesar (son of Cleopatra), see Caesarion

Ptolemy Apion 10, 165

Ptolemy (*dioecetes*), see Ptolemaeus

Ptolemy of Cyprus (brother of Ptolemy XII) 14f.

Ptolemy of Mauretania 231

Ptolemy Philadelphus (son of Cleopatra) 150, 163–6, 231, 267f.

Publicola, Gellius, see Gellius

Puteoli 16, 18

Pythodoris 230

Pythodorus (husband of eldest Antonia) 186, 188, 230

Quirinius 88, 102f.

Ra 45, 99, 103; see also Amon

Rabirius Postumus, Gaius 13, 16f., 55, 61, 252

Rameses II 8, 45

Raphia 41

Rashid, see Rosetta

Re, see Ra

Red Sea 33f., 90, 140, 176, 218f., 229, 269

Regulus, Lucius Livineius 262

Rhacotis 31, 256

Rhine, River, see Germany

Rhodes 16, 21, 38, 61, 73, 116, 128, 219

Rhodon 218, 229

Rhoemetalces 274

Rhosus 177, 264

Romulus 88, 102

Rosetta (Rashid) 41, 233

Roxana 271

Rufilla 185

Rufio 80

Rumania, see Dacia

Russia, see Bosphorus (Cimmerian)

Sabaeans 215

Sabinus, Julius 260

Sabinus, see Calvisius

Sais 25
Salvia Titisenia, see Titisenia
Salvius 57
Samos 61, 196, 216, 219
Samosata 131
Sara 96, 261
Sarapion, see Serapion
Sarapis 43f., 46, 120, 133, 143, 161
Sardinia 129
Sarmentus 204
Saturn, see Kronos
Saturninus, Julius 271
Satyrus 262
Save, River 156
Scarpus, Lucius Pinarius 207, 217, 220
Scellius 211
Scipio Africanus junior (Aemilianus), Publius Cornelius 9f., 38
Scribonia 127, 129, 264
Sebek 268
Selene, see Moon
Seleucids 7ff., 12, 17, 41, 48, 65, 75f., 110, 158, 168f., 172, 253, 268, 276
Seleucus I 251, 268
Seleucus (commander at Pelusium) 220
Seleucus Cybiosactes 17
Seleucus (treasurer) 180
Semele 23
Semiramis 178
Senmet 256
Septimius, Lucius 57f.
Septimius Severus, see Severus
Serapion (envoy) 70
Serapion (governor of Cyprus) 101ff., 121, 261
Serapis, see Sarapis
Sermylo 271
Servilia Nais, see Nais
Servilius Casca, see Casca
Servius 198, 275
Sesostris III 8
Seth 118
Severus, Septimius 257
Shakespeare, William xvi, 5, 7, 66, 123, 152, 195, 224, 242f., 276f., 280
Shaw, Bernard xvi, 16, 87, 258
Sibylline books, oracles 172, 235
Sicily 11, 36, 63, 105, 129, 149f., 190, 205f., 208
Sicyon 126
Sidney, Sir Philip 242
Sidon 135

Silanus, Marcus Junius 272, 274
Sinai, Mount 140
Sinope 129, 256
Sisyphus 270
Smyrna 102
Socnopaeus 268
Socotra, see Dioscuridou Nesos
Socrates of Rhodes 116
Sol, see Sun
Somalia 33f.
Sophocles 21
Sosigenes 89, 260
Sosius, Gaius 129, 132, 134, 166, 191f., 203, 206, 210f., 265, 273
Sotades 27
Spain 78, 90, 218
Sparta 204
Statianus, Oppius, see Oppius
Strabo 4, 34, 138, 178, 226, 240, 265
Strouthon 252
Sudan, see Ethiopia
Suetonius 78, 81, 91f., 185, 243
Sulla, Lucius Cornelius 11
Sun (Helios, Sol) 120, 142ff.
Syme, Sir Ronald 234, 279
Syria 6, 9, 11f., 16, 19, 36, 40, 42, 70, 74, 110, 114, 120f., 123f., 127, 130f., 133, 137f., 141, 145, 151f., 155, 157f., 165, 172, 175, 180, 194, 219, 255; see also Phoenicia
Syriac 141, 256

Tacitus 189, 234
Taenarum, Cape 103, 203, 212
Taposiris Magna 177, 255
Tarcondimotus I Philantonius 274
Tarentum (Taras) 20, 85, 132, 198
Tarn, Sir William xvi, 234, 236, 277
Tarquinius Superbus 202
Tarsus 111f., 115, 120f., 124, 135, 176, 180
Ten Cities, see Decapolis
Terentilla 185
Terracina 89
Tertia 95
Tertulla (mistress of Octavian) 185
Tertulla (wife of Cassius), see Tertia
Thapsus 85
Theadelphia 15
Thebaid (Upper Egypt) 9, 34f., 41f., 46, 49, 51f., 81, 100, 231, 255
Thebes (Karnak, Luxor) 45f., 256, 261

Theodorus 230
Theodotus 61, 257
Theseus 23
Thessalonica 52, 57, 262
Thessaly 57, 96, 214
Thothmes III 8, 45, 259
Thrace 206f.
Thucydides 243
Thyrsus 221
Tiber, River 87, 89, 91, 202
Tiberius 240
Tibur 155
Tigellius Hermogenes, Marcus, see Hermogenes
Tigranes I the Great 268
Tillius Cimber 93
Timagenes 181, 279
Timon, Timonium 217
Tinteris 49
Tintyra (Dendera) 42, 99, 256, 261, 263, 268
Titiopolis 272
Titisenia, Salvia 185
Titius, Marcus 155f., 192
Titus 268
Toryne 205
Trajan 243
Tralles 186, 188, 194
Transylvania, see Dacia
Trebonius, Gaius 93
Tripolis 115, 265
Trogodytes 34, 256
Troy (Ilium) 92, 222
Tryphon 252
Tumilat, Wadi 90
Tunisia, see Africa (Roman province)

Turnus 277
Turullius, Decimus 153, 194, 220, 230, 273
Tusculum 114
Tyre 31, 85, 121ff., 135, 177

Upper Egypt, see Thebaid
Urmia, Lake, see Matiana

Varro, Marcus Terentius 90
Varus, Gaius Vibius, see Vibius
Velleius Paterculus 161f., 205, 240, 275
Ventidius, Publius 131
Venus, see Aphrodite
Vergil, see Virgil
Vestal Virgins 91, 152, 193
Via Egnatia 198, 205
Vibius Varus, Gaius 264
Virgil 127, 188, 198, 201, 214, 227f., 235f., 244, 264, 277
Vitruvius 126
Voltaire 20

Wilhelm II 188

Xerxes 198

Zacynthus 129, 132, 166, 203, 265, 273
Zela 85
Zeno 255
Zenobia 233
Zenodorus 265
Zeugma 146
Zeus 25, 27, 31, 43, 137; see also Hadad, Jupiter
Zosime 86